UNMANNED

Also by William M. Arkin

American Coup: How a Terrified Government Is Destroying
the Constitution

Top Secret America: The Rise of the New American Security State
with Dana Priest

Divining Victory: Airpower in the 2006 Israel-Hezbollah War

Code Names: Deciphering U.S. Military Plans, Programs,
and Operations in the 9/11 World

Operation Iraqi Freedom: 22 Historic Days in Words and Pictures
with Marc Kusnetz and General Montgomery Meigs

The U.S. Military Online: A Directory for Internet Access
to the Department of Defense

Encyclopedia of the U.S. Military
with Joshua Handler, Julie A. Morrissey, and Jacquelyn Walsh

Nuclear Weapons Databook: Volume IV—Soviet Nuclear Weapons
with Thomas B. Cochran, Robert S. Norris,
and Jeffrey I. Sands

Nuclear Weapons Databook: Volume III—U.S. Nuclear Warhead
Facility Profiles with Thomas B. Cochran, Milton M. Hoenig,
and Robert S. Norris

Nuclear Weapons Databook: Volume II—U.S. Nuclear Warhead
Production with Thomas B. Cochran, Milton M. Hoenig,
and Robert S. Norris

Nuclear Battlefields: Global Links in the Arms Race
with Richard Fieldhouse

S.I.O.P.: The Secret U.S. Plan for Nuclear War
with Peter Pringle

Nuclear Weapons Databook: Volume I—U.S. Nuclear Forces
and Capabilities with Thomas B. Cochran and Milton M. Hoenig

Research Guide to Current Military and Strategic Affairs

UNMANNED

DRONES, DATA, AND THE ILLUSION OF PERFECT WARFARE

WILLIAM M. ARKIN

LITTLE, BROWN AND COMPANY

New York • Boston • London

Little, Brown and Company
Hachette Book Group
1290 Avenue of the Americas, New York, NY 10104
littlebrown.com

First Edition: July 2015

Little, Brown and Company is a division of Hachette Book Group, Inc. The Little, Brown name and logo are trademarks of Hachette Book Group, Inc.

The publisher is not responsible for websites (or their content) that are not owned by the publisher.

The Hachette Speakers Bureau provides a wide range of authors for speaking events. To find out more, go to hachettespeakersbureau.com or call (866) 376-6591.

Chapter epigraphs are from *The Epic of Gilgamesh*, translated with an introduction by Andrew George (Allen Lane The Penguin Press, 1999; Penguin Classics, 2000; Revised, 2003). Copyright © Andrew George, 1999. Reproduced by permission of Penguin Books Ltd.

ISBN 978-0-316-32335-2
LCCN 2015931408

10 9 8 7 6 5 4 3 2 1

RRD-C

Printed in the United States of America

To Rikki and Hannah, Luciana for everything; and Watt,
for making me think deeper about Gilgamesh

Contents

Contents

UNMANNED

INTRODUCTION

Only Shamash the hero crosses the ocean:
apart from the Sun God, who crosses the ocean?
TABLET X, *EPIC OF GILGAMESH*

Held up by three lawn mower–sized wheels, two of them attached to the slimmest of metal poles bolted to its fuselage and the front one strengthened by struts and shock absorbers, the Predator drone has been described as "spindly," as if something weighing more than a ton and standing higher than a tall man, with wings extending the length of four automobiles, should nevertheless be thought of as fragile. The lone push propeller at the rear gives off the familiar whirr and swoosh of a baseball bat, and the engine whines away as it prepares for takeoff. The drone's body is all curves and humps, with that unmistakable rotating bug eye protruding under the cockpit up front, except that there is no cockpit, just as there is no pilot on board.

With its characteristic inverted-V tail, the drone trundles down the taxiway looking from a distance like any commuter plane, slightly flapping as the body turns. But when it takes off, with surprisingly little runway, those long wings capture the friction just perfectly to provide lift. Every second of every day, about fifty of these Predator-type drones are airborne worldwide, over Afghanistan and Pakistan, quietly flying over Yemen or Syria, working in Africa and Latin America, patrolling the US border, monitoring the oceans, conducting civilian and scientific missions of all kinds.[1] These airplane-sized drones, which have become so much the staple of American military power, have amassed over a million flight hours in the past decade, hardly the toil of something fragile. They fly at an altitude of 15,000 to 40,000 feet and can stay airborne for as many as forty-five hours. Though they have been flying for over twenty years, they are also hardly static. Constantly updated models and accessorized packages leave the secret showrooms for duty, videotaping anything that goes on below, some even in high-definition. They have sensors that can see both day and night, in clear weather or in sandstorms, at narrow views or at wide ones. Some contain equipment that can listen in to radio and cell phone communications, even precisely locate where these communications are coming from.

The US military operated fewer than 200 unmanned aerial vehicles—drones[2]—when the World Trade Center and Pentagon were hit in 2001; today, in addition to some 500 of this Predator class, it possesses well over 11,000 other kinds of drones.[3] From just 50 remotely controlled unmanned ground vehicles enlisted to serve at the beginning of the Afghanistan war, the number grew to over 8,000.[4] At sea, the navy employed a fleet of 70 unmanned surface and undersea craft at the time of 9/11; they now have over 500.[5] Walking robots, unmanned ground sensors and surveillance towers, and reconnaissance blimps abound, not to mention satellites of an unprecedented variety, large and small, in high and low orbit around Earth. Government funding for drones and other unmanned systems increased from about $350 million at the time of 9/11 to well over $5 billion a year by 2013; even with defense budget reductions that come from the "end" of two wars, that spending is projected to surpass $4.5 billion annually through 2018.[6]

Though one might conclude from the global drone debate

that the United States is the sole owner of aerial unmanned vehicles, eighty-eight other nations also operate drones, and fifty-four nations manufacture their own. Italy and the United Kingdom fly their own Predator-type drones. The European countries, propelled by their involvement in Afghanistan and Iraq, built up an inventory of over 3,500 unmanned aerial vehicles (or UAVs) in a decade of fighting.[7] France has even flown its own lethal drone missions in Africa. Smaller countries strapped for manpower but heavily invested in their militaries—Israel, Taiwan, South Korea, Singapore, and the United Arab Emirates, to name a few—play an outsized role in unmanned research, development, and adoption. The unlikeliest of US allies in the "war against terror"—Burundi, Uganda, Yemen, and of course Afghanistan and Iraq—fly American-made drones. China, Russia, Iran, and North Korea have healthy unmanned programs and innumerable growing inventories. And all these countries don't just *have* the drones: China uses them to spy on Japan near disputed islands in Asia. Bolivia uses them to spot coca fields in the Andes. Hamas in the Palestinian territories and the Lebanon-based Hizballah state-within-a-state both have and have used Iranian-made drones, Hamas even armed ones. Even NATO ally Turkey pilots drones that increasingly cross its neighbors' borders, American style.

Meanwhile, the unmanned civilian "market" quickly evolves into law enforcement, scientific research, industrial and consumer services, education, and even entertainment. Border agencies and local police have begun emulating their military brethren in acquiring drones not just for bomb disposal and other dangerous missions, but also for intelligence collection and surveillance. UAVs are playing greater and greater roles in agriculture, in weather forecasting, in identifying and locating forest fires and oil pipeline leaks, in assisting archeological and environmental research, and in relaying radio signals, and are increasingly present in businesses from real estate to journalism.

Like the military, the civilian unmanned world is also not just in the skies: Rovers explore the planets and the universe. Unmanned undersea vehicles abound, whether the Jacques Cousteau sort or mini-subs like the one that discovered the wreckage of Amelia Earhart's airplane, lost for almost a hundred years. Self-driving cars are almost in the rearview mirror: Google's experimental versions have already covered half a million miles under computer control. Wheeled and walking robots are no longer just the stuff of gladiator competitions and science fairs; they are increasingly smarter and more adaptive and flexible, and are now taking up regular jobs dispensing medications and even teaching languages. Scores of universities are acquiring their own unmanned vehicles, beefing up their robotics and aerial vehicle programs, some chasing the almighty dollar in homeland and national security grants but many just hungry to pursue the final frontier. And who hasn't seen the news stories about novelty drones delivering pizza, about Facebook buying its own fleet of Internet-in-the-sky drones, or about the promised fleet of Amazon *super-primes* supplanting the postal service and UPS? Civilian technologies and potential commercial applications have expanded so much and so rapidly that it is no longer the military that is driving technology development in this field, not even after a decade and a half of war.[8]

To many, this is just the arc of the future, with efficiency and a level of network interconnectedness merely paralleling the Internet of Things: a set of machines literally doing the repetitive and dirty work too dangerous or too boring for humans. To others, all of this is ushering in some nightmare of government spying and killer robots and autonomous decision-makers. "Drone" itself has become a sizzling curse word that for some invokes post-9/11 ethical failure and lawlessness. Predator's deathly name, one critic writes, "conjures images of a science-fiction dystopia, a 'Terminator Planet' where robots hover in the sky and exterminate humans on the ground"; the critic adds for dramatic emphasis that "this is no longer science-fiction fantasy."[9] The skyline is so seemingly clouded with the unmanned that communities and states have begun restricting drone use, while gallant citizens declare their intent to do their own hunting, to literally shoot airborne intruders on sight.

Washington (and other governments) meanwhile doggedly and fiercely defend ubiquitous surveillance and targeted killing, claiming they are not only necessary for security but also legal. "It's the only game in town," former CIA director Leon Panetta famously said in 2009;[10] "game" was an unintentional label but flippant enough wording to confirm the worst for those who already see this mode of warfare as too careless and remote.

"Remote" describes precisely the way many military and intelligence officers think about public misgivings. Sure, everyone wants less war, but do they really want more risk? Do drone critics really desire less precision, or decisions taken with inferior intelligence, or the greater number of casualties and destruction that would come if somehow the world went backward and returned to the grinding industrial warfare of the twentieth century? A 2013 Army War College study sums up the moment as seen by those who are unruffled by the advance of the unmanned:

> Drones place no U.S. military personnel at risk. They do not require a large "footprint" of U.S. personnel overseas. They are armed with accurate missiles that have the capacity to target individuals, automobiles, and sections of structures such as rooms in a large house. Perhaps the most consequential advantage of drones is their ability to integrate intelligence collection with decisions to use

force. These characteristics...make drones especially effective at targeting only the individuals against whom the United States wishes to use force, and minimizing harm to noncombatants.[11]

It is a rousing defense, and yet it is totally off the mark. The argument that drones place no US military personnel at risk is not only exaggerated but is also an evasion of much larger issues, such as who is ultimately at risk and whether the resulting mode of low-cost perpetual warfare really safeguards any lives in the long run (or indeed even contributes to the long-term security of the United States or the world).

And despite the 2010 withdrawal of US forces from Iraq and the end of conventional combat in Afghanistan, no one believes that the United States has really reduced its footprint overseas. The smaller number of troops is more indicative of a twenty-first-century reality, which is the end of the industrial era and the ability to generate even greater combat power than in yesteryear with fewer and fewer soldiers. But while fewer boots, fewer trainees, and fewer deaths and injuries are supposed to mean less human hassle (and less expenditure on people), the strategy is really a Washington bookkeeping trick. Machines do more of the work, but an invisible multitude of civilian contractors has quietly replaced soldiers. What's more, the United States hasn't earned any particular points for a softer touch or greater care; indeed, most people doubt that precision has genuinely been achieved, given the narrative of constant civilian casualties embedded within a competing legend of all-knowing intelligence. Nor has terrorism been defeated; some even argue that the threat from terrorism hasn't even diminished.[12] And whatever the actual numbers of terrorists, the Muslim world (and much of the rest of the world) remains unpersuaded about the supposedly benign designs of

American empire, even if the foot is smaller and the stomp is more of a grind.

Government propaganda, the mainstream news media, and Hollywood special effects merely add to unrealistic images of what "unmanned" means by characterizing drones almost solely as high-flying hunter-killers or all-seeing and instantaneous answer machines. Yet only about 5 percent of the 11,000-plus drones owned by the United States are airplane-sized.[13] An even smaller subset—just a few hundred craft worldwide—are the infamous armed Predator types that garner so much public attention. And yet even one as supposedly knowledgeable as former secretary of defense Robert Gates has described the entire class of drones as "man hunters."[14]

In fact, far more than nine out of ten of the world's drones are small, short-range, and unarmed. The vast majority of these are no larger than a remote-controlled model airplane. In the United States military, most are just one type of drone, a 4.2-pound little spy machine called Raven.[15] These and other personal-sized devices are little more than standard government issue for soldiers these days, the modern equivalents of binoculars or radios. They are increasingly ubiquitous, to be sure, but one could say they are remarkable merely in the same way that smartphones and inter-connected everythings are: omnipresent, attention-grabbing, ultra-convenient, annoying, distancing, challenging to privacy and security, definitely exerting some kind of influence on our society even if the ultimate outcome is unclear. And whether or not weapons of today or tomorrow can fly through windows, the belief in such a vision of warfare has itself spawned the explosion of data collection and a shift in focus to information-based hunting. After all, now the military and intelligence agencies have to know where all the windows are. And there are a lot of windows.

The one characteristic that makes aerial drones so different from manned aircraft—a characteristic shared with robots and unmanned undersea vehicles—is that, relieved of the human being on board, they can loiter. They can linger aimlessly, moving about in a slow and idle manner and making purposeless stops in the course of a trip. Before the military started using the buzz-phrases "persistent surveillance" and "perch and stare" to atomize intelligence and envelop the drone as just another one of the guys, they used the word "loiter"—as with Panetta's word "game," thereby saying way more than was ever intended.

Now, the reader might think I bring up the term "loitering" to suggest a metaphor for some sort of crime being committed, when in fact it is the aimlessness that I want to focus on. Loitering, drone war advocates say, provides "a clearer picture of the target and its surroundings, including the presence of innocent civilians." The danger is that this very confidence in "surgical precision"—this "laser-like focus," to use the words of drone war architect and CIA director John Brennan—self-validates the use of drones. Proponents argue that because the United States is taking unprecedented measures to be both discriminating and meticulous in its pursuit of terrorists, it is therefore doing the right thing.[16]

Defenders might argue that I am being unfair, that thirty hours hanging out on the aerial corner is neither random nor idle: like the window, that corner has to be carefully selected, the occupants cataloged; every pedestrian and automobile that goes by has to be identified. And the drone doesn't loiter at just any corner and start looking for bad guys, they'd say; the very driving factor is the bad guys, not the corner. Nothing is left to chance given the variables, they'd argue; the whole process is precise, and tens of thousands of operators and analysts are the human decision-makers and controllers. They'd say that intelligence-driven drone warfare is not harassment of vagrants or dispersal of hooligans or preying upon some poor corner dwellers. It is the very opposite of the indiscriminate slaughter perpetrated both by suicide bombers and by armies of old, they'd argue. Every alternative to airpower and drones—from ground combat to in-your-face counterinsurgency strategies that involve gaining and holding neighborhoods, villages, areas, provinces, countries—increases death, damage, and the level of harm to civilians. The absence of an alternative becomes the justification.

But it is still just targeting that is going on. This thing called targeting is not intelligence collection in any classic sense or with any purpose toward warning or greater understanding or even keeping (or creating) the peace. The so-called intelligence that is being collected and analyzed is just data, raw data that turns into reports, and geographic information that turns into data sets and ginormous multidimensional Libraries of Congress' worth of databases. Information is sought to make the battlefield maps more precise, to map the windows, corners, streets, houses, families, tribes, and social networks. It is a process intended to separate the combatants from the noncombatants, to be sure, to minimize harm to civilians in the crossfire, to let those who are innocent pass, but it is also an approach without a strategy, a patient precision that so much develops its own rhythm and automatic decision-making that it has become antiprecision.

Just as "intelligence" has been turned into little more than targeting data, so too has the human element of intelligence been devalued. "Human intelligence" is most often described as an antidote to technical collection, as a post-9/11 boots-on-the-ground rejection of relying too much on technology and remoteness. But soldiers who do HUMINT, as it is called, are mostly checking identifications and inquiring as to relationships to collect more data. The subspecialty called counterintelligence ends up being little more than local screening of the backgrounds of potential insider threats, natives needed in the fight to better infiltrate cultural and familial black spots. "Identity" intelligence has emerged as a new discipline, the automation of knowing someone without knowing anything else. The field of forensics flourishes on this new battlefield as well, with literal police work now being undertaken by men and women in uniform who are valued neither for their guns nor for their brains; they are just the live robocops closest to the fray. The data that the so-called analysts inspect is disconnected from any particular country or culture or even security outcome. Analysis is reduced to the work of marketing specialists mining transactional data to find their next customers. Country and regional expertise is leadership profiling, countercorruption, counterthreat finance, a bigger set of brains and a bigger set of tools to handle all the incoming nonbattlefield data, as vague and unmeasurable as the war on drugs or the fight against organized crime in ridding civilized society of drugs or crime. As we will see, in this world of loitering, any effort to produce insight and reflections—call it soft power, the battle for hearts and minds, nation building, getting at the root causes, it doesn't matter—has not just been a huge bust; it has been completely lost in the shuffle.

Hundreds of thousands of maintainers and scientists and analysts and technicians (unlaborers, I'll call them) are involved in the process, which isn't unmanned at all. And we have made it global: we have extended the battlefield to every corner and expanded the target lists beyond just terrorists. In this domain wholly given over to targeting, waiting for (or creating) an opportunity to find and to kill has become the preferred and seemingly the only option, whether at the American border or in the remotest corner of Syria or Pakistan. Loitering facilitates and even encourages a perpetual effort. Though humans operate the Data

Machine, with collection and analysis and collaboration occurring at all levels, the only real intervention of decision-making occurs when production falters. On a typical day, there is high anxiety, and there are real dangers for many, but if everything goes right, if a prospective operation doesn't portend too much danger, if a prospective strike doesn't equal x-number of calculated potential civilian deaths, if no public controversies arise and there are no leaks, then no real decisions are made.

No one would dispute that warfare has become more information-centric. This data-centric, keyboard-oriented style of warfare also happens to suit the cadre of digital natives who have supplanted the bricks-and-mortar warriors of the previous era: young people who joined the military after 9/11 now make up well over 90 percent of everyone in uniform.[17] Military studies point out that 80 percent of these natives, sometimes called millennials—people born between 1980 and 2000—live in households with 24/7 computer and online access, and that 92 percent play video games. By college graduation, the typical digital native has logged 10,000 hours with a joystick of some sort. The military labels these digital natives "information hounds" with "lofty expectations."[18]

When you talk to military elders about their cadre of digital natives, they describe them as those who "want to do, not to be told." With connectivity as their hallmark, they expect to jump right into a new piece of equipment, a new website, or a new game, learning the controls through trial and error. And not only that— digital natives value team learning, and they achieve and improve naturally through social media. When you visit a military unit or a command post these days, it's quite noticeable to a grease-pencil-trained analyst like me that the ubiquitous accoutrement of modern-day war-making is social media, from the common operating picture to the multiple open chat sessions connecting highly dispersed information workers. And yet this instant messaging, which has all of the immediacy, abbreviation, and fleetingness of teenage texting, goes on in a secure and hidden world and concerns matters of life and death.

These digital natives are supported by hundreds of thousands of devices—handhelds, tablets, laptops, smart thises and thats—and are in constant contact with each other through gigantic communications networks. Every soldier everywhere is called a sensor and a contributor. Each of them sits at his or her console, and collectively they drive a transformation of the world's premier hierarchical institution into one of open information and egalitarian involvement, with civilian leaders at the top and generals commanding the information machine, automated and increasingly autonomous, tended to by a cadre of war-surfers. In fact, for the modern military, almost every aspect of recruitment and training, and increasingly the way operations themselves are carried out, caters to the expectations of these digitally addicted multitaskers.[19]

In the decade following 2001, almost any contraption or method that might help the US military combat terrorism with less human exposure was also accepted into this fight. Predators and their brethren were acquired to penetrate denied physical space. The mini- and microdrones and the robots and the myriad associated appliances operated at all other altitudes and in all other conditions to put "intelligence" everywhere: the hidden, buried, flying, crawling, and riding sensors peering over the next hill, sniffing and warning of dangers, pulling guard duty, scouting the roads to provide warning for convoys, approaching improvised explosive devices (IEDs) and unexploded bombs.

In Afghanistan and Iraq, and then in new battlefields in Yemen and Pakistan, everyone was told that this was going to be a new kind of war. The United States wasn't going to win the fight against terrorism through defeating an army on the battlefield or attacking some set of traditional targets with bombers. The new mission was going out and hunting. Special operations forces and secret agents—that is, the small-scale and elite fighters like the Navy SEALs of the individual commando variety—would lead the fight, and more activity would take place in the shadows than in the light. Information would be as valuable as any bullet. Humans are engaged in this effort, and there are those individuals who actually go out there and risk their lives. But the irony is that this very human-centric design of hunter-killer special operations, these particular types of boots on the ground, require far more exhaustive preparation and microscopic-level intelligence information than industrial armies ever needed. Thus the technological effort and the human effort demand the same data, a circular requirement that has become the dominant activity.

Arguments are put forward in policy circles around Washington and by the drone manufacturers that unmanned systems merely offer gigantic cost savings or protect the lives of soldiers. Unbelievable advances in information technology, nanotechnology, and even genetics, together with the continued miniaturization of nearly everything, propel unprecedented and constant acceleration. The future already promises personal drones of amazing sophistication weighing just a gram.[20]

Some might say that these advances merely repeat the historical cycles of technological innovation that every war produces. But that is dangerous thinking. Every element of what has emerged in this increasingly unmanned world is dependent on civilian technology and, in fact, civilian infrastructure. Nothing happens in this world without the Internet, even if private pipelines and superencryption are the way that the military facilitates its own secure enclave within the network. As a result, private and public communications have become one. Developments in the processing and handling of big data, the use of the cloud, and information analysis move forward in parallel military and civilian worlds and at breakneck speed; the best of what is civilian is readily adapted for the military, whereas the robustness of what is military is desperately needed to protect networks that are no longer just civilian.

As civilian melds into military, naturally the number of civilians in the fight also increases. (Some technologies are just too new or too complex for a cadre of eighteen-year-old military gamers to master.) Civilian expertise, though, even when it's from dragooned academic and civilian specialties like anthropology or sociology, hasn't resulted in a better understanding of any country, nor of radical Islam or terrorism. But there has definitely been a mastering of the task of hunting as more and more of the old human tasks—finding and tracking, translation, navigation, even killing—are done more competently, even if in the service of an ultimately automatic Machine.

Though there is a pretense of flattening and greater collaboration through networking, in reality a two-tiered system has emerged. Centrally controlled information and networks akin to public transportation grids deliver big data and the big picture while every digital native gets their own equivalent private vehicle, not only constantly connected but also in control of their own little dashboard, with their own headphones, and their own high-powered flashlights to surf into the unknown. Everyone serves to defeat al Qaeda and other terrorists and enemies, but the actual effort is multitiered, the elite (and truly the few) doing the hunting and killing while the rest busy themselves in social net-warring: guard the bases, secure the supply lines for the convoys that deliver the water and fuel, thwart the IED networks that exist to thwart them, reduce human exposure. Warfare hasn't completely transformed into an endeavor where *everyone* on the battlefield is merely there to sustain being on the battlefield, but the ratio of those actually doing the fighting to those processing the information and operating the Machine is at historical extremes. It is hard to quantify, but during the Afghanistan war, only 1.6 percent of the supplies shipped to the battlefield comprised ammunition, and less than 1 percent was repair parts. Fuel, on the other hand, constituted almost 39 percent; water, food, clothing, and personal items made up another 55.4 percent.[21]

Although the intelligence produced by this phantasmagorical network is constantly depicted by Hollywood as having brought anything and everything just a mouse click away, or, more ominously, as having achieved a comprehensive and undifferentiated police state sprung from Edward Snowden's worst nightmare, the facts are contrary to both of these common pictures. The size of the Data Machine reflects its immaturity and the struggle to tame its subject matter more than its omniscience. Few inside the military or the world of public policy seem to be able to pinpoint this core problem because today's data collectors—military and civilian, government and commercial, public and private—all have one thing in common: whether through personal smartphones or through the most sophisticated hyperspectral imaging sensors, they accumulate unprecedented amounts of data. Think about your own information glut: texts, e-mails, photos, videos, music, paper mail, lists, and books residing on multiple appliances that are impossible to shut off, ponderous to categorize, and difficult to find.

The government effort costing hundreds of billions of dollars, constituting tens of thousands of sensors and hundreds of thousands of human operators and analysts, is barely able to keep up with the task of finding and monitoring a few thousand people. And that's the point: monumental leaps have occurred, both in technology and in the ways of war, but they have all been to achieve a very limited objective. The military has been transformed and become hyperprecise, but it also has become able to do only one thing: drill down to the individual—a terrorist, a car, an armored vehicle, a window in an office, the most hidden or fragile heart or brain of a machine or a network. Data feeds this incredible targeting machine, which goes about its work with such economy that it is sometimes not even apparent what is being destroyed, let alone why. It is such a new way of warfare that every death—friendly and enemy—is enormously magnified. Ours is a numerically anomalous tragedy; theirs an exaggerated and over-magnified victory.

Almost a decade and a half after 9/11, when I look at the digital legions splayed out on a truly global battlefield, I see drones and the Data Machine they serve—the unmanned with all of its special and unique ways—as the greatest threat to our national security, our safety, and our very way of life. If drones instantly didn't exist, the black boxes that are at the heart of the Data Machine would still equip manned aircraft and satellites, and would even be propelling themselves around on the ground. And yet drones are the proper place to start thinking about our illusory pursuit of this brand of perfect war, both the godlike endeavor to root out evil and the increased unwillingness to suffer human sacrifice in the course of making war.

CHAPTER ONE

Search of the Wind

...Heaven cried aloud, while earth did rumble.
The day grew still, darkness came forth.
There was a flash of lightning, fire broke out.
[The flames] flared up, death rained down.
TABLET IV, *EPIC OF GILGAMESH*

To really begin to understand drones, you have to understand Gilgamesh.

The *Epic of Gilgamesh* is the world's oldest work of literature, going back in Mesopotamian oral tradition more than 5,000 years.[1] Though unknown to many in the West, its narrative has influenced countless themes of humankind: there is a great flood, and there was an ancient time that existed before the deluge; there is a serpent that upends immortality; there are parables and rules that suggest moral codes for living one's life; and there are warnings of the dangers of absolute power on earth. Gilgamesh's story is so universal that references to it reached thousands of miles away into Egyptian and Hittite courts, into Greek and Roman literature, and even into the two great Judeo-Christian and Islamic books. "Gilgamesh links East and West, antiquity and modernity, poetry and history," writes one contemporary scholar.[2]

The *Epic* begins by explaining that Gilgamesh, one part man and two parts god, thought he "was wise in all matters on land

and sea," but had to endure friendship, loss, and transformation to find a cautious peace with himself.

Gilgamesh was the king of Uruk, striking in his looks, the fiercest of all warriors. But the young king was also a selfish and rapacious ruler. To teach him lessons of humility and mortal rule, the gods decided to create a friend and equal, Enkidu: a being made of clay and water and dropped into the wilderness, "innocent of mankind."

Let them contend together and leave Uruk in quiet, the gods said.

Enkidu was feral and free-living with the gazelles and the beasts, knowing nothing of the world of men, an enduring figure of the primeval and an archetype that persists in stories through *Tarzan of the Apes*.[3] One day a hunter spies the enormous and hairy Enkidu taking water with the wild animals and goes to tell Gilgamesh of this beast that is frustrating his hunt.

A wild one, a star fallen from heaven, strong and free? Gilgamesh exclaims. He's had a dream of this unconquerable equal, two parts man and one part wild creature.

The king bids Shamhat, a courtesan of Ishtar's temple, to go and embrace Enkidu, to teach him the art of the women "so that a man he will finally be." The two lie together for six days and seven nights. When Enkidu is finally sated, he is also transformed. When he returns to the wild, the creatures run away. "Enkidu was grown weak, for wisdom was in him, and the thoughts of a man were in his heart," the *Epic* says.

Shamhat then tells Enkidu about Gilgamesh, the king who is also perfect in strength and could be his equal in all respects. On the way to Uruk, Enkidu is literally transformed into a man— shaved, clothed, taught to speak, to eat, to enjoy the pleasures of beer—and he also learns of the king's wicked rule. When he arrives, the first thing he does is intervene to stop Gilgamesh from taking a virgin bride from her betrothed on their wedding night, a privilege the king reserves for himself. The two wrestle in a titanic bout, knocking down walls and destroying buildings. And though Gilgamesh prevails, he is deeply moved by Enkidu's courage and strength, and they immediately develop a profound friendship, becoming brothers-in-arms.

Bored with his existence in Uruk, Gilgamesh then decides to challenge Humbaba, the devoted demon of the gods and protector of the great cedar forest. Gilgamesh and Enkidu journey many days to what is assumed to be today's Syria or Lebanon to cut down the coveted trees to adorn Uruk's palaces and temples. They encounter and then slay Humbaba, but only together, and then only really with the intervention of the gods.

When they return to Uruk, even Ishtar, the goddess of love, is so stunned by Gilgamesh's conquest and his beauty that she proposes that he become her lover. But Gilgamesh spurns and shames the deity of Uruk: "Which of your lovers did you ever love forever?" he asks, recounting a string of men and their pitiful ends at her hands.

Ishtar is so incensed that she demands that her father send down the Bull of Heaven to teach Gilgamesh a lesson. When the bull arrives, he stamps the ground and opens a chasm to the underworld, killing hundreds in the city. He drinks of the Euphrates River and reduces its level by many feet. Another epic battle ensues. Fighting together, Gilgamesh and Enkidu slay the celestial bull. But Enkidu goes too far at the end and heaves its flank at Ishtar on her temple walls.

Is it Gilgamesh's contempt or Enkidu's brutal act that provides the reason for punishment? In either case, the gods decide they must teach Gilgamesh a lesson, and Enkidu is given an illness that eats away at him. He dreams of the "house of dust" that awaits him, the netherworld. And on the twelfth day, as he is dying, he beseeches Gilgamesh: Do not forget how we fought together. "I shall not die like a man fallen in battle," he cries, shameful that his end comes merely from a sickness.

Gilgamesh's heart is shattered with Enkidu's death. He goes off in search of immortality, believing now that his life is meaningless unless it can be made eternal. He returns to the wild, clothing himself in animal skins and seeking out Utanapishti, the legendary man who reputedly survived the great flood with "the seed of all living creatures," to find out how he too might escape death.

At the edge of the world, Gilgamesh overcomes the scorpion men who guard the Mashu district, the mountains where the sun rises and sets. At the waters of death, he impetuously kills the odd stone oarsmen of Urshanabi, the ferryman, almost destroying all chances of crossing. During a great sea journey, Gilgamesh's and Urshanabi's punting poles are eaten by the death waters, and the two bind their clothing into sails. Finally arriving before the great prophet, Gilgamesh learns the knowledge of all the times before the great flood. And he learns that he cannot live forever. Defeated, he returns to Uruk with the knowledge of mortality and settles into his role as wise ruler, satisfied that his tale will live on in the stone tablets he leaves behind.

Someone with a sense of antiquity, or irony, gave the name Gilgamesh to an actual device that is one of the top secret tools of the modern-day Data Machine. Developed and fielded for the National Security Agency in 2006 to hunt terrorists, Gilgamesh the black box is attached to unmanned Predator and even larger Reaper drones, where it performs a very specific task in "signals intelligence," seeking out the faintest and most fleeting of buried digits emanating from the contemporary netherworld and performing the alchemy needed to precisely place them.

By itself, Gilgamesh the black box is just a laptop-sized hunk of metal and circuit boards. But when combined with a host of other similarly named devices—ARTEMIS, Gemini, Nitro, Temptress, Nebula—the gathering horde of sensors, receivers, processors, direction finders, decoders, and recorders accumulates both a greater synergy and a higher vision. This is warfare truly transformed. Though many make the mistake of assuming that what has changed since 9/11 is global terrorism—nonstate actors or an Islamic jihad or even "asymmetrical" warfare—the enduring transformation, that which will affect human history from now until all eternity, is not the enemy but the world that Gilgamesh the black box represents.[4] It is not a weapon per se, nor is it a game-changer of blatant historic note. Gilgamesh is also not merely the kind of joystick-controlled robot that so many have put forth to punctuate their distaste for war and ancient blood-lust. In fact, military historians and buffs will probably never speak of this Gilgamesh in the same way they speak of Enigma, blitzkrieg, Little Boy, precision, stealth, or any other war winners of any of the Great Wars. Gilgamesh's setting, moreover, will never have the heroic distinction of a Waterloo or a Gettysburg or a Normandy. Not only is Gilgamesh virtually invisible due to crushing government secrecy, it also floats above and is disconnected from the very geography it meticulously catalogs; it is difficult to make concrete as what we think of when we think of an army, or warfare, or even a place.

Gilgamesh is an obscure cog in a bigger system of systems and a network that is the heart of what I call the Data Machine. I call Gilgamesh itself a black box, the term attached to a flight recorder on an aircraft but also, according to the dictionary definition, any complex piece of equipment, typically a unit in an electronic system, whose contents are mysterious to the user. Part eye, part ear, part balance and sensing, Gilgamesh is just one of thousands of pieces of what military command and control experts call the "sensors, actuators, and data layer" of the Global Information Grid (GIG), a military combination of all networks, mobile and landline, voice and data.[5]

Just as "black box" is an imperfect representation because Gilgamesh needs to be conceived as more anthropomorphized than a mere box, the Machine that Gilgamesh attaches to has to be seen more like a living body made up of organs and bloodstream, each part cellular and complex and interconnected. This Data Machine— the national security complex, US intelligence, spying and killing, targeted death—grew and improved as needs presented themselves, as technologies emerged, and as computing power increased. But it has never been nurtured, or, to extend the analogy even further, it has been raised in the wild, magnificent and hairy but lacking in those attributes that make for a thoughtful human endeavor. Those in charge speak of the GIG's "architecture" as if someone started with a blueprint, but as retired air force chief General John Jumper said more than a decade ago when describing the growing machine: "You wouldn't dare buy a house that your architect couldn't draw for you first." And yet, as he says, "We're buying parts and pieces of our military without having a picture of the house."[6]

Like the *Epic of Gilgamesh*, the earthly world of Gilgamesh the black box comprises an expansive cast of characters—some with mythical names, some felicitous, some warlike and ominous. Each black box character plays a distinct role in each stratum of digital war-making. And in the way that Gilgamesh the actual king is recorded in Sumerian history as having ruled for 126 years, Gilgamesh the black box has to be thought of in a very contemporary time frame. The niche capability that this and other black boxes provide might last only 126 days, but that's an eternity in our information age. Think of them as the latest smartphone or app in the form of specialized wiretaps or spy cameras. There's a demand for a one-off to be fabricated and put in place to exploit some opportunity or fill some intelligence blind spot. But the hunted quarry is also ever-changing, adapting or making use of new methods to exist, communicate, travel, or hide within a bigger digital background that is itself constantly undergoing growth and change. So when the target or the technological or computational conditions change, the inventors go back to their shadowy caldrons, and another specialized Gilgamesh comes along to take the place of the outmoded one. Black box Gilgameshes that each play a specific role in intercepting and precisely geolocating a potential target thus emerge whenever and wherever there is a need. The type of data being collected constantly mutates as new sources and methods of collecting and deciphering are discovered. There are countless other secret sensors like Gilgamesh of the black box variety—ACES HY, Lynx, Dragonfly, Pennantrace, Silent Dagger, Star Sapphire, Airhandler, Viper Reach—each a platoon mate, each slightly different and able to "see" or "hear" or untangle some identifying characteristic of an electronic morsel to penetrate into the most unconventional of domains. Black boxes process imagery—photos in the visible spectrum, infrared images, synthetic aperture radar, light detection and ranging, or spectral renderings—scrutinizing each frame as it floods in, tagging and sending the take either for immediate use or for retrieval later. Other black boxes act as secret agents that can suck down the contents of a computer hard drive: more data to be sent off for processing and use. Sound waves, facial recognition, smells, infinitesimal changes in chemical makeup or landscape, the special and unique gait of an individual's stride, can all be collected and measured in some form of digital indicator. Searchers seek even to capture and characterize innate emanations: a dormant cell phone, a computer keystroke in front of a screen, a microprocessor within an automobile, some oscillating or unintentionally revealing digit that might indicate a presence and an identity even when the mechanical and corporeal world is seemingly silent. Data is the prize, but the path to getting it is the task.

The collectors would be nothing without the processors, the members of another black box tribe: Alaska, Association, Final e Curfew, Gargle8 and Garuda, Temptress, and Witchhunt. These tools characterize and analyze the collected data, peering into pixels and wavelengths and binaries, triaging and fusing information to discover or figure out an identity and then its place in a larger social network. Sharkfinn, Chalkfun, and Goldminer, part of the Real-time Regional Gateway (RTRG) family, push intercepted communications to battlefield users. Specialized brethren such as Thunderbunny and Metrics do specific tasks such as computing the connections between one electronic device and another: "call chaining." Dishfire, Octave, Contraoctave, Broomstick, and Taperlay store the voluminous material. Stratus and Turretfire keep it in the cloud. As digits are logged, translated, parsed, sorted, and displayed, hundreds of additional specialized and secret applications arrange them by date, by location, by language, by voice, and by subject. Incompatible software and formats are threaded together through other sets of black boxes, software, and widgets.[7]

Each of these ingenious Gilgameshes represents tens or hundreds of millions in invested dollars and hours by some government laboratory or (more often) private company of IT geniuses unlaboring away in obscurity. But this is not a tale about industry or money. Gilgamesh and its kind are not only almost universally absent from the public debate about warfare and targeted killing, but no one is really privy to or can fully grasp the totality of the new indecipherable, not the users, not the managers, not the decision-makers, and certainly not the elected officials.[8] This is a world beyond "death TV," as it is sometimes referred to, the now-familiar black-and-white renderings of full-motion video that have become all too common in describing a singular eye in the sky as just "drones." It is a world beyond voice transmissions or even the so-called metadata that is attached to every piece of digital communication and that most people just associate with the NSA. Struggling with its own definition, the military sometimes calls it intelligence mission data.[9] "The speed of technical innovation and the complexity of modern weapons systems are creating ever-increasing demand for specialized intelligence mission data to feed sensors and automated processes," a 2013 Pentagon report says.[10]

Feed me! Is this the human condition of intelligence, of the Data Machine? That the Machine churns on because it serves no purpose except to ingest everything? Does it churn because in political terms, leaders are afraid they will be punished after the next spectacular terror attack if they have failed to detect that specific something that might have made the difference? Or is it just data, and are they merely sucking up everything simply because we can, "a growing amount of surveillance, communications, and intelligence work...being performed by unmanned aircraft and satellites"[11] disconnected from a human endeavor, even one as repugnant and glorious as war?

In the closed community of Gilgamesh the black box, in locked rooms inside barricaded and guarded compounds, the relentless Machine churns. The cameras and the sensors and the listening devices are carried aloft by another family—Predators, Reapers, Global Hawks, little Ravens, manned Liberties, Rivet Joints, Senior Scouts, and Dragon Ladies (U-2s). The unmanned "platforms" like Predator that have become so well known, however, are, as the label "platform" suggests, merely hosts—kind of like flying buses—carrying the army of passengers (certainly more often black boxes than bombs or missiles) that collect the digits.

The essential finishers are the wizards of geolocation—ARTEMIS, Displayview, Foxmill, G-box, GEGS, Nemesis, Talonview, Toxicaire, Typhon, and Worldwind—more black boxes and software workers that—or is it who?—perform direction finding and triangulation, comparing the times and frequencies from signals as received at different collectors, pinpointing the location of something even when an object is moving, even performing geolocation when only one vertex in a triangle is known.

When Gilgamesh seamlessly meshes and everything is revealed, when digital markers can be calculated and timed and fused with change detection histories and "pattern of life" databases, it is relentless exactitude from the heavens. The end result is labeled High Value Target (HVT) assured pursuit, "assured pursuit" being an official buzzphrase used to describe a very specific and very secret achievement: the finding and killing of the enemies of the state. In this top secret world, "Assured Pursuit Certified (APC)" is even something one can actually put on one's résumé; it is a kind of marksmanship badge meaning that one has mastered the use of all the modern-day black boxes and is privy to the secrets of the gods: how to conduct the meticulous work of human archeology that has come to be at the center of perpetual war.

Gilgamesh the black box is at the center of our story, but it isn't the hero. Given the totality of the Machine, there isn't really a single hero in the world of black boxes. This is not to impugn some leader or general or commander or scientist or analyst or pilot or soldier, nor is it to question or doubt the human sacrifices of the killed and injured or the exceptional bravery of the actual fighters who indeed go out and take the greatest risks. But Gilgamesh is, in the end, just one of thousands of components; and though we have way too much of a tendency, in our struggle to grasp modern warfare, to reduce the world of drones to those Cessna-sized Predators that we imagine are guided by some joystick-wielding adolescent, the truth is that except for the few who actually hike and hide and sweat, the few who actually have to go outside the wire and beyond the barricades to the edge of the world in the quest, the vast majority of humans are a removed network of technicians—unlaborers—who outnumber old-fashioned fighters tens of thousands to one. Two parts machine, one part man: the fight is truly unmanned.

"We should join together and do one thing, a deed such as has never (before) been done," Gilgamesh says to Enkidu in Tablet IV of the *Epic*. It could be the motto for this extraordinary search party. *It* never has been done before, not on this scale, not with this ambition, a global network that seeks the most elusive morsel in an infinite information universe, searching deeper and deeper into every buried recess, processing all for the singular purpose of locating an enemy—the unanticipated and diabolical that forever eludes.

The cold truth is that the endeavor is irreducible from the Machine and its network.[12] Feeding the Machine, and the enormity of the mere task of integrating it all, overwhelms. The culmination is not some final battle per se, it is the distillation of the military's efforts into some 3-D model or PowerPoint briefing or even video simulation to evoke a decision to kill, a process that has "crisp efficiency" and an inexorable quality, as one veteran of targeted killing decision-making said, that "left him feeling more like an observer than a participant."[13] It's therefore hard not to see the Machine as kin to some kind of divine execution, hard not to label it all godlike, hard not to decry a robot takeover or some sanitized video game, warfare stripped of all the humanity.[14]

Who other than Gilgamesh can say "I am king without equal"? the *Epic* asks.

And thus our story begins, an effort to fathom our descent into the world of the unmanned and our servitude to the Machine. Our modern-day Gilgamesh travels leagues, and journeys to unknown places in the beyond. It exists in a world of warfare, but also a world inextricable from our society and its struggles with the information age. It is a world where human interventions in the decisions of life and death are essential and where the entire enterprise is indeed man-made, but where the Machine's purpose is to eliminate the weaknesses and errors of human input.

CHAPTER TWO

Dead Reckoning

Shamash roused against Humbaba the mighty galewinds:
South Wind, North Wind, East Wind and West Wind,
Blast, Counterblast, Typhoon, Hurricane and Tempest,
Devil-Wind, Frost-Wind, Gale and Tornado.
TABLET V, *EPIC OF GILGAMESH*

H e will take you to the Garden of Eden," the Iraqi general said.

Word preceded my arrival in the small southern backwater, a decrepit village located at the point where the Tigris and Euphrates Rivers meet to form the Shatt al-Arab.

Two days earlier, I had been farther north, in Amarah, listening to a diatribe by a Saddam crony who said the United States had dropped colorful "mines" intended to attract the attention of children and animals and then to automatically explode when they got near. I was in Iraq just months after the 1991 Gulf War ended, working as the sole military advisor to the so-called Harvard Study Team of medical professionals and lawyers, the first team inside Iraq to survey the civilian effects.

"You'll have to prove that," I said, and the Saddam henchman turned to one of his aides and issued some order in Arabic. The next morning, my team and I accompanied an Iraqi general and his gun-toting entourage into the barren desert west of town.

Scattered about on the scrub-covered and clay-cracked expanse as far as the eye could see were hundreds of bright-yellow soda-can-sized objects, surely an odd sight to behold in the expanse of brownness. I could tell from the size and shape of the objects that this was a graveyard of BLU-97 bomblets, the unexploded remnants of larger cluster bombs. Since the bomblets are designed to explode right above the ground or on contact, there were many questions: Was it a weapons malfunction? Was it a dumping ground for leftovers jettisoned after missions farther north? And what about the Iraqi claim that the bomblets were still going off and killing civilians? How volatile were these devices now, after having sat and baked in the sun in the months since they had first been dropped?

The ground reminded me a little of northern New Mexico, where wide expanses on both sides of trickling streams can instantly turn into raging rivers and then recede, leaving behind a parched arroyo to be baked, curling clay a couple of inches thick, rock-hard on the sun side, still moist underneath. And that's sort of what happened in Iraq in January and February 1991, a particularly rainy season. Months of standoff starting with Iraq's August invasion of Kuwait took place over a line in the sand in a parched and largely featureless geography called the Syrian Desert, a lifeless quarter that occupies parts of Iraq, Kuwait, Saudi Arabia, Jordan, and Syria, ancient lava fields covering 125,000 square miles, the size of Great Britain, or New Mexico. For five months, Iraqi forces dug in. But by the time the war started in mid-January, Desert Storm only partially lived up to its first name. Rains swept over the Mesopotamian interior, the lands between the Tigris and Euphrates Rivers, north and east of the Syrian Desert. And not only that, but 1991 was a particularly harsh and wet winter.

Since the time of Gilgamesh, the coming of the rains and the flooding that often resulted changed the fortunes of civilizations that occupied this Fertile Crescent. Old Assyrian texts mention that trade resumes in the spring after the "opening of roads," a process necessary after winter rains covered everything with water.[1] The courses of the great rivers themselves changed many times. Ancient Uruk—Gilgamesh's kingdom—was once on the bank of the Euphrates and is now just an archeological ruin deep in the desert. As civilization came, so to speak, roads were built up on high embankments, with bridges and culverts crossing rivers and their tributaries, but also over dry riverbeds (wadis), allowing the flooding to pass. Hence these low-lying areas adjacent to the roads that filled with water in the winter months. Now, six months after Desert Storm bombing, the waters around Amarah had long ago seeped into the ground and evaporated, exposing thousands of unexploded bomblets. Were they duds simply lying there because they had failed to detonate when they landed in the water?

Randomly—and, in hindsight, stupidly—I approached one near the road where our convoy parked, took pictures, got down on the ground and wrote down the serial numbers, inexpertly thought about the amount of explosive contained inside, imagined the scored and crenelated steel canister designed to break up into thousands of tiny pieces of killing metal, and figured that the bomblet, if it exploded, would form a conical shape dispersing upward. I backed up about twenty-five feet, which was how far away I thought we would have to be to escape any shrapnel that would fly overhead. I shooed everyone else behind me, including the general and the soldiers, who obediently scattered, and then I threw a rock.

The next thing I knew, I was flat on my back, blood gushing from my mouth, painful shrapnel and bits of incendiary zirconium wafer embedded in my lip and right arm. By the luck of the gods, I wasn't so short as to have shrapnel hit me in the eye. My translator, Zena, also was a dentist by training, and, by sheer coincidence, we had dined the previous day with an English-speaking surgeon at Saddam General Hospital in Amarah, which was where we headed. I don't remember much from that moment on, but Zena rendered immediate first aid, washing the wound with our stockpile of bottled water, and held my lip together as we careened east to the hospital.

"I have killed my American," I remember the general whining repeatedly.

As soon as we got to town, Zena called her father in Baghdad and told him to find plastic surgery thread and bring it down to Amarah, about a four-hour drive from the capital. They didn't have those delicate supplies at this provincial civilian hospital, nor did they have antibiotics or much of anything else. But by midafternoon, the British-trained surgeon was sewing my lip back together and removing fragments from my arm.

Stitched, bandaged, and in throbbing pain, I continued my mission the next day. And there in al Qurnah, though I wanted to see the al Hartha electrical power plant, newly built and destroyed by US bombing in another puzzling anomaly, my Iraqi host had a far more special treat for his American guest, the man now famous for hurling the stone. He would take us to see "the tree."

In the middle of a garbage-strewn and abandoned portico at the confluence of the two rivers south of town, there is a ten-foot-high bleached and shriveled skeleton of a shrub. The general referred to it as Adam's tree and insisted that this very place was the cradle of civilization, the location where the Garden of Eden once was, and the source of all mankind. Feral dogs pacing the perimeter snarled; the midafternoon sun beat down, activating a putrid smell of urine and feces, all creating an overall ambiance that made it kind of hard to fully appreciate.

Little did I know then that this tree was also a confluence and a path to this story: as I pieced together my own fragments, I learned why there was such a large number of unexploded bomblets clustered along the roads of Amarah. The answer wasn't malfeasance, and though mistakes were made and technical problems revealed, focusing too much on them obscured more important lessons. There was a logical reason why cluster bombs had been used here and why they had such a high dud rate as a result of landing in water, but the why and the aftereffects were practically invisible to both Iraqi and American military men. And so I learned that the minute details really mattered, that secrecy and compartmentalization were as much a curse inside the system as they were outside, and that the lowly implementers (Iraqi missile men or American pilots) had a job to do and couldn't see the big picture. But most important, to understand the evolution of the unmanned and the Data Machine, I learned that though politicians and people with axes to grind might scream bloody murder, the technologists always—always—seek to make killing ever more discriminate and precise.[2]

From Amarah I learned as well that hardly anyone, no matter how high his or her rank, has a complete picture or really knows what is going on outside his or her specific organization. It was an experience that would shape much of my struggle to understand the secret world over the next two decades, in part because it taught me to scrutinize action and reaction not just to determine what went right and wrong, but also to look for the big picture in the small technological and operational details.

During the 1991 war, Saddam's forces shot Scud missiles from western *and* southeastern Iraq, and though army general Norman Schwarzkopf, the Desert Storm commander, dismissed them militarily as not being able to hit the broad side of a barn—and the

US Air Force saw the missiles as a diversion from their choreographed bombing campaign of Baghdad—a top priority in Washington was keeping Israel out of the war. Aircraft were thus sent out to find Saddam's missile launchers, but they kept coming. When Iraq shot missiles at Saudi Arabia, the missiles originated from hide sites west of Amarah and north of al Qurnah, setting up quickly, firing, and moving. Infrared sensors on faraway satellites recorded the launches, some nights transmitting the data quickly—but never quickly enough.

The Scud "hunt" accelerated, but finding the launchers proved impossible, even after pilots observed a missile being fired 15,000 feet below.[3] The hunt became a matter of pride for the air force; failure to find the Scuds would be such a contrast with its success in otherwise employing stealth and laser-guided bombs. Scud-hunting aircraft were kept airborne continuously to enhance response time. A sort of chess game pitted American technology against an unsophisticated yet wily opponent, Iraq exploiting American blind spots and willing to operate contrary to standard military doctrines to deliver the only kind of hurt it could.

Fifteen percent of all air missions into the Iraqi interior ended up being diverted to counter the Scud—a huge demand for resources if nothing else—but no one particularly anticipated that the weather would have such an additional impact. Rain and fog, high winds, battlefield obscurations natural and man-made wreaked havoc. Hundreds of attack sorties and a significant number of entire mission packages were canceled because parts—aerial tankers or supporting reconnaissance—weren't available to accompany the attackers. And since most aircraft were already operating at medium or high altitudes, outside the range of the bulk of Iraqi air defenses, poor visibility became a double problem. Low clouds, which were present about a third of the time, meant that pilots couldn't see much on the ground.

If air war strategists and targeters could not precisely locate the mobile Scud missile launchers but knew generally where they were firing from, they surmised that this knowledge could, at the very least, help them to limit the Scud movements. Consequently, they started dropping cluster bombs along the roads and embankments where launchers were suspected. With a dispersal area approaching the size of a football field, even a single cluster bomb was thought to have an impact.[4] Targeters particularly sought road bridges in the areas to limit where these modern-day monsters could rampage.[5] This ended up including the Amarah city bridge just a few hundred feet from Saddam General Hospital, a bridge that otherwise would have been on no target list. The bridge wasn't completely destroyed in the attack, but it was damaged enough to stop a multi-ton transporter from crossing. The blast from the bombs also blew out windows, cracked walls, and showered the interior of the hospital with shards of glass and debris.

The failure to find Scuds became legend in the antiairpower annals and among military historians schooled to believe real wars only happen on the ground. Airpower advocates had answers and rationalizations galore: after overstating how many Scud launchers they had succeeded in destroying, they argued that they had kept Israel out of the war and reduced Iraq's ability to fire missiles. Mission accomplished. They had similar arguments about Saddam's survival, about his massive stockpile of weapons of mass destruction discovered after the war, and about civilian casualties and so-called collateral damage. They argued that they hadn't killed Saddam because they hadn't really been trying to, and that they hadn't destroyed WMDs because the intelligence people hadn't known about them. In both cases, it was someone else's fault. "Pictures of bombs threading their way down ventilator ports, elevator shafts, and bunker doors demonstrated more eloquently than any amount of written analysis how effectively and devastatingly air warfare could strike," an official air force report bragged later,[6] ignoring all the Scudiness. If their method of bombing hadn't completely eliminated civilian casualties or damage, it had, airpower advocates argued, at least produced historically low levels. These advocates couldn't necessarily substantiate or convince anyone of the veracity of these claims, but they formed the basis for weapons improvements and technological advances over the following two decades to overcome weather constraints and improve accuracy and timeliness of attacks.

Many would focus on the war's role in exorcising the ghosts of Vietnam—clear mission, superb army leadership, no micromanagement from the top, and absolute victory. Many of the same guardians of the senior service and the sanctity of military history also looked up at airpower and sensed an appropriation. They disparaged the remote instrument, the pretense of spotless surgery, the video-game war, even the moral flaw of an unfair fight. Whether it was in the space-age Patriot antimissile missiles or the stealth fighter, critics felt comfortable in the realm of arguing that things didn't work or did not go as planned, as if somehow things going wrong in warfare were an attribute unique to airpower.[7]

Iraqis also shared this disparaging view, which slowly took hold in the Arab and Muslim world. Airpower—the instrument that was indifferent to geography, the new mode of warfare that could compress distance and reach out practically impervious to countermeasure—came to symbolize American arrogance and subjugation. Historians used to telling the war story through War 1.0 heroics and chivalry on the ground were flummoxed by airpower and the emerging unmanned system, which had neither a Gilgamesh-like hero nor a human story line.

Adam's tree thus wasn't just some kitsch fascist monument invented by Saddam, or, as the army Strategic Studies Institute would interpret it even a decade later, Baathist propaganda falsely trying to connect Iraq to "some of the greatest civilizations in ancient history beginning with Sumer and Akkad, then Babylon, Assyria, Chaldea, and the Abbasid caliphate."[8] Adam's tree was an essential window into why Iraqis thought of themselves as different and special, and how they also measured the flow of history and their place in it on a very different scale from the moment-by-moment American ethos. I saw this on the ground but also learned that it is the very kind of insight that isn't attainable from the air, the very understanding that we think of as "intelligence," which has increasingly become impossible to pick up in our era of drones and data.

"Mesopotamia has been the venue for many onslaughts and wars," Saddam later told the Turkish newspaper *Hürriyet*. "Nevertheless, a new civilization emerged after each onslaught and war, and God willing we will establish a new Iraq."[9] Everywhere I went in Iraq, I heard people echo a similar narrative, a kind of defense of Iraq's behavior, even those who vociferously opposed Saddam himself. I heard rationalizations for the invasion and for the destruction of Kuwait's oil wells, and justifications for Iraqi intransigence in not cooperating with the international community now that the shooting was over.

Who would expect little Iraq to prevail against the onslaught of the entire world's military machine and its superior arms? Saddam said, and normal Iraqis echoed him. Of course the tiny country would lose in a battle against a country both larger and technologically superior. That was just a matter of physics. But if Iraq had withdrawn from Kuwait under threat of war from the United States and the United Nations, that would have spelled a great moral defeat, would have compromised Iraq to political calculations rather than to its historic destiny. The United States— the West—with its superior technology could destroy the modern infrastructure of Iraq—wasn't that even the intention behind goading Iraq into Kuwait in the first place? they'd ask, with a nod and a wink—but the land of the great rivers would still be there when the nations we were currently familiar with were long gone. In this land inextricably tied to civilizations going back before Gilgamesh all the way to Adam, defeat was transitory, a mere moment in the great sweep of mankind.

The Institute for Defense Analyses later analyzed the Scud hunt with a strictly technological focus. High flying in itself didn't reduce the effectiveness (or accuracy) of smart weapons, but laser-guided or remote-controlled (say, from a television camera) precision relied on continued visual contact with the target.[10] Slow response times, limitations in sensors, problems with distinguishing targets from decoys, and precise geolocation also proved wanting. It all came down to mastering the holy grail of time-dependent targeting: "Airborne sensors stayed out of Iraqi airspace, marginalizing their coverage, and strike aircraft received inadequate cueing from satellites due to sensor limitations." An average of sixty minutes was needed to collect and disseminate information on located Scud missiles. But by then, the Scuds were gone.[11]

Over the next decade, while Iraq decayed under sanctions and military pressure, the technologists sought to perfect the ability to dispense with pulsating air defenses and the hoary Humbaba launchers of the industrial era, or, for that matter, with any other mechanized army like Iraq's. That desert of frustration outside Amarah spurred on new weapons, better sensors, more robust communications capabilities, all with the goal of improving the methods and compressing the time needed to find a target, to more precisely locate it, and to kill it in any weather. These became the elements of advanced precision warfare in Afghanistan and the next Iraq war more than twenty years later; what today has an initialism of F3EAD—Find, Fix, Finish, Exploit, Analyze, and Disseminate—but in those days could barely be spelled out.[12] Technologies just then emerging—computing power, digital optics, satellite navigation, ubiquitous (and cheap) long-range control, a worldwide and robust network of communications—would form the back end of every military and civilian development to follow.

As I visited Iraq again later in the 1990s, it was plainly evident that hundreds of thousands of Iraqi young men who had experienced and survived Desert Storm had gone home with a reluctant but healthy respect for the awesomeness of the American military and its technology. Sure, there was anger as well as a continuing sense of dogged resignation that Iraq's greatness was more tied to its past than to its future. Iraq's army had been soundly defeated in battle, defeated by an opponent that it could not reach or equal. And it was equally clear that although the country had once been modern (or at least modernizing), with hospitals and superhighways and a communications and electrical grid that the US military had considered worth bombing in the first place, it was now disintegrating, a fact that highlighted Iraq's defeat while everyone else seemed to be marching forward.

The terrorists who would emerge in the next decade didn't have much affinity for Saddam Hussein's plight, nor did the Iraqi experience of utter defeat inculcate much respect on their part for the United States. They saw the new world order and the West as the new rapacious rulers of planet Earth, cravenly hiding behind a shield of superior technology. The significance of Scud missiles, those clumsy and inaccurate terror weapons of an earlier era, was that they inspired those who wished to fight the magnificent King, whether in the development of suicide bombers, airliners as weapons, or later improvised explosive devices. None of these weapons would ever really threaten the West or directly defeat the modern military, but they would force those operating out of reach to come down to the human level of carnage and feel its effect.

CHAPTER THREE

Fire and Forget

I examined the look of the weather.
The weather to look at was full of foreboding,
I went into the boat and sealed my hatch.
To the one who sealed the boat, Puzur-Enlil the boatman,
I gave my palace with all its goods.
TABLET XI, *EPIC OF GILGAMESH*

O ne can almost hear the adolescent guffaws in the American telling of the first Gulf war, locker-room swagger that glosses over all the difficulties involved in preparing to fight the *fourth-largest army in the world*. Gone and forgotten are the many drills in anticipation of chemical weapons or worse, the thousands of body bags shipped to Saudi Arabia for the expected corpses, the fear that the new smart weapons would not work, and the many frustrations when the likes of Scud missiles stymied the best of plans. All was miraculously expunged at the end of forty-three days, and making fun of the hapless opponents, with their mismatched uniforms and meager supplies, became the new narrative, the impetuous and thoughtless heaving of the severed flank of the Bull of Heaven at the gods was the taunting of the enemy.

Perhaps one of the saddest pretenses is in the urban legend of Iraqi soldiers being so stupid that they tried to surrender to a drone. It was on one of the last days of the conflict. An unmanned

Pioneer, its snowmobile engine screeching away at about 2,000 feet, overflew Kuwait's Faylakah Island, taking video that included footage of Iraqi soldiers waving white flags in the air.

The footage was beamed back to a US Navy battleship and went viral in military channels. The story, which was quickly embellished, became lore not just of Iraq's easy dispatch but also of the magic of the unmanned.[1] Remote images of the enemy surrendering!

In 1991, live video was virtually unheard of outside highly classified intelligence circles, and now the hierarchical bottom-dwellers had their own eyes in the sky. No longer did they have to wait for information to come in from distant agencies—agencies that would package this information without regard for the consumers.[2] It wasn't quite real-time surveillance in the way we think of that today, but it was a taste. Users fell in love with the pictures. General Walter Boomer, the top marine commander, labeled the Pioneer drone "the single most valuable intelligence collector" of Desert Storm.[3]

But this wasn't really the case. On the contrary, drones were actually a scant footnote in the war, deployed in limited numbers and of marginal utility. One-way kamikaze-like electronic fakers were used by air warriors to deceive Baghdad air defense systems on the opening night of the war.[4] But other than that, the only notable contribution was made by three dozen 400-pound Pioneers, which flew a total of 330 missions, spending about 1,000 hours in the air.[5] Working for the army and the marines, these short-range drones went in close where it was thought too dangerous for man to venture, and in a couple of instances scored some tactical success, perhaps auguring what was to come with greater reliability and integration in the future.[6] But in actuality, the majority of Pioneers belonged to the navy and spent most of their time out of harm's way and supporting a sideshow, lurking over a Kuwaiti mudflat jutting into the gulf. There the most for-saken of Iraqi infantry remained trapped and cut off from com-munications and supply, bit players in an American pretense of pinning down coastal forces by deceiving them into thinking an amphibious invasion was coming. In reality, those soldiers were Saddam's cannon fodder, pins on some craven general's map.

"Exceptional utility," Vice Admiral David Jeremiah, then vice chairman of the Joint Chiefs of Staff, said of Pioneer's role when the war was over.[7] The Pentagon's postwar report on unmanned systems lauded the "unprecedented success" of the drone, which it said proved "the utility and importance of UAVs in combat." Only one was shot down, the Defense Department crowed.[8] "Pioneer became a legend," said another analysis.[9]

Without digging further, uncurious historians refer to "Pio-neer's ability to spot each sixteen-inch round fired by U.S. battle-ships in real time," thereby increasing "the accuracy of the big guns."[10] "Ability" is the key word here: there is no evidence that the Pioneer did more than fly and film. And "accuracy" also has a very strange definition; the obsolete and inaccurate projectiles hit the ground, but we don't know much more about what happened to these shells, which weighed as much as a Volkswagen Beetle. They barreled down to earth with all of hell's fury, the very antithesis of precision and a leftover of another epoch, America's own version of Scud terror. In fact, over a period of sixty hours, from February 23 to 26, almost six hundred parcels of retribution — more than half of all the projectiles fired during Desert Storm and nearly as many shells as American battleships fired during the last fifteen months of World War II — rained down on the coastal "defenders."[11]

The official military justification was to deceive Iraqi troops into thinking an amphibious invasion was coming and thus pin-ning them in place. But the real purpose was a form of brutal housekeeping: away from TV cameras and probing eyes, the battleships were pulled out of the old industrial closet and deployed. The United States was able to landfill the old ammunition abroad, rather than having to dispose of it back home.[12] Faylakah was the perfect venue for our leftovers. In fact, fighters bombing Iraqi targets farther inland also dropped bombs on Faylakah Island upon returning to their aircraft carriers from unsatisfying missions — the planes couldn't land on the ships with external bombs still slung under their wings, so they had to go. They could have been jettisoned into the water, but why waste a bomb? Even the incident involving Iraqi soldiers surrendering to Pioneer has an explanation. A Pioneer launched from the battleship *Wisconsin* became uncontrollable and headed off over Iraqi positions, positions that had already been subjected to heavy bombardment. Iraqi troops poured out of their bunkers and trenches, waving any white material they could lay their hands on in a desperate bid to surrender before — they assumed — the arrival of yet more sixteen-inch shells. Flying at a low level and out of control, the drone had developed a mind of its own and must have appeared particularly menacing — at least before it ran out of fuel and crashed.[13]

The boosters crowed about Pioneer's debut, but the actual record of its performance and its overall military contribution tells a different story. This would be the usual case as warfare moved from the industrial to the information era, this dichotomy of everything going as well as could be expected, or even better, the technology working perfectly, and yet that fact is completely divorced from any complex and larger outcome. This phenomenon has become even more pronounced with drones and the world of black boxes, where in addition secrecy and novelty aggrandize so much attention, obscuring and even erasing the reality on the ground.

So despite all of the quotes from the generals, Pioneer wasn't any kind of magic bullet; in reality, ground commanders and operators alike found Pioneer difficult to employ and limited in its usefulness. The army's Pioneer didn't arrive in Saudi Arabia until a week after the shooting began and did not fly a mission until February 1.[14] The 100-mile range and three-hour endurance were really too short to support ground forces at distances where they needed reconnaissance the most. The drones also demanded constant radio line of sight from the operator, and had communications lines that were both limited and vulnerable to jamming. It was supposedly a dangerous place to be, exposed to Iraqi antiaircraft guns. Thus, the claim that only one drone was shot down would be impressive were it not for the fact that Pioneers flew only in airspace where defenses had already been beaten back by other aircraft and artillery. In fact, more than a dozen Pioneers ended up lost not to enemy action, but to operator error or mechanical failure.[15] Since imagery feeds via satellite links had not been developed yet, data transmission of what Pioneer could see was also limited.[16] If two Pioneers were flying at once, the imagery could only be viewed from one at a time. Insufficient infrared cooling systems hampered nighttime viewing, and operators never quite knew precisely where the drones were, lacking as they were in both precision navigation and onboard geolocation. With a small engine that was overstressed and required special 100-octane gasoline, and with little ability to maneuver, flying was also hazardous.[17] Rain eroded Pioneer's laminated wood propellers.[18] "If it's raining... or even drizzling, we aren't flying," said one navy Pioneer operator.[19]

Pioneer wasn't the only system hindered by weather conditions. Even the latest aircraft and laser-guided weapons were flummoxed by rain and moisture, dust and smoke. Half of the missions of the star of the war, the F-117 stealth fighter, were aborted due to weather. The problem was mostly the laser-guided bombs the

F-117 carried, predominantly the GBU-27, the newest-generation 2,000-pound munition designed specifically for use by the stealth fighter and its advanced target acquisition system.[20] Laser-guided bombs work by using an onboard seeker that responds to reflected laser radiation at a certain frequency. The seeker sees the target as a bright spot and sends signals to the bomb's basic steering mechanism to orient the direction of flight toward the target. But low visibility and moisture in the air interfered both with basic laser performance and with the aircraft viewing system. Even when weapons were launched, the success rate of synchronizing and then "locking on" the laser spot with the seeker was compromised.

It was a mass of frustrations — the need to counter Iraq's Scud missile maneuvers, the weather limitations, and the promise (and limitations) of Pioneer and other drones[21] — driving what airpower expert Barry Watts calls the development of "a true reconnaissance-strike complex able to find fleeting or time-sensitive targets and strike them in near–real time."[22] Needed first was something that would allow aircraft and weapons to simply receive coordinates on the ground and home in on that location. The navy's Navigation Signal Timing and Ranging Global Positioning System (NAVSTAR), which later went by the acronym GPS, provided the geographic transparency.[23] After Desert Storm, the air force also accelerated development of a new bomb called the Joint Direct Attack Munition (or JDAM, pronounced "jay-dam"), a weapon dependent on GPS and one that eventually paved the way to making geolocation the most important objective in warfare.[24]

Developed by Boeing, JDAM is a conversion "kit" for dumb bombs that gives any aircraft an all-weather precision strike capability, requiring only that the weapon senses where it began and where the target is in geographic coordinates. And at less than $30,000 per kit, JDAM cost one-twentieth of what a laser-guided bomb cost and one-fiftieth of what a cruise missile cost.

Of course, nothing is that simple, especially once an active, mobile enemy is involved, but as long as the position, speed, and heading of the aircraft are known and communicated to the weapon; as long as JDAM can acquire and track the signals of four GPS satellites once it leaves the airplane; as long as the coordinates of the target on the ground are accurate; as long as the release mechanism on the airplane, the computers, the mission planning software, the fuses, and the bomb all work; as long as no human error is made in "fat fingering" data into computers, then JDAM is able to fly itself to the given coordinates and hit the target, exploding within about forty-five feet of any intended location on earth, regardless of weather.[25] This is officially labeled "near precision," which gives some sense of how much perfection was sought.

After all of the unexpected weather interferences of Desert Storm, JDAM quickly moved forward in development. During testing, weapons recorded 95 percent system reliability while consistently landing one-third closer than the design specifications demanded.[26] Amidst testing, on June 26, 1993, the twenty-fourth GPS satellite was launched into orbit, completing the worldwide network. Each satellite carries a time code and a precise data point that when triangulated allows a receiver to calculate position, speed, and time to the nearest few feet. The extremely precise time lag—measured in fractions of a second—between the satellite transmission and the receiver is converted into distance to each satellite. The minute difference between signals is then used to calculate the receiver's position.[27]

JDAM kits were developed to go on 2,000-pound, 1,000-pound, and 500-pound bombs. The navy joined the program, and GPS receivers were installed in aircraft of all stripes, and a massive program was started to verify and make target coordinates on the ground up-to-date and superprecise. Time-critical targets, then identified as ballistic missiles (like the Iraqi Scuds), also demanded ways of transferring target data from real-time intelligence systems to the attacking aircraft even after the aircraft had taken off.[28]

In 1997, the air force received its first operational JDAMs. By then, the United States had been patrolling the skies over Iraq for six years, enforcing no-fly zones and occasionally bombing targets on the ground. Development of JDAM followed big-war visions, which of course meant big numbers. According to one air force briefing, incorporating JDAMs into B-1 bombers would represent 78 percent of the air force's payload, or the ability to deliver 2,280 JDAMs by ninety-five bombers in a single attack,[29] more than all of the weapons delivered by the entire stealth fighter force in forty-three days of Desert Storm. General Buster Glosson, the operational deputy of the first Iraq air war who went on to head the air staff's development directorate, described JDAM's potential, based upon testing in Nevada, as a single bomber being able to "destroy" twenty-four separate targets in a single pass.[30]

The astuteness behind developing JDAM was seen in 1999, when Operation Allied Force, the air war over Kosovo, began. Weather conditions over Serbia and Kosovo were at least 50 percent cloud cover more than 70 percent of the time, and only twenty-one days out of a total of seventy-eight days of bombing were clear. In addition, Serbian ground forces and paramilitaries baited and vexed air planners, moving in the literal fog, hiding under trees and in urban areas, not to mention using human shields to instill hesitation in NATO's committee-based decision-making. Yet while 16 percent of all strike sorties were lost to poor weather, JDAM never faltered. Forty-five B-2 stealth bombers, flying arduous round-trip bombing missions all the way from Missouri to Europe, delivered 656 JDAMs day in and day out.

Despite the poor weather conditions, the JDAMs performed flaw-lessly, according to air force reports.[31]

The reaction from military pilots was no different than some dot-com boomers gushing about their new inventions. "Weather and other battlefield conditions that might obscure a target do not affect JDAM," one air force pilot said.[32] "JDAM solves the prob-lem of bad weather, camouflage, [and] excessive winds aloft and night," said another.[33] Appearing at a Pentagon briefing toward the end of the conflict, Brigadier General Leroy Barnidge, Jr., the B-2 wing commander, told reporters, "I've seen zero collateral damage" from JDAM strikes.[34]

So many bombs dropping on so many precise targets: that was the public picture. But the true behind-the-scenes goal was a scram-ble to obtain and generate sufficient targets, thereby increasing the capacity of bomb-damage assessment in wartime: Did the bomb hit its desired impact point? Did the bomb detonate as planned and with full force? Did the bomb fuse function as intended?[35]

By the time JDAM proved itself, the simplicity of black box advancements like GPS was already resulting in revolutionary changes in automobiles, telephones, and other civilian gadgetry. Many senior leaders, even senior airmen, tried to temper the notions of weather being brushed aside, of darkness being turned to light, of perfect warfare emerging in a simple three-step pro-cess of finding the target, locating it precisely, and destroying it. It wasn't just that the networks and black boxes would themselves be potentially vulnerable to a competent opponent. The Data Machine to support the overall endeavor was still in its infancy. Unmanned technologies were becoming more and more domi-nant, but, like modern-day Gilgameshes, the military still needed to make a long journey.

CHAPTER FOUR

Trojan Spirit

[Said] Ur-shanabi to him [to Gilgamesh],
"Set to, O Gilgamesh! Take the first [punting pole!]
Let your hand not touch the Waters of Death,
lest you wither [it!]"
TABLET X, *EPIC OF GILGAMESH*

P redator's journey from invention to implementation is less clear than that of JDAM. Some insist that Predator originated in the mind of a Baghdad-born Israeli turned mad scientist named Abraham "Abe" Karem; or that a courageous CIA engineer named "Jane" defied the bureaucracy and made it so. Then there's a retired air force colonel known to all by his call sign, Snake, who spearheaded Predator's development by cutting through the bureaucracy. Another member of the cast is an army weapons expert who goes by the nickname Boom Boom, who integrated the Hellfire missile and changed the game completely. Lurking nearby is another woman called the Black Widow, who figured out matters of temperature and torque. Or maybe it was retired navy rear admiral Thomas J. Cassidy, who became CEO and president of General Atomics Aeronautical Systems, Predator's California birthplace. Others say it was CIA director R. James Woolsey; or Secretary of Defense William Perry; or Under Secretary of Defense (and future CIA director) John Deutch. Air force aficionados say chief of staff General Ron Fogleman had the vision of a reconnaissance platform in an era of disappearing planes and declining budgets. Others say it was General John P. Jumper, European commander and later chief of staff, who experienced all of the limitations of Bosnia and Kosovo and then went on to champion an armed drone, a system conceived and developed because of the vision of this one man.[1]

None of these characterizations tells the whole story, but they do suggest that *someone* is responsible, that "drones," despite the name, were spurred by imagination and courage; that there is a hero. Except that in the case of Predator, modern-day historians have a hard time putting a face to the machine. When I told an air force friend of mine, an airpower historian and teacher, that I was writing a book about drones, he responded that they had a pretty uninspiring history—"maybe for want of people."

Absent a discoverer or single champion, the alternative is to personify some organization as birthing and nurturing the drone. As with all military history intent on a human face, there is a subtext here as well: that Predator represents the vision of a network of courageous souls working in and across organizations; or the opposite, that Predator or some forerunner was shortchanged or squashed by evil bureaucrats and self-interested organizations who weren't a part of the advance, the desk-bound armed only with a *non-concur*, like scorpion men standing in Gilgamesh's way on his journey to the end of the earth, guarding the Mashu of advance.

And then there's the tendency to do the thing that comes with the recounting of any controversial program, which is to paint it as unexceptional. That's how, when one reads about Predator, one also hears of Compass Arrow and Combat Dawn, of Albatross, Condor, Prowler, and Praerie, Teal Rain and AARS, Amber and Gnat-750, the begetters of more modern iterations. These are all just characters, however, in an epic that conveys the message for fans and critics alike that nothing is ever really new and that therefore Predator per se shouldn't be criticized, shouldn't be singled out, that since everything is a continuum, there is no good or bad, even in weapons. There are only good and bad actors and bad historians intent on promoting their theories. Meanwhile, the Luddites and dreamers and enemies all play politics in the face of the need for national security combined with the given of unstoppable technological advance.

Many feel compelled to tell the Predator story by meandering through aviation history and insisting that the unmanned we see today are merely the progeny of balloons of the 1800s or remote-controlled thises and thats of the industrial age going back to the First World War; or heck, even that Nikola Tesla came up with the whole idea and it was stolen from him. Drones became so hot in 2013 that the news media, searching for any angle to bring the heroless machines alive, dug up the historical tidbit that Marilyn Monroe was "discovered" while working in a drone factory during World War II. And yes, indeed, Norma Jean was photographed at the Radioplane Munitions Factory in Van Nuys, California: one of the riveters putting finishing touches on an OQ-3 drone.[2]

But comparing the OQ-3 to the modern-day Predator is kind of like comparing a firecracker to an atom bomb: not only does it ignore all of what makes the two so very different, but it also conveys that tired Washington message that always accompanies the public's discovery of anything that's controversial, namely, that Predator is nothing new, that drones have always been with us; that they are neither an invention of 9/11 nor of the war against terrorism. In other words, what's the big deal?[3]

It's actually tricky and complex to say exactly when any weapon is "invented," and Predator is no exception. Where exactly do you start the story? Do you start it on July 3, 1994, under brilliantly sunny skies in El Mirage, California, where the prototype made its first flight? It flew for less than twenty seconds before gravity brought it back to earth.[4] Virtually everything that has been written since about this drone ignores real facts, even sometimes avoiding July 3 altogether. After all, there's no good way to start a glorious legend with a crash.[5]

A good place to intercept history, then, is probably the Vietnam War, when the dangerous work of manned aerial reconnaissance over North Vietnamese skies meant much loss of life and lots of political pain, as the names and faces of fallen soldiers and captured pilots ate at the nation's soul. Unmanned technology had been used in Operation Crossroads, when remotely piloted aircraft took air samples during the atomic bomb tests of 1946–47, but that was basically secret history. In the late 1950s, with spy satellites still not yet launched and the U-2 the only reliable reconnaissance platform that could penetrate deep into Soviet and Chinese territory, work intensified on an unmanned solution that could fly lower and avoid human loss. Drones started flying as replacements for manned aircraft, and reconnaissance drones began regularly penetrating enemy airspace, flying more than 3,000 sorties in North Vietnamese skies, with losses of about 15 percent. But only about 40 percent of the missions were successful in returning reconnaissance images, and the cost (in dollars) was five times greater than a manned mission.[6] Only, or that's the very point of the unmanned, that despite the percentages, no one was killed or captured.[7]

Eventually, the technological challenges experienced during operations led to a system of constant upgrade, with each variation overcoming some limitation of the previous model. The Reagan era then brought increased secret budgets, with companies being founded and sold, one system building upon another, many crashes and many kinks working their way into usable systems.[8] In 1983, drones mounting low-light-level video systems were used to track infiltrations into Honduras along the Nicaraguan border.[9]

Long-endurance reconnaissance drones that might replace manned aircraft were funded by the CIA, defense agencies, and the armed services. There was a profusion of code names and programs, and experimental birds exceeded altitudes of 68,000 feet, flying for over forty hours. But here are the words and phrases that really mattered: composite structures and lightweight materials, flight controls and computers, high-lift wings, fuel economy, electric motors, communications, bandwidth, navigation, geolocation.[10]

As airpower historian Tom Ehrhard says, Predator became a *part* of the air force, but in fact it emerged from the intelligence community—from the CIA—and drone development was initially dominated by the army and navy.[11] During the Cold War at least, the air service was bombers and missiles, and *the* mission was nuclear deterrence. Drones were merely a sideshow, an expense not central to the industrial meat grinder of accumulating awe-inspiring numbers and capabilities to keep the Soviets at bay. At that time, even the *manned* fighter community battled to earn the same national recognition of SAC, the Strategic Air Command. Then, and now, an "off-budget" program would be allowed breathing room for science experiments and a high-risk development environment. In this world, there were fewer meddlers and no interfering newspeople to answer. Just a few in Congress were briefed and co-opted, none of them in a position informed enough to ask questions. The practical benefits were obvious, but the downside is autonomy itself, with technological pursuits being driven forward because we can and because we must—leaving the arguably more important matters of public trust, reason, and national purpose behind on the ground.

US military operations in the former Yugoslavia began in July 1992 with Operation Provide Promise, a humanitarian airlift of food and medical supplies to Sarajevo that eventually surpassed even the Berlin Airlift of 1948–49 in the amount of materiel delivered. Colin Powell, then chairman of the Joint Chiefs and veteran senior military officer from Desert Storm, called for the development of "more than episodic reconnaissance" over the Balkans: he wanted loitering surveillance.[12] Reconnaissance satellites couldn't provide continuous coverage of mobile targets, and the imagery produced was too highly classified to be quickly disseminated to allied partners or actual soldiers. Manned aircraft were of limited endurance and only available in small numbers; and, most important for political war, they came with the additional danger of the possible loss of an aircrew over hostile areas. It seemed that only a family of long-endurance unmanned systems could fill the gap.[13]

The most promising immediate platform was the Gnat-750, a high-flying long-endurance drone that the CIA funded out of its research budget.[14] Lucky for everyone, the new president, Bill Clinton, chose the most unlikely of candidates to be agency director—R. James Woolsey, a hawkish Republican Washington arms-control lawyer—a national security feather in Clinton's cap, but also a man who would become famous for being the consummate outsider. Woolsey was a technical man and "long fascinated with the notion of a long endurance unmanned reconnaissance vehicle."[15] When briefed on Gnat, he immediately agreed to support development, even after one of two prototypes crashed in California because of a software error during initial testing.[16] In roughly six months, a CIA-operated Gnat was flying 25,000 feet over the Balkans, operating clandestinely from an airfield in Turkey and from the Croatian island of Hvar.[17]

Miniaturization of electronics, improved sensors, development of reliable and jam-resistant data links, and improvements in navigation accuracy overcame many limitations of earlier systems.[18] Gnat, which did not yet have a satellite link, had to receive flight commands and relay data through a nearby ground station or a manned airplane flying within line of sight. Yet when the manned airplane was used, it could remain at its post relaying communications for only a few hours at a time. Gnat also only successfully launched two-thirds of the time, with many missions being scuttled because of technical problems or bad weather.[19]

General Atomics was awarded its initial military contract for an upgraded version of the Gnat in January 1994; the firm called it Predator.[20] With Gnat and operational experience under its belt, the San Diego–based company was able to deliver a "system" of three vehicles in less than a year. It extended Gnat's fuselage, put on a longer wing and a better engine, and thereby tripled the earlier drone's ability to carry a payload. Predator exceeded all of Gnat's specs, including a fuel capacity that allowed for up to twenty-two hours' endurance.[21] And where Gnat sounded like a lawn mower in the sky, Predator had a quieter engine.[22] The drone itself had a bulbous nose that integrated satellite communications into the forward fuselage.[23] The ground control system, fitted into a single trailer, contained two main consoles, one for the pilot and one for the sensor operator, who regulated imagery functions and camera settings, switching from the visible to the infrared spectrum and taking single photographs. Another trailer housed the Trojan Spirit, which transmitted and received both unclassified and encrypted communications from voice, wire, digital, and satellite sources and was the conduit used to relay commands and disseminate intelligence.[24]

The most important innovation in the Predator, though, was the satellite links, both GPS for navigation, and communications data links to commercial satellites that were connected to the ground control station and could relay images to users.[25] For the first time, military drones could be controlled from up to 400 miles away.[26] Now an unmanned machine could range far away, stay up longer, and send back motion imagery in near–real time like a television camera in the sky.[27]

Starting in August 1995, Predator video from Bosnia dazzled. Special lines were set up to relay the intelligence to Langley and right onto Woolsey's desk.[28] The CIA director recalled that he watched foot traffic over the Mostar Bridge while communicating with the forward ground station over an early form of chat software.[29] Later he gushed: "I could sit in my office, call up a classified channel and in an early version of e-mail type messages to a guy in Albania asking him to zoom in on things."[30]

Unmanned aerial vehicles became the best potential source of intelligence without undue risk.[31] Commanders needed some way to improve their ability to monitor safe areas established around Bosnian cities. UN peacekeepers on the ground couldn't do it, and manned reconnaissance wasn't abundantly available, nor could it loiter, particularly given the low level of risk NATO was willing to take with its pilots.

This, at any rate, was the theory behind the use of drones and the requirement for them, but Predator was still in its infancy and nothing was quite instant or consistent: the initial three vehicles deployed didn't have ground-mapping radar (which would allow the system to "see" through bad weather), forcing them to fly beneath the clouds, where they were also more vulnerable to Serb guns and missiles.[32] Two of the three airframes were lost in the first month: one was shot down while flying at just 4,000 feet, the other scuttled due to an engine failure.[33] At 120 knots maximum speed (138 mph), Predator also struggled to make progress in the face of strong headwinds. The drone's very large wings allowed it to fly more like a glider than an airplane, and that was the secret to flight endurance, but at lower altitudes it also made the drone more sensitive to wind and turbulence.[34] In-flight icing, precipitation, and cloud cover also hampered operations.[35] Would technology ever overcome the force of Mother Nature?

The convention at this point, which I will honor, is to recount the limitations of the machine itself. And indeed Predator emerged with the expected hiccups that plague any system as it grows into its skin. The drone's initial flaws were legion:[36] despite their range and endurance, the vehicles still needed to be placed close to their targets to begin their missions. And because of the two-second time delay in the satellite signal, direct radio-controlled takeoff and landing had to be managed by close-in pilots and maintainers — in other words, bases, which in the case of Balkan operations meant clandestine relationships or diplomatic arrangements with countries like Albania, where US forces didn't formally exist. The ground presence was also substantial,[37] not necessarily a flaw but a surprise to some who had a vision of one-man, one-joystick, one-vehicle operations.[38] Cost, the air force found out, was ten times what many assumed.[39] In fact, despite the term "unmanned," maintaining Predator proved more labor-intensive than manned operations, not even counting how many people were needed to handle the incoming intelligence, which just kept increasing in volume.

As with the performance of Pioneer in Desert Storm, it is hard to really say what bigger difference the 128 Predator missions and their 850 hours of video made in Bosnia.[40] One air force study points to September 5, 1995, when NATO was dithering over renewed bombing, the decision hinging on whether the Serbs were withdrawing heavy weapons from the Sarajevo safe area. Based on Predator motion imagery that day, the study says, the US commander advised his NATO counterpart: "No intents being demonstrated; let's get on with it!"[41] Predator was also credited with monitoring mass grave sites near Sarajevo, helping search for downed pilots, and providing real-time bomb-damage assessments of air strikes.[42] When Pope John Paul II made his visit to Bosnia in April 1997, a Predator flew two dedicated security surveillance missions totaling 22.5 hours.[43] One military writer even says that Predator provided NATO commanders with the "critical intelligence to begin a bombing campaign that, in turn, led to the Dayton Peace Accord signed in December 1995."[44] Whatever the truth, wherever Predator video was delivered, particularly to the desktops of generals and admirals in the chain of command or to the Pentagon, the phones started ringing: *Fly over this, fly over that, what's that?*[45] The hypnosis was beginning.

For the military, Predator was the first of the modern-day "advanced concept technology demonstrations." These were boutique and one-of-a-kind experiments. They did not approach the multibillion-dollar fighter planes or fighting ships in cost or visibility, nor were they the stuff of engineering drawings, where methodical testing was required before a production model could roll off a mass assembly line. Initially, in fact, no two systems were exactly alike. Think smartphones today: they can be externally identical, and yet how fast the processor is, how many gigs of memory, how many megapixels the camera, and what software and apps it runs, mean a world of difference. These early Predators were ad hoc and quick reaction and more lost in the books than off the books. That pioneering quality—flying by the seat of the pants, even if no one was flying—opened the door for the entire family of fathers, cousins, uncles, and advisors to stake a claim. As the Institute for Defense Analyses would later say of Predator, it never met the "requirements" set down on paper and yet still flew and flew, and flew. "It supports the argument that deploying a less-than-perfect system is better than deploying no system," the think tank concluded.[46]

"Less than perfect" also meant that no specification was set in stone: when Predators first emerged to fly over Bosnia, they didn't even have operator's manuals. The concept of operations (or CONOPS)—the very centerpiece that tells everyone from the grease monkey on the flight line to the general in the command center how the system fits in and what is expected—was considered a "living document," undergoing endless iterations in response to both failures and successes.[47] Retired admiral Cassidy even accompanied the first group of Predators to Albania to ensure that the system would perform as promised, and he brought along a gaggle of company civilians and engineers (the first generation of the ubiquitous contractors to come). Without the manufacturer on the scene, the system couldn't even have flown.[48]

After the first Gulf war, reviewers were already noting the dangers of this new feature of ad hoc weapons development, which manifested itself in Desert Storm not just in science experiments rushed to the battlefield but also in an unwritten scourge—which at that time birthed the cult of the military recording everything in a forever-changing PowerPoint briefing rather than writing things down on a piece of paper.[49] Long before anyone heard of Internet addiction, before people were saying they would feel panicked and naked if they lost their mobile phones, Predator was flying into our culture. Being incommunicado was no longer an option, waiting was already become exasperating, quietly thinking was dying, paper was on its way out, and everything was becoming data, precisely located and instant. Right down to their desktop monitors in Washington, decision-makers could be perpetually plugged in and as much a part of the day-to-day battle as anyone else. It was the birth of an age of what I'll call vextering (vectoring in an era of text), with an infinite gamescape of data and targets just around the corner.

CHAPTER FIVE

Dialogue of the Deaf

He saw what was secret, discovered what was hidden....
TABLET I, *EPIC OF GILGAMESH*

No target ever died in the collection process," General Jumper, Air Forces in Europe commander, said at the time of the Kosovo conflict in 1999. "We don't pop the cork when the picture arrives; we pop the cork when the target is dead."[1] It was pre-9/11 and Jumper wasn't even talking about killing terrorists or individuals; a target is a target, an airfield, military barracks, troops in the field or on the move. An air force does many things, but in the end, it's all about killing the target. From a military perspective, intelligence — air intelligence — is useless unless it contributes to the demise of a target. All capabilities are nurtured and perfected for this singular task, a focus that has evolved from cities to factories to bridges to the individual tank to the individual on the corner.

In our era of perpetual warfare, smooth-talking generals repeat the catechism of the day, which is about nation and capacity building, and about supporting the troops on the ground. But the honest and true-blue airman is trained and prepared to drop the bomb. You want it done more quickly, safely, and effectively, with fewer civilian casualties and collateral damage? he asks. Just give me the tools, provide me with the intelligence, point me in the right direction, and let me do my thing. It doesn't matter whether the target is another airplane in the skies, a tent in the desert, or even someone's cybertransmissions. War is ugly, and airpower is the modern lead. So an airman says tell me what the target is, even tell me what level of damage you want, and get out of the way.

It shouldn't be too surprising, then, that before anyone in Washington was focused on Osama bin Laden, before the politicos "thought of" putting a missile on Predator, before bureaucrats advanced their counterterrorism covert action programs, before anyone started fretting about overflying Taliban-held Afghanistan or taking out any princely phantom, air warriors were already thinking about the means: put a weapon on the new Predator, and not only can you conduct reconnaissance and find a potential target, but you can also do something about it right then. You can do it against air defenses that might be too lethal for manned aircraft, and you can do it against Scud missiles that shoot and scoot. And with the right weapons and the right black boxes, it can be done in the dark, in the rain, and a world away.

From the very beginning of drones' development, the idea of arming them had been experimented with.[2] Amber — the immediate predecessor of Predator developed for Cold War duties against an industrial army — was conceived to include a loitering model that would find the target and then turn into a kamikaze missile.[3] In some ways, then, the saga of getting drones from just looking to looking and killing is unexceptional in every way. Sure, Predator (and later types of unmanned drones) had to overcome dozens of technological and institutional hurdles — even some from inside the air force itself, who bristled at the unmanned quality. But then, every new capability has to fight to gain traction in a world of tribes and limited resources: bomber versus fighter, combat versus support, intelligence versus operations, conventional versus unconventional.

There were people like General Jumper who genuinely had vision and sensed how the unmanned could fill a void.[4] Musing about Predator long before it was armed, Admiral William A. Owens, the vice chairman of the Joint Chiefs of Staff and one of the original proponents of network-centric warfare, said that Predator "was flying over an area...at 25,000 feet....It had been up there for a long time, many hours, and you could see the city below, and you could focus in on the city, you could see a building, focus on a building, you could see a window, focus on a window. You could put a cursor around it and [get] the GPS latitude and longitude very accurately, remotely via satellite. And if you passed that information to an F-16 or an F-15 [fighter flying overhead] at 30,000 feet, and that pilot can simply put in that latitude and longitude into his bomb fire control system, then that bomb can be dropped quite accurately onto that target, maybe very close to that window, or, if it's a precision weapon, perhaps it could be put through the window...."[5] It would be many years before that vision would be even close to realization, but after the concept of loitering unmanned reconnaissance was "proven"[6] in Bosnia, money began flowing: the Pentagon alone spent more than $3 billion on unmanned aerial systems in the 1990s.[7] Much of that money went to fund even higher-flying, longer-range, stealthier, and far more expensive drones than Predator. More than a decade's work lay ahead in perfecting an aerodynamically and militarily robust flying machine that would reliably be able to kill the target.

The black box rides alongside as the silent partner: a military is remarkable for its men and its machines, not for its accessories. Predator is just Predator to all but the experts, extraordinary for its flying and enthralling for its video output. But nothing happens without the peripherals and the payloads, and each year of Predator operations, different types and generations of black boxes accumulated—all with different objectives. Each accessory represented a modification and an expense. Each meant a penalty in weight, a new demand on limited onboard power, and an entire new family of corporate and government partners. So though it was still just Predator, in the course of three years from when it first flew, the drone's service ceiling was increased to 45,000 feet and the payload expanded from 400 to 750 pounds. A new engine was installed while additional accessories needed to kill the target quietly burrowed into the fuselage and the Machine.

When the 1996 model of the Predator started Bosnia duty, certainly the most important black box was its new synthetic aperture radar (SAR), the very ground-mapping capability which allowed the drone to see day or night, through cloud cover and during inclement weather. SAR works by transmitting sharp microwave beams (pulses) to "illuminate" an area and then receive and process the reflected signals.[8] The first SAR mounted on Predator was called the Tactical Endurance SAR system (TESAR) and provided continuous, near-real-time strip-map (wide-area) imagery. The radar allowed the identification of objects viewed from 25,000 feet within an area as small as one square foot.[9] The continuous sweep was formed on board Predator, compressed, and sent via data link in a scrolling manner called a "waterfall display" to the ground control station, where dedicated computer stations and special software were used to reform and display usable images. Analysts on the ground could then select one-by-one kilometer stills for further exploitation.

At 165 pounds, TESAR was an engineering marvel, not the first of the Gilgamesh generation of black boxes by any means, but certainly the most influential in opening up the world of seeing beyond the optical, not just into the fog but also increasingly into other spectra. Some panned TESAR's scrolling output because that streaming waterfall display could be read only by trained analysts and was thereby useless to the average viewer.[10] But multiple generations followed: the Lynx SAR and then the Starlite black boxes that produced a more pleasing display at a fraction of the price, with multiple channels instead of one, with spot map and moving targeting indicator modes in addition to strip-map mode, at a third of the weight, with four times less power consumption, at ten times the resolution, a thousand times more user friendly. These are the very tablets of our modern era, the revelation of all that is hidden.

The air war over Kosovo started in March 1999, and by then, Predator (and its predecessor the Gnat-750) had been routinely flying in congested airspace across national boundaries for four years. During the seventy-eight days of bombing, seven Predators flew alongside a navy Pioneer detachment operating from ships in the Adriatic Sea, and the army flew Hunter (a drone a third of the size of Predator and the first army drone to fly in real-world combat).[11] Problems related to weather and technology led to many cancellations and losses, but the fleet still managed an average of six one-to-three-hour missions daily, largely thanks to black boxes. Predator transmitted near-real-time imagery directly to users and acted as a "second set of eyes" on targets.[12] And most important, Predator video fed the chain of command, appearing live on screens in Belgium, Italy, and Germany, at the Pentagon, and even in the White House Situation Room.[13]

The Serbs had become proficient both in hiding from drones and in shooting them down when they wandered too close, honing their experiences during Bosnia. Still, as air force chief of staff General Michael Ryan quipped: "[Drones] go out there and die for their country—and we don't mourn."[14] Given that mission number one for the international coalition was zero friendly casualties, and that the road to winning the war against Serbia was continuous flying and bombing until Slobodan Miloševic cried uncle, not mourning really mattered. And despite their limitations, drones could do things that manned aircraft couldn't. They could linger and spot targets in hollows or other shadowy areas where reconnaissance satellites or manned aircraft couldn't see. They could assess bomb damage in near–real time by loitering above the bombers. They could linger and search for mobile targets that the Serbs otherwise ably camouflaged.

In Kosovo, General Jumper credited Predator's long loiter time as a key element in allowing targeters to distinguish civilians from fighters and paramilitaries. "We have documented instances of Serbian special police using the very tractors that the civilians were using to go from house to house to burn and to kill," he said.[15] But Kosovo was also the first true global information war. Every image of American and NATO destruction on television and the Internet heavily influenced a nervous European public, scoring a direct hit in the battle for hearts and minds. It didn't matter that this was the very war where B-2 bombers and their weather-defying JDAM bombs shifted the percentage of weapons dropped squarely into the precision column. The debate about civilian casualties and collateral damage grew red hot.

Despite their frustrations about the political constraints on bombing, the military remained focused on the job they had to do when they could fly: killing the target. Predator in its 75 sorties and 870 hours of flying proved more promising than ever, but the senior leadership was also aware that it wasn't yet the optimum tool. Jumper called the problem the "dialogue of the deaf": a Predator team would locate some target of opportunity with its camera, circuitously relaying the information to tip off some nearby strike asset, and then a frustrating exchange would ensue. That was because the sensor operator of the Predator was looking through what is called a "soda straw" optic at 10-power magnification. He'd say: "Well, if you look over to the left, there's a road right beside the two houses. A tree line is right next to that. A river is running nearby." The pilot nearby saw an endless sea of red-roofed buildings and countless roads. Forty-five minutes later, the sensor operator and the pilot might have talked their way "into the same Zip code," Jumper said, but by that time, the jet would have had to leave the target area to refuel. "You'd have the Predator up there looking at targets, but you had no way to get that information, other than verbally, to the airplanes that were going to attack those tanks."[16]

So once again, a black box stepped in.[17] Off the books and unrestrained by bureaucratic red tape, the technologists who serve to arm the cutting edge recommended that Predator's first-generation rotating camera ball be replaced with one that would offer both a camera and a laser illuminator—just like the one on a combat airplane. That would allow the drone sensor operator to observe a potential target and put a laser "spot" on it on the ground for a nearby fighter pilot to instantly see. A Raytheon-made turret, intended for use by navy helicopters, already existed, its sole downside being that it had only an infrared viewer and not a daytime camera.[18] That wasn't so bad, however, particularly since "hot" hiding tanks were *the* target of the moment, and now Predator could spot a target's heat signature and put a laser on it.

"Things moved with what became legendary speed," one study recounts. "The laser designator was obtained from the navy only 18 hours after the recommendation was approved. Testing was accelerated, and the first laser-equipped Predator was deployed to Kosovo just 38 days later."[19] Two airframes (nicknamed WILD, for wartime implemented laser designator) were ready for combat on June 2, and the drone was now bulked up with a targeting black box.[20] There was one successful test in which a WILD Predator lased for an A-10 that night;[21] Miloševic accepted NATO's demands for ending the conflict the next day.[22]

But the vision was solidified. WILD transformed Predator from "just a pure surveillance system into something that actually… directs weapons on the targets," Jumper said.[23] When he returned to the United States months later, he inquired as to the further development of more WILD Predators, only to learn that bureaucrats had not only squashed the retrofit of Predators with the new laser designators, but had even ordered the laser ball turrets taken off the WILDs because they weren't a validated official requirement. Jumper was "furious"[24] that "the tyranny of our acquisition process" had mindlessly excised a capability.[25] Air force bureaucrats maintained that "there was general concern for the lack of proper training and employment/tactics to use the laser designator" and that Predator had three different configurations, each of which required a different set of technical orders, whereas there needed to be one baseline system.[26]

I don't want to understate the impact of an unthinking bureaucracy or the passive-aggressive tendencies of all government infighters. Bureaucratic shenanigans and rivalries are common, and they are hardly unique to the air force. But here's the point: this is the *why* of why the black box world exists. In Washington things rarely get done unless they happen off the books and in the underworld. Nothing happens without top cover support of someone in a position of leadership, like a Jumper, or the outside lobbying of self-interested voices. Nothing happens unless a special organization with special authorities does it. A black box solves so many problems. And black boxes are so good at then becoming both darling (and star) for those special few in the know.

The black box hovers above and rides parallel to all that is unspecial, not just adding to the allure of the next black box, but also leaving behind unanswered bigger questions. In the American narrative, it's hard not to see Predator and other hunter-killers—unmanned and manned—as the spindly loners wielding justice: the very embodiment of some laconic Clint Eastwood hero or some futuristic and noisy Luke Skywalker breaking the rules but fighting the fight against the dark side.

How, though, do others see the black boxes and the unmanned? When I visited Serbia immediately after the Kosovo war, the impact of an airpower-only war was palpable. After seventy-eight days of air attacks but with no ground fighting and political capitulation by Slobodan Miloševic after he failed to outlast NATO's bombing, the people on the streets (pro- and antigovernment alike) were outraged. The United States was cowardly, they said, and since the United States with all of its technology was all-seeing, the only conclusion they could draw was that the United States had intentionally decided who would die and who would live, creating civilian casualties to instill fear and uncertainty, punishing the Serbian people but not even saving the Kosovars, because the real purpose of the war was to teach Serbia a lesson and subordinate it to modern Europe. Thus the shape of the post-9/11 world was already forming. Black box operations were starting to demonstrate a speed and flexibility that matched the emerging information culture. Unmanned war machines were showing real promise not just in sparing human lives but also in filling gaps in capabilities. And though the objective of hitting the target—anywhere, anytime, in any weather, and now even with exactly the political modulation suggested—was undeniably reducing collateral civilian harm, warfare was becoming remote and baffling and even opaque, pulling it more and more into secret recesses and therefore further away from human intervention.

CHAPTER SIX

Another Plane

...like a wild bull lording it, head held aloft,
He has no equal when his weapons are brandished....
TABLET I, *EPIC OF GILGAMESH*

After five years of Bosnia and a war over Kosovo, after Somalia and Haiti, amid covert action and high-wire diplomacy and the maintenance of a constant military shield around Saddam Hussein and Iraq, al Qaeda finally forced itself into the Clinton administration's in-box. Those leading and attracted to al Qaeda chose, for their own epic, Afghanistan, where they (or their glorious elders) defended Islam against the modern-day crusaders and brought down the superpower. It wasn't that they had any particular kinship with Saddam and his secular socialist state; it was that they saw Iraq's defeat (and the defeat of Bosnian Muslims at the hands of Christian Serbs) in the same way they saw themselves: humbled and subordinated. Theirs was a movement imbued with god-driven justifications as old as mankind.

Bin Laden raged. He raged against Israel, but also against the Saudi royal family—for its collusion with Jews, Christians, and Crusaders. He condemned the Communists in Yemen and the secular states of Iraq, Syria, and Egypt; he longed for an Islamic sanctuary in Afghanistan. But an al Qaeda theme from the very beginning—before anyone in the West had even heard of bin Laden—was that the US military presence in Saudi Arabia, which had started as a reaction to the Iraqi invasion of Kuwait in 1990, was an invasion into the most holy place of Islam.[1] Through years of standoff with a weakened Iraq and aborted involvement in Somalia, al Qaeda also developed a theory of American moral weakness.[2] It declared war on the United States in August 1996.[3] "With small capabilities, and with our faith, we can defeat the greatest military power of modern times," bin Laden later said in a message to his followers.[4]

Al Qaeda mounted many aborted, attempted, and annoying attacks against its long list of enemies, but it was the devastating and deadly simultaneous bombings of two US embassies in Nairobi and Dar es Salaam in 1998 that signified the true beginning of the age of terror. *Act of war,* bin Laden screamed, and *Act of war,* the Clinton camp rejoined.[5] Tomahawk sea-launched cruise missiles were fired in retaliation against targets believed to house bin Laden himself, an unmanned attack that satisfied some bloodlust and purported to represent some policy, a public act yet also one with all of the trappings of covert action, an act at all because the unmanned technology (even if it was then in the form of a long-range cruise missile) meant safety and a small price. Everything now was outside age-old conventions of war. Military acts on both sides occurred seemingly unattached to armies; there was a complete disregard for borders and airspace, and the distinction between who was military and who was civilian became blurred. As for the United States, a state decision was made without the input of the people.

In compartments above top secret, and in circles extremely limited, the Clinton White House and the CIA terror-hunters increasingly became fixated on Osama bin Laden as the new target. The missiles slammed into al Qaeda training camps, but the circle of Washington knowers convinced themselves afterward that the "problem" with the cruise missile strike when it didn't kill Osama bin Laden was that the intelligence information on bin Laden's whereabouts just wasn't good enough (and not that the strategy or the inherent secrecy of covert operations was flawed). The capabilities to track an individual, an individual target, had to be developed.

The capabilities of a different kind of war accumulated: meetings were held with a host of clandestine partners who might help, moneys were exchanged, forward bases were set up, and covert assistance was provided to governments and anti-Taliban groups alike; equipment for better tracking, long-range optics, and intercept devices was developed, and some was shipped and set up on mountaintops and on hidden corners; there were safe houses and backup plans, a CIA plane to fly bin Laden out should he be captured, a hostage rescue plan to protect Americans in Afghanistan.[6] All were needed just to facilitate any kind of action in this remote part of the world, and each had its own supply line and ecosystem, the means of the doing becoming the activity as much as the doing itself. And most important, some kind of network of communications was needed to bring it all together, for the purpose, after all, was to improve the intelligence, to collect and move it almost immediately from the battlefield to the altar of the temple and back so that the target, now one individual, could be killed, either by the US military or by its proxies increasingly commanded by the CIA.

Al Qaeda consolidated and matured while the scheming unfolded. The Tomahawk cruise missile strike, of course, signaled to bin Laden that *he* was now an active target. Subsequent schemes to enlist the help of old Afghan allies and the spymasters of Pakistan also sent whispers back to al Qaeda. And then there was the buildup of American capacity on the ground. A secret

American base in Uzbekistan, though opaque in Washington, flickered on al Qaeda's radar screens, signaling gathering threats and the need for greater defenses (and, as would be seen, offense).

As clandestine capabilities moved forward, there were significant dissenters. When the head of the CIA's bin Laden unit came up with a scheme to use Afghan proxies left over from the anti-Soviet days to kidnap bin Laden and deliver him to Egypt, where he would quietly disappear, the top FBI counterterrorism official furiously objected. "I'm a lawman, not a killer," he is said to have responded.[7] Attorney General Janet Reno, the nation's top law enforcement official, also took the unusual step of informing the CIA that she didn't support tacit presidential approval authorizing Afghan proxies to kill Osama bin Laden if his capture was not possible. In the top secret halls of government, she even labeled any explicit CIA plan to kill bin Laden "illegal," a declaration that might otherwise be thought of as the kiss of death no matter what the exigency.[8] Inside the CIA itself, David Carey, executive director and the number three man at the Agency, also saw covert action and technological solutions as a "distraction" and too much of an attention grabber and time suck, diffusing people and resources from worldwide disruption operations against al Qaeda—that is, from trying to uncover and stop immediate and future attacks.[9]

But PowerPoint and background papers flew, focusing everyone more on the question of feasibility and choreography than on legality or wisdom. The circle of decision-makers, already quite small, got smaller and even tighter, everyone in that circle being there precisely because they accepted the validity and exceptionality of their mission. So it came down to killing.[10]

The "debate" about using so-called "lethal force" against Osama bin Laden devolved into a bureaucratic exercise to ensure that the presidential finding authorizing the action was worded properly to protect everyone involved, including the president himself: capture would be preferable to killing, and killing would be judged acceptable only if capture was not feasible; the Afghan partners—euphemistically labeled "the tribals" to suggest some circle of indigenous wagons defending against outside marauders— would be paid only if bin Laden was captured. Bin Laden was declared an imminent threat to the United States. The right of self-defense was invoked, granting permissions and immunities. Before the 9/11 Commission three years later, CIA director George Tenet portrayed the covert action agency as the protector of the laws and status quo—rather than the president's law-breaking arm, which is in fact what it is—claiming that "CIA leadership...felt it important that there was a full understanding by the President and the National Security Council" of another attack or an assassination.[11] Yet when the president's authorization allowing the agency to kill the Saudi man was finally granted, only four decision-making officials outside the White House (or the CIA) were even allowed to read it; and none were allowed to keep a copy or discuss it with their staffs.[12]

By then this small circle of secret warriors in the White House had discovered Predator. The "Predator project is our highest near-term priority," wrote the head of the Small Group, the formal interagency chamber beyond top secret, in April 2000. The CIA would fly the air force drone over Afghanistan to gather real-time information on the whereabouts of the al Qaeda head, so as to provide the intelligence needed to make that next attack a successful assassination. The still-developing capability was taken out of any normal chain of command and career path to become part of a high-priority White House program now labeled Afghan Eyes.[13]

Again there was considerable opposition. James Pavitt, the head of the Agency's clandestine service, even argued that if Predator fired a missile at bin Laden and responsibility for the use of lethal force was laid at the Agency's doorstep, it would endanger the lives of CIA operatives around the world.[14] But the response of the Predator's supporters was ruthless, a machine now being placed in harm's way, dissenters turned into weak and visionless bureaucrats. "You know," White House blusterer Richard Clarke is quoted as saying, "if the Predator gets shot down, the pilot goes home and fucks his wife. It's OK. There's no POW issue here."[15] No loss of American life, or so it seemed, meant there was no issue of any kind.

By mid-August 2000, the White House approved deployment of Predator to Uzbekistan. The CIA wouldn't fly the Predator. Air force pilots on loan would man the controls, together with the technical specialists who were still working out the kinks of the communications and imagery network. And there would be civilian contractors from General Atomics as well.[16] It would be an extremely complex operation: two combined teams—from the CIA, the air force, the technologists' secret cauldron called Big Safari, and the manufacturer General Atomics—would be needed, together with security, housing, feeding, etc. One team would operate in Uzbekistan to launch and recover the Predator drones and maintain them before and after each mission. The other team deployed with the ground control station to a secret base—in Germany, the secret being that the German government wouldn't be told.[17] It was the first attempt at what the air force called split operations, with forward takeoff handed off to active mission control over a thousand miles away once the drone was at stable altitude.[18]

On September 7, the first Predator mission was conducted from Uzbekistan: the drone was launched and made the three-hour flight to Kandahar in southern Afghanistan.[19] In a memo to national security advisor Sandy Berger, one of the White House staffers suggested that an emergency committee be established to act on any video that might come in if the reconnaissance drone locked in on bin Laden's location. Much discussion ensued about how Afghan tribals would be rushed closer, about how US special operators might swoop in, about how more Tomahawk cruise missiles might be spun up and sent off to get him this time, even how a manned air attack might be undertaken; the only "implications" of the now-accumulated capability that were raised were whether surveillance could determine whether bin Laden actually remained in place or moved.[20]

About two weeks later, they thought they had found their quarry.[21] Loitering over Tarnak Farms, a walled compound and old Soviet agricultural commune east of the city and one of bin Laden's residences, the Predator sensor operators saw "a security detail around a tall man in a white robe." It was probably bin Laden, those read in at the CIA assessed; it *was* bin Laden, the staff at the White House concluded.[22] The video was labeled "truly astonishing," the whole enterprise taking on the merriment of total victory. After a second bin Laden sighting was supposedly made,[23] staffer Richard Clarke wrote to Berger that "it might be a little gloomy sitting around the fire with the al Qida [sic] leadership these days."[24] A stylized video show of the two missions was prepared for President Clinton, who was personally walked through the 15,000-foot sightings.[25]

The second sighting of bin Laden came a week to the day after Congress authorized approval for the air force to arm the Predator, releasing funds from the public treasury to do so. The program had been initiated by General Jumper upon his return to the United States, and development of a Hellfire missile capability on the Predator was moving along.[26] But since the missile was considered a "new start" under the law, air force attorneys forbade any "touch labor" by government employees until approval was received. There was also a legal issue as to whether an armed Predator violated the Intermediate-Range Nuclear Forces Treaty with the Soviet Union. That 1987 treaty banned ground-launched cruise missiles, and the question was whether the drone was being given characteristics that would classify it as a cruise missile, albeit a reusable one.[27] While awaiting resolution on the treaty issue, lawyers counseled that no missile could actually be attached to a complete Predator airframe. A wing was removed from a Predator and propped up on sawhorses; the engineers ran wires from the launcher to a flight control computer in the disassembled Predator's fuselage to check whether the systems would work.[28]

Sounds ridiculous, no? Momentum was building to kill bin Laden and change history and a bunch of bureaucrats, lawyers, and green-eyeshade penny pinchers were being punctilious? That was certainly the way conventional wisdom would frame the conversations after 9/11 as to why Predator didn't just go on and do its thing against bin Laden right then and there.[29] The participants told tales of bin Laden being caught on tape during the first flight, and even convinced the 9/11 Commission that that was what happened.[30] But the truth of Predator's capabilities is that the drones were far less advanced than advertised, and there was no particular culprit, except maybe secrecy, for the failure to eliminate bin Laden. Richard Whittle, in his book *Predator*, demonstrates how tentative the capability was. The former chief lawyer of the CIA agreed, later writing that "drone technology was still a work in progress; it was not yet certain that it would be lethally effective."[31]

In fact, no one delayed needlessly. Any hesitation or caution about whether a mission over remote Afghanistan could be successful was legitimate. By mid-2000, almost a quarter of the five dozen Predators that had been delivered to the air force had been lost in operations.[32] During two deployments to the Balkans, three exercises in the United States, and one demonstration at the United States' southern border, weather caused the cancellation of 17 percent of planned missions, and there was an early return to base in 19 percent of the others that got off the ground.[33] Over the former Yugoslavia, from 1996 through the end of 1999, only about half of Predator missions were completed. Enemy action was one cause, but operator error equaled weather as another.[34] The official operational test and evaluation, completed in October 2000, said that Predator was "not without limitations and difficulties," in part because "reliability and maintainability problems persist."[35] Flying over Afghanistan at that point also had a very real, tight time constraint, as bad weather over the northern Hindu Kush mountain range would start to creep in in October (as was seen exactly a year later when US special operations helicopters flying from Uzbekistan had a hard time making it to the Panjshir Valley after 9/11).

The Taliban also detected the high-flying drone on radar, and early on launched a MiG fighter to attempt an interception.[36] Though air analysts went to work at the Pentagon to determine whether the ancient Soviet jets could indeed shoot down a drone, it was now clear that the Taliban (and al Qaeda) knew that the reconnaissance missions were being flown. A glimmer of triumph might have flickered with those in the know, but the mission was also made exponentially more difficult because the other side knew: the tall man in white robes was never seen again.[37]

This is sometimes the disremembered reverberation of covert action, which is always sought when the president and his advisors can't change the facts. And then, as the covert action itself unfolds in a secret chamber, for all the covertness, changes in the direction of the winds or ripples in the sands also act to provoke countering actions on the part of those who are being hunted. In "normal" channels, even in the development of revolutionary technologies that are highly secret (such as, for instance, stealth in the 1970s), a part of the process is to create equal and parallel countermeasures programs to ensure that a high level of classification doesn't inadvertently result in a lack of independent review and outside criticism regarding what an adversary might be doing to counter the goal.[38] But this was not the case with the Clinton administration's growing "war" with al Qaeda.

Gilgamesh the black box, then, is not the only manifestation of a secret world that lies beyond. A black box can also be thought of as policy. There is all of what happens in the open—Congressional appropriations, foreign policy, boots on the ground, bombing, navies showing the flag here and there—and then there are the supplements and appendages that make up special operations and covert action and psychological warfare and the newest member of the black family: cyber. Although throughout this chapter I have used the terms "air force" and "CIA" and "White House" to suggest some coherent council, in fact it was not *the* CIA but simply the counterterrorism-dedicated elite *within* the CIA, and to apply even that term before 9/11 is an erroneous characterization. They were hardly elite, which means they had to operate black box style in order to out-elite the other elites, often against the prevailing views of the CIA's own leadership. In the black box world, the result is incredible secrecy and an alliance with people more powerful than those in delegated positions of power. Which brings us to the *who* of the more powerful people. It wasn't *the* White House, the public place, or the government on record, but the black box operators who were members of the staff of the National Security Council, which in those days meant people who were desktop warriors—memo-writers and meeting-goers who know how to guide decisions without making them, and who would never claim to be operators of anything, because they also need to avoid the stain of Oliver North and the legacy of White

House operators mucking about in the business of open government. And they are mere staffers when diffidence matters, especially when there is a need to foist off disasters or unsuccessful projects on their bosses. But paper tigers they are through and through, because they don't have any authority to order anything or spend any money, not without the okay of some department or agency that actually has a budget. So their only avenue of do, derring-do or just plain do, and certainly the easiest, is the black box, which always means "segregated" and sometimes means "in a vacuum and cut off from what is going on outside closed worlds." Those working in the open world are also unaware of what goes on in the black box, or the when and the why of the rules being suspended. This is the genesis of warrantless surveillance or enhanced interrogation techniques (torture), each a black box pursuit and off the books. And the public consequence is not only to make drone attacks seem out of the blue and out of context, but also for the compartment to fail to enlist the greatest minds in thinking through the overall problem and the proper response.

At this point, merely telling the Predator story in isolation is, well, a bit isolated—because a week after the second (and last) sighting of the tall man in the white robes and just a month after the secret start of Predator flights over Afghanistan, a small dinghy carrying two men and a load of explosives rammed into the middle of the destroyer USS *Cole* in Aden harbor in Yemen, killing seventeen sailors and injuring thirty-nine others.

The immediate impulse for the residents of the secret chambers—for those in Washington who had been living and breathing Afghan Eyes, snatch and grab, Predator, and the man in the white robes—was to attempt another retaliatory strike: a faster one, a better one, a bigger one. They agitated for it and then lamented not getting it, blaming sticklers and lawmen and those too weak to have vision, who were still standing in the way.[39]

"We were shocked to learn that the Navy was even making port calls in Yemen," counterterrorism staffer Richard Clarke later wrote,[40] revealing what a vacuum the bin Laden quest existed in. General Anthony Zinni, the overall commander for the Middle East region, was labeled "culpable" by two others working in the White House circle.[41] Michael Sheehan "was particularly outraged" that neither Zinni nor anyone else in the US military pressed for implementation of existing terrorist retaliation plans, that is, for an immediate attack.[42] The government, even most of the intelligence community, was criminally stuck on a peacetime footing, the residents of the black box fumed. It was all the military's fault for taking al Qaeda too lightly, they said. The dots weren't connected even before America knew there were dots.[43]

For America, the attack on the USS *Cole* came out of the blue, sending people running for their atlases to check where Yemen was, and scratching their heads to fathom how the US military could have been making such an ill-prepared and unprotected port visit in such an obviously dangerous part of the world. And just a month away, America had a presidential election—a hotly contested one.

Volumes would later be written as to whether terror is a crime or an act of war, about the namby-pamby pre-9/11 reactions, about the failures of intelligence and government that led to the 2001 attacks, and then about the turnaround and all the supposed correctives that followed. But there is no denying in hindsight that by conferring warrior status upon al Qaeda, the United States also conferred the age-old mantle of the military on a bunch of criminals, even if they were archcriminals. Like the goddess Ishtar throwing a tantrum that resulted in Enkidu's death, the black box reared its mighty pencil and took on the role of judge and jury—and more, claimed the essential authority and power of the gods. None of it would have happened without unmanned systems—first the long-range Tomahawk cruise missiles that could be fired from the Indian Ocean deep into Afghanistan, and then Predator, which now proved that it could range anywhere, and also could soon do so with its own weapon.

I hate to say that regardless of the outcome of the 2000 elections, al Qaeda had gained advantage and the embassy bombings and the attack on the *Cole* were huge victories for bin Laden. As Lawrence Wright says in *The Looming Tower*, "al Qaeda camps in Afghanistan filled with new recruits, and contributors from the Gulf States arrived carrying Samsonite suitcases filled with petrodollars, as in the glory days of the Afghan jihad."[44]

It was all just part of a continuum, the focus on the best way to "fix" and "finish" the enemy, from Iraqi Scuds in 1991 to those Serb tanks in Kosovo in 1999, but soon enough, the focus was on taking out one leader at a time, and then even one terrorist or insurgent at a time. As some have suggested, it was not just an overreliance on technology and a descent into an all-consuming black box that blinded the government to broader threats, but also an automaticity that suggested that public servants and even the president had no choice in the matter, that indeed our entire system of national security was in its way becoming autonomous and unmanned.

CHAPTER SEVEN

Inherit the Wind

[I will] curse you with a mighty curse,
my curse shall afflict you now and forthwith!
A household to delight in [you shall not] acquire,
[never to] reside in the [midst] of a family!
TABLET VII, *EPIC OF GILGAMESH*

In his first regular meeting with the Bush White House after the inauguration, CIA director George Tenet raised the question of who would be in command of Predators flying over Afghanistan, particularly since they would soon be armed.[1] He got no answer. Less than a week later, he raised the same issue in his first private meeting with Secretary of Defense Rumsfeld.[2] Tenet asserted that the experiences of the previous year hunting for bin Laden demonstrated that, in the case of another sighting, the US government wasn't ready.[3] Rumsfeld, who was ultimately in command of the air force's Predator, was noncommittal and fails to even mention any pre-9/11 deliberations in his own autobiography.

On February 16, 2001, less than two weeks after Tenet delivered his talking points at the Pentagon, a Predator flying over the Nevada desert launched a five-foot-long Hellfire laser-guided missile against a stationary tank target. Under the most carefully chosen conditions of clear skies and calm weather, the ninety-eight-pound Hellfire left its position under the wing and found the laser spot "painted" on the turret of the stationary hull. Seventeen seconds after ignition, the missile struck the tank turret about six inches to the right of dead center, spinning it around about thirty degrees. The unarmed Hellfire "made a big, gray dent in the turret—just beautiful," the test director said.[4]

The newly promoted General Jumper, now the top air force man, had initiated the program. He made it his mission to solve the puzzle of hitting fleeting and time-perishable targets. "It seemed obvious to me that if you have a vehicle out there that is staring at a target, it probably ought to have something on board that can do something about it," he later explained. He admitted to the "culture clash" between intelligence and operations people in mixing the two functions so closely together—collection and action—but also recognized that central to the air force's ultimate acceptance of any major investment in unmanned platforms was going to be their ability to carry a weapon and hit the target. [5]

Predator's manufacturer had anticipated that a weapon might be added. Engineers designed the wings with powered hard points to carry payloads that might include weapons. Unlike earlier drones that were more model airplanes than real aircraft, the very concept of a larger and more capable Predator was to be a drone that acted more like an airplane. "What do airplanes do?" They carry sensors, video, and electronics. And some of them carry weapons, General Atomics CEO Tom Cassidy later recalled.

Predator's weapons would have to be extremely light, less than 200 pounds if two were carried, one under each wing. The technologists who were secreted away in the black box recesses of weapons development went to work—one option would cost tens of millions and be ready in five to seven years; another was more than a decade away and would cost hundreds of millions. The army's missile was initially passed over as an option by many in blue because they didn't want to have to deal with and be beholden to the missile's owner. The navy, on the other hand, had already experimented with Hellfire and the very same laser designator the air force had used on WILD Predators. Though there was a "shit storm" of a fight inside the flying service over new versus old, Jumper was unabashedly in favor of the navy configuration with the army missile: right weight, combat proven, and available in abundance right away.[6] "Take three months and $3 million, and you go do it, just do it," he told his subordinates in June 2000.[7]

The engineers went to work on integrating the missile into the aerial system's electronics and then incorporating the targeting and fire control black boxes needed to make Hellfire work. Would the force and the torque of a weapon be too much for the delicate airframe? How would the missile's rocket plume affect the drone?

On February 21, five days after the inert test, a Predator flying at 2,000 feet fired the first live Hellfire, this time using its own Kosovo ball to self-designate.[8] Like the earlier test, the missile used was a low-altitude C-version, originally designed to be delivered from attack helicopters at treetop level against armored vehicles.[9] Additional testing of the more expensive K-version would be necessary at higher and higher altitudes, and there would have to be testing under more realistic conditions and in real weather, as well as shooting against a moving target.[10] But the system was moving forward.

Many would later blame Rumsfeld or the Bush administration for some failure to take advantage of a magical system right then and there, for not deploying Predator to Afghanistan in early 2001 and killing bin Laden.[11] Yet there was no political holdup. Joint air force and CIA tests starting in May showed a Hellfire problem when fired from higher altitudes: the CIA provided the specifications and funding to construct a building at the China Lake range in California that mimicked bin Laden's home (though what was built resembled nothing of the sort).[12] The story goes that Hellfire, optimized for armor penetration, punched right through the roof and burrowed into the ground. Work started on a fragmentation warhead with a larger lethal radius and an improved fuse that would detonate the explosives in the milliseconds that the missile was inside the structure.[13] The technologists, moreover, were working to devise a way for Predator to be operated from a ground control station in the United States. Some said that long-range remote split operations, which would entail routing the Predator's signal to a satellite, then cross-linking to another satellite, then to an antenna on the ground in Europe, and then across the Atlantic Ocean via fiber optic cable, wouldn't work.[14] But they did.

By mid-2001, Predator was one of only three operational unmanned aerial vehicles in the US military (the marine corps still flew short-range Pioneers of Desert Storm fame, and the army flew its midrange drone called Hunter).[15] Predator had participated in combat actions in Bosnia and Kosovo, started flying over Iraq in 1998 as part of enforcement of no-fly zones (and was still doing so right up to 9/11), and even returned to the Balkans for a deployment in early 2001.[16] Especially flying over Serbia (and Iraq), the system was considered highly vulnerable to enemy air defenses and radar-guided air defense missiles. And the sortie rate per airframe was frustratingly low if it was to be considered a reliable standard weapon.[17]

Another unmanned drone under development, far more promising and expensive, was Global Hawk. Global Hawk flew higher and was much larger than Predator, a super and robust intelligence platform that by its very design and blue-chip manufacturer (Teledyne Ryan, and later Northrop Grumman) suggested *strategic* and superior.[18] Where Predator provided what was called a soda straw field of view, Global Hawk provided a wide field of view. Though we may think of Global Hawk today as an integral element of the terrorism search, its origins were actually wholly conventional and orthodox; it was intended for major wars to support time-sensitive targeting against the usual list of mobile prey.[19]

The original concept that was percolating at the end of the first Bush administration was to create a complex duo of a stealthy and highly cutting-edge drone (called DarkStar and being developed by Lockheed Martin)[20] and a more conventional Global Hawk. The plan was that they would ultimately supplant penetrating reconnaissance aircraft, that is, replace the manned U-2s of Cold War fame and possibly even some satellites.[21] The initial prototype Global Hawk, which was rolled out of its California laboratory in February 1997, was 44 feet long, with a wingspan of 116 feet and weighing 26,750 pounds at takeoff. The flight vehicle was to be able to cruise to a target area 1,200 miles from the launch site, loiter on station for twenty-four hours at an altitude of about 65,000 feet, and then return to the takeoff point. It was more than twice the size of Predator, with a capacity to carry 1,900 pounds (almost quadruple Predator's payload), flying at almost three times the altitude and for more than twice the distance. Perhaps most importantly, Global Hawk could provide coverage of up to 40,000 square nautical miles per day.[22]

By flying at 65,000 feet, above all civilian aircraft (Predator flies in the same airspace as commercial traffic), Global Hawk could position itself over an area of interest, achieving a degree of persistence not obtainable from either manned aircraft or satellites. Global Hawk was also fundamentally different than Predator in that while Predator flew with a man-in-the-loop, that is, with a pilot constantly at the controls, Global Hawk was flown autonomously. Equipped with an automatic takeoff and landing system, Global Hawk followed a computer-controlled flight plan once launched. Only if an emergency developed or the preplanned mission was overridden by a higher priority did an operator take over.[23]

Global Hawk made its debut flight at Edwards AFB in California in February 1998.[24] Several problems arose in flight, but none were so serious that the system operators couldn't handle the airframe using manual override.[25] Besides, the whole idea behind Global Hawk was to develop the system while flying, updating it as the airframe and the various black box payloads evolved. Some called it "spiraling," with version A (the RQ-4A) slated to be fielded as soon as possible and then replaced as new models emerged.

In April 2000, Global Hawk began an extensive demonstration, flying to Florida and transmitting images of shipping activity in the Gulf of Mexico to the coast guard, continuing up the Atlantic coast and wowing army and navy image recipients at Fort Bragg and in Norfolk. It then flew across the ocean, where it transmitted pictures of ship movement north of the Azores; overflew the coast of Portugal, where it imaged a NATO amphibious landing exercise; and then flew back to Florida, for a total of twenty-eight hours in the air. A month after Global Hawk entered its formal engineering, manufacturing, and development phase in March 2001, another demonstrator model touched down in Australia after a flight of approximately twenty-two hours and 7,500 miles without refueling, becoming the first unmanned vehicle to cross the Pacific Ocean. None of this is to suggest that the program didn't have its challenges: one of seven airframes was lost in an early crash, and another had an accident on the runway that destroyed its sensor assembly, the only one installed on a developmental system at the time.[26] Still, the new system exceeded even the most optimistic expectations.

There is no evidence that Donald Rumsfeld, micromanager par excellence, made any significant decisions regarding Global Hawk before 9/11 or even noticed the drone. The Pentagon "approved" production of six Global Hawk aircraft three months into the Bush administration for a prospective initial operational capability a year or two out; home basing in California was announced in July; the drone was a living and breathing system that would incrementally acquire better airframes and incorporate imagery and signal intercept capabilities as they became available.[27] A long list of black box suitors wrote their names on Global Hawk's dance card. Beginning in 1998, a mountain of PowerPoint briefings accumulated, suggesting new packages to attach: a new and superior Advanced Synthetic Aperture Radar System (ASARS) Improvement Program, or AIP; an Interferometric SAR (InSAR), an array of optics and radio frequency probes that use interference phenomena structures to obtain higher resolution; a better Moving Target Indicator (MTI) that promised detection of any moving object down to 2.5 mph; multispectral and hyperspectral sensors; a foliage penetration (FOPEN) radar; a bomb damage impact assessor; a Nuclear, Biological, and Chemical (NBC) detection kit; a Boost-Phase Intercept (BPI) missile defense capability; an extended air surveillance and airborne targeting and cross-cueing system (ATACCS); a signals intelligence (SIGINT) intercept capability; and an Airborne Communications Node (ACN).[28]

Global Hawk went on its world tour, and throughout the summer of 2001, Predator cooled its heels, operating over the former Yugoslavia and supporting the no-fly zone imposed over southern Iraq.[29] Resumption of Predator flights over Afghanistan continued to be hotly debated inside the new administration, but the Pentagon took a decidedly passive backseat in the deliberations. Tenet suggests that the operational and policy questions of killing bin Laden held things up. "What criteria would we use to shoot? Who authorizes weapons firing? What are the implications of a successful firing and of an unsuccessful firing?"[30] But the CIA and the Pentagon both wanted to hold off on sending Predator back to Uzbekistan until the armed version was ready.[31] When the Bush National Security Council authorized deployment on September 1, the policies regarding the CIA's use were still unresolved, and Uzbekistan had not yet granted permission to allow flights by weapons-carrying aircraft. The decision was put off until after the Labor Day weekend.[32]

After 9/11, many wondered why there wasn't instant retaliation. An initial target list for Tomahawk cruise missile attacks was produced on September 12 that included Taliban air defense stations and military barracks, as well as al Qaeda camps.[33] The Central Command (CENTCOM) headquarters in Florida produced three military options: a cruise-missile-only strike à la Clinton; a cruise missile strike plus manned bombers in a three-to-ten-day air campaign à la later Clinton; and a cruise missile and bomber package plus "boots on the ground," a plan that would employ not just special operations forces but also the army and marine corps.[34] Option three was selected. "This time," President Bush said, "we're not just going to pound sand."[35]

With a public war now declared against al Qaeda, the contrast between the CIA and Rumsfeld's Pentagon was stark. Largely shut off from the black box deliberations and the grand covert action before 9/11, the bulk of the Pentagon was wholly unprepared. On the other hand, the CIA carried around "a briefcase stuffed with top-secret documents and plans, in many respects the culmination of more than four years of work on Osama bin

Laden and the al-Qaeda network."[36] Yet even with war, the allure of covert action persisted. On September 17, President Bush signed a top secret "Presidential Finding" authorizing an unprecedented range of operations against al Qaeda, as well as the use of lethal force against bin Laden and his terrorist leadership.[37] "I had never in my experience been part of or even seen a presidential authorization as far-reaching and as aggressive in scope," the top CIA lawyer said.[38] By that time, three weaponized Predators were at an isolated airfield in Uzbekistan.[39] A thoroughly reeling and arm-twisted Pakistan also granted blanket overflight and landing rights for all necessary military operations against the Taliban and al Qaeda.[40] On the same day that President Bush signed his finding, Islamabad airport was closed for two hours to allow an initial wave of US military transports to land.[41] Predators were moved to Shahbaz airfield in Jacobabad, just 300 miles southeast of Kandahar.[42] The drones and operators were on the ground before the engineers and support personnel.[43]

Aircraft carrier battle groups, amphibious ships, and submarines left their ports and stations for the Arabian Sea and the Indian Ocean. B-2 and B-52 bombers and long-range fighters gathered from the Indian Ocean to Turkey and congregated around the Gulf states. Oman granted permission to host special operations forces at Masirah Island, and AC-130 gunships staged there.[44]

It wouldn't be much of an exaggeration to say that machines outnumbered men. The world of the unmanned was already playing an outsized role: on the first night of attacks on October 7, fifty Tomahawk sea-launched cruise missiles were fired from four surface ships and two submarines (one the Royal Navy's HMS *Trafalgar*), and the majority of the bombs dropped were the satellite-guided Joint Direct Attack Munitions (JDAMs) first introduced in the Kosovo war. In fact, the first operational task of the CIA Jawbreaker team on the ground inside the country was taking GPS surveys of Northern Alliance frontline positions opposite the Taliban for use by the JDAMs.[45] Almost everything was now about the data.

When bombing began, US intelligence had no clue where bin Laden was, so Mullah Omar, leader of the Taliban government, became the highest-priority target. Two Predators were flying over Kandahar the first night, keeping a watchful eye on locations where Omar might be. One Predator, which was launched from Uzbekistan, was armed and belonged to the CIA. The other was unarmed and had been launched by the air force from Pakistan. Soon after bombing began, the Predator teams were monitoring a Mullah Omar house when several vehicles left, driving west of the city.

Kandahar is an ancient place built on the ruins of Shahr-i-Konah, said to have been founded by Alexander the Great three hundred years before Christ, a ruin today located about four miles west of the city center. When I first visited Kandahar in 2002, the same two main streets that anchored the original city were still there, one running from the Kabul to the Herat gates of the old walled city, the other crossing at a ninety-degree angle and running from the Shikarpur gate to the ancient citadel. The city was a jumble of disrepair and destruction, the famed arched dome long gone, the ancient stone reservoir neglected, the headquarters of the Ministry for the Propagation of Virtue and the Prevention of Vice instead sitting on the northeast corner of Kandahar's heart, the building itself now a bombed-out shell.[46]

On that first night, while a Predator was tracking a convoy thought to be associated with Mullah Omar, the SUVs and pick-ups ended up at a residence near the old ruins. I visited this residence in March 2002; it was an isolated complex given the label Objective Gecko by the US military. Omar's fortress was surrounded by a low-slung wall, with the single entrance road criss-crossing berms and skirting around dirt-filled fifty-five-gallon barrels that served as barriers to prevent any high-speed approach. The compound was topped with antiaircraft guns and shielded on two sides by abrupt hundred-foot boulders. When I visited, it had already been thoroughly bombed, the only incongruity being that the main buildings were gaily painted in pastel hues and adorned with weird faux minarets and fake palm trees.

That night, at the CIA, at the White House, at the Pentagon, at Central Command in Florida, and at forward command centers, everyone was watching the video, and there was intense discussion regarding the probability that indeed the convoy carried Mullah Omar. Many of those in the intelligence fields admitted that it was more supposition than certainty. Permission to attack the house identified as Mullah Omar's residence was denied, or so it seemed to many—and there were many—who stayed glued to this single platform's reality show. Unbeknownst to many participants, including the air force head of the operation, the CIA mission commander in Virginia nevertheless was given orders to engage. One of the presumed security forces' vehicles parked at the edge of the compound was hit with a Hellfire.[47] It was the first operational firing of a weapon from a Predator drone.

The compound wouldn't feature in the official war story until twelve days later, and no official history and no announcement at the time mentions the inaugural "combat shot" of Predator or an attack at Mullah Omar's compound among the thirty-one targets attacked on October 7.[48]

The New Yorker later carried a much-quoted article by Seymour Hersh that said that an armed CIA Predator identified an SUV convoy carrying Mullah Omar on the first night of the war. According to Hersh, CENTCOM—Tommy Franks's command—wouldn't "push the button," unsure of positive ID and concerned about civilian collateral damage in Kandahar. The Predator then reportedly tracked the convoy to "a building" where Omar and his entourage took cover. When General Franks finally gave permission for the drone to fire a Hellfire missile in front of the building to see who came out, Mullah Omar supposedly scooted out the rear.[49]

After the *New Yorker* story came out, Rumsfeld, the White House, the air force, politicians, and the news media all roared disapproval. Military lawyers were blamed for their punctiliousness, and Franks was criticized for screwing up the mission, for micromanaging, for slowing down the campaign, and for demanding unnecessary target approval. Political leaders were criticized for not providing timely approval and imposing excessive collateral damage constraints in the first place. Rumors circulated that CIA intelligence *analysts* sitting in Langley were the problem, thinking that the building the Taliban took refuge in was a mosque. The CIA meanwhile whispered that they had thought it was Omar for sure, placing the blame squarely back on the shoulders of Central Command and the military.

No one came off looking smart, and the incident and reactions surrounding it were a surrogate for much bigger battles being waged in Washington. I experienced my own unsolicited lobbying from air force leaders and Deputy Secretary of Defense Paul Wolfowitz, who called me at home and tried to convince me that the problem was the CIA or even "the army commanders" (read General Franks) in charge of a new technology that they neither understood nor appreciated. Predator didn't kill the target, and everyone spent an inordinate amount of time with their new black box, specially cleared to enter a still-restricted chamber. The dynamic itself, the stimuli of action creating crisis and decisions, obscured both the power and the cost of going at it unmanned, and made the mission seem more than it was, as if the death of Mullah Omar would have untangled the United States from Afghanistan for the next decade and a half or stopped terrorism.

Days after the bombing of Afghanistan commenced, a military aide came into Donald Rumsfeld's office at the Pentagon to advise him that the IT wizards could hook up a special monitor at his desk so he also could watch real-time video from Predators flying half a world away. The vernacular of the irascible defense secretary's response is lost to history: "That's not the job of the Secretary of Defense," he is blandly quoted as replying. "That's General Franks's job and the job of our field commanders."[50]

Rumsfeld's instinct about the danger of micromanagement was right, even if he and everyone else would soon get all tied up by Predator's inaugural use. In his autobiography, General Franks would later tell some tall tale about intentionally choosing not to bomb Mullah Omar's house on the first night of the war, "hoping it would serve as a magnet for Omar and his deputies..." later on.[51] For some reason, he forgets that a Hellfire was fired at that very house, and he gets the location of Objective Gecko wrong, saying it was in downtown Kandahar.[52]

The air force types who hated Tommy Franks for having a typical man-in-green blind spot when it came to anything that wasn't boots on the ground couldn't wait to tattle. Though Rumsfeld blithely labeled Predator video and control of the drones Franks's job, they whispered that the field commander went overboard in trying to put himself in the pilot's seat. Not only did he watch the Predator feed himself, talking directly with the pilot regarding picture quality, fuel status, and even how the Hellfire missile might work, but he also personally directed the strike on the very vehicle that he would later forget was even bombed. "This sequence took over 90 minutes to complete and at multiple points the CENTCOM/CC [General Franks] was talking directly with the pilot of a single aircraft and directing aircraft tactics based upon the Predator video," a key air force participant later wrote.[53]

The blood between the services became so bad that after Franks heard that air force chief of staff General John Jumper had watched the first-night attack unfold on video from the Pentagon, he ordered that his feed be removed.[54] Thus the inaugural use of an armed Predator ended up being an introduction to the fundamental divide that exists between the world of the manned and the unmanned, as war begins to slip dangerously into the realm of video games and button-pushing murder. There are wars and secret wars, special and unspecial operations, civilians acting as military men and the actual field commanders being constantly diverted to tend to some promised silver bullet. It would happen again and again, this intrinsic fight between history and secret history. Unmanned warfare—safer, more flexible, newer, and certainly more alluring—might demand greater human attention but also starts us down the road of devaluing human input.

CHAPTER EIGHT

My Back Is Killing Me

...he took up his axe in his hand,
he drew forth the dirk [from] his [belt],
forward he crept and on [them] he rushed down.
Like an arrow he fell among them....
TABLET X, *EPIC OF GILGAMESH*

It is perhaps a minor point, but the sources are practically unanimous, and they are almost all wrong: in the first weeks of the war against terrorism, the experts and articles and studies say, a Predator drone (not just a Predator but a *CIA* Predator) killed—and not just killed, but "assassinated"—Mohammad Atef, the al Qaeda military operations chief and World Trade Center attack commander.[1] Atef was killed on November 3, 2001, or maybe it was the thirteenth or late November, or at least in the month of November; in Kabul, near Kabul, south of Kabul, in Gardez, in Jalalabad in eastern Afghanistan; at a house, in a hotel, while on the run. As people fled, the Predator opened fire on them as well; Atef was killed along with "close to a hundred" other al Qaeda members. So say the history and law professors; the pro-drone analysts; the antidrone activists; the industry of terrorism authorities; the Congressional Research Service; the former chairman of the Joint Chiefs of Staff; the infamous lawyer John Yoo, author of the torture memos; the *New York Times*; and pretty much everyone else.[2]

Mohammad Atef did die — that we know. He was the first and highest-ranking al Qaeda man to be killed after 9/11 and the first to be killed in any kind of air attack that specifically targeted an individual. But he wasn't killed by a drone. Is this the way we want to leave the history of something so controversial: with wrong assumptions and messy scholarship? And even if Atef had been killed by a Predator, is it proper to call his death assassination, during a war, or to pin it on the CIA, as if the intelligence agency is somehow independent and not just some secret-agent warrior in our wholly transformed hybrid of a military? Does it matter that the story is engaged as highbrow ammunition for a particular argument or that it is mangled in rumor and a massive game of Telephone? I think it does matter, but as I tell the story, I just ask the reader to remember the telephone and not the Predator: Mohammed Atef was killed because of the black box and the phone.

Mohammad Atef was described as "a very striking-looking person, tall and slender with bright green eyes, dark-skinned, bearded, full of youth and vigour," by Abdel Bari Atwan in *The Secret History of al Qaeda*. "He was modest, extremely radical and exceptionally polite."[3] A lot can be said about Atef, but the most important fact for this story is that he had a bad back, a really bad back. He was practically immobile, and US intelligence has since concluded that he was likely bed-bound, so when other al Qaeda leaders and fighters evacuated the Afghan capital, Atef stayed behind.

I've been to the house in Kabul where Atef was killed. I didn't know that at the time; I had been directed to a nice residence in an upscale neighborhood by locals when I was leading a bomb damage assessment on behalf of the nongovernmental organization Human Rights Watch. The house had obviously been bombed, and not just promiscuously; it had been intentionally targeted and directly attacked with multiple bombs; the adjacent houses had been damaged only by the blast and flying shrapnel, the telltale signs of a precision attack. It was one of a dozen or more locations I probably visited that day in March 2002, looking for and verifying civilian casualties and trying to make sense of the targeting choices in Operation Enduring Freedom. In Kabul, eyewitnesses said the house was hit on November 12 or 13. Taliban forces were retreating from the Afghan capital, and the Northern Alliance was coming in from the Shomali Plain to the north; there was chaos. The early-morning hours of November 13 also turned out to be the final major urban air attack of the initial post-9/11 campaign. It was the same day, sources said, and I have confirmed, that the offices of Al Jazeera television nearby were also attacked.

When Al Jazeera was bombed, it was immediately reported in the news media. "We had identified two locations in Kabul where Al Jazeera people worked, and this location wasn't among them," Colonel Rick Thomas, a Gulf-based spokesman for Central Command, told the Associated Press the same day. The attacked structure, he added, was "a known al-Qaida [sic] facility" in downtown Kabul. Thomas said that the United States "had no indications this or any nearby facility was used by Al Jazeera."[4]

That morning, Pentagon spokesman Rear Admiral Craig Quigley happened to be conducting a briefing at the Foreign Press Center in Washington and was also asked about the attack. "I have seen the news reports...that some sort of weapon went awry and destroyed those facilities," he said, suggesting a malfunction. Adding that the United States only hits "military targets," Quigley surmised that perhaps "weapons have failed" or "human errors have been made," with perhaps "targets being struck that we did not intend to strike."[5]

But Mohammed Jassim al-Ali, Al Jazeera's managing editor, claimed in an interview that the strike must have been deliberate. "They know where we are located and they know what we have in our office and we also did not get any warning," he said.[6] Colonel Brian Hoey, another spokesman for CENTCOM and located in Florida, then contradicted Quigley and said that the building in question had been deliberately attacked, but said the attack was based on "compelling" evidence that it was being used by al Qaeda and not because it was Al Jazeera. At the time of the attack, Hoey added "the indications we had was that this was not an Al Jazeera office." The US military, he said, "does not and will not target media. We would not, as a policy, target news media organizations— it would not even begin to make sense."[7]

Despite denials and explanations, to outsiders the attack on Al Jazeera looked absolutely intentional. The Arab network had become famous for reporting on civilian casualties from inside Afghanistan, a role similar to the one that Radio Television of Serbia (RTS) played in the 1999 Kosovo war. Given that NATO intentionally bombed the Belgrade headquarters of the RTS during Operation Allied Force, it was easy to speculate that Al Jazeera was targeted simply for reporting a side of the war that the United States wanted suppressed. The Committee to Protect Journalists in New York protested, putting out a warning that a "deliberate attack on a civilian facility is prohibited under international humanitarian law." No less than General Tommy Franks responded to the committee by letter six months later, categorically denying that Al Jazeera facilities "have ever been intentionally targeted by coalition forces."[8] In a letter to Al Jazeera dated December 6, 2001, Assistant Secretary of Defense Victoria ("Tori") Clarke stated that "the building we struck was a known al-Qaeda facility in central Kabul," adding that "there were no indications that this or any nearby facility was used by Al-Jazeera."[9]

Around the same time, I was contacted by a team of air force analysts who were working on the lessons learned, trying to reconstruct and analyze the bombing campaign, what went right, what went wrong. They'd heard I had pictures; they'd heard I knew things, and they wanted to compare notes. We agreed that they would break the rules and invite me into the classified realm to combine the official target lists, pilot mission reports, and poststrike assessments with my observations and data from the ground. What we pieced together was that on the night of November 12–13, the United States undertook a meticulously planned attack on at least three dispersed houses, each coded as being associated with al Qaeda leadership. Three were identified on the target list as:

- Kabul Residence (AOM 666)
- Kabul Probable Arab Residence (AOM 532)
- Kabul Suspect Residence (AOM 597)

These were all preplanned attacks, that is, the targets were identified and selected based on intelligence reporting that associated the locations with al Qaeda at least twenty-four hours beforehand: they went on a validated target list, as opposed to being time-sensitive (or fleeting) targets chosen because conditions on the ground or contemporaneous intercepts indicated that they were active, though, as we shall see, that played a role as well. As best as it can be reconstructed and understood by me, as the numbers would suggest, there were hundreds of prospective targets in this category, and on the thirty-fifth day of bombing, with rapidly changing circumstances and al Qaeda leadership on the move, this was probably close to a last chance to bomb in Kabul (Kandahar in the south was still contested, as were most of the cities and villages in the east). War planners were still uncertain whether the city would indeed fall and how quickly US special operations forces (and "other government agencies," as they like to say of the CIA) would make it into the city to reconnoiter and exploit al Qaeda and Taliban places of interest.

The squadrons and pilots in these cases received the air tasking order with their assigned targets, time of attack, designated weapons, and special instructions. Target study was done, in the sense of identifying the object to be attacked on a map and on satellite imagery and special graphics, and the planners at CENTCOM and the attacking squadron applied effectiveness methodologies to calculate the optimum angle of attack, the specific aimpoint, and the bomb and fusing that would be required to maximize the specified damage while minimizing collateral damage to adjacent areas.

According to the classified air tasking order (ATO) for that evening, three targets were attacked by US Navy F/A-18 Hornet fighter aircraft armed with 500-pound GBU-12 laser-guided bombs. Since all of the targets were located in densely built-up and heavily populated areas, the smallest laser-guided bomb in existence at that time was chosen. The pilots had to locate their target through their viewing systems, align their aircraft to be able to shoot a laser beam to the intended aimpoint, and, while flying at more than 500 mph, release the laser-guided bombs in the right "envelope" in order for the weapon to detect the laser reflection, which then guided the bomb to the intended aimpoint.

According to the classified pilot mission reports, two of the three targets—Kabul Probable Arab Residence and Kabul Suspect Residence—were hit nearly simultaneously at 14:04 and 14:20 Zulu time (Greenwich Mean Time), or 18:04 and 18:20 local time. The third target, Kabul Residence, was hit at 20:39 and 20:49 Zulu time, or 12:39 a.m. and 12:49 a.m. local time, in the early-morning hours of November 13. Kabul Residence was hit with four GBU-12s, two each separated by ten minutes.

Using the coordinates listed on the ATO and mission reports and comparing them to satellite imagery and GPS coordinates I collected on the ground, a fourth target also appeared. Air force analysts labeled it Building 4. It appeared that Kabul Residence (AOM 666), a house quite some distance away, was not bombed by an ATO asset that night after all. Building 4 turned out instead to be a house containing the offices of Al Jazeera television, that is, based upon the coordinates my team derived on the ground and seemingly the targets the navy fighters attacked based upon the time of attack, even if their official mission reports said they attacked AOM 666.[10] AOM 592 and 597, the latter closest to the main avenue and located at Wazir Akbar Khan Street No. 13, according to my notes, were two adjacent houses practically opposite the Wazir Akbar Khan hospital complex. The air force analysts concluded that Mohammed Atef was in one of those two houses. An FBI special agent who later exploited the house confirmed the location based upon my pictures.

But there was a limit to what the military records revealed, at least in air force and CENTCOM records outside compartmented worlds. Whether AOM 666 was bombed at all remained unclear; it was a house that once was the residence of the Kabul mayor but far away from the Al Jazeera office (Building 4) or Mohammed Atef's house. We scoured the air tasking order to see if some other attacker, particularly a CIA Predator drone, was also flying in the area at that time. My air force friends made inquiries up the chain of command. After months of work, we concluded that there was a single armed CIA Predator there that night that might have been involved in the bombing of AOM 666.[11] It was pretty clear that Building 4 *was* Al Jazeera, and it was pretty clear that the F-18 dropped at least two of its four weapons at the moment it was attacked. But how did it get on the target list? Did the navy pilots get a time-sensitive target change while they were in the air and then attack Building 4? Their postmission reports didn't say. And what was the role of the Predator, which almost everyone claimed killed Atef?

Rear Admiral Quigley later stated that the United States intentionally targeted the residential building that housed Al Jazeera (and indeed it was just a house), the target we were now calling Building 4. He said the house occupied by Al Jazeera "had been, and was at the time, a facility used by al-Qaida." According to the *Guardian*, Quigley said its "military significance" made it a "legitimate target."[12] He took back his earlier presumption that there was any error, and stated that US intelligence had confirmed that the house was an al Qaeda facility. Quigley also said that the United States never knew the house was Al Jazeera's office, and that the compound had a "different intelligence signal completely."[13]

I visited the Al Jazeera house (Building 4) as well, and with Al Jazeera papers strewn everywhere amongst the rubble, and a large satellite dish in the courtyard, it was indeed being used by the Qatari-based network. But reconstructing any event is difficult, as I would find out once again, even when one has the best of information. They don't talk about "fog of war" for nothing, and there's always something one doesn't know, especially in this new style of warfare, where intelligence information is as important as operations, where military and CIA overlap uncomfortably and where decisions are split second. But remember the telephone? When Quigley and other spokesmen referred to "compelling evidence" and called the Al Jazeera office a "command and control" facility of "military significance," this was code for an emanating signal, what Admiral Quigley elliptically referred to as the house's "intelligence signal." But "intelligence signature" is the correct term, and I later confirmed with the admiral that he had not misspoken, so I assumed that the *Guardian* reporter just got the transposition of the term wrong in his notes.

This is the world of the NSA that we have become so familiar with since Edward Snowden sprang onto the scene. But NSA is also like a character in a favorite television drama: there is a real person behind the character, and the character is also only playing a role, even if he or she perfectly inhabits that role. In the real world of NSA, even going back fifty years or more, history is silent on what the eavesdroppers were specifically listening to at any one time. There are incidents such as the USS *Liberty* or USS *Pueblo* or Flight 007 that are dissected (and butchered), but by and large, the most historians learn is that "a signal" or an intercept, or a decryption, provided some breakthrough.

Abdel Bari Atwan, in his *Secret History of al Qaeda*, claims that Mohammed Atef telephoned the newspaper *al-Quds al-Arabi* before he was killed,[14] but whether that is true or not, what seems clear is that on that day, at that moment, the center of Kabul was a pretty quiet place electronically, and the use of any satellite telephone would have been picked up by the American ear. One air force officer who was in the command center on November 13 said, "We sat there with report after report after report of thousands of vehicles leaving Kabul" on the southwestern road leading east, but airstrikes were restricted because of concerns that "civilians might be mixed in" with the possibly escaping al Qaeda and Taliban.[15] So though every possible eye was mobilized, ears proved the most revealing of a potential target in this chaotic environment, providing that "second source" or positive ID that is needed for any sensitive attack. Thus the activation of any signal, including an Al Jazeera signal, might have been, in this final night of Kabul bombing, enough of a tip-off to "flex" to the target, as they say. Especially if it is true that the United States didn't know that

Al Jazeera was at that specific structure, at that moment. Or if the United States knew, but also knew that al Qaeda was borrowing (or commandeering) Al Jazeera satellite circuits to communicate.

Admittedly, that's a lot of *ifs*.

Ali Soufan, the former FBI agent who was involved in post-war exploitation of al Qaeda material, says definitively that Atef was killed in an airstrike in Kabul on November 13, 2001, unable to evacuate from the city because of his chronic back problems.[16] Peter Bergen, bestselling terrorist expert, also says that Atef stayed behind in Kabul because of a back problem, and that a prominent Pakistani surgeon, Dr. Amer Aziz, was summoned to Kabul "in early November 2001" to treat him.[17] The 9/11 Commission lets slip in a footnote that various al Qaeda materials were "found in the rubble of Atef's house near [sic] Kabul following a November 2001 airstrike, together with a martyrdom video of [Ramzi] Binalshibh," one of the 9/11 key planners.[18] Another official source refers to the success of immediate follow-on counterterrorism operations in Malaysia and Singapore based upon the exploitation of material taken from Atef's house.[19] I know that his death was confirmed on the ground and that the house was exploited, and I know from my own sources that it was the exact house I later visited.

The role Predator played that night is exquisitely dissected by Richard Whittle in his *Predator: The Secret Origins of the Drone Revolution*. The air force–flown CIA Predator over Kabul that day and night, equipped literally with a Radio Shack black box receiver, picked up radio signals from an evident al Qaeda convoy and tracked it to Wazir Akbar Khan Street, the targets labeled AOM 592 and 597. Air force F-15Es flying in the vicinity were called to attack the target, Whittle writes, based upon his sources, and bombed it twice, contradicting what the paper trail said; but the F-15 mission was later also lauded in a semiofficial air force his-

tory, "the longest fighter combat mission in history."[20] The important point, though, is that the Predator didn't fire on Atef's house,
instead going on to shoot a single Hellfire at another house—
AOM 666?—that a group of people escaped to from Atef's house,
watching them as they ran through the streets of Kabul.[21]

For reasons that probably have mainly to do with the desire
for some charmed epic, the legend would become that Predator
killed Atef. The *New York Times* first reported it based on which-
ever administration or intelligence official heard the rumors and
passed on the magic. Even former chairman of the Joint Chiefs of
Staff Dick Myers later says in his autobiography that Atef "had
been killed in a CIA Predator strike that had targeted his Kabul
home with a Hellfire missile."[22] And Peter Bergen goes even further, saying that Atef's "death, though initially reported to have
come in a U.S. air strike, was later confirmed to have been the
result of a drone strike."[23] But manned airstrike it was; of that
there's no doubt.

Though the Afghanistan war fully opened the door for our
current drone wars, the lesson of the killing of Atef is once again
that it is the target and not the means of attack that is the remarkable part of contemporary warfare. My air force analyst friends
and I later marveled at how many unknowns persisted, the how
and the why of the Predator rumor, and we speculated over beers
whether the "information ops" types at the CIA or some other
black box channel didn't secretly borrow the navy F-18s that night
to intentionally bomb the news media, though when asked, a
high-level intelligence source countered that it was perfectly jus-
tifiable to bomb and cut off one of the last communications paths
that might be used to transmit al Qaeda's latest orders—a justification that might hold up in the court of law and public opinion,
the mere bonus being that the bombing of a "command and control" target also served to silence a disagreeable Arab station.[24]

Though the lessons learned report I helped with was classified and never publicly released, the air force, like the other services, sponsored a variety of official and approved histories of the kind that tell varnished war stories, the ones that fawn over command brilliance and are filled with institutional heroics. One states unambiguously that Atef was killed in a manned strike, and not only that, but by an air force plane.[25] Though I generally remain skeptical of the common assumption that the fighter pilot community that dominates the air force works against Predator and the unmanned, drones *are* second-class citizens, not just because they are not citizens at all but also because they inhabit unfamiliar space between sensor and shooter, a funny military way of describing two human attributes. For the air warriors, it isn't just their love affair with manned flight that tends to make them opposed to unmanned killing—it is also the universal discomfort with a process of seeing a prospective target during a war without being able to kill it. And of course, there is the unsatisfying legend that comes from the world of the unmanned: that the network killed Atef; that it was fast computer work; that it was merely the physics of triangulating a telephone call; that it could all have been done by machines.

CHAPTER NINE

The Machine Builds

[Wild Cow] Ninsun was clever [and wise, well versed in everything,]
[the mother of] Gilgamesh....
She smothered the censer and came [down from the roof,]
She summoned Enkidu...
TABLET III, *EPIC OF GILGAMESH*

The Afghanistan war in its first few weeks just about con-
founded everyone—after all, there was no industrial
military opponent à la Serbia or Iraq, and there were no discern-
ible targets. But the official public utterances were right on. "I
want to remind you that while today's operations are visible, many
other operations may not be so visible," General Myers said at the
podium of the Pentagon press room on the first night.[1] The next
night on the *CBS Evening News*, Rumsfeld added: "We're so con-
ditioned as a people to think that a military campaign has to be
cruise missiles and television images of airplanes dropping bombs,
and that's just false. This is a totally different war. We need a new
vocabulary. We need to get rid of old think and start thinking
about this thing the way it really is."[2]

Yet despite attempts by Rumsfeld and Myers, the story of war
continues to be all about bombs and bullets. In this version of war,
friendly versus enemy hardware is stacked up on two sides of a
ledger, with divisions of men mobilized and trained and prepared

to move to some front line where they engage in battles that look largely unchanged from those that took place thousands of years ago. Rumsfeld and company stressed all of the right points in arguing that this was not going to be our forefathers' war. But even they could not anticipate how different this war would be, and how the Data Machine—and its vast collection of intelligence—would begin to take over, even as the public narrative of war stayed largely stuck in the industrial age (and on the ground).

This is the essence of the wars the United States now fights. Individual targets—fixed, mobile, and now even individual humans— are identified and validated and located and tracked from the ground or the sky; they are identified through imagery, electronic emissions, communications, or other intelligence. In this kind of war, the strikers are more abundant than good targeting information, and the data itself, like a camouflaged enemy, masks the intelligence. The magic is melding what satellites and high-flying aircraft can see and hear, fusing together audio and video, the visible and invisible electromagnetic spectrums, and then processing and moving all of the information literally around the globe in seconds to make decisions. The key is to have strikers on station above or in close for that moment in time.[3]

In a place as far away and isolated as Afghanistan, whether cruise missile strikes or manned bombing are involved or not, the data scouts—both human and machine—at the edge of the Machine are almost always there first. These are the intelligence collectors who map enemy air defenses, the spy planes that listen in on radio communications, the photographers who image military installations and enemy concentrations. In 2001, Predators were sent out to do reconnaissance. They first overflew Afghan airspace before anyone else did, with an air force–led crew operating the now-veteran drone from an improvised ground control station in a wooded area on the CIA's grounds in Langley, Virginia.[4] But at that point, the majority of the scouts (if you don't count reconnaissance satellites) were almost completely manned. America's "strategic" intelligence collectors, all manned, air force RC-135 and navy EP-3 signals intelligence planes and the high-flying U-2s, began patrols around the periphery of Afghanistan almost immediately after 9/11 to sniff out prospective targets; they would penetrate into Afghan airspace soon thereafter.[5] Manned navy P-3C Orion airplanes, meanwhile, normally used for anti-submarine warfare and maritime surveillance (and also equipped with a full-motion video camera similar to the Predator's), leap-frogged closer to the potential battlespace, where they would join the others overflying the Taliban from forward air bases in Pakistan.[6] When the air force squadrons and the aircraft carriers arrived, EA-6B, ES-3, and specialized F-16 planes brought in electronic warfare capabilities and other black boxes. The Royal Air Force brought its own equivalents as well: Nimrod R1 electronic intelligence aircraft, the Canberra PR9 reconnaissance aircraft, and an E-3D AWACS flying radar. The French air force contributed the Mirage IV reconnaissance jet.[7]

"For the first time in the history of modern warfare," Ben Lambeth wrote in his semiofficial history of the conflict, a war "was conducted under an overarching intelligence, surveillance, and reconnaissance (ISR) umbrella that stared down relentlessly in search of enemy activity."[8] There was a lot of ISR, but "relentlessly" is pure hyperbole, and the initial small contribution of the unmanned goes by without remark. It was the amount of ISR overhead that would become a measure of success; it was the ability of each collecting platform or its black boxes to collect the right data to serve the needs of the specific weapons or the characteristics of the specific targets. And those needs were becoming more and more exacting. Bombing, the visible element of the conventional war model, initially unfolded with the attack on fixed targets associated with the Taliban and then moved to troops in the field. But the satellite-guided JDAM bombs—precise and economical—had taken on a meticulous singularity, each a product of a specific GPS coordinate rendered by some human. *You want the bomb where? At that spot on the front lines? On that mortar position?* So one bomb was delivered. But government officials were not impressed with one bomb—no matter how precise it was. They wanted more. In fact, the day after bombing commenced, the head of the CIA team inside northern Afghanistan wrote that the "disappointment with the Northern Alliance's senior ranks to the first night's bombing was palpable....News from the NA commanders on the Kabul front reported no bombs falling on the Taliban or Arab positions." Intercepted radio communications from Taliban positions on the front lines also "indicated a sense of relief among the Taliban forces at the low level and limited impact of the bombing."[9] Four days later, the CIA station chief in Islamabad further sent a cable labeling the military effort in southern Afghanistan even worse and a "political disappointment."[10]

The Northern Alliance probably would have been ecstatic if B-52s and "dumb bombs" had come in instead and carpet-bombed their archenemies into dust, as was the case through the end of the war in Vietnam. But regardless of the emotions of 9/11, something crucial had changed, and practices lacking in a precision result had become antithetical to the airpower creed. Despite all the anger unleashed by the World Trade Center and Pentagon attacks, despite a Bush administration that beat its breast, bellowing that it would break with the recent past of controlled bombing to introduce "shock and awe," the same unmanned Tomahawk cruise missiles dominated in the first few days, and air attacks remained as controlled as they had been at any time in the Clinton administration. The Bush White House—or at least someone with a political eye to the future—restricted attacks in urban areas and imposed collateral-damage and civilian-casualty restraints not much different than those used in the Balkans.[11]

Even General Tommy Franks called the beginning of Operation Enduring Freedom the "ten days from Hell,"[12] demonstrating that his lifelong artilleryman's viewpoint was even more habituated to imagining blistering bombardment. Rumsfeld was putting constant pressure on Franks, particularly apoplectic that the CIA was getting all the credit because military special operations forces hadn't yet arrived. It appeared that perhaps a frustrated nation and a wholly changed military would still reach back into the deep past of carpet-bombing to mete out a little more old-fashioned killing.[13]

For almost a week nothing changed in the design or pace of the war, but then on October 16, manned AC-130 gunships took part in the air campaign for the first time, attacking Taliban frontline positions.[14] Gunships operated by the Air Force Special Operations Command would become the most lethal assets available to the CIA and special operations forces working with the Northern Alliance (and later with Karzai's Pashtun fighters in the south) in the weeks ahead, supporting nearly every major offensive in strafing Taliban troops and pulverizing prepared defenses. With a legacy of nicknames like Puff the Magic Dragon, Angel of Death, Ultimate End, and Equalizer, the gunships delivered old-fashioned bloody vengeance. Each plane was armed with a side-mounted 25mm Gatling gun capable of firing 1,800 rounds a minute, a 40mm cannon—think machine gun firing small artillery shells—and a 105mm howitzer that fired 33-pound shells. These were said to be so accurate and fast that a single airplane could put one round in every square foot of a football field in seven seconds. If anyone argued that bombardment of that sort wasn't precision, the airpower advocates would counter that these were "special" operations. They hardly had to argue; the missions were secret.

Doctrine was for the gunships to fly a racetrack pattern above the battlefield, but the lumbering aerial battleships, flying slowly and at low altitude (and with a crew of fourteen) were consequently also vulnerable to missiles and gunfire from the ground (one was shot down over Kuwait during Desert Storm). So despite the passions of 9/11, the vulnerability of these manned aircraft restricted their operations. Crews were also having a problem in sparsely populated and mountainous Afghanistan: the sound of their presence traveled great distances at night, when the AC-130s flew for greater protection and safety. During orbits to line up their targets, the crews would often watch enemy fighters scatter in their infrared scopes.[15] To give the gunships a leg up in defending themselves and in preparing immediate fire, the technologists furiously worked to bring a live feed from a Predator already overflying Taliban defenses that would then prep the planes while they were as far as 100 miles away. The addition of the black box in November had an immediate payoff. Now, rather than the aircraft gunners looking through their own television viewing system and infrared detection sensors to find targets, or making contact with a ground spotter who would literally have to talk the aircraft gunner onto a desired target, those in the plane had their own unmanned scout and could see exactly what the drone saw, arriving ready and blasting away.[16]

It wasn't until October 16, the same day AC-130s began flying, that military special operations forces staged in Uzbekistan were also finally given the go-ahead to insert into the Panjshir Valley as well.[17] Then on October 19, in the *first action by US ground forces*, special operators flew in four specially configured MH-47 helicopters from the aircraft carrier USS *Kitty Hawk* in the Indian Ocean, overflying Pakistan to penetrate deep into Taliban country. Officially it was a mission to "disrupt Taliban leadership and AQ [al Qaeda] communications, gather intelligence and detain select personnel." AC-130 gunships and heavily armed MH-60 Blackhawk helicopters peppered the objectives with artillery and missiles moments before the assault.

Really, it was a demonstration, an isolated operation to put boots on the ground, one intended to send a signal both to the enemy and to the American people. For General Franks and the other ground force leaders in the US military, and for the Bush administration, the departure from cruise missile strikes and airstrikes represented the important break with the recent past. So on October 19, when the parachutes opened and the helicopters roared, old-fashioned images of real war were finally registered. The assault was directed at two objectives—one Gecko (Mullah Omar's house west of Kandahar) and the other Rhino, an unused airfield in southern Afghanistan. The special operators spent a total of an hour on the ground at Gecko, some collecting whatever was left to collect, but most just manning security positions to protect everyone until the show was over.[18]

With the infiltration of military special ops and the "success" of October 19, though, bombers and fighters shifted from hitting preplanned fixed targets to flying "flexed" missions against Taliban troops: opportunistic strikes.[19] As more and more US special operations soldiers arrived to accompany anti-Taliban forces, highly specialized ground controllers (called Joint Terminal Attack Controllers, JTACs—pronounced "jay-tacks") also arrived. With their GPS and laser designators and black boxes connecting them to the precise maps and all of intelligence in the GIG, there was an immediate increase in the lethality of JDAM strikes.[20] If the Taliban reinforced their weak points or moved to redeploy, they only exposed more targets for aircraft—which were now practically circling overhead in wait—to attack.[21] After ten years of overflying Iraq, every one of those fighter jets and most of the bombers also brought with them their own black boxes, external pods and data links that gave them photographic and radar capabilities better than any spy plane of old. The attacker and the scout were also increasingly integrated, the synergy meaning that every individual mission had greater effect even as fewer weapons were expended.

Still, the anxiety among the government and the American population on the whole about military progress continued to rise. At a National Security Council meeting on October 24, President Bush shot a "barrage of questions at Rumsfeld and Myers" about whether the Pentagon had a "winter scenario" to go after cave hideouts, the assumption being that the war would go on for at least several more months. National security advisor Condoleezza Rice even "suggested to the president the possibility of changing the strategy and Americanizing the Afghan effort by adding large numbers of U.S. ground forces."[22] That anxiety was reflected in the public debate as well. Senator Joseph Biden, chairman of the Senate Foreign Relations Committee and future vice president, told the Council on Foreign Relations that the air attacks were making the United States look like "a high-tech bully." On *Face the Nation*, Senator John McCain said the United States was "going to have to put troops on the ground." The war would involve casualties and "it won't be accomplished through airpower alone."[23]

On October 26, 2001, nineteen days into Operation Enduring Freedom, the young Machine almost at full bore, Donald Rumsfeld signed a deployment order to send the Global Hawk unmanned aerial vehicle to Afghanistan. The drone was still experimental, and only two airframes were ready—no one had ever flown it in any kind of combat environment. By the first week of November, Global Hawk was overflying Afghanistan at 60,000 feet, giving commanders something they had never had before: a persistent wide-angle view of the battlefield.[24]

By the first of November, twenty-three days after combat began, CIA teams on the ground reported intercepted Taliban radio communications "full of panic and fear..."[25] The Machine was demonstrating its economy, and JDAMs were hitting their targets. And then it was dramatically over: bombed and harried, greased by CIA money and fighting their brethren rather than Americans, the Taliban disintegrated. Mazar-i-Sharif fell, and then Taliban forces started retreating from Kabul. The western city of Herat also fell, followed by Jalalabad and finally Kandahar. Taliban government ceased to exist, and al Qaeda leadership fled to the eastern mountains and Pakistan.

And then, ironically, though precision airpower had worked while the Taliban defended their turf, it turned out that once Taliban forces left their prepared defenses, that same machine faltered. Both sides were out of uniform; both insisted on using military and civilian vehicles; the battlefield extended into cities and towns, and fighters freely (and even intentionally) intermingled with civilians. This shift to the long war of individual targeting occurred silently. And with it came the need for those very ISR assets not only to be able to linger much longer, but also to exist in such abundance that each would serve as a replacement for a human spotter (or fighter) on the ground.

Special operations and airpower seem to be the easy answer to the question of future US military strategy, even if one considers the enormous US and international ground forces that would follow over the next decade and a half. Those small-scale forces were leveraged by what the military calls "persistency over the battlefield" and "highly adaptive planning,"[26] which colloquially can be translated to mean almost limitless options at any time or place, as long as reliance is not too heavy on forward-deployed forces, which tend to suck up as much energy to sustain and protect as they exert additional combat power in this kind of frontless battle. None of this strategy could be implemented without black boxes and drones. As military attention shifted from Afghanistan to Iraq, true star status was conferred on Predator. General Franks called the drone "my most capable sensor in hunting down and killing al-Qaeda and Taliban leadership," and General Jumper declared it "the ideal weapon"[27] to "take care of a range of targets that we called fleeting and perishable—ones that get away quickly."

But in 2002, Predator was ideal more in potential than in reality. The drone continued to be plagued by the weather; it could not take off or land when crosswinds exceeded 17 knots, and at least three Predators crashed in Afghanistan between October 2001 and February 2002 because of bad weather and ice.[28] Global Hawk, in fact, only flew seventeen missions and was grounded between January and March 2002 after one of two crashed (a second crashed in July 2002).[29] Drones didn't get Mohammed Atef, and no one of any consequence was hunted down by Predator until November 2002, when a CIA drone flying from Djibouti made its first kill in Yemen.[30]

But the Machine was an immature prodigy. Every part was producing or moving information and adapting inside a growing network. Communications had moved a long way since Desert Storm in 1991, when there was a negligible spread between voice, video, and data needs. Most people did not have e-mail, and the World Wide Web had yet to be invented. The army corps commander was limited to being able to fax one sheet of paper to each of his division subordinates to send written orders,[31] and the daily air tasking order telling all planes where to fly and what to bomb had to be printed out and each copy ferried to aircraft carriers and outlying air bases via courier because the file was too large to transmit over existing lines. In the entire Gulf War of 1991, to support more than half a million troops on the ground, the total data rate used by the entire US military was 99 megabits per second (Mbps).[32]

The demand for bandwidth to support military operations increased from 99 Mbps in Desert Storm to 250 Mbps in Operation Allied Force, the seventy-eight-day Kosovo war.[33] That was two and a half times as much bandwidth, but it was to support one-tenth as many soldiers; hence, it was 25 times as much bandwidth per soldier on the battlefield. Much of that increase was caused by the need to move digital intelligence data. To operate two Predators simultaneously required 12 Mbps.[34] Maintaining a quality link to Beale Air Force Base in California (where imagery was being processed) "remained problematic throughout the campaign."[35] Even with only a few drones operating, one study concluded, "communications systems were stressed to the point that operational trade-offs were required and some activities had to be delayed or cancelled."[36] Video teleconferencing also came of age in Kosovo and became all the rage for political consultation and micromanagement, sucking up additional satellite bandwidth, particularly when the meetings were held at the top secret level and took over specialized communications networks. And even simple networked changes in ways of doing business demanded more bandwidth; the shift from maintaining huge stockpiles of munitions and supplies to what is called "as needed" transport, even basic bar code and GPS tracking that provided greater visibility over supplies, demanded additional bandwidth.

In the weeks before Operation Enduring Freedom, the Afghanistan war, Central Command projected that its network data needs would peak at 500 Mbps—it was already routinely using about 100 Mbps before 9/11 just to support day-to-day operations and the Iraq no-fly zones. Yet shortly after Afghanistan operations commenced, the military realized that its forces would need much more than 500 Mbps and potentially more than one gigabit (one billion bits) per second (Gbps).[37] In just two years, from Kosovo to OEF, the network requirement almost tripled. And that was while the "force" on the ground also declined by more than 95 percent in terms of the number of human beings.

More and more unmanned vehicles were also not just creators of information, but also voracious users. Within three weeks of 9/11, the Defense Department leased its first commercial satellite transponder just to accommodate the bandwidth demands of one drone—Global Hawk. Before the end of 2001, the commercial bandwidth capacity for CENTCOM support surged to more than half a gigabyte; and the Pentagon paid over $300 million to lease (and reserve) capacity on civilian satellites.[38] On the East Coast, four commercially operated gateways were added to the existing military teleports, quadrupling capacity.[39]

One postwar lessons learned report says: "The dominant transformation feature throughout the campaign...whether technological, operational, or organizational in nature, was the contributory role of information over kinetics—'brains over brawn.'"[40] Some would confuse the change as a simple combination of airpower and special operations. Some would chalk up the victory to covert action, money, and some unique attribute of the Afghan people. Why wars are won and why this campaign signaled such a false picture of successful conclusion will be debated for years. What can't be debated is that no one really understood what "brains over brawn" meant in practical terms.

By Thanksgiving 2001, planning for an Iraq war started, slowly beginning the process of bleeding away intelligence assets from Afghanistan.[41] The network formed for the initial advance on Baghdad mostly built upon what had been created for the war against al Qaeda and the Taliban, and though few additional unmanned systems were fielded between two wars, a networked and fully tracked ground force of 350,000 soldiers to invade Iraq demanded 3.2 gigabits per second (3,200 megabits per second), four times the bandwidth that was used in Afghanistan.[42] Lieutenant General Harry Raduege Jr., director of the Defense Information Systems Agency, said of the first few months of war in Afghanistan that "we're supporting one-tenth the number of forces deployed during Desert Storm with eight times the commercial SATCOM bandwidth."[43] Compared to Desert Storm twelve years earlier, the data requirements per soldier in Gulf War II grew exponentially. The growing number of Predators[44] and Global Hawks was greatly increasing the amount of data used, but it was more that each new black box upgrade demanded yet more data as well.

On August 1, 2003, the first of forty-eight initial Global Hawk production models rolled out at Northrop Grumman's plant in Palmdale, California. The data rate requirement to process intelligence collected by Global Hawk was ten times the bandwidth demand of Predator.[45] The next growth modification of Global Hawk would require 1.1 Gbps, *per drone*, ten times the total bandwidth used by the entire US military in the first Gulf war; double that used for operations in Kosovo.[46] Fewer men, more links, more black boxes, more data, more unmanned collectors—the Machine itself was beginning to determine the design of the very campaign that would unfold.

CHAPTER TEN

The Split

My friend, I have had the fourth,
it surpasses my other three dreams!
I saw a Thunderbird in the sky,
up it rose like a cloud, soaring above us.
TABLET IV, *EPIC OF GILGAMESH*

The drive from El Mirage, California, to Las Vegas is bleak, crossing the Mojave Desert and the Providence Mountains at nearly 5,000 feet. In January 2002, three months into the war against terrorism and more than a month after the Taliban had abandoned Kabul, an SUV left the General Atomics test site in El Mirage on a rogue mission with three passengers: the company's lead hardware engineer, an air force civilian scientist, and an army Special Forces warrant officer named Chris Manuel. A Predator drone flying high overhead was transmitting motion imagery of the hangars and other buildings at the test site back to its ground control station.

On the engineer's lap was a Panasonic Toughbook laptop that was receiving constant updates from the Predator feed. Manuel had spent months in the mountains of eastern Afghanistan tracking down al Qaeda fighters and was on home leave in Ohio when he decided to offer a field operations perspective. Using his military ID to get onto Wright-Patterson Air Force Base but bearded and in civilian clothes, he walked into the Big Safari office. He'd served in Bosnia, where his "special reconnaissance" teams operated deep behind enemy lines and clandestinely "exfiltrated" digital stills and video.[1] Later he saw Predators transmit motion imagery back to command centers during the Kosovo war, and then he'd heard that the technologists in the secret recesses had equipped each AC-130 gunship with its own special antenna, black box, and monitor to bring the Predator imagery right into the plane.

What the units on the ground needed, he told his wary air force listeners, was a direct feed from the Predators or other sensors flying overhead, not just some voice report coming through an intermediary or liaison. "I know these guys are flying up there," he said, referring to Predators. "I just want to see the video before my team arrives at its objective so that we know what we are getting into. Couldn't something like the black box installed on the gunships be given to the troops?"

Eight days later, he was in the SUV as it drove north on Interstate 15. When they were 117 miles from El Mirage, as the car went through a mountain pass, the General Atomics engineer proudly announced: "We got it." There in the backseat, they were watching what the Predator was watching.[2]

They called the black box ROVER, the Remotely Operated Video Enhanced Receiver, neither a drone nor a weapon and yet eclipsing both in the relentless quest to leverage America's technical advantages. ROVER brought the extended eye everywhere and made the job of targeting even more individual and intimate — the army of hunters in the field were equipped with the same information that the deskbound had back at home; the imagery product from on high was melded as an integral part of operations. And that created an expectation and then a requirement that everyone have their own eye, their own drone.

It wasn't always that way. When I was a young intelligence analyst in West Berlin in the 1970s, "bandwidth" wasn't even a word and index cards were still *the* database. Intelligence was hierarchical and material. Oh, our command on the front lines of the Cold War collected—we had listening stations and our own little reconnaissance planes and human intelligence of a surprising variety. Raw reports were filed, sometimes at FLASH precedence over teletype during a crisis, but the intelligence was mostly delivered in typed reports and hard-copy photos and occasional artifacts and then turned into articles and charts and products created and delivered by people at higher commands.

Everything in my upbringing as a student and as an intelligence analyst in the army in the days of index cards was that information delivery was serial in nature: one completed a project before one moved on to the next—until war and contact with the enemy provoked "tactical" intelligence, that is, movement and changes of immediate significance. With few alterations, this basic Cold War, pre-Internet design remained in place through Desert Storm: layered intelligence was employed to collect its small bit, each echelon from the platoon all the way to the Pentagon seeing a bigger and bigger view of the battlefield, with the "fusing" of all only occasionally achieved; the scarce (and expensive) collection resources were carefully doled out and carefully marshaled. The result was hardly ever pretty.

Think television before cable: the intelligence agencies were the networks. There were only so many channels, and you watched what they broadcast. They decided what you needed to know. Anything we produced in Berlin was just their fodder for potential remanufacture into one of their broadcasts. Every once in a while, something rocketed right to the top because it was truly consequential, but compared to the broadcasters, we were more akin to some obscure webcast with a very specialized following.

Predator and ROVER couldn't have emerged without the larger network architecture, the multiuse fiber and satellite communications pathways, literally a larger "enterprise" supplying the means, bandwidth, routing, and distribution that link platforms, sensors, operators, and consumers. Miniaturization of electronic components and advances in detection, guidance, and networking technologies facilitated generational leaps after Desert Storm, the effect being that the process of finding, fixing, and tracking a target could be completed faster and more cheaply and no longer depended on either expensive stand-alone platforms or the high priests of analysis at the top echelons. The true advance came not in intelligence sensors per se, not even in the unmanned; it came in the form of the black box, literally plug-in and plug-on avionics modules and pods (strap-on appendages for aircraft, usually attached to the wing or fuselage). Though a number of pods were in use starting with the Vietnam War, and select aircraft in Desert Storm could carry single-function targeting pods for reconnaissance or laser designation,[3] the introduction of the Low Altitude Navigation and Targeting Infrared for Night (LANTIRN) in 1991 changed the capability of the individual: the pilot could now see in the dark.[4] The eight-foot-long LANTIRN Forward Looking Infrared (FLIR) sensor and its Terrain Following Radar (TFR) enabled pilots to fly at low altitude at night and view the forward terrain. An integrated laser designator and range finder allowed the crew to self-illuminate or mark the target and then deliver its own laser-guided bomb—collecting, processing, and killing a contemporaneous target all in one process.[5]

Second- and third- generation black box pods emerged that had imagers with higher resolution, greater magnification, and multispectral capabilities; automatic target recognition software; GPS capability (eliminating the need for a separate navigation module); and two-way data links. Many automatic functions were introduced, decreasing human workload, particularly for single-pilot aircraft, "allowing attack of targets with precision-guided weapons with only a single pass."[6] The Nite Hawk laser designator/ranger and thermal imaging FLIR was introduced to marine corps aviation in 1993.[7] Litening added an optical imager (allowing daylight operations) and was introduced on F-16s in 1999.

Even before 9/11, most of these capabilities had been extensively used in Iraq. In a decade of supposed military stagnation and neglect, aircraft evolved from dumb to versatile precision platforms through black box modifications. Multimission strike assets developed capabilities and tactics to image, pass video, and send secure e-mail, as well as to transfer data between fighters, command planes, other intelligence assets, to their home bases and even back to the command centers.[8] They even became reconnaissance platforms similar to Predator with their own motion imagery cameras.[9] Thus, without the introduction of a single new major weapons system, a combination of one new satellite-guided weapon (JDAM), ubiquitous GPS, improved sensor performance, and processing bandwidth resulted in an exponential increase in military capability.

As aircraft were flying regular patrols over the Balkans and Iraq, hardly ever dropping a bomb or engaging in an air battle, the new black boxes were called upon more and more to report intelligence. Aircraft up in the air, just flying, were collecting data, data that could be turned into intelligence that was of potential use to others. These new capabilities came to be known as non-traditional intelligence surveillance and reconnaissance (NTISR), an advance barely recognized outside the air forces and one that generated initial disapproval from the fighter pilot community.[10] But NTISR compensated for shortages of traditional intelligence collection assets (whether they were satellites, aircraft, or Predators), while also directly integrating with the strike function.

"Before NTISR, we had fighter aircraft with surveillance capabilities burning holes in the sky, just waiting to be tasked by ground
commanders," an intelligence officer said. "Instead of wasting these
resources, we've begun to use them to fill some of the gaps in our
traditional ISR [intelligence, surveillance, and reconnaissance]
operations."[11] By 2001, roughly 400 air force manned aircraft had
data links that fully allowed them to carry pods and other emerging
black boxes.[12] It would be years before anyone even uttered the
dream of every platform (human, drone, or airplane) a sensor, which
would later become the central pretense of the Data Machine.

Before devices like ROVER appeared on the scene, Predator
video was downlinked to the ground control station, which was
collocated with its own satellite transmitter. At the station, analysts annotated the video with a classified voice overlay in near–
real time to describe what they saw. The encrypted classified
video and audio were then uplinked via a commercial satellite to
an intelligence base in the United Kingdom. From there, the data
was sent back to a broadcast management center in the Pentagon
through ground lines and fiberoptic submarine cables that went
across the Atlantic Ocean. Then the video and audio were uplinked
to satellite using a dedicated three-million-bits-per-second (3
Mbps) channel. It was initially called the Joint Broadcast Service,
and it was awfully similar to the commercial Direct Broadcast
Satellite service introduced in 1994. In fact, it was DBS with the
same kind of dedicated video channels and military encryption
added. In April 1996, the Bosnia Command and Control Augmentation was turned on, a one-way broadcast network capable of
sending imagery products and large amounts of data and video to
two dozen Europe-based receiving sites that could pick up the
secret channels.

All that information was now freely flowing, but it was too
much for an individual pilot or even a pool of analysts in some

forward unit to fully exploit. And so before anyone had ever heard the word "enterprise" or understood how the cloud worked or how common processing, storage, and retrieval gave everyone the same service, the ISR community activated a very necessary $760-million machine. Deployable Ground Station-1 was a 250-man processing and analysis unit established in July 1994, capable of receiving multiple imagery and data streams in real time and spitting usable intelligence back in minutes.[13] In October 1994, the Virginia-based unit moved to Saudi Arabia to take the feed from U-2s and the new NTISR assets for the Iraq mission.

The shift in doing that work back in the United States rather than in the combat zone was precipitated on June 25, 1996, when a US Air Force housing area in Saudi Arabia was bombed, killing 19 and injuring 500 others: 24 intelligence analysts and officers from DGS-1 were killed or injured.[14] DGS-1 moved back to Virginia but continued doing the same job from there, connected back to the air command center not just via satellite but also via computer chat and a common operating picture—that is, everyone was looking at a similar map on the same network at the same time. DGS-2 was activated in California, picking up the full-motion video (FMV) exploitation function for Predator. By 1999, a "comprehensive intelligence capability" was declared operational with DGS, allowing the processing of multi-INT: multiple forms of intelligence. The air force could now deploy a relatively small number of people forward and relay much of the analytic effort to a global federated enterprise, the lion's share of the work being done as part of what became known as the Distributed Common Ground System, or DCGS.

Conceived as a centralized way of tasking sensors, conducting analysis, and disseminating intelligence, mapping, and weather data, the two initial DCGS sites grew to nine by the time of the 2003 Iraq war, all interconnected.[15] By then, data taken from drones, from U-2s, from Global Hawks, and from imagery collected by purchased commercial satellites was all interlinked.[16]

Like Predator, like DCGS, like the aircraft pods themselves and almost all of the black boxes that would follow, the ROVER viewer evolved in generations of new models as well, never with a fixed blueprint or a final design.[17] In fact, ROVER never became a "Program of Record" belonging to any one of the military services, nor did it occupy a special line item in the budget, as might have happened with a normal piece of equipment of the past. It never went through the Joint Chiefs of Staff or Defense Department requirements process to determine whether it was needed. It has never been formally tested or certified for military or joint use, and it has not been officially standardized by NATO.[18] Think of it, then, as more akin to a new smartphone with its cascading and overlapping generations of hardware and software, except that ROVER is applied to matters of life and death, with the "testing" taking place in the field. And yet, without formal requirement and largely without bureaucratic involvement, in less than a decade from the first desert experiment, over 15,000 ROVERs were delivered to the US military, and the militaries of at least fourteen other countries fighting alongside the United States adopted it as well.[19]

At nearly fifty pounds, ROVER II, as Chris Manuel's component was called, needed some work. Only 147 were delivered to special operations ground controllers. A backpack-portable and more rugged ROVER III followed in 2004. It was capable of receiving on multiple bands and could be powered from a vehicle battery, processing video through Windows media commercial software, displaying the picture to a laptop or other viewing device: 2,331 units were delivered. ROVER IV came the next year, even smaller than ROVER III, with two-way communications and a point-and-click feature that allowed a ground spotter to designate a target on the integrated display, the very same map displayed in a fighter or bomber cockpit overhead—another 1,169 units were delivered. In 2008, the One System Remote Video Terminal (OSRVT), a modified and improved ROVER III, was also introduced for the army, capable of receiving full-motion video with metadata, something the ROVER III couldn't do.[20] Then ROVER 5 began production in November 2008: this was the so-called John Madden version, with a menu-driven touch screen and telestrator-like interface that allowed annotations, enabling ground controllers to "drop" points on the screen and draw lines to make notes or communicate with other operators. Now the ubiquitous device had a look and feel familiar to any video gamer, weighing in at just four pounds. It was followed by Rover 7 and even smaller and more specialized VORTEX receivers for special operations.[21]

By 2008, the various ROVERs were receiving real-time video not just from Predator, but also from five other unmanned systems—Hunter, Fire Scout, Pointer, Raven, and Shadow—as well as from AC-130 gunships and navy P-3 Orion aircraft, and from specially equipped Scathe View collectors on C-130 transports. ROVER receivers appeared on laptops, in aircraft and helicopter cockpits, on ships, in vehicles, and in command posts—video and imagery and the magic data stream delivered from over forty different platforms, all fused together, one image under God.

Between split base operations controlling Predator flights and the increasing real-time dissemination of intelligence information through ROVER and its cousins, through the movement of all of that data around the battlefield and around the world, the capacity of the Data Machine's hidden back end (today called PED, for processing, exploitation, and dissemination, and involving the conversion of raw data into usable intelligence) began to be both the limiting and the leading factor.[22] Of course, there is never enough of the right intelligence at the right time to satisfy any commander or soldier on the battlefield, but now the full effect of the shift from the industrial era, from the paper world to the world of digits, began to exert additional power and effects. Massive numbers of secure and reliable communications pipelines going to obscure areas of the world were needed; Predator and its various intelligence-collecting brethren were voracious users of bandwidth for piloting and control, as well as for transmission of their product.

It is an exaggeration to say that Predator changed everything, but the loitering platform—and the introduction of the personal intelligence video screen—emerged at a moment when it became technologically possible not just to link the inputs of all sensors for immediate consumption but also when there were sufficient collection assets to allow smaller and smaller organizations, even individual operators in the field, to possess almost everything they needed. ROVER enabled the "elusive goal of instantaneous attack by finding a target, matching it with a weapon, shooting the weapon, and observing the resultant effects," an unofficial air force history said.[23] And when the immediate needs weren't met, more black boxes were brought in and connected to the Data Machine.

Real-time access to a view from above, the air force wrote in 2006, allows commanders to see and react "with a level of speed and accuracy unheard of five years ago."[24] By 2010, they were even calling some smaller drones and obscure black boxes "personal ISR," too numerous to count in the bookkeeping of the central Machine. "In the past, we have always relied on something associated with a time delay," says one air force general. "A third party was always involved in distribution." That was an enormous frustration during Desert Storm, when it often took days for intelligence experts to complete their analysis and obtain the clearances to deliver targeting information back to the pilots who needed it. "Now," says the general, "there's no intel geek involved in the processing."[25] "Customers" of the new Machine started at the top, at the president and his decision-makers, and extended downward to commanders, pilots, and the digital natives all the way at the bottom, even to the last soldiers at the edge.

Intelligence for the "commander," and yet each user in possession of data became their own decision-maker. The first taste of live video, followed by the broadcast system that allowed anyone to watch, and then ROVER with its personal eye's view, changed everything. Given how much more lethal and exacting every weapon was also becoming, the numbers were turned upside down — that is, one bomber became equal to ten or fifty or a hundred of a half-century earlier; one Hellfire-type missile could do what thousands of bombs couldn't even do in the past: kill the target. The equation of how many people are needed to make war shifted from warriors to data processors and unlaborers. The changing of the doing itself thus also changed the very nature of war.

There was a transition period between the Cold War and merely war, to an era of wars of policy rather than wars of necessity. And there were changes in society, coincident or as a consequence, whereby the assumption of universal military service was abandoned for a volunteer and professional military (though I would argue, and I have, that society overall has become much more militarized).[26] And, of course, there was just the reality of societies' movement to the information era and the age of the digital self. The shift to the unmanned is therefore not merely some post-9/11 phenomenon. The Data Machine wasn't the product of any diabolical mind or plans of the Bush administration. Predator was not some invention intended for al Qaeda. Targeted killing is not just some macabre Obama pastime. *Unmanned* is warfare changed with society and then accelerated in more than a decade of warfare that was hardly ever industrial in nature.

After Desert Storm, two worlds emerged. One marched down Fifth Avenue and celebrated; the other quietly moved into the geography of permanent war. America took down its yellow ribbons, but the Machine stayed in the Middle East and enforced a no-fly zone over Saddam's Iraq and supported the endless United Nations search for WMD. But the imposition of a no-fly zone over Iraq wasn't merely a policy. People stayed in Kuwait and the Gulf states and Saudi Arabia to oversee and fly, but more and more of the work of war started to shift geographically far away. When the Khobar Towers bombing occurred, it was only natural that in the shrapnel that flew was also the question: Did anyone really need to be forward and present at all?[27] The Machine was starting to answer.

CHAPTER ELEVEN

The Explosion

Enkidu began to speak to Gilgamesh:
"My brother, this night what a dream [I dreamed!]
The gods . . . [held assembly],
and Anu spoke unto Enlil: 'These, because they slew
the Bull of Heaven, and slew Humbaba . . . between these two
[let one of them die!]' "
TABLET VII, *EPIC OF GILGAMESH*

It was almost biblical, and looked that way—the massive sand-storm that engulfed southern Iraq starting on March 26, 2003, seven days into the second Gulf war. For three days, day-light turned an opaque orange, and the epic storm—some said the worst in 100 years—seemingly halted army and marine forces, their visibility reduced to less than ten feet. Units on the ground lost their ability to communicate. The news media reported that the storm prevented troops from calling in artillery and even forced a halt to airstrikes. Ground assaults were canceled. The anxiety of war, already at a fever pitch, provoked imaginings of native Iraqi advantages seized and another quagmire: speculation mounted that as soon as US forces crossed some imagined red line, Saddam would unleash chemical weapons, a gas in a cloud in a fog in a storm that would upend everything.

But no one had yet heard about Grumpy. That was the nickname for Air Vehicle-3, the third Global Hawk ever built. The drone was given the nickname because it displayed all of the crankiness of a prototype, demanding loving care and constant tinkering. It was the same airframe that had gone on a world tour before 9/11, the same that had first flown over Afghanistan, and now it was back over Iraq, souped up with better black boxes, flying overhead and sweeping aside all that Mother Nature could throw at it.

Though some might imagine that during the second Gulf war, US forces were backed up by an army of drones now doing much of the work, in early 2003, the US military was still pretty much where it had been with unmanned systems after 9/11: lots of promise but an inventory that didn't match the hype. Only eight Predators flew, and the ground forces deployed only about 100 other drones—Hunter, Pointer, Shadow, and Raven with the army, Desert Hawk with the air force, Pioneer and Dragon Eye with the marine corps, Phoenix with the British army, and Silver Fox with special operations forces.[1] And there was only one fully equipped Global Hawk: Grumpy.

But Grumpy was such an asset. Grumpy flew day and night, regardless of weather, a single eye in the sky, high above everything else. It flew fifteen days in a row over Iraq, a quiet and unexpected member of the team, doing things it really was never intended to do. But it couldn't do anything without what was now a truly global network. The launch and recovery team was at Al Dhafra Air Base, about an hour outside Abu Dhabi in the United Arab Emirates. The mission controllers, "flying" the Global Hawk with keyboard and mouse and operating the sensors, were at Beale Air Force Base in the California desert, halfway around the world. Imagery from Global Hawk was transmitted via satellite to California and then relayed to another base, in Reno, Nevada. There analysts from the 152nd Intelligence Squadron of the Nevada Air National Guard scrolled through the incoming data and sent on-the-spot analysis to the Global Hawk desk in the air command center back in Saudi Arabia (which was also receiving and could consult a simultaneous secondary feed). If a particularly time-sensitive target was observed, the Global Hawk liaison would tip off the interdiction desk on the command center watch floor, which would then transmit the information to an E-3 AWACS command and control airplane flying over Iraq and directing traffic. If a fighter or bomber on station was already in the loop, the command center in Saudi Arabia could speak directly to the pilot. A chat line was always open between all of the players on the ground, the phones were sometimes used, and secure e-mail over the Internet transmitted actual photos, even to the cockpit.[2]

A lot had been learned in a year and a half of flying over Afghanistan, the most important lesson being that when there was a battle on—"troop in contact"—everything else was secondary and everyone wanted pictures. Though Global Hawk was intended to fly a route planned in advance and to take a set of specific images based upon formal collection requirements, in actual operations it ended up being used as much for ad hoc tasking, often deviating 100 miles or more off its course to put eyes over a developing battle or look at something interesting called in by spotters on the ground. During the Battle of Tora Bora, Global Hawk dropped its planned imagery collection profile altogether and started tracking Taliban and al Qaeda positions and cave entrances, either using its infrared camera to detect campfires or receiving tip-offs to take a closer look with its sensors into crevices and cracks off angle from satellites. Aircraft and AC-130 gunships in the area would undertake airstrikes, which Global Hawk could then instantly confirm via star-shaped infrared flashes, recording bomb explosions, the sparkle of success.

Such instant gratification made quite a contrast with doctrine and even practice before the 2003 war: in old-fashioned war, the army corps commander, in charge of three to five divisions, would rely upon his own intelligence units—either field artillery radars or organic collection assets—out from the front. A fire support team would determine the best way to attack beyond the range of the divisions. If airstrikes were desired, a liaison would nominate the target through higher headquarters to the daily targeting board at the air command center, which would then task flying squadrons, which would fly the requested missions anywhere from one to three days later. If the target was mobile, the nominated target would have to be meticulously tracked and its position updated to the air guys as many as three times a day. The obvious question then asked in the fall of 2002 was "When we find a target, why not just kill it right then?" Capabilities and communications had certainly improved; what was needed was closer cooperation at the working level and a change in practice to reflect the new capabilities of the Data Machine.

In Iraq, a beefed-up air force support unit arrived at the army corps headquarters to figure out exactly how to deliver instant support, and it became fully integrated into the command post. Ground forces were planning to move rapidly and skirt most Iraqi defenses, but ahead of the pack were special forces and long-range reconnaissance elements stealthily operating in areas where attacks needed to take extra care. So in addition to the normal concerns about civilian casualties and collateral harm, immediate attacks on midrange targets of importance to the ground force needed to be carefully cleared to avoid friendly fire. The rules were that either a forward controller (a JTAC) or a pilot had to *see* a target or that the intelligence needed to be confirmed by two sources in situations where neither a JTAC nor a pilot could see it, the latter turning out to be the case in more than 90 percent of the attacks that would take place in March and April 2003.[3]

The Rand Corporation would later write of the 2003 war: "U.S. forces encountered little resistance from the Iraqi Army during the invasion."[4] And despite the sandstorm, at the crucial moment of seeming crisis for the offensive, the Machine didn't stumble. With hundreds of embedded reporters scrutinizing every battalion and company's moves, it truly looked like the offensive had stalled. When the skies cleared, the press corps heaved a sigh of relief for the 5th Army Corps.

But Grumpy had been overhead all along, nudged north of the thirty-third parallel within fifteen miles of Baghdad before any other airborne intelligence asset, and Grumpy flew over the epic storm as well. It wasn't just Grumpy. Predators had flown over Baghdad since before the shooting started.[5] But once the storm developed, Grumpy dominated, along with two manned airplanes: the JSTARS (Joint Surveillance and Target Attack Radar System), with its gigantic moving target indicator radar that could track vehicles, and the RC-135 Rivet Joint, which collected Iraqi signals and electronic emissions. Grumpy was the only platform that had uninterrupted endurance, and it flew in near space far above the storm, where other aircraft didn't operate. Peering down, its optical and infrared sensors were blinded by dust, but its synthetic aperture radar was able to see through the muck and provide continuous coverage, reconstructing changes on the ground, particularly movement of armored vehicles.

Silently, or at least with all eyes focused on the men and women on the ground, the Machine went into action: aircraft flying overhead couldn't see either, but then, all they needed were geographic coordinates to deliver their JDAM weapons.

Using the storm as a shield, Iraqi units east of the Euphrates River changed hide sites and redeployed, constantly being bombed as they did so. Irregular fighters, the Fedayeen Saddam and the Quds Force, flooded south, as did elements of two Republican

Guard divisions, moving from near Baghdad to reinforce the Medina Division, which was defending the Euphrates River crossings. They too were constantly bombed.

As the sandstorm dissipated, the 5th Army Corps prepared five simultaneous attacks on Iraqi forces stretching from Lake Razazah in the west to Samawah in the east, the main effort intended to skirt Iraqi defenses to the west and swing around to enter Baghdad through what the US military called the Karbala Gap. However, it looked to a blinded Iraq as if the US force would cross the Euphrates River and mount its main offensive up Highway 8, driving straight for Baghdad. On the morning of March 31, intelligence reports started coming in that the Hammurabi Republican Guard division — equipped with tanks and other armored vehicles — was moving to shore up the defense of that route. Grumpy and JSTARS and Predator and the rest of the sensor pool tracked every move. Within minutes of detecting each moving armored formation, bombs arrived. Fighters and bombers dropped satellite-guided 2,000-pound JDAMs on the Iraqis, pilots plugging in coordinates in the air. Linking directly to the bomber cockpits via chat, the Global Hawk desk provided a "last-look" assessment to confirm that Iraqi tanks were still on the intended aimpoints. Predator, together with shorter-range Hunter drones, sent back immediate bomb damage assessments. Counting tanks, artillery, armored personnel carriers, and wheeled vehicles, the Medina division was reduced in strength from 92 to 29 percent of its equipment and personnel. Forty-eight hours later, the US 3rd Infantry Division was at Saddam International Airport in Baghdad.[6]

All eyes stayed on the ground as the army and marines blew into the Iraqi capital. The statue of Saddam Hussein was toppled and "Mission accomplished" announced just three weeks later. Everyone on the field of battle, and certainly everyone in the command post, knew that none of it would have been possible without Grumpy and the Machine.[7] The army later calculated that of the Iraqi forces in front of the 5th Corps, 421 of 660 tanks were destroyed by air attacks; 423 of 843 artillery guns were hit from the air; overall, 1,144 pieces of equipment, more than half of the Iraqi force facing the US corps, were destroyed in the most lethal air attack ever.[8]

"We did massive damage to the Iraqi maneuver units to the point that in the interviews later [Iraqi officers]…said they just walked away from their equipment because they knew if they stayed with it it was going to be hit," General Jumper said at a postwar meeting of air force commanders.[9] Compared with Desert Storm, where less than 10 percent of the air weapons expended were precision-guided munitions, 71 percent in the twenty-one-day battle were precision.[10] But as even the army said, it was more than just numbers: "The traditional means of summarizing combat effectiveness, and particularly the recitation of gross tonnages of ordnance dropped, are meaningless as a way to measure."[11] In this new form of warfare, it was precision rather than gross tonnage that would provide a clear testament of success. And not just precision, but the individual target now measured in personal-sized ways. The air force declared it the beginning of the age of "mass precision," claiming that the three Republican Guard divisions were destroyed before the army and marine corps even made "ground contact" with them.[12] Major General David Deptula, the air command center operations director, said of Grumpy: "Because we controlled it…we could put it where we needed it, when we needed it, and for the duration we needed it."[13] The performance of the ISR platforms during the dust storms, General Jumper added, proved to be "a major turning point" in the war.[14]

"We," of course, meant the air force, factual but very unbrotherly in a singular military that later faced the consequences of less money and thus more unmanning. "The war," of course, would go on for another seven years, and the bigger question—whether the offensive was secured by the Machine or by the troops on the ground—was never resolved. In twenty-one days of fighting, Grumpy provided 3,700 images,[15] and Northrop Grumman claimed that the single drone, flying approximately 5 percent of the surveillance missions, accounted for more than 55 percent of the information to facilitate time-sensitive engagements, finding 40 percent of Iraqi armor formations, or 300 tanks in total.[16]

Of course, there were the usual problems: bugs required recoding. A Predator was shot down on March 28, showing vulnerability and the need for a faster and more robust platform. The 5th Corps' Hunters, the midsized twin-boomed drones equipped with electrooptical and infrared sensors and able to stay airborne for eighteen hours, provided a soda straw view of the battlefield, pointing to the need for a wider view on this particular drone, akin to another Global Hawk.[17] And as for the newer unmanned systems like Raven and Dragon Eye that were seeing some of their first combat? Well, there just weren't enough of them.

Before the situation in Iraq went all to hell, the Defense Science Board assessed the state of the unmanned, concluding that "little doubt remains as to the operational utility and military worth of UAVs," particularly for the "all important persistent surveillance of the battlespace."[18] Still, the board pointed out that despite experiences in Afghanistan and their incorporation into the Iraq war, only 175 drones were yet operational.[19] The board echoed an earlier Defense Department study that concluded that the Pentagon had spent more than $6 billion on unmanned systems and had fewer than 100 large vehicles to show for it.[20] The board tried to settle many of the earlier hesitations of the services in adopting drones—technologically and culturally—pointing out that the loss rates of the Predator and Hunter—even of the ancient Pioneer—were comparable with military and general aviation aircraft per 100,000 flight hours.[21]

As the board is chartered to do, it also made recommendations for future technologies, some of them quite tantalizing. Bandwidth came first, the board fully recognizing its centrality to the operation of unmanned vehicles and the now-regular practice of reachback. The board also predicted that with the emergence of a single network under the Global Information Grid initiative, there would be "a marked improvement in the available bandwidth." There still needed to be a much greater integration of sensors with combat troops, whether that came through data links that automatically transferred information between systems, or through ROVER-like black boxes that instantly facilitated the movement of the video and pictures.[22] And even with GIG deployment, the board pointed out that movement of intelligence over the "last tactical mile" to remote operators, whether they were navy ships operating in distant waters or special forces teams in the mountains of Afghanistan working at the edge of the network, demanded some kind of communications adjunct. The board recommended greater investment in the use of drones to create its own Internet in the sky.[23] And finally, to reduce Predator's and Global Hawk's voracious appetites for bandwidth, as well as the increasing manpower demands associated with analyzing the Niagara of data now coming in, the board recommended the development of some kind of "on-board target recognition," that is, "algorithms to survey large areas and reliably select only targets of interest for transmission."[24] In other words, the drones themselves would look at the video and imagery, sounding an alarm and tipping off analysts and fighters when they detected something of significance. It wasn't exactly autonomous killer robots, but it certainly had some similarities. The scientists recommended based on cost-effectiveness and supposed logic, the developments all followed without consideration of ethical or policy implications. After all, this is a *science* board.

The board recommended more of everything, from "fighter-like air vehicles for lethal missions" to "small or micro-UAVs for urban combat."[25] Still, the board observed the chaos associated with a system that had gotten used to building a house without an architect: the system relied on spiral development, the process by which new black boxes and capabilities were added as they became available, and it used developmental prototypes rather than programs of record (which coincidentally allowed piecemeal buying rather than presenting Congress with a total program cost). "There are so many different UAV systems in various stages of development," the board said, "that they are outstripping the ability to evolve standards and approaches for common mission management."[26] Investments in Predator and Global Hawk were skyrocketing, but the rest of the program was largely parochial and uncoordinated.[27] Still, no one anticipated how rapidly and how large the drone force would grow and what its demands (and effects) would be.

Iraqi resistance to the American military occupation stayed "at a low, relatively tolerable level" through the fall of 2003 and even into 2004, Rand said,[28] with the Iraqi fighters dismissed as "dead enders" and "former regime elements" by the Bush administration. But by the time Saddam Hussein was captured on December 13, it was clear that the United States didn't understand the sociopolitical circumstances of the country, including the deep divisions between Sunni, Shia, and Kurd that war and regime change had helped to unleash, as well as the sentiments against this occupation. At the end of March 2004, Iraqis attacked a group of four Blackwater contractor guards in Fallujah, an industrial town west of Baghdad. The four were brutally killed; the crowd burned their bodies beyond recognition, then hanged two from the girders of a main bridge, where citizens celebrated.

The Battle of Fallujah began that November, led by US Marines to retake the city. Elsewhere, the United States battled Shia militia associated with Muqtada al-Sadr. The forces in Iraq increasingly also focused on "force protection"—protecting the troops and their bases from insurgent attack. Presence outside fortified bases was inconsistent and often involved ineffective door-to-door raids. But the real issue for the human presence was supply. Main supply routes from Kuwait and from US-occupied bases became a favorite target of anticoalition forces. The first American casualty from a roadside improvised explosive device occurred in June 2003, and that July, in an announcement of a soldier's death, the military used the term "IED" for the first time. By the summer of 2004, insurgents began to lay "daisy chains" of roadside bombs (multiple, interconnected weapons) in more-precise attacks. The Rand Corporation later said that the United States had a hard time "recognizing the nature of the problem," choosing a technology effort to counter IEDs, while ignoring violence and suicide bombers who were increasingly terrorizing the Iraqi civilian population, thus creating more chaos.[29]

Technology advanced, both on the air force side to handle the high volume of precision-guided weapons that were now being employed—everything needed precise coordinates—and on the ground as well, where the tools like ROVER were opening up eyes to real-time and personal intelligence and a world of black boxes just beyond the reach of the normal soldier.[30] The Machine was expanding to the edge.

CHAPTER TWELVE

Flock of Birds

"Who goes in front saves his companion,
Who knows the road protects his friend."
Let Enkidu go before you,
He knows the journey to the Forest of Cedar.
TABLET III, *EPIC OF GILGAMESH*

Until the IED became the everything and the only thing for US ground forces in Iraq, the old Pioneer from Desert Storm remained the most ubiquitous drone for ground forces, having flown in Desert Storm in 1991, in Somalia, Haiti, Bosnia, and Kosovo, and again in Iraq, starting in 2003. Pioneer wasn't the first drone, not even of the modern era, and though two decades after the first Gulf war, it was still there and dominant,[1] no one outside of those who had a vision of airpower rallied behind either unmanned systems or the power of the Machine— that is, until the unexpected shift from big war to civil war, from mechanized protection to guerrilla vulnerabilities, made things so lethal. And then what happened was right out of Genesis: the tribe expanded, begats upon begats raising a nation of unmanned.

Pioneer begat Shadow.[2] Pioneer veterans grumbled that Shadow's flying range was 60 kilometers less than Pioneer's.[3] And whereas Pioneer had to be launched by a rocket-assisted catapult

147

contraption and landed in a large net, Shadow...well, had a similar bulky and complicated launch and recovering process, using
arresting gear similar to jets on the deck of an aircraft carrier,
demanding a flat, cleared space the size of a soccer field to
operate.

But in those twenty years, the technologies had transformed,
and everything about the modern drones reduced infant mortality to almost zero. Shadow was lighter, had a more powerful
engine that used motor gasoline readily available to ground
forces, and could fly 4,000 feet higher than Pioneer and loiter for
six hours, almost a third longer than its forefather. The first version of Shadow (referred to as the Shadow 200) was thus a substantial advance in all aspects, and the range didn't particularly
matter because it was no longer just *the* pioneer, the only drone in
the hands of the troops on the ground; it was part of a growing
family. Its range, in fact, matched the distance covered by typical
army brigade-level operations, the highest echelon to which it was
assigned.

The army chose Shadow not just to replace Pioneer but also
eventually to replace Hunter; the marine corps shot for an improved
Shadow-B with three feet of additional wing to increase fuel storage for greater range and payload to match its tactical needs; and
the navy began the search for a vertical-takeoff-and-landing
alternative that could operate from ships (initially Fire Scout).

In the world of unmanned systems, Pioneer and Shadow are
called small unmanned aerial systems (SUAS), that is, more than
4.5 pounds but less than 55 pounds.[4] They are also sometimes
called tactical unmanned aerial vehicles (TUAV): directly supporting those at the edge of combat. But neither title quite
explains their position in the network of drones as so many more
have emerged. These Shadows in the middle, not too large and
not too small, are operated by a platoon of men to support the

intelligence needs of a fighting brigade of some 3,000 to 3,500 men. The unit is assigned four drones, two ground control stations, one rail launcher, and eight HUMVEEs (a Shadow unit requires three C-130 air transports to deploy it).[5]

"Medium" doesn't mean just right, though, as each size has not just a different function at a different echelon in the military but also different owners and sponsors, each with their own priorities (and budgets). Shadows are thus far larger cousins of the Class 1 UAVs, or the small drones, and even there "small" doesn't mean micro- or nano, which would come later. Their story begins with—if there is ever a beginning—Pointer, another patriarch introduced in the late 1980s. Pointer was a two-man-portable, hand-launched 8.3-pound drone, with a nine-foot wingspan—it was essentially a remote-controlled sailplane powered by a small electric motor. Pointer served with the army and marine corps in Desert Storm and was used by special operations command in the 1990s as a test bed for miniaturized sensors. The standard Pointer, with its tiny electrooptical and infrared camera, or alternatively with a chemical agent detector, had an endurance of approximately two hours flying at an altitude of about 500 feet, feeding its images directly back to its operators, where they were recorded on 8mm tape. One of the operators could also use a microphone to annotate the video while it was being recorded if it was to be further distributed.[6] The first special operations units to go to Afghanistan in 2001 took the latest generation of Pointers with them, now integrated with a GPS-based autonomous navigation unit. Word soon spread that individual soldiers were successfully using and controlling their own drones in an austere environment, and the demand for personal eyes in the sky was created.[7]

Pointer was also cousin to Flashlight, which was part of the Pathfinder tribe of experimental platforms, all hand-built prototypes born of 9/11 and made for special operations and shipped out into combat for the express purpose of testing and gaining user feedback; the plan from the very beginning was to spiral and spiral until a production model was finally determined. Along the way, Pathfinder begat Puma and WASP; and from other parts of the military and intelligence community came Buster and Silver Fox, which begat Swiper, which should not be confused with T-Hawk or Manta or Coyote or SuperBat or Urban Canyon, and which are all a different clan than Desert Hawk or gMAV; but I'm getting ahead of myself. Pathfinder begat Raven in 2002, a veritable monster at double Flashlight's size, but the drone that would become the most ubiquitous personal ISR vehicle ever.[8]

Puma emerged as a significantly upgraded Pointer, a spiraling off initially for special operations use, while Raven, a completely new design, was smaller, lighter, and more capable. Dragon Eye was selected as the marine corps replacement for Pointer and deployed the same year. Backpack-carried and battery-powered, it was used in the initial Iraq invasion as well, the marines planning to purchase 300 until it too was scuttled in favor of Raven. And then the ultraquiet Dragon Eye ATR version was demonstrated, flying off of a submarine two years later, providing security as it entered port.[9]

I've never been much of a weapons buff, and I know all of these begats and ancestral genealogies could get a bit confusing and even tedious, but the details are important. I'm not directing your attention to what provides the usual fanfare in histories and press releases and news stories—the airframes and their performance stats and mankind's ongoing love affair with flight—but to the black boxes and how each generation of drone, how each spiral of development within the same airframe, solidified the presence of the unmanned, infiltrated further into military and intelligence society, and consequently put more and more eyes on a truly global battlefield, which then demanded more and more care and feeding of the overall Data Machine. Moreover, the growing IED problem and frustrations in Afghanistan and Iraq led to an entire other class of unmanned systems to be developed: ad hoc, irregular, special, secret. To understand drones, then, and therefore to understand the world of Gilgamesh that has emerged, the details (and the chaos) of these hydra-headed developments are essential. The black boxes and their variety and versatility have been not just the hidden history but also, as we'll see, the makers of the future.

So even smaller than the family of drones in the mini category are the microdrones. The Wasp Micro Air Vehicle (MAV) is part of this family, just eight inches long and weighing 15 ounces (430 grams), with an endurance of over one and a half hours. Wasp can be manually operated or programmed for GPS-based autonomous navigation from takeoff to landing. Its synthetic materials act as both battery and main wing structure. The Battlefield Air Targeting Micro Air Vehicle (BATMAV) competition actually begat Wasp, which started as yet another experiment, spawning competitors and spiraling until it became its own first cousin. Wasp, of course, begat Wasp AE (all environment), which begat a slightly larger Wasp-III/BATMAV, weighing in at a lovely 16 ounces. Air Force Special Operations Command started getting Wasps in 2007, issuing them to ground controllers, the JTACs calling in airstrikes to give them greater situational awareness. It wasn't a true micro, but most important, it was built to utilize the same common ground station as its larger and dominant cousin, Raven, and thus could become a full member of the Machine. Wasp is described as "expendable," and "micro" sounds sexy and futuristic and conjures all sorts of science fiction images of a barely observable object weaving its way into rooms. But at $50,000 each, it is neither expendable nor sneaky.[10]

Raven, all 4.2 pounds (1.9 kg) of *smartdrone* perfection, is certainly not as famous as any of the larger drones, yet it has become *the* drone — at least 14,000 Raven were deployed by 2014 around the world; three-quarters of the US inventory of all drones is Raven, the most common in all the world's militaries. With a wingspan of 4.5 feet and a 3-foot length, Raven looks like a remote-controlled hobby plane. The drone flies day or night as high as 500 feet, manually via wireless link or autonomously through a set of preprogrammed GPS waypoints. At 27 to 60 mph maximum speed, Raven can range as far as 10 kilometers from its base station, with an endurance of 80 to 110 minutes from a single-use battery (the endurance drops to 60 to 90 minutes with a rechargeable, but then that battery can be recharged by a HUMVEE anywhere).

At two-thirds of the size and weight of Pointer, and with 50 percent greater endurance at twice the altitude of Dragon Eye, it's no wonder that Raven has become so popular.[11] A single fully operational model still demands two people to carry, the multiple suitcase load including the airframe, camera, batteries, erectable antenna, laptop ground control station, mission viewer, network hub, cables, and spare parts. Raven can be prepared in the field in as little as fifteen minutes, the act of launching it sort of like heaving a javelin. One person prepares and controls the aircraft, the other the ground control station and antenna link. A triangular scope that looks like an old-fashioned slide viewer with an attached darkening eye cover is used to operate the drone and "see" exactly what the Raven sees, the handheld console ("hand controller") about the size and shape of a video game controller, with three buttons on each side to manually fly it. The laptop incorporates an overlaid digital map and has a touch screen used to set the waypoints.[12] The ground control station also observes the wind speeds and directions, and monitors the computer data from the drone itself: speed, altitude, battery level, magnetic heading, direction from the home waypoint to the drone, wind direction, and bearing to the target. Operators can take still pictures and transmit them or even go back in the motion imagery if they miss something. Raven shares its common ground control station not just with Wasp and Puma, but also feeding independently into Company-level tactical command centers, where the imagery can also be simultaneously viewed.[13]

Raven is so simple to use that any soldier can be trained in eighty hours to be a certified operator. The training is almost all hands-on, perfect for the digital natives. Raven operators say it's all about flight hours and finesse to develop what they call "muscle memory," getting to the point, like when they're playing a video game, where they know where the buttons are and what to do without even thinking about it.

Raven lands through what can only be described as a controlled crash (officially it's called "stall and disassemble on impact"). The operator has a throttle button that can be kicked on and off, and there is an auto-land mode; but still, the airframe almost always breaks apart. But the all-important data link and camera are mounted in a Kevlar-armored coffee-cup-sized nose that is easily removable or can even be jettisoned. If there are any downsides, they are the noise, the vulnerability to ground fire, the restrictions in operating in poor weather or high winds, and, at 14,000 feet maximum, the launch altitude. In theory, Raven ought to be ineffective in a mountainous place like Afghanistan,[14] since it was originally conceived as a system for urban use.[15] In actual combat, however, operators found Raven far better suited for use in a rural environment "where interference from buildings and various electromagnetic signals were not as prevalent."[16]

Raven A, with separate daytime and nighttime camera mounts, was first flown in 2001 and fielded the next year. Raven A begat the Raven A+, which begat Raven B in 2005.[17] AeroVironment, the California manufacturer, received its first full-production US Army contract in October 2005 to supply 2,358 basic Raven systems, each including a ground control station and three air vehicles. Since then, it has received dozens of additional production and spiral contracts. The marine corps, air force, and special operations command all started acquiring their own Ravens; and civil agencies like the US Geologic Survey also began using the drone. And Raven was purchased and started flying with the militaries of Australia, Burundi, the Czech Republic, Denmark, Estonia, Iraq, Italy, Lebanon, the Netherlands, Norway, Saudi Arabia, Spain, Thailand, Uganda, the United Kingdom, and Yemen. The official sticker price is $35,000 per drone, but the entire basic "system" costs upward of $250,000, making the cost per drone closer to $75,000. Gimbaled Raven, the latest, is almost double that in expense.[18]

Another member of the Raven family, Puma, at thirteen pounds with a nine-foot wingspan, was introduced in 2001 to serve as a quiet alternative, allowing surveillance while avoiding detection. First fielded by the army's 101st Airborne Division in Afghanistan, it was really intended for use by special operators who couldn't accommodate themselves to the hum of the Pointer or the buzz of the Raven. Puma, while heavier, is also more portable, fitting into a set of rucksacks and thereby movable off-road without a vehicle. The drone has a communications range of 15 km and flight endurance of two hours; and it can be put into an auto-loiter mode at a programmed sensor point of interest. Puma also incorporated the gimbaled sensor package—the rotating eye—so that it is able to fix on a designated point and provide a steady, constant image while compensating for airframe movement.[19]

Formally, the army describes the family of small drones that includes Raven and Puma as occupying the bottom of the hierarchy; Shadow at the brigade level in the middle; and its own version of Predator—Gray Eagle—is at the division and above. Until it is fully retired, there is also Hunter, which today includes a signals intelligence black box and even a weapon and is assigned to four corps-level military intelligence units. Hunters are slated to continue flying until 2022, eventually to be replaced by Shadow or some Predator derivative.[20]

As the Raven standard caught on, marine corps ground forces also gravitated closer to the army's standard—WASP and Raven at the battalion level and Shadow at the top—but in the middle, they are adopting their own STUAS—small tactical unmanned aerial system—called Blackjack (Integrator). Blackjack is a 135-pound drone with a 16-foot wingspan, and as a "standard" piece of equipment intended to be assigned to every division, is more "expeditionary" than Shadow, which is to say, it doesn't require a soccer field for recovery.[21] But even there, it uses the same launch and recovery system as another drone called ScanEagle, which flies at the same echelon.

The Boeing-produced ScanEagle had long been used by the United States in experimentation and is perhaps one of the most interesting cases in the flock, for though it starting flying combat in 2004, it was not even owned by the government. It was the first of the generation of drones rented by the hour from the contractor as "needs" on the battlefield outpaced the ability of the acquisition system to supply them. In Iraq, the United States began renting drones like ScanEagle (as well as manned reconnaissance aircraft), the promise being a surge capability that could be easily demobilized when the need disappeared. ScanEagle flew alongside the marines, first in Iraq and then in Afghanistan. The Australian army later rented it as well. Blackjack/Integrator was meant to be the permanent replacement for ScanEagle.[22] But as the machine continues to move forward regardless of war, ScanEagle was purchased by the United States anyhow in 2012.[23]

At this point, an eagle-eyed reader probably is asking why I've stressed the importance of the black boxes, yet have hardly mentioned them at all so far, nor described in any detail the sensors on all of these drones. In my defense, I say that even untangling the various tribal affiliations and the interlocking networks of all of these drones, to say nothing of the question of their actual roles and impact, is hard enough. It's not as though drones just appeared. "Tribal representatives," as General Jumper called the various operations, intelligence, and support communities, are made up of people in different career fields who each have their own ways and systems and their own interests.[24] Nor were they whipped into a mad frenzy simply because of corporate tycoons intent on making money. More accurately, they emerged because people were dying, because there was a sense of threat and frustration, and because there was a need to protect people—to sacrifice anything other than a human being. One could chalk it all up to bureaucratic politics or the military-industrial complex or even technology run amok, but the very human striving of terror versus the machine and the machine versus terror is the most accurate genesis. War didn't begin on 9/11, nor will the warring end anytime soon, so it is only fitting that the lineage of drones has become as zigzagged and irregular as the master they serve.

In the spring of 2004, General John Abizaid, the CENTCOM commander who followed Tommy Franks, wrote to Secretary Rumsfeld calling for a "Manhattan-like Project" to counter IEDs, which were the "number one killer of American troops" (and of Iraqi civilians) at the time.[25] Insurgent attacks sharply increased after August 2003, tripling by December 2004, remaining at the high level after the Battle of Fallujah, and including suicide bombings and hostage beheadings.[26]

At every level all the way down to the platoon and company,

the priority became immediate and preemptive lifesaving, each unit focusing on its own challenges.[27] The more distant high-value target search effort for the 9/11-related terrorists was given over to the CIA and the growing world of black special operations. At home, the Joint Improvised Explosive Device Defeat Organization (JIEDDO, pronounced "jy-aid-oh") was created and large IED-oriented task forces were established in Iraq and Afghanistan to focus the effort. Nothing was seemingly outside the purview of the new counter-IED crusade, and JIEDDO became the premier off-budget sponsor. Task Force ODIN in Iraq (Observe, Detect, Identify, and Neutralize), first established in 2006, and then other counter-IED task forces, overt and clandestine, ended up being a mini-US government and a mini-United Nations. They built up their own air and ground force, their own intelligence establishment, their own research department, their own special operations, their own schoolhouse, their own interrogators, even their own police and bomb squads with laboratories and evidence rooms, the grander theory being that "giving lower-ranking tactical commanders the real-time persistent surveillance typically reserved for senior leadership and strategic decision makers" would turn the tide.[28]

The drone ranks opened to almost any volunteer. Standards were lowered and widened because IEDs had become so lethal. The perfect example is ScanEagle itself. Initially developed by Insitu Group (eventually partnered with and then bought by Boeing) in 2002 to be another begat in the medium competition, it was the smallest drone equipped with a stabilized gimbaled camera with more than twenty-four hours of endurance.[29] It just didn't get any traction with the Pentagon. That is, until the demand for more eyes in the sky, and a sense that the air force was holding back on its Predator support for the troops, led to the idea of a fee-for-service drone. Contractors would fly and maintain the thirty-eight-pound ScanEagles, while the military would supply the mission commanders and analyst support. Fee-for-service caught on; the military didn't have to *buy* the platforms, it could lease them. For JIEDDO, it was also all their own: imagery, the signals, the data—anything that would support the new boundless appetite of the counter-IED war. For NATO countries, leasing reconnaissance was capability without commitment to fill the gap until they acquired their own large systems.[30]

It isn't the origin of every irregular or unconventional drone like the ScanEagle, but scratch the surface of Aerosonde, Buster, Swiper, Shrike, Tiger Hunter II, GhostBat, Silver Fox, Golden Eye, Green Dart, Tigershark, T-Hawk, Freewing, Scorpion, Hummingbird, gMAV, or Rmax and you will find birth or rebirth in some IED justification. Each platform and each black box, regular or not, off-budget or leased, open or secret, constituted a "host" for yet more data gathering, even as they also meant an enormous human investment as much to operate as to incorporate into the Data Machine. JIEDDO wasn't averse to buying or using the standard-issue Shadows or Ravens or Pumas, but it was intent on creating its own focused capability. Thus it would take a Puma and put its own experimental counter-IED black box on it: hail CEASAR (the Communications Electronic Attack with Surveillance and Reconnaissance) and VADER (the Vehicle and Dismount Exploitation Radar), each another warrior thrown into the fight. Nor were drones some cowardly emissary: slow-flying manned aircraft were also purchased and stuffed with "modular" equipment, black boxes: ARMS, MARSS, Highlighter, Liberty.[31] The black box, more than the platform, determined where manned or unmanned would go. Soon enough, the army and marine corps, air force and navy, special operations community, JIEDDO, and "other government agencies" were doing the same, buying their own "special" capabilities to pry open and go into the enemy underworld.

Still the wars continued, and as the same enemy IED tactics migrated to Afghanistan and other parts of the world, crude detonating devices became more sophisticated and attacks turned into "complex events" of multiple explosions, with the enemy ranging from individual suicide bombers to sophisticated cells utilizing command-detonated roadside bombs triggered by cell phones and garage door openers.[32] Pretty soon, no ground force commander, no matter what echelon, wanted to or would conduct an operation unless he was assured of the availability of airborne full-motion video overhead.[33] Manned airstrike sorties, normally a twelve-to-one ratio over intelligence and surveillance flights, shifted to a ratio of two to one.[34] These fighter jets were not only valuable for patrol or when troops were in contact; the imagery they provided with their NTISR pods and their contribution to the network were what was most important. In one year, dropping bombs went down precipitously (for example, in one F-16 wing in Iraq, in 2,500 sorties, only 45 of the flights resulted in munitions being dropped, a rate of less than 1.8 percent).[35] The toll on the drones was also felt. From June 2004 to June 2005, the Predator fleet flew more than 27,000 hours over Iraq and Afghanistan—almost triple what it had flown just a year earlier.

Money flowed and gadgets appeared; rapid-reaction and emergency systems of acquisition sent almost any black box or newfangled collector they could get their hands on to get more, master the data, and win the war. It is another indecipherable thicket of everything from specialized vehicles to microwave, laser, and sound weapons; from specialized robots to aerostats, even a pack of beloved tactical explosion detection dogs; thousands of jammers; and, of course, drones; a vast experimental whirlwind of over 70,000 black boxes.[36] Everything was tried, but as the Rand Corporation later explained, "offensive 'left of boom' targeting measures…were employed too late and with little effect."[37] There was growing recognition that the task was identifying and targeting not just bomb makers but the entire network of individuals involved in the production, transportation, and emplacement of IEDs; going right of boom, before the soldiers ever had the misfortune of coming upon the end product.

Prepare the Force, Defeat the Device, Attack the Network: that became the multibillion-dollar creed and the three pillars of counter-IED. With IEDs accounting for up to 80 percent of soldier casualties in Iraq by 2007, $10 billion went into the lifesaving spree.[38] Then the order came down from the Pentagon to shift from armored vehicles and jammers and drones to the new number one, "attack the network." So in the middle of the biggest buying spree in the history of drones, in the middle of acquiring more and more platforms to reassure the industrial army that it too was armed for the information era, the order came down from the Pentagon to "Stop Buying Platforms."[39] It was a frustrated recognition that no one knew how many collection platforms were actually out there or whether the data being collected by them was being used adequately, or being used at all. The order wasn't to stop buying platforms and solve the information glut problem. It wasn't an order to stop relying on technology. No one made any move to halt the growth of the Data Machine. Stop buying platforms: it is itself an industrial cry, and though it might not have been mistaken in any way, it was a cry for help that just couldn't recognize how much things had changed.

CHAPTER THIRTEEN

Mind-Set over Mind

As the Bull of Heaven snorted a pit opened up,
One hundred men of Uruk fell down it.
The second time it snorted a pit opened up,
Two hundred men of Uruk fell down it.
TABLET VI, *EPIC OF GILGAMESH*

The epic battle between the army and the air force started as most fights do, with a big misunderstanding. Troops were dying and getting torn apart by IEDs daily—hourly—and the air force wouldn't give more. It wasn't aircraft or bombs that were most needed: it was intelligence. That was how the army saw it. And that was how the new secretary of defense, Robert Gates, saw it, labeling the standoff between the two military branches an "unseemly turf fight" in which the air force wanted "absolute control of a [drone] capability for which it had little enthusiasm in the first place."[1]

In the first place goes back to an anecdote Gates loves to repeat, which is that, as CIA director in 1992, he had tried to enlist the air force in the Agency's secret drone program, only to be rebuffed. People join the air force to fly airplanes, Gates later wrote, a "mind-set" he found still prevalent when he came to the Pentagon in December 2006.[2] Further, Gates found life in the Pentagon to be "largely business as usual," a "damnable peacetime mind-set" oblivious to two wars going on.³ He openly took the army's side in an ongoing fight over Predator support, aligning himself with the troops on the ground. Gates loved being known as the Soldiers' Secretary, the regular-Joe advocate, and the un-Rumsfeld, even if in truth he was every bit the Washington animal and still very much stuck in predigital turf. Part of that role for Gates was to actively align himself with everyone's pre-conceptions of the enduring problem. He attacked government waste, dismissing gold-plated weapons and obstreperous bureau-crats. But his own understanding of the military was stale, oblivi-ous to the new truth of the unmanned, which was that the flying service wasn't stuck in the past and the army really yearned to be more like the air force, which ultimately meant less tethered to the ground and closer to the heart of the Data Machine.

The army. A single archetype can represent that gigantic institution as well as "silk scarf" can accurately portray the air force. Fewer than .5 percent of the people in the air force actually fly fighter jets, even if they are a self-selected elite. The army has its own power elite—commanders of infantry and the other com-bat arms—and "boots on the ground" is a national purpose that seizes everyone even as *the army* has changed and the military has become a tangled mass of soldier, civilian, contractor, and techni-cian. But for the army commanders, the direct supporting cast also includes the air force, the youthful invention of the twentieth century, the adolescent who broke away from military history, an institution that can be misread as *only* coveting the latest swoosh when in fact it wants whatever technology does the job—even if that means without the troops. Unbound by the constraints of distance and even geography, the airpower ethic is to use the information advantage—going above and beyond the territory of ground forces, going behind enemy lines, even penetrating into the mind of an enemy. When a quicksand-stuck army adopted "attack the network" as its counter-IED strategy, it was merely pursuing the air force aesthetic boiled down to its very essence. And this was the aesthetic not just of the air force but of the modern fighting force in general, dominated as it is by the Data Machine and its army of unlaborers and technicians, who vastly outnumber those flying fighter jets or actually doing combat in ground units.

If "attack the network" was going to be the task, and counterinsurgency tactics were emerging that valued synchronized and heartfelt action over combat, not-killing over killing, winning hearts over stopping hearts, then what was really behind the army–air force tension was a result of years of history. As far back as late 2003, said Lieutenant General Richard Sanchez, the first postcombat commander in Iraq, the army admitted to itself that it was completely unprepared for the task beyond invasion and conventional war. We were "completely lost in a totally different operational environment," Sanchez said.[4] Brigadier General Martin Dempsey, then a brigade commander in Baghdad and later chairman of the Joint Chiefs, agreed, saying that the frustration in this new kind of nonwar was that "we're either fighting for intelligence or we're fighting based on that intelligence."[5]

Intelligence, specifically tactical intelligence—that which takes place at the company, battalion, and brigade level—had to shift from merely being a part of operations to *leading* operations—and creating actionable opportunities to kill the target. Everything from basic analysis, human intelligence, and network connections to the Data Machine was beefed up as the army scrambled to adjust.[6]

And the army looked around: with Predators above and thousands of ROVERs peeping into someone else's window, constantly reminding the GIs that they were the lowest on the totem pole, they coveted the big eye that would allow persistent surveillance and the entire targeting cycle all the way to their own kill. And they wanted the capability to see and kill at a distance. And there was this centralized air force operating completely at the beck and call of the ground commander and political masters, and yet seemingly unable to support the troops while the army was just trying to get through the day, dependent on others for its intelligence and airpower. Surveillance desperately shifted to the unmanned. And drones began to arrive in greater numbers. It wasn't seamless; accident rates were high, as becoming more like the air force demanded different skills. The troops were also scared. "We don't go out the gate without our drones," the rule for today became. Said one army general: "We can send a UAS down an alley, use it to look around corners, or look on a roof to see what's up there, dramatically increasing Soldier protection and preserving the force—a vital force multiplier in this era of persistent conflict."[7]

"Over time, as other commanders saw what these ISR capabilities were, the demand for more of them for regular combat operations and for force protection grew exponentially," Gates later wrote.[8]

And that was the point: looking outside the gates, the air force had its *own* set of eyes—but for what? Special operations forces had their own everything, with their own budgets, as did the counter-IED task forces, which weren't focused on every individual combat outpost's protection but on some bigger (almost air force–like) ephemeral network, while soldiers were dying. Even the marines were able to sustain wall-to-wall drone coverage of Fallujah for months on end in 2004, and they had their own full-spectrum aviation. And the CIA and the DEA had their own reconnaissance. The poor army guys at the bottom just had model airplanes.

If all of these incongruities weren't enough to appeal to the new secretary, he started in office with two troubled wars and a bad taste in his mouth regarding the basic health of his military. Though to many he was a godsend, especially after Rumsfeld, he just seemed oblivious to the true struggle and the resulting larger transition that was occurring as the Data Machine exerted greater influence. First, he should have understood that the dogfaces on the front lines are always bitching and that dealing with what they think they need at any moment is a sensitive and almost parental balancing act. Second, he should have fully understood that no amount of blaming bureaucrats was going to change the immediate circumstances on the ground. And third, he should have had an inkling that the true crisis wasn't with machinery or data— which meant the corporeal side of ISR—in other words, there was now so much data and so many eyes, the true problem wasn't even the size of the Machine but its appetite, an appetite that excreted an abundance of intelligence, none of it clearly pointing to a losing endeavor.

In the ways of Washington, on June 28, 2007, Gates received a bracing letter from two powerful senators, Joe Biden and Republican Kit Bond, a communication from outside the family that forced him to take some kind of action. "We are concerned that the Department is failing to respond to urgent warfighter requirements because of unconscionable bureaucratic delays in Washington," the two said.[9] From commercial radios and GPS units to homemade armor needed for army vehicles, soldiers were still scrounging around and going outside normal channels to get what they needed. The battle against IEDs consumed all—the Joint Improvised Explosive Device Defeat Organization was reaching $10 billion annually in emergency expenditures. But now that "attack the network" was the strategy, along with the surge of troops and the new charismatic commander in Iraq practicing something called counterinsurgency, what they needed more than anything else was intelligence. Or so it seemed. And that meant drones.

Maybe it was the army's still-simmering resentment that it had lost Predator control a decade earlier,[10] maybe it was its attitude that the air force existed solely to support it, but the whispering campaign began: the air force wasn't providing *the troops* with sufficient Predator sorties or hours. And now the cerebral general David Petraeus, the field commander and matinee idol, was raising the need for more ISR, intelligence, surveillance, and reconnaissance, in every conversation with the new secretary.[11] "While investments had been made in remotely piloted vehicles (drones)," Gates observed, "there were no crash programs to increase their numbers or the diversity of intelligence, surveillance, and reconnaissance capabilities for commanders."[12]

It was a ridiculous statement given the clattering flock that was emerging, given the directions that the air force was already heading in.[13] But unbeknownst to Gates, the army was already flying its own version of Predator, having established Task Force Observe, Detect, Identify, and Neutralize (Task Force ODIN) in Iraq, an organization that would use manned and unmanned platforms together to provide persistent surveillance and what the army was now calling manned-unmanned teaming (or MUMT). An army aviation commander described MUMT as the "preferred method for supporting dangerous missions in today's conflicts."[14] The misunderstanders wrote that ODIN existed precisely because of "the limited numbers of USAF Predator UAVs in Iraq, and consequent refusal of many Army requests" for support.[15] Many in Congress and the Pentagon became convinced of some intentional slight in not supporting the troops. More surveillance, the attitude was, would mean "more lives would be saved and the fight against insurgent led IEDs could be defeated."[16]

Did Gates not know that the army was completely focused on building the flock of smaller drones like Raven to issue them to every company?[17] Did he not see the army's own compartmented developments, or the way the counter-IED and special operations worlds were just going in their own directions? Did he not know that by the time he became secretary, there were still only 150 various drones, including Predators, deployed forward, a decision made not by the air force but by higher-ups in the operational chains and a decision driven by the capacities of the Machine? And as for the air force, did he not see that when US forces invaded Iraq in 2003, the air force flew Predators as much as it could out of Kuwait and that a single Global Hawk named Grumpy had worked tirelessly on behalf of the troops? Did he not know that overall, over 90 percent of *all* air force intelligence collection worldwide was being thrown into the fight?[18] This is the ultimate scourge of black box policies and technologies: that no one really knows the totality of the system. Gates came into office with his own history and biases, and responded to the squeakiest political wheel. The troops and their sense of neglect in the new world of the Data Machine were the squeakiest, and the most politic to go the extra mile for.

The army's move to acquire its own Predator started in 2001, before 9/11 and before "IED" was even a term. The service was defining requirements for a replacement for Hunter, which then was less than a decade old but was considered to be an intelligence asset of limited usefulness in network-centric warfare. Various alternatives flocked about, but in March 2003, the same month the second Iraq war started, the army purchased three Improved-Gnat Extended Range (IGnat-ER) drones from General Atomics, an upgrade of the CIA Gnat-750 flown over Bosnia a decade earlier. It did so not because it anticipated deadly roadside bombs or the fight ahead; on the contrary, the army was doing what Gates said he abhorred about the air force—it was planning for the future. That meant the Future Combat System, a digital-network-centric force still of boots, but in which the ground was more ephemeral and expansive. IGnat-ER began flying in Iraq in early 2004.[19]

Extended Range/Multi-Purpose (ER/MP), the army's formal name for its generic and formal requirement to replace Hunter, emerged the next year. Again, this was just the normal flow of modernization, but amidst a declining situation on the ground in Iraq, everyone outside the army thought it might be seeking to duplicate existing capabilities, and though the army argued it was entitled to replace an aging and obsolete system, it actually rebuffed a formal "analysis of alternatives," happy to use magic adjectives to tug at the heartstrings of troop-loving Washington— urgent requirement, quick reaction—that would push their way through the bureaucracy and Congress.[20]

ER/MP continued forward to fill the operational requirements and specifications set down on paper for the far future, but in August 2005, General Atomics won an army contract and seventeen Warriors were purchased. Warrior was a green version of Predator and was more capable than IGnat-ER and in many ways more capable than even early air force Predator models. Again, the army and the air force argued over the new model—its capabilities, its controllers, how fancy all of the black boxes needed to be. And by early 2007, the disagreement over these big drones and central control had reached a boiling point. At an April 19 hearing, Representative Neil Abercrombie of Hawaii, chairman of the armed services subcommittee dealing with airpower, complained that no one was in charge, that no one in the Pentagon was exercising control over competing programs.[21] Sky Warrior Block 0 emerged during this interservice battle, with the army flying a dozen of them in Iraq.

All of this went down before Gates even became secretary, before he demanded anything. Air Force chief General T. Michael ("Buzz") Moseley, who had been the air commander working with the army during the invasion, went public with a tone-deaf argument that the air force should become the overall "executive agent" for all medium- and high-altitude drones flying above 3,500 feet. "Demand for UAVs currently exceeds supply, and it will continue to do so even after all the Services have fielded all their programmed" capabilities, he wrote. "My proposal...is all about getting the most 'joint' combat capability out of these limited Intelligence, Surveillance and Reconnaissance (ISR) resources, while promoting Service interdependence and ensuring the best stewardship of America's tax dollars." [22] On September 28, 2007, Gates called a meeting of senior department officials "to read them the riot act" and urged them to apply "a sense of urgency and a willingness 'to break china' to get more materiel to the field faster."[23] According to Gates, the problem was that the air force was only providing eight Predator "caps" (combat air patrols)— each cap twenty-four hours of coverage with three drones—and had *no plans* to increase that number. "I was determined that would change," he said.[24] He directed an increase in the number of caps to eighteen, demanding a plan by November 1.[25] After Moseley directed a study on how this order could be implemented, Gates thought the air force was still moving far too slowly. And the secretary says he was further frustrated that all Moseley and Air Force Secretary Michael Wynne could seem to talk about was a new bomber and more F-22 stealth fighter jets, neither of which, he said "were playing any part in the wars we were already in."[26]

Standardization, deconfliction, elimination of duplication,

avoiding friendly fire, all the more magic Washington arguments were put forward, but it was a conflict already reduced to the simplistic explanation that the air force was lacking in support for the troops. "I'm pursuing the UAV EA [executive agent] role to make the Joint Force—not the air force—more combat capable," Moseley responded.[27] Joint Chiefs chairman General Peter Pace, US Marine Corps, agreed that it made sense to have all flights in common airspace under one authority as long as that did not "override the needs of the troops on the ground."[28] The Joint Requirements Oversight Council agreed, forwarding its recommendation that executive agency be assigned to the air force.[29] But the army mounted a vigorous and effective rebuttal, arguing that its Shadow drone, organic to the division, already flew over 3,500 feet and that flying in accordance with a centrally controlled schedule would shortchange the troops. Deputy Secretary Gordon England, the man generally responsible for the business side of the Pentagon, sided with the army, and that was the end.[30]

But after visiting the Predator and Reaper home base in Nevada on January 8, 2008, Gates became even more convinced of a lack of enthusiasm and urgency in the air force.[31] Drone personnel assignments were sluggish and seemingly second-tier; quality of life for his troops, even these video monitoring unlaborers, was shockingly subpar. A week later he wrote to Admiral Michael Mullen, chairman of the Joint Chiefs of Staff, that he wanted any materiel requests from Iraq and Afghanistan ground commanders brought to his attention. The "immediate problem," Gates said, "was the difficulty we were having in meeting our field commanders' need for intelligence, surveillance, and reconnaissance (ISR) capabilities: a mix of unmanned drones, propeller-driven reconnaissance aircraft, analysts, linguists, and data fusion capabilities that collected and fed critical battlefield information— including intercepted phone calls of terrorist leaders and live video transmission of insurgents planting IEDs—to military commanders, who could then act on it."[32]

Even though the flock migrating to the battlefield was mind-boggling in numbers and diversity, that picture of want—not control or numbers—drove the crisis. "The true metric that gauges the power that these systems bring to our current fight is the insatiable demand by our commanders for these assets," a top army general observed.[33] Now that unmanned systems and the Data Machine had become the latest superweapon, there was no way of saying that enough might be enough. Or more pointedly, there was no way of challenging the trend of the army slowly turning itself into a self-contained killing machine, usurping centralized functions into the ground combat forces and transforming itself into an intelligence-dominated (and unmanned) Machine.

On April 28, 2008, Gates appeared before the students and faculty at the Air War College in Montgomery, Alabama, and let loose on the service for not doing its part, for being "stuck in old ways of doing business." With respect to drones, he said he insisted that more Predators needed to be deployed but that getting them has been akin to "pulling teeth." He announced the creation of a high-level ISR Task Force above the services, one that would "find more innovative and bold ways to help those whose lives are on the line."[34]

To refute Gates, the air force said it was already doing everything he complained it wasn't: reprogramming over $2.3 billion for fiscal year 2007, opening the way to double its Predator coverage for combat operations in Iraq and Afghanistan, a move initiated before he became secretary. On May 1, the air force said, it would be providing twenty-four Predator caps, and it was working to expand to thirty-four caps by the end of 2008.[35]

But Gates was on a tear. He formed a new ISR Task Force, with a mandate of commonality and resolving the army–air force dispute, another ad hoc institution given rapid acquisition authority.[36] And so while the air force was redoubling its efforts, while JIEDDO was still buying every new product coming its way, and while the army was already independently buying the outlines of its own Predator force, the task force became yet another offline slush fund. In August, Gates approved seventy-two new drone and black box initiatives at a cost of $2.6 billion, more off-the-books programs that he later bragged about, saying he was able to maneuver spending without congressional approval for three years.[37] By 2012, the task force had spent over $10 billion.[38]

Despite the army's continued scramble to get its own Predator no matter what, IGnat-ER cum Warrior cum Sky Warrior Block 0 cum Warrior Alpha cum Sky Warrior Block 1 moved forward.[39] Block 0 was followed by Sky Warrior Alpha, one foot longer with engine, avionics, and data link enhancements, incorporating the automatic landing system, with a deicing capability. Weapons capable Block 1 became the next iteration.[40] The objective model for the army, an improved Predator now renamed Gray Eagle, would be 100 percent soldier maintained instead of contractor operated. Gray Eagle was armed with four Hellfire missiles, not just the two on air force Predators, and had a complete point-and-click flight system, and high-definition TV—the very capability the army originally said it didn't need. We're just fulfilling the secretary's desire to field "75 percent solutions" quickly rather than 100 percent solutions on some distant horizon, an army spokesperson said.[41]

In Iraq, it wasn't really Predator-type drones per se that were needed or were making a difference. The very concept of "attack the network" connoted not just a shift from operations to intelligence, but also a lessening of the importance of the physical dimension of the battle. The army, like the air force, started to use the terms "effects based" and "strategic effects" to connote this shift. In the so-called Battle for Sadr City in April 2008, a Shia-dominated northeast slum of Baghdad, a variety of drones—army Ravens and Shadows, air force Predators and Global Hawks, special operations Predators and secret Green Darts—maintained overwatch and were sent forward to scout for Apache attack helicopters and other army ground-based precision guided weapons. No one thought for a moment that Predator or Global Hawk would be doing anything different than the army's own drones. "Supporting this one brigade, 24/7," General Petraeus later said, "were 2 [Air Force] Predators (armed with Hellfire missiles), Shadow and Raven UAVs, aerostat blimps with optics, RAID [surveillance] towers, three air weapons teams (of two AH64 Apache [attack helicopters] each), and two additional UAVs [drones] with special capabilities [the Green Darts and special operations drones]." Also in support were air force close air support fighter jets, Petraeus said, "and the national, strategic intelligence platforms," including satellites, the fleet of large manned intelligence aircraft and U-2s. "We gave the brigade more ISR than any unit in history," the "we" being the joint military, though not necessarily, or not particularly, the air force.[42] That battle included no army IGnats or Sky Warriors, either; they were actually unavailable to the joint commander because they belonged to the counter-IED tribe and were withheld.

When Gates became secretary, the air force was able to provide a total of eleven caps over the battlefield, split between two countries and carefully marshaled for maximum availability. By the Battle of Sadr City, the same month that Gates would let loose on the air force institution, they were on schedule to triple the number of caps to thirty-three.[43] Even Gates admitted that by June 2008, the air force was able to report it was "dramatically" increasing the number of Predator patrols.[44] And in fall 2007, the air force had also deployed the first of a new generation of

Predator-like drones, the MQ-9 Reaper, which was a vast improvement in capabilities and combat power over the original Predator models.[45]

By the start of the Battle of Sadr City, the army was also bragging about its drone accomplishments: in less than a year in Iraq, the army's Sky Warrior A was involved in 148 sensor-to-shooter target handoffs, resulting in hundreds of IED emplacers being killed, injured, or detained. In fact, now, with its flock of everything from Ravens to Sky Warriors, the army could even say that it outpaced the air force in drone hours flown at the height of the insurgency from 2005 through 2007.[46]

The air force valiantly fought back against the slur to its honor (and the facts). Officials pointed to the fact that although Predator's first 100,000 hours took over ten years to attain, increased operations tempo meant that the next 100,000 hours would be reached within six months.[47] The first 250,000 hours took twelve years; the second 250,000 took eighteen months and were completed in 2008.[48] It had become some strange battle of the numbers, this disagreement. And then in the middle of it all, with the situation in Iraq so dire, the army assigned its version of Predator to the 82nd Airborne Division in September 2007, to fly in *Afghanistan.*[49] It was inescapable: the army drones would act on behalf of the Machine as well.

On June 5, in an unprecedented move, the secretary of defense unexpectedly relieved both the secretary and chief of staff of the United States Air Force. Gates insisted that the sole reason was a failure to safeguard the nuclear arsenal, a Washington nightmare scenario that trumped all others and became blaring headlines after a bomber unit in the United States mistakenly transported real live nuclear weapons from one base to another.[50] The seed for the June massacre, though, was Predator and the unshakable view that the flying service provided inadequate support to the army.

The nuclear mishap, Admiral Mullen wrote to Gates, "is representative and symptomatic of a greater decline, for which I believe our Air Force leadership has to be held accountable."[51] At the field level, the final break with the notion of a centrally controlled intelligence capability was made. Everyone was now their own intelligence service, intelligence of course meaning data and targeting, and service of course meaning service to the Machine.

CHAPTER FOURTEEN

Gilgamesh Calling

Shamash grew worried, and bending down,
he spoke to Gilgamesh:
"O Gilgamesh, where are you wandering?
The life that you seek you will never find."
TABLET IX, *EPIC OF GILGAMESH*

At 4:45 p.m. on the afternoon of June 7, 2006, two air force F-16C fighter jets flying over Baghdad got a call to proceed to a safe house in a date palm grove outside the provincial capital of Baqubah, forty-five miles northeast. It wasn't an IED event or troops in contact but a possible strike on a high-value target. No more needed to be said; they were there.

A precision mission like this just doesn't happen: there is a supported commander somewhere with an objective, even if that commander is *the* commander in chief. There are decisions made as to who is high-value, with input from everyone from strategists to lawyers. There is intelligence information on each individual target, whether that is a person on some list to achieve a national objective or only a local bomb-maker or insurgent of importance to the smallest unit on the battlefield. There are a mix of forces available locally, regionally, and even globally, hopefully all trained and up to the task, and these forces demand countless decisions and preparations over years to produce tangible capabilities. There are commanders at all levels who survey their people and capabilities, gauging the whole, not just intuiting the bravest and the smartest but also assessing qualities of the heart and mind. All of this needs to be brought together at a place and at a point in time, with the capabilities and priorities all in order, so that when the call does come in, there is not only someone to answer—someone who has the smarts and skills—but also someone who can act, if necessary.

And then there's an enemy. As General Norman Schwarzkopf once famously said: People may think of war as if it's a ballet, "like it's choreographed ahead of time, and when the orchestra strikes up and starts playing, everyone goes out there and goes through a set piece." Well, he said, "It is choreographed, and what happens is the orchestra starts playing and some son of a bitch climbs out of the orchestra pit with a bayonet and starts chasing you around the stage. And the choreography goes right out the window."[1]

On that day, at that time, in that place, the air force F-16 two-ship was merely flying a routine anti-insurgency mission, which meant that they were slotted into a designated orbit for a scheduled period, armed and ready to provide air support of ground forces if they were called. There was literally a schedule—a plan of the day—and based upon location and the availability of resources, and taking into consideration the projected needs of tomorrow and the day after, and considering the immediate priorities of commanders from the very top to the very bottom, as many of the available capabilities were allocated as possible. This thing we call war is a vast machine of which the Data Machine is but one element; it should also be noted, however, that the data is most ephemeral. For while those F-16s were available in exactly the same way Predator or other ISR would be, the F-16s were tangible and came without controversy. And as the capability to neutralize the target (and the objective isn't *always* to kill) has become more and more exacting, the role that data plays not only grows as well, but also the speed of decision-making becomes superhuman.

On that day, those two F-16s flying their scheduled mission had no prior tip-off as to what lay ahead. Befitting a half-trillion-dollar machine, the jets were each fitted with a Litening targeting pod, a 400-pound black box with a rotating sensor similar to the bug-eyed device on Predator's chin. Seven feet long, stuffed with computers and bristling with TV camera, infrared detector, laser range finder, and marker (or designator), it is one of those unheralded and little-known transformative nonweapons of networked warfare. Litening is but a minor outpost of the overall Machine, hardly noticed by people at the top, and yet this black box exponentially increases the sheer military capability of already capable airplanes.

Litening links the pilot and his jet to the larger network and transforms its host by giving pilots additional eyes beyond the visual. It acts at once as navigator, gunner, engineer, and weapons technician. This single man and his black box assistant are now driver, collector, scout, and shooter; intelligence and operations; air defense and attack; interdiction and close air support. What were once separate disciplines that all required hundreds of different platforms and human beings are now reduced to one. Litening is still hostage to the numbers: the probability of kill is determined by endless calculations that factor in everything from the airplane to the network to the fuse on the bomb itself, but it is a concentration of greater combat power in one platform that is constantly being increased.

With Litening, the pilot can examine objects and terrain below, the central brain projecting a map-enhanced picture to the heads-up display, a yellow-cast transparent scene floating above the instrument panel. With embedded intelligence information and symbology from stored geographic information systems and automatically receiving up-to-the-second updates via data links to a myriad other intelligence sources all feeding the same net-work, the F-16 can precisely attack with laser-guided bombs, with GPS satellite-guided JDAMs, or even with conventional "dumb" bombs (though that is more and more rare). By 2006, with weapons that were tested and tweaked to near perfection; with the black boxes on board serving as adjutant, intelligence officer, and IT department; and with a pilot cadre that was combat experienced, attacking that target was possible with a very high degree of probability under all weather conditions, day and night. Everyone took it for granted, and *that's* a decade ago.

At the main command center in Qatar and at forward command centers at Balad Air Base to the north, where the F-16s originated, and at reachback stations in the United States and at other manned fusion nodes in the Data Machine worldwide, those responsible on that shift were completely focused on this one event, even as computers spoke to computers, with the supplemental imagery and signals coming in, some being fed automatically to the jets' data links and to Litening, some moving via chat and e-mail and even radio, one giant confederation primed to support the same objective.

Speaking to the air operations coaches, the F-16s stayed at medium altitude, where they had a reduced sound signature, so as to not tip off the high-value target. The pilots soon discovered that there were special forces below with eyes on target, convey-ing 100 percent certainty not just that the target was in the house and hadn't moved, but that the stealthiness of the fighter jets could be verified from the ground. More backroom work-ers calculated blast and explosive effects of the weapons on board; others busied themselves with target study: the house was a rebar-reinforced concrete structure, isolated, with zero civilian collateral damage concerns.

With the aid of mapping programs, the precise coordinates of the target were relayed to the plane's central computer, and the pilots jetted to the area, surveilling the surroundings, checking their magnified visual image taken with Litening's sensors against other imagery already linked into the fighter's brain. The soldiers on the ground, a Predator drone flying above, and the listening planes and satellites even farther afield were all focused and contributing, duty officers and commanders now on the phones and in chat windows talking to additional players in Washington and Florida. At 6:15 p.m., ninety minutes after the call came in, having locked in on the correct house and with all permissions granted and precautions taken to protect the American operators in a hide site not far away from the house, the pilots received their "GO" order to attack. The explosive would be fused to punch the bomb inside the structure before it detonated, a matter of milliseconds' difference. The lead plane lased the target—that is, pointed its laser marker on the intended aimpoint on the house's roof—and dropped one 500-pound laser-guided bomb. In less than two seconds, the bomb scored what appeared to be a direct hit, at least as much as the pod sensors could tell from the explosion and the washed-out sparkle on the infrared viewer.

The Predator watching from above, which belonged and reported to a higher-level special operations commander far away, saw things just a little differently. Or someone on the ground did. It didn't matter; someone else made the call. Within minutes, an order came back to hit the target again, and the F-16s circled back around, this time delivering an even newer 500-pound GBU-38 JDAM, steered solely by precisely matched coordinates, now a dust-and-debris-muddled place that might defy visual observation and laser designation.[2]

The high-value target, Abu Musab al-Zarqawi, murderer, beheader, archterrorist, and leader of an organization loosely called al Qaeda in Iraq, was killed.[3] It was the culmination of a four-year search, but in a world that loves its perpetual firsts, this was another one: the headlines screamed *terror mastermind killed*, and story time at the air force became simply how a Predator overhead cued expert pilots to perform their professional craft, just a little bit ignoring the men below. But even the special operations world did the same; the dogged investigators and true leads in the effort feathered their own caps with a narrative that stressed the success of human cunning and derring-do where the conventional army bumbled or the remote fly-boys were just too far away. But everyone was a little bit right. Except that the true achievement in the slaying of Zarqawi was the triumph of the Data Machine in finally making its way through its rigorous murder boards. The capacity had been growing for years, but now there was no denying anywhere that minute geolocation, the finding of an individual almost no matter where, had finally found its place. The final chapter of killing the target was a meticulous and automated piece of cake.

Geolocation became a massive issue from the moment the Afghanistan war began in 2001. Accuracy was measured in yards, a distance still too great to target an individual and ensure minimal harm to the surroundings when using precision guided munitions. With black boxes playing a larger role in the process, the NSA created a separate geolocation unit to advance the craft. Drone or not, it proved itself in the killing of Mohammed Atef in November 2001 when it locked into telephone calls; and it proved itself months later when 9/11 chiefs Abu Zubaydah and Khalid Sheikh Mohammed were captured in Pakistan.[4] After the death of Zarqawi, with Iraq at the apogee of unscripted chaos and Afghanistan increasingly unraveling, and with the tricks of black box eyeballing and eavesdropping starting to consistently work, the former CIA *and* NSA director, retired air force general Michael Hayden, told a military audience that the capacity to physically destroy the target had indeed reached its apogee: "Whether it's some idiot in a cave in Waziristan or rather some small WMD production facility," the target is easy to finish, he said. "They're just damn hard to find."[5]

The find. The task of precisely locating and identifying a target parallels the development of longer- and longer-range weapons and the maturation of the Machine. In the late 1990s, finding became a discipline all its own when sophisticated sensors and intercept devices were first enlisted as the means to provide geolocation sufficiently accurate for emerging satellite-guided JDAM bombs. Each development in this discipline, like all of the others, followed the same path, not just of technological advance and miniaturization, but also of the reduction in the number of people demanded to do the job. That is the essence of unmanned.

"Find 'em, fix 'em, and fuck 'em over!" was a motto used in Vietnam by radio intercept and direction finding units, the mission wretchedly similar to that performed forty years later. Armed with the PRD-1 black box affectionately known as the Purd, "radio research" operators would wade out into the swamp and seek out Communist guerrilla infiltrators, the still-physical act with earphones rather than keyboard, three sites working in unison to triangulate enemy transmissions, the interactions spotty, the probabilities low.[6] For the non–mathematically inclined, it is a simple task—except that the art has been supplemented over decades by larger receivers with more sophisticated techniques. Miniaturization meant that the black box material could increasingly be fit on a tripod or attached to a drone or even a networked pod like Litening flying overhead. Triangulation wasn't just the intersection of three lines but also became a function of movement and synchronization with other networked interceptors, the ear ubiquitous and the sound no longer just produced by radio waves.

Precision improved over the years as the errors involved in measurement and interference (noise) declined. Geolocation and direction finding are old cousins, but geolocation is more realistic and distinguished from DF by determining a meaningful location rather than just a bearing or a set of geographic coordinates. That means geolocation is always tied to a road, a house, or some scrutinized place. The techniques rely on space, time, and frequency, or a combination. The radio transmission, use angle of arrival, time of arrival, time difference of arrival, and differential Doppler (also called frequency difference of arrival) are calculated from movement or change in the radiated electromagnetic energy (the transmitter) and the receiver (or receivers).[7] Each of these methods has advantages and disadvantages. Computers and advanced mathematics are used to create exact coordination of the signals between the receivers and the fusion node that is computing the position, as well as precise synchronization among the receivers, thus increasing emitter position estimation.[8]

Whether in Vietnam fifty years ago or in the modern-day Middle East, the collectors have to be close enough (or strong enough) to detect the signal. These days, low-power devices (emitters) such as cell phones, cordless phones, wireless routers, walkie-talkies, and even garage door openers can be detected, demonstrating the huge advances that have been made in characterizing and locating even the faintest of clues. This task is made even more difficult in urban environments, where buildings can cause interference, though everywhere these days there can be an abundance of emitting devices (and thus interference). From Desert Storm through Kosovo to Iraq 2006 and into the current day, whether the task is synchronizing or searching deeper, the black box has grown smaller and smaller as the individual and minute target has also shrunk, all while operating on a larger and larger battlefield.

As General Stanley McChrystal, the overall Zarqawi attack commander, describes it, after the Battle of Fallujah in 2005, a major effort was undertaken to refine the ability to map and geo-locate targets of all kinds. At the Machine level, a mosaic was built: a "patchwork of movement from our eyes in the clouds," the picture given even greater fidelity when combined with "signals, human, and other intelligence disciplines" all melded into a com-mon picture. Pattern of life analysis and positive identification needed to target an individual that just a year earlier took weeks was compressed into days or even hours. A months-long cam-paign stripped Zarqawi of his cadre of mid- and senior-level lieu-tenants, causing a slow erosion of his network and thus closer and closer geolocation of an increasingly nervous center.[9]

The CIA and McChrystal's national counterterrorism task force loosely under the Joint Special Operations Command[10] had been working at a higher level than either the air force or the reg-ular army or other special commands in tracking the Jordanian national since even before the invasion of Iraq. And it was not just a technological effort. Along the way, there were many successes in collection, in analysis, and in breakthroughs that came from exploiting each new piece of information that came in. And in the end, US and Jordanian intelligence officials tracked the move-ments of Abdul-Rahman, one of Zarqawi's advisors, just as they tracked bin Laden's couriers later, locating the safe house and waiting patiently until the two met there.

That day on the ground, McChrystal's army Delta Force commandos were lying in wait. Once the house was bombed, they swarmed the target, picking through the rubble, confirming Zar-qawi's death and retrieving the body. There had been days, weeks, and even months of effort on the part of the so-called black special operators, the hero hunter-killers of a growing enterprise and the very human and heroic embodiment of millennia-old warfare. Yet in this new war no names were divulged, not even of the pilots. The general narrative isn't erroneous—it was indeed one team doggedly and bravely risking it all, vanguards of an entire nation even if they were all made into invisible and masked ninja warriors. In a world full of terrorists, the good guys have been made faceless, further enhancing the preeminence of the Machine. I know the justification: that the military is merely protecting the fighters and their families from the repercussions of a globally transparent world that could place them at risk from terrorists even while at home. In this era of global targeting and surgical geolocation, the importance of the "sanctity of the home" has diminished. There is an erosion of the distinction for both sides as to what is military and what is civilian, and one can now be targeted while in the "safety" of one's own home.

Stanley McChrystal was the closest one could label as the first chief American home wrecker. When the general took command of the Joint Special Operations Command (or JSOC, pronounced "jay-sock"), he knew he wanted to turn his hunter-killer operation into a little bit of a machine. "We needed to become networked together," he noted about his command. And so he moved himself and the fighting headquarters to Balad Air Base, naming the forward command Task Force 714, seeding liaison officers everywhere, connecting with every possible organization, and inviting outside fighters and intelligence specialists into his previously closed-off command post.[11] Chat room connections among the command centers, liaisons, reachback centers, platform crew, and even soldiers on the ground were made.[12] Frustrated with the lack of Arab linguists, McChrystal connected directly to Washington and turned his headquarters into a mere operating node of an enormous exploitation community, "a powerhouse of capabilities we could never have created ourselves," he says. Soon linguists in the United States were translating documents, and technicians were examining the insides of other materials collected in raids.[13] And the Distributed Common Ground System (DCGS) was modified as well—collection at that point was really limited by exploitation capacity. A special operations forces unique enclave was established, with new ground stations activated, and with imagery analysis shifted to stateside reserve and National Guard units to relieve the burden and spread around the network. The NSA hub at Fort Gordon in Georgia was fully given over to constant detection and translation on behalf of Middle East missions.[14] McChrystal also wanted his men to see raw intercepts the moment they were collected, even from satellites, a chain of custody that the NSA initially resisted until it began to "believe in the network premise itself."[15] The frustrated McChrystal "resorted to buying, borrowing, leasing, and modifying an odd array of substitutes" for intelligence, surveillance, and reconnaissance, what the black operators amusingly called their Confederate Air Force to describe its otherwise motley array of manned aircraft and unmanned drones.[16] The end result, McChrystal says, was "turning a hierarchical force with stubborn habits of insularity into one whose success relied on reflexive sharing of information and a pace of operations that could feel more frenetic than deliberate."[17]

In late 2004, McChrystal's command got its hands on what he called a "game-changing" technology—NSA's latest—one that would capitalize on Zarqawi and his lieutenants' own use of technology, specifically the cell phone. In Iraq, public cell phones hadn't even existed five years earlier, but they were now a key tool not just for terrorist command and control but also for communicating propaganda and even threats from Zarqawi to the now fully connected Iraqi people.[18] The NSA itself called the development the Little Boy of signals intelligence, equivalent to the world-changing impact of the bomb dropped on Hiroshima for what it did to targeting.[19] Simply, though by now we know that nothing is simple, the intelligence people in the field working with the NSA figured out a way to find individual cell phones down to the most minute of corner locations, by figuring out how to geolocate devices even when they weren't in use or the caller didn't answer.[20]

Dana Priest and I described the development of the hunter-killer capability of the US military and dissected it in *Top Secret America*, but still some insist that a single drone-based black box capability called Distantfocus enabled geolocation and that somehow this new capability was so promiscuous and so much lower in accuracy or even chivalry because human beings weren't directly involved in the find.[21] The truth is that it was a set of black boxes, on Predator and Reaper and on newly deployed manned aircraft, confederate and union alike—Airhandler, Gilgamesh, Pennant-race, Nebula, Windjammer—all working in unison and melded together as part of the network, with McChrystal's command certainly showing the way, but ultimately providing neither the inventors nor the dominant operators.[22] In fact, in the fall of 2006, JIEDDO, the counter-IED off-the-books organization, began fusing data from everywhere—Multi-INT—to attack the network at the lowest level.[23]

For national assassinations, Gilgamesh the black box would make the call by performing *active* geolocation like a radar pulsing an emitter, in this case a device with a unique identifier, not its telephone number but its underlying identity of hardware and software, an identity that allows the cell phone system to find the phone and call it whether the owner answers or not. Flying overhead, just like the overhead fabric of invisible digits that has become a ubiquitous part of our modern-day lives, Gilgamesh would mimic another phone, and in the way of black boxes, it would extract just the information it needed to secure positive identification and precise locating.

Though the relationship between intelligence and operations was already being turned on its head, after the successful full court press against Zarqawi everyone was saying operations *was* intelligence.[24] "We found ourselves largely focused on the fix and the finish—the tactical strikes—even though the exploit-analyze portion of the cycle would determine our success or failure," said McChrystal.[25] The success in getting Zarqawi, McChrystal's intelligence chief and the future head of the Defense Intelligence Agency said, showed that "successful counter-network operations that used the new combined arms team of operations and intelligence" were the only way forward.[26] Air force secretary Michael Wynne congratulated the "ground commander" for thinking "spherically," with Zarqawi's death standing as proof that the military depended as much on intelligence, surveillance, and reconnaissance as on strike.[27]

Addressing the specific tracking and killing of Zarqawi, Major General Bradley Heithold, commander of the air force ISR Agency, said that Predator flew twenty-four hours a day, seven days a week to pinpoint the terrorist's location. "It's a huge effort to find where they are," he said.[28] It was, in fact, 6,000 hours of Predator time, said Lieutenant General David Deptula, Heithold's boss and head of air force intelligence.[29] That's approximately three Predators operating 24/7 for about thirty total days. Of course it wasn't just Predator, though the air force found itself both promoting and defending its still-limited asset. And the case for drones wasn't difficult to make. An F-16 can loiter over a target for about an hour, burning about 1,000 gallons of jet fuel before needing refueling. An unmanned Predator can loiter for twenty-four hours, burning only 100 gallons of fuel. Keeping two F-16 fighters in the air that long would have required about 120 tanker trucks' worth of fuel and cost ten times as much as a drone.[30] And it wasn't just jets versus drones.

"We still rely too much on outdated industrial processes," says Lieutenant General John F. Kimmons, the head of army intelligence. "Our computers don't do enough work for us." Kimmons called for "intelligence access for all, including the Soldier," to make great quantities of information available faster, with computer-to-computer communications similar to that facilitated by Litening and with similar data link black boxes becoming the norm not just for special forces but for the nonspecial as well. "If it takes too long to create an assessment of a problem, then the technology is not relevant or applicable," Kimmons said.[31] It wasn't some Luddite statement: all of the Gilgameshes would have to be enlisted in the singular task.

And by the time Gilgamesh the black box emerged—to find and exterminate the designated targets with minimum human risk—it wasn't alone. The network had grown from megabits to gigabits and then even terabits of calculated righteousness, the Data Machine only one part human, if that. Gilgamesh was at the center, fighting in unison not just with its signals intelligence brethren but also drawing on a family of models—each focused on some different digit for support—Airhammer, Amberjack, Chrysalis, Growler, Hybrid, Kingfish, Nightglow, Temptress, Whami, Salem, Witchhunt, and Smite.

The killing of Zarqawi, McChrystal said, laid the foundation "for a machine that would become larger, better synchronized, and smarter in the years ahead."[32] For the task in Iraq, as well as in Afghanistan, Pakistan, Yemen, and elsewhere, demanded "radically faster and often very precise execution."[33]

From then on, everyone clamored to adopt *the model* of

finding, fixing, and finishing the target, what the air force had been striving to do since Desert Storm in trying to find Scuds and then Serbs and then *the Sheikh*, what the army wanted in becoming more like the air force in adopting precision and targeting, what the counter-IED empire was doing in acquiring its own drones and inventing "attack the network" to thwart later roadside bombs, and even what special operations forces and the CIA were learning to perfect in their perpetual pursuit of each individual high-value target to be ticked off an endless list. The Zarqawi mission would augur and be a miniature version of the killing of bin Laden that would take place seven years later. And it would set the stage for President Obama to hold back on action in Iraq almost a decade later; "boots on the ground" was no longer the standard for measuring American military capability, certainly not in the case of going after the ISIS fighters. But, as in Vietnam, finding, fixing, and finishing the target can also be magnificently immediate while taking on a kind of vacant quality separated from any larger human endeavor or achievement.

CHAPTER FIFTEEN

Beyond the Speed of War

He is fair in manhood, dignified in bearing,
graced with charm in his whole person.
He has a strength more mighty than yours,
unsleeping he is by day and by night.
TABLET I, *EPIC OF GILGAMESH*

I n an obscure office building tucked behind the Fair Oaks
Mall in Fairfax, Virginia, and at highly secure data centers in
a half dozen locations from Maryland to California, is the national
signatures pool, a massive electronic library that catalogs hundreds of thousands of signatures, the digital marks of our entire
world.[1] The signatures database, which has been meticulously
collected for decades, catalogs the distinguishing features of
everything, civilian and military, foreign and domestic, from
weapons to vehicles to fabrics to vegetation to individual people.

Everything gives off a spectral signature—a house, a car, a
knife—observable in countless regions of the electromagnetic
spectrum. As one official of this secretive world says, a signature
"is a distinctive basic characteristic or set of characteristics that
consistently re-occurs and uniquely identifies a piece of equipment, activity, individual, or event."[2] Because all material reflects,
absorbs, or emits photons as a consequence of its molecular

makeup, a high-resolution deconstruction of the intensity of these materials can form a rendering unique to any given material.[3]

The collection of signatures goes back to the days when the Soviet enemy was behind an iron curtain and the intelligence wizards needed to come up with innovative and even elliptical methods to acquire information. The earliest days of atomic fission spawned a special type of sleuthery, with aircraft and satellites sniffing out rare isotopic concentrations to discover the existence of nuclear tests and then even to characterize the makeup and capabilities of hidden nuclear weapons. These techniques of scientific detection and technical intelligence took on the name measurements and signature intelligence (or MASINT).[4] MASINT collection and analysis never had the allure of human intelligence, the wonder of imagery, or the capacious plenty of signals intelligence, even if it did provide the possibility of seeing into the beyond. Instead, it served as a kind of technical back end of the nuclear age, with every enemy weapon given added character by its radioactive return or other chemical signature; every target characterized not just by location and size but also by its physical composition. Finally, friendly weapons systems were made "signature dependent," that is, sent off to find and attack through progressions of sensing enemy signatures and making arcane calculations to precisely find, locate, attack, and assess—each act building on the last.

Detection augmented normal seeing and hearing: infrared detection of the plume of a missile, acoustic detection of the sound emitted by a submarine, electrooptical detection of laser light, materials sampling to detect the presence of chemical or biological agents. At the height of the Cold War, the emerging "INTs" that built into the whole of MASINT spawned highly qualified scientists with a wide array of specialties.

Scientists are needed because MASINT differs from "normal" intelligence in that with MASINT, what is seen is inferred from the physical characteristics—it is not just what something looks like to the naked eye. By way of explanation, photographs rely on the literal extraction of information by a human. MASINT deals with nonliteral exploitation.[5]

Any kind of sensor, as determined by its size, weight, and sophistication, measures reflective energy based upon spectral and spatial resolution, observation time, and frequency of observation, processing the resulting data to highlight different spectra against a static background.[6] Every sensor collects energy that bounces off an object. And in the electronic era, every sensor converts its returns into digits, a series of picture elements (or pixels), which are themselves just zeros and ones.[7]

Unless a target is visibly observed by the human eye, something has to translate what a nonliteral sensor detects into what we "see" when we think of seeing. When normal people think of radar, they imagine pulses of energy sent out and a simulation of a physical shape formed in the reflective returns: it's an airplane in the sky, a tank on the ground, etc. And that's indeed how it all started. What is physical and can be seen, even at long distances, is what is reflected. But fast-forward to the modern day: What if the object you are trying to "see" is tiny, or nonreflective, or moving? And what if you can't send out a beam of energy to pulse it because that would make you vulnerable to observation and attack yourself? There are a gazillion permutations and steps in the underlying physics, but that's basically how nonliteral detection emerged as a supplement to the visual and the physically reflective.

Now to see it: the reflected energy travels in wavelengths and must be received by a sensor that can translate those waves into something understandable to humans. What is visible to the human eye are three bands of electromagnetic energy almost in the middle of the electronic spectrum; red, green, and blue (known as RGB). An infrared sensor measures wavelengths adjacent to the visible bands in the spectrum.[8] A multispectral sensor can monitor reflected energy in ten spectral bands of visible and infrared light. Hyperspectral imagers, the most complex and with the broadest view, monitor spectral bands numbering up to 200 or more. This includes reflected energy in the ultraviolet (UV), visible, near-infrared (IR), and short-wave infrared (SWIR) portions of the electromagnetic spectrum, as well as the *emitted* energy in the mid-wave infrared (MWIR) and long-wave infrared (LWIR) portions of the infrared spectrum.[9]

Multispectral imaging (MSI) has been used in the civil world for decades to observe everything from general land cover to detailed species identification. In the 1960s, scientists confirmed that reflectance measurements by multispectral airborne and space sensors permitted the identification of the mineral makeup of rocks, soils, and vegetation. In weather forecasting, MSI is used to detect cloud droplets, ice particles, dust, ash, and smoke, each of which can then be associated with specific frequencies. MSI can also monitor wavelengths over broad areas to characterize terrain and man-made features, a technique in widespread use by the military in mapmaking.

Hyperspectral imaging (HSI), on the other hand, collects the energy of a wider section of the electromagnetic spectrum and from many narrower bands simultaneously, from infrared across the visible to ultraviolet. Because hyperspectral sensors can sample spectral signals reflected and emitted from the same area, a sensor can even separate atmospheric signals from ground signals, thus allowing the sensor to essentially "see" through clouds.[10] It wasn't until 1989 that the first hyperspectral imager was flown,[11] and today, it is the most complex form of MASINT.[12]

To fully understand the world of signature-derived intelligence, it is useful to think of the domain name system that orders the Internet. When a Web address (a URL) is typed into a browser or clicked on as a hyperlink, an international library of numeric Internet Protocol (IP) addresses is instantly searched, returning the Web server associated with each address. That way, the IP address—the site's signature, if you will—can be a public and easily remembered name translating the domain name. And given that the DNS system is its own network, if it is unable to translate a particular domain name, it asks another at a higher echelon, and so on, until the correct IP address is returned.

A hyperspectral signature can be thought of in the same way. Since every object reflects and absorbs light in different ways, the amount and type of radiation reflected directly relate to an object's surface chemical and physical characteristics, illumination factors, and atmospheric properties.[13] In intelligence terms, the ultimate goal in imaging is to produce a complete reflectance spectrum for each pixel, an achievement that can only come from hyperspectral imaging.[14]

Hyperspectral imaging then can simply be described as a type of remote sensing that uses powerful information contained in the full-spectrum signature of an object (that is, its total reflective makeup). Not surprisingly, the most important feature of hyperspectral imaging for military and intelligence purposes, in addition to its complexity, is that there are just a few highly expensive black boxes on a small population of highly classified platforms that are able to practically collect and translate into images.[15] HSI is a multistep process involving an enormous amount of imaging and computing, but in the end, say for instance in the case of IEDs, spectral signatures related to bombs and techniques to hide them are collected and validated against ground truth to populate data sets of objects of interest. What makes the data instantly available and militarily relevant is the database of spectral signatures that underlies the whole process.

While a multispectral sensor might indicate the presence of an object such as a vehicle, a hyperspectral sensor can also detect whether it's metal or plastic, what kind of metal it's made from, the color and type of paint it has, and the amount of moisture it contains. A multispectral image might differentiate between desert and farmland, separating features in the near-infrared region because the chlorophyll in the plants is reflected to a far greater extent than any other feature. A hyperspectral image of the same farmland can differentiate a barley crop from potatoes, detect stressed vegetation, and even determine soil composition.

The Pentagon first actively initiated research on a hyperspectral sensor that would be able to return near-real-time data in 1991, initially to fill a need experienced in Cold War Europe and later in Bosnia and Kosovo, which was to see what was hidden in shadows and under trees.[16] The Hycorder black box was flown in October 1994 and June 1995, the first of an unmanned hyperspectral generation that would begin to open the way for the fighting man to see in a completely new manner. The imaging radio-spectrometer was fitted on board a navy Pioneer drone that flew over the White Sands Missile Range in New Mexico and Yuma, Arizona. Reflective targets with known signatures were precisely placed on the ground, and the spectral information was downlinked to a visualization and analysis system that processed the continuously running video using the finest computer of the day, a Pentium Pro PC. Desert Radiance, as the experiments were called, proved the feasibility of detection of a tactical target by use of its unique spectral signature.[17] Desert Radiance was followed by Forest Radiance, Island Radiance, and Littoral Radiance, each planned collection operation a proving ground for the calibration of aerial sensors and processors and the building of a larger and larger signature library.

As part of the Hyperspectral MASINT Support to Military Operations (HYMSMO) umbrella program started in the late 1990s, different hyperspectral sensors were flown to explore tactical detection and classification of potential military targets. Hyperspectral imagers were placed on manned aircraft and in space,[18] each attempting to increase spatial resolution and signal-to-noise ratios to militarily useful levels. In each case, a series of runs were flown in which tanks and other military vehicles were precisely placed on a targeted terrain, or fabric and painted target panels were used to simulate camouflage. Ground truth measurements were also taken simultaneously, from towers and other airborne platforms, to compare the reflectance of the surface to the energy recorded by the imaging sensor. And in 1997, blind testing was introduced, that is, hyperspectral imaging used to find hidden objects. Overall detection success rates were nowhere near the level needed for combat.[19] And HSI continued to be conceived in Cold War terms, detecting the evidence of weapons of mass destruction manufacture or deployment through the presence of plumes or runoff; or in strictly conventional military terms, as countercamouflage—detecting objects that were intentionally hidden from sight.

The WARHORSE black box flew on board Predator a year before 9/11.[20] It's another acronym, of course, for Wide Area Reconnaissance Hyperspectral Overhead Real-Time Surveillance Experiment. It is a hyperspectral sensor that images from approximately 10,000 feet, with a collection process that entails[21] a massive amount of data, far beyond anything seen with Global Hawk imagery or synthetic aperture radars or even operational multispectral sensors.

Just one frame of a hyperspectral imager is on the scale of 20 gigabytes or more. Before WARHORSE, this huge amount of data was stored on digital tapes, which were then mailed to the appropriate organizations for processing, with intelligence returning days or weeks or even months after the image was taken.[22] With WARHORSE, the data were collected, calibrated, corrected, and presented so that when a spectral signature in the stored database harmonized with something being processed (or in other words, when the IP address of a sought-after website was matched), a camera on board Predator simultaneously took a still image (or "chip") of the same scene, the image itself being modified to create false color variations so that it was visible to the human eye. In this way, WARHORSE could provide tip-offs or cueing of other sensors. However, the hyperspectral data was still so complex that it needed to be processed elsewhere for further exploitation.

Enter the Signatures Support Program. A program that had always been dominated by strategic nuclear and "national" collection shifted to conventional and even unconventional war in the late 1990s. The decades-old collection of signatures started to look at dynamic phenomena, that is, the signatures of real-time events and activities immediately relevant to the fighting man and woman.[23] Hyperspectral imaging, if it could be made practical and cost effective, would allow a way to see through clouds and under trees, to detect what was underground or underwater, to find what the enemy was trying to hide, and even to rescue a friendly downed pilot hiding behind enemy lines (by detecting a previously applied reflective "tag").[24] But the only way that hyperspectral imaging could be turned into anything beyond a science project was to rely on onboard processing of the enormous amount of data generated to extract only the bits needed to identify prospective targets. WARHORSE was the first step.

When war in Afghanistan began in 2001, every form of intelligence collection in this remote and unknown land was employed, including experimental hyperspectral sensors. First to enlist in Afghanistan was NASA's satellite-based Hyperion sensor, which was used to assess pre- and postbomb damage by comparing before-and-after scenes of difficult places that had been bombed, such as tunnels and caves.[25] Hyperspectral imaging was also able to detect concentrations of carbon dioxide in cave-riddled areas and thereby possibly signal the presence of humans.[26] When the first sensors were applied for tactical detection, in Afghanistan and then in Iraq, they were also shown to be able to detect buried IEDs by detecting the presence of disturbed dirt or by using "change detection" techniques to go back and see anomalies of military significance. Common types of IEDs were also directly detected through signature matching, particularly as the IED library grew.[27]

Hyperspectral products were not quite in the hands of the war-fighter because of security classifications and scarcity, and a real challenge to overcome was bandwidth, given how much data was demanded and had to move through the networks. But the Pentagon, sufficiently optimistic about the prospect of real-time imaging, in 2002 approved the HyCAS or Hyperspectral Collection and Analysis System technology demonstration, a five-year program that would assess the feasibility of spectral data as a source of regular tactical intelligence, while also figuring out ways of incorporating HSI sensors into the day-to-day workings of the Data Machine.[28] As Sue Payton, the Pentagon's head of advanced systems, said upon unveiling HyCAS, the United States now had hyperspectral sensors on aircraft and even in space. HyCAS included sensors on Global Hawk, on Predator, and on manned navy P-3 aircraft.

In 2007, the US Geological Survey conducted HALO Falcon, a sweeping hyperspectral survey of Afghanistan that collected data from an altitude of 50,000 feet.[29] The public announcement was that the mission was designed to assess Afghanistan's natural resources, such as coal, water, and minerals, and that no less than President Karzai had requested the mission.[30] The true purpose of the mission was to build a complete snapshot signature of the country in order to form a baseline that intelligence collection of the future could rely upon. In other words, the purpose was to create a library of the entire country's broad signature.

Experimentation in the United States continued as collection accelerated in Afghanistan and Iraq. The signatures experts processing the volumes of data that were newly arriving purchased and fabricated the materials that made up such things as military vehicles, camouflage, fabrics, and paints, in order to conduct spectral characterization and add to the library. At black box laboratories, work accelerated not just on new means of collecting and processing hyperspectral data, but also on reducing signal-to-noise ratio (false alarm rates), on improving spectral and radiometric stability and image quality at high altitudes, and on improvements in computational capabilities and communication that would make it possible to overlay hyperspectral data with imagery or eavesdropping. MASINT was becoming the new everything, and new standards were created for all kinds of multi- and hyper-spectral collection.[31] Partly driven by war, partly driven by the promise—any promise—of support for the troops in the counter-IED battle, partly just reflecting the incredible pace of techno-logical change in the information field, and partly prompted by the unappeasable ambitions of the Data Machine, a new vibrancy pulsated through the signatures world. The main air force signatures data center in Tennessee filled to capacity, and "automated scene detection" was slowly developed to ease the processing burden.

It didn't take long, but it also didn't happen overnight. Within two years, the processing time of HSI collected data declined from eight hours to less than a minute.[32] Sensors became so small, and processing so advanced, that even ground-based hyperspectral sensors were introduced that could be used by reconnaissance troops. The troops could use the new set of eyes to identify very small targets at a distance of a mile or to detect spectral signatures associated with programmed patterns of anomaly detection. The ground prototypes incorporated automated software that allowed for data to be automatically processed "without a human in the loop."[33] You don't have to be a PhD optical scientist, one company official said. "You just push a button, algorithms are processed and you see the target on the screen."[34]

The military mission of finding people through spectral imaging did not start with terrorism or al Qaeda, but was part of a sacred task at the core of all organized and honorable fighting. Antiseptically labeled "personnel recovery," it is the very emotional task—the promise—not to ignore a fallen comrade on the battlefield and never to leave anyone behind. The unique capacity of hyperspectral images to detect, locate, and identify materials associated with a downed pilot or a captured soldier made long-range search and rescue an early articulation of mission need, a capability made all the more practical with the development of specially formulated material (called taggants) with exact spectral features, material so small that it could be worn or carried by a pilot and yet also detected in real time by a hyperspectral sensor.[35] As part of the HyCAS program in 2003, taggants that the human eye could not readily detect were tested and successfully identified in airborne surveillance.[36]

From this use of hyperspectral imaging and identifying taggants came the next step: "noncooperative identification." It too was initially applied to creating capabilities to identify and track friendly forces and to avoid friendly fire. The military called it combat identification[37] until the Iraq war in 2003 introduced ubiquitous blue-force tracking, which entailed automatic satellite collection of the locations of select vehicles by pulsing the special tags they mounted. The noncooperative part comes in the ability of systems to interrogate without human action or knowledge. Complex coalition operations, working behind enemy lines, demanded black box devices that enabled war-fighters to identify friendly, enemy, and neutral forces for "shoot/don't shoot" instant decisions.

As counter-IED and counterinsurgency doctrines took over in Afghanistan and Iraq, noncooperative identification was looked to as another intelligence application of hyperspectral imaging, both in signature development and to directly enhance both targeted killing and the counter-IED "attack the network" strategies. Another INT emerged, biometrics-enabled intelligence, which is defined as the intelligence information "associated with and or derived from biometrics data that matches a specific person or unknown identity to a place, activity, device, component, or weapon that supports terrorist/insurgent network and related pattern analysis; facilitates high-value individual targeting, reveals movement patterns, and confirms claimed identity."[38] As the head of the Pentagon's biometrics agency said: "The department has unique military requirements to collect biometrics from unknown individuals in all tactical environments, to transmit and store that collected data and to fuse intelligence, law enforcement, and administrative databases to provide the contextual data that will enable timely identification of unknown individuals on the battlefield."[39]

As the HyCAS experiments reached their conclusion in 2008 and as the next generation of hyperspectral sensors was preparing for deployment even as the Iraq war was coming to an end, the signature support specialists began putting more and more effort into what is called remote biometric feature extraction or soft biometrics. This is noncooperative identification to the extreme, the biometrics not of fingerprints but of gait, body markings, vein structure, heartbeat, and even odor—all things that might be detected and identified at a distance, all things detectable by hyperspectral means.[40]

In 2006, the first hyperspectral camera experiments were conducted to detect human skin spectra. The methods are only hinted at in secret documents: nonobtrusive biometrics, multimodal biometrics fusion, biometrics-at-a-distance, iris-at-a-distance, stand-off/remote facial recognition and matching, remote biometric feature extraction, spectral facial recognition, Cognitive Counter-IED Integrated Signature System.[41] As one biometrics briefing asked about processing intelligence from a terrorist attack site: How do you classify an anonymous individual? By something he's wearing? By something he's carrying? By who he is associated with? By where he's been?[42]

By "where he's been."

That puts the entire Data Machine, not just drones, at the service of the new assassins. To find individuals and aid in the targeting, whole new fields of intelligence exploitation emerged at about the same time. It was referred to as Advanced Geospatial Intelligence, the quantitative analysis of data combining types of sensors, but also all types of information technically derived from the processing, exploitation, and nonliteral analysis of the data.[43] One intelligence industry executive calls Advanced Geospatial Intelligence the "power of place."[44]

One could say in the end that it all goes back to killing the target, the mobile target, the fleeting target, the difficult target, approximating the capacity of the human brain while at the same time brushing aside all of the essential and crucial decisions in order to just push the button when the data lines up. Perfecting targeting to an individual level entails using all means necessary. And sometimes backtracking becomes the only way forward. It is a shift in the temporal promise—using where he's been to predict where he'll be—that requires connecting the dots at such hyper-speed and in so many dimensions as to replace the retrospective with the prospective, the estimative with the actually prophetic.

CHAPTER SIXTEEN

X-Men

The young men of Uruk he harries without warrant,
Gilgamesh lets no son go free to his father....
Tablet I, *Epic of Gilgamesh*

A shipment of plastic men's sandals stamped MADE IN CHINA and common in South Asia goes on sale in Peshawar. A wafer-thin tagging device no bigger than a business card has been embedded during manufacture, China being only a stamp. Some of the tags are passive and will register when they pass by special readers, with the location of the shoe transmitted to a central tracker. Others are active and will transmit a signal that can be picked up from tuned receivers, even in space. It's a long shot, but the shoes will do the talking: when they cross the border or visit certain locations, the unknown wearer will be identified as a person of interest.

A sensitive-site exploitation team moves to search suspect buildings, leaving behind tiny motion-activated surveillance cameras. A grid of clandestine unattended motion-detecting ground sensors—eyes on the ground—is also left behind, blanketing the neighborhood with visual, acoustic, and seismic informants.

From more than one kilometer away, a close-access target reconnaissance team watches a suspect compound. A high-value individual on the target list has been followed off and on for weeks by Predator, and now a cell phone call locates an associate. Utilizing their long-range sensors, the team gets a decent biometrics profile of two individuals—height, estimated weight, 2-D facial, hyperspectral signature—and transmits the files to the tactical operations center, where it is relayed to the Biometrics Fusion Center in West Virginia for second-phase analysis and confirmation of identity.

Predators flying high overhead establish pattern of life, identifying a truck never before connected with any known bomb-making network. Predator footage, together with archival satellite imagery, feeds into geolocating software that determines the truck's coordinates with one-foot accuracy. A small drone is then launched, a very special drone with a classified name. It silently lands near the truck, dispensing its micro morphing air-land vehicle, which skitters to the truck and then crawls underneath. Its camera, which normally faces forward during flight, flips up and gathers images of a bomb that has been placed on the truck's underbelly.[1]

"Going Hollywood," military people call it, when politicians and bureaucrats, inspired by movie and television special effects, propose some harebrained mission, their own imagination creating the illusion that anything is possible. Army General Henry "Hugh" Shelton, chairman of the Joint Chiefs of Staff during the late Clinton years and himself a lifelong special operator, says he was constantly baffled by the parade of counterterrorism schemes offered up from the safety of desks at 1600 Pennsylvania Avenue, often by people who were seemingly indifferent to the life-threatening circumstances pursued on behalf of what he and others in the Pentagon felt were low-priority objectives.[2] "You know," Clinton is said to have told Shelton after one frustrating meeting, "it would scare the shit out of al Qaeda if suddenly a bunch of black ninjas rappelled out of helicopters into the middle of their camp."[3]

The decision-makers, for their part, have never really understood the military's passive-aggressive resistance to their civilian masters, thinking it mere alpha male posturing—we don't do windows—or even risk aversion. What's the use of having a superb military if it goes unused? Madeleine Albright once asked.[4] Various military officers expressed their distaste, though, for the prospect of being turned into mere assassins. So it shouldn't have come as much of a surprise to the civilians when one officer, after being badgered as to why the military seemingly couldn't come up with *any* plan for counterterrorism short of war, answered: *"That's what we do, sir. If you want covert, there's the CIA."*[5]

Unable to resolve the bigger question of whether terrorism was a form of warfare, gross criminal action, or some shadow confrontation meant for intelligence operatives and not the military, the clashing decision-makers lurched forward. Something *had* to be done, and the dynamics of endless briefings and proposals in secret echo chambers was that data ultimately determined the doing: thus the final arbiter of approval for any Hollywood-like mission invariably came down to the quality of the intelligence information needed to maximize success and minimize danger. It was a battle between *Can you assure me that he's there?* versus *"You fuckers won't bust down the door unless we can tell you what color bin Laden's socks are!"*[6] Then 9/11 came and, well, apropos our story line, everyone gained a greater appreciation for improving the means to confirm that he's there *and* for the importance of knowing the color of his socks. A new class of warrior emerged, not quite military, not quite CIA, and certainly not lawmen. I call them the x-men.

During the Clinton administration, one replete with these very battles, a whole new field labeled "special reconnaissance capabilities" emerged. When operations were required in what are called denied areas or politically sensitive territories, when everything from terrain to reality got in the way of conventional solutions, when socks were uncertain, special reconnaissance kicked in.[7] Operations behind enemy lines, these missions always demanded the best of the best, but now just a little bit of Hollywood was adopted. Equipment played a larger and larger role, special reconnaissance being described as "employing military capabilities not normally found in conventional forces."[8] That meant black boxes.

Where mechanical eyes and ears fail, where the Data Machine stumbles, or where the cloud fills to bursting, something akin to the dark arts begins. These are the most secret of all secrets: the *how* of how the United States and its allies find and confirm individuals, *the* individual, when satellites and drones overhead or intercepted digits just aren't enough. The starting point of such a mission could be a tip-off from sensors demanding positive ID and greater precision, or it could be just a name leading to a link leading to a link, and on and on and on, as the global hunt proceeds to find the body. This is the cutting edge of what is both manned and unmanned. And not only that, but this is also where the seams are: these black ops—military operations—exist in a gap where things are neither strictly military nor strictly covert, nor in the realm of law enforcement. The lanes of the road separating those communities—soldiers, spies, cops—used to be clearly marked, and for good reason—military was military, civilian was civilian, war was war, and assassination was something that didn't happen within war's rules. Even if military special operations worked clandestinely, they weren't covert, that is, operations where the United States sought to hide its involvement (and those operations were once solely the domain of the CIA). And the CIA wasn't the military, that honor being reserved for those who operate in the open. Military special operators and CIA people might work together, and lawmen might even be brought into a hostage rescue or an individual takedown, but the basic distinction of each of their roles pretty much held up until 9/11. A conventional fighting force pursuing an unconventional foe just couldn't do things in the old ways in the hopes of stopping terror (or later even just stopping IED attacks) before it occurred. Or more precisely, while conventional military forces fought in the light, another war went on in the dark.

Dense government budget documents, obscure PowerPoint briefings, corporate job postings, and coded insider language hint of what lies on this other side. It is practically indecipherable terminology, a fragment of a tablet of a larger body that doesn't exist in the light. I've learned over the years to sniff out the signs of these secret programs: like rare birds, they lurk deep in jungles behind euphemisms: sensitive activities, technical applications, technical support, signature support, special technical operations (or STO), special communications enterprise, special capabilities. More recently, euphemisms include tagging; tracking and locating (or TTL), including hostile forces TTL and clandestine TTL; and close-access target reconnaissance. This is the territory literally of the x-men, the intelligence and operations staff offices called G2X or G3X (or N2X/3X in the navy and J2X/3X in joint organizations). These x-divisions have been newly established within directorates and secreted behind the STO door or inside the SAPF, the special access program facility, an organizational component attached to almost every battlefield organization.

Dispense for a moment with the jargon and the acronyms and just think special effects: an old house crackling in the night as humidity and temperature change. A wafting pheromone that imperceptibly stimulates on a meandering vapor that floats from neck to nose. We all know that dogs can hear what humans can't, that flies or bats can see or sense in amazing ways, that animals and insects and plants have evolved to armored and camouflaged perfection. The digital world is no different, with its hidden messages and sixth-sense attributes: metadata, impulse, emanation, heat signature. The digital creak from integrated circuits or even in a carbon-based life-form can signal a dramatic presence; a scent can mystically identify a particular person, even a particular feeling. Electronic devices, even when not powered on, emit unintentional electromagnetic energy, a passive electromagnetic signature that can be used to characterize and eventually to detect and identify. If multi- and hyperspectral sensing is the height of computing and physics in the world of imagery, this is alchemy, part science and part divination. Everything reveals if one can get close enough, close enough to get a special tag onto a car or into the heel of a shoe, close enough to get between a cell phone call and its nearest cell tower to intercept the call, close enough to actually listen to the voices or take a picture.

Tagging, tracking, and locating (or TTL) can be broadly defined as a set of unmanned technologies used to physically mark a target while providing a means of tracking it at the same time. This is the world of BORAT, Gecko, Perseus, Wolfhound, Orion, Talon Sabre, UniTrac, Shadow Wolf, Jabiru, Kestrel, Silent Partner, Pinpoint, Datong, and Q Electronics tracking systems; such a nice list of black boxes that hints of the diversity, effort, and secrecy in this multihundred-million-dollar program.[9] The tag is attached to whatever item is to be located or tracked. But the tags are not always exactly tags, and they can be either active devices (radio-emitting) or passive, that is, readable through interrogation. Passive tags can also be chemical (such as infrared fluorescent), dynamic optical, or biological in nature ("spy dust," biochromophores).[10] Passive tags are not unlike those now used to scan almost every postal shipment. The most complex tags can also be manufactured from phosphors, dyes, and nanomaterials, substances that show up when exposed to air or light or are viewed by special sensors or by multi- and hyperspectral imagers. Perhaps the most tantalizing advance of all is in the field of nanotechnology, where a class of nanomaterials is called quantum dots. By using quantum dot (QD) technology taggants, which can be aerosolized or dispensed in an inconspicuous powder, friendly and suspect individuals can be uniquely marked and covertly tracked. The tags are undetectable in the visible-light spectrum, and they dissolve, minimizing detection in the long term. A lightweight laser interrogator can simultaneously identify QD-tagged objects from as far away as two kilometers.

Since the early 1900s, bird-banding programs have been used to keep track of winter migrations and territory. Scientists started using radio transmitters to track wildlife in the 1950s, a tactic that went worldwide in the 1970s when the Argos satellite was launched, then achieved high resolution with GPS in the 1990s.[11] Aided by improved communications and vastly shrinking everything, tagging and tracking has become a common and fully networked scientific discipline.

Industry also started using tagging technologies to track shipping containers, cargo, and other important assets, a field generally called Automatic Identification Technology (AIT).[12] The military used GPS satellite technology and radio-frequency identification devices (RFIDs) to monitor convoy logistics, munitions, and hazardous materials.[13] By 2007, the US Army operated the largest active RFID system in the world, over 3,000 read-and-write sites and more than two million tags. Information stored on the tag and affixed to an object like a pallet is remotely detected by specialized readers whenever they are within range, the small battery on the tag allowing it to transmit a signal. No one needed to point a gizmo at the bar code, and active tracking became a normal way not just to monitor movements but also to receive health status reports of sensitive shipments.[14]

Of course, the same technologies migrated to the secret world. Long before 9/11, law enforcement agencies like the Drug Enforcement Administration and the FBI began using microprocessor-based vehicle tagging and tracking systems, and the DEA even created a black box that could process the propeller noise of a small plane and identify it by the specific signature it emitted, based upon minute variations in balance and torque. Scientists at the CIA developed elegant covert agent communications, listening devices, and clandestine surveillance (remember Afghan Eyes from the pre-9/11 bin Laden search). Night vision and forward-looking infrared, and the entire world of search and rescue beacons, advanced on the military front. When the new black commandos of the Joint Special Operations Command were given the "national" assignments of hostage rescue and weapons of mass destruction search and recovery, no expense was spared and any potential technology was considered. And just to illustrate the utter irrelevance of any one administration, if it isn't already obvious, the weapon's developers began working on long-range facial recognition (the Human ID program) before Bush II came along, at first under laboratory conditions, until Afghanistan and Iraq became the laboratory.[15] The capability to find a face, locate the eye, and focus for an iris capture was achieved at one meter, and then at three meters, and then went longer and longer until biometrics at a distance was a reality.[16]

At the end of 2004, with the bloom off the rose of victory in both Afghanistan and Iraq, the Defense Science Board assessed the state of TTL and special activities, the phrase that refers to all clandestine and quasicovert military action. A "Hostile Forces

TTL Capability Development Document" had been approved at the Pentagon, and the tags-on program of tracking suspected terrorists and their networks of facilitators—clandestine TTL—became "SOF-operator defined," that is, in direct support of the one-percenters already moving into clandestine battlefields like Pakistan and Yemen and East Africa.[17] Special Operations Command told Congress that year that it needed to address "surveillance inadequacies in the Department of Defense's ability to collect timely, actionable intelligence on difficult-to-access, high-value targets and on tagging, tracking, and locating (TTL) vehicles, aircraft, vessels, containers, and individuals."[18] The Defense Science Board didn't mince words as to its sense of urgency: the Pentagon's highest scientific advisors called for a new Manhattan Project to focus on programs that would find, identify, and track individuals. Having fully supported drones and all of the latest black boxes through hyperspectral experimentation, the board wrote: "We need close-in, terrestrial means. We believe an integrated, coherent approach is required in order to develop identification, tagging, tracking, and locating (ID/TTL) capabilities that will give U.S. military forces the same advantage finding targets in asymmetric warfare that it has in conventional warfare."[19] By February 2006, the SOCOM (Special Operations Command) commander General Bruce Brown designated TTL the highest-ranked capability need of his command.[20]

It would never quite become a Manhattan Project, but in five years, the special reconnaissance world moved more and more into TTL techniques as part of common operations, with pattern of life drone study from overhead, close-access target reconnaissance looking through the windows, and TTL and its supersecret methods going inside. Like the counter-IED empire that produced flocks of drones and other black box devices, a TTL patron emerged as well, this one with a budget of $450 million. Special reconnaissance capabilities rebranded itself Special Reconnaissance, Surveillance, and Exploitation (SRSE), and in August 2010, its portfolio of developing new tagging, tracking, and locating sensors expanded to encompass the biometrics and forensics systems, the edge-of-intelligence work, and much more akin to what straight-up policemen did.[21] State-of-the-art "technical surveillance collection" also moved forward under the x-men banner, a term once reserved exclusively for bugs planted behind light fixtures and vents, now including so-called technical audio and video systems used for reconnaissance and targeting, all, of course, made mobile and networked for remoting and reachback. At each step along the way, the black boxes of special reconnaissance needed to be more capable, be undetectable, have longer battery life, and be able to communicate outside normal networks. Man-carried devices also had to be smaller, smaller, and smaller, even to the point of being "wearable" by a soldier, the epitome being lightweight, low-power, body-worn cameras, eavesdropping and TTL command centers. The human was now the bug and the furthest forward probe of the unmanned Data Machine.[22] A specialized unattended land mesh network for high-data-rate, long-range persistent communications was created; TTL at the edge would demand robust wireless communications.[23]

In those same five years, more than 2,500 regular soldiers, sailors, airmen, and marines completed the close-access target reconnaissance course, and the less secret and more rudimentary tools of TTL proliferated to white special operators and intelligence units. As early as 2004, the Hostile Forces Integrated Targeting Sub-system (HITS) was up and running, melding geolocation computations of raw data with radio frequency modeling and error estimation, bringing black and less black together. Then came SpotterRF, the world's smallest surveillance radar, a low-power unit that weighs about four pounds and can fit into a backpack. In February 2007, TTL was being heralded as "influencing the battlefield by providing location and intent of hostile forces." Operatives could now contribute to persistent surveillance while collecting and extracting information "from denied areas." The community of x-men merged with the "interagency partners" of the CIA and FBI to synchronize capabilities that would perpetuate counterterrorism and killing operations even after the troops were gone.[24] The next month, John Young, the director of Defense Research and Engineering, testified that research was emphasizing "advanced nanotechnology, biology, and chemistry to give us a means to find, identify, and track individual human beings with minimal exposure of our forces and with an ability to project this capability into areas of limited access."[25]

Manned close-access target reconnaissance — combining the four main technical surveillance disciplines (electronics, video, audio, and TTL) — puts the x-men in the riskiest positions, whether in penetrating deep into the mountains of Pakistan on lone missions, or in going into the urban areas of Fallujah and Baghdad (or even into cities and places not yet on the public target lists). But the development of these technologies and the risk assumed can also obscure the true transformation here and the ultimate hallmark of the x-men: They cross the lines. They go where others can't. They are soldiers, policemen, and covert operators all rolled into one. No border holds them back, and similarly, no conventional law applies. They have ridden the wave of post-9/11 jingoism, of connect the dots, and they march forward on the simplest explanation of why those attacks came. They are armed with technologies that are only tangentially arms. They have access to nanotechnologies and MASINT and the sciences of biometrics and forensics, which previously were available only in the security and law enforcement domains. And they are the answer machines: what used to be complementary and a mere adjunct to traditional intelligence is now more often than not *the* second source, the positive ID or the right-down-to-his-socks conclusion that decision-makers and x-men use to pull the trigger, acting as both intelligence collectors and executioners. These nonsoldiers, nonlawmen are all-in-one: a manned unmanned.

In special corners of the Machine, special corners only hinted at in the killings of Zarqawi and bin Laden, the x-men incorporate an everything portfolio, "technical support systems, special communications, SIGINT, and satellites,"[26] building a self-contained world. The tools have accumulated, just as the data that the NSA collects worldwide accumulates, almost to the breaking point. And yet still there is a deficit—the urban hunt, the global hunt, the jungle hunt, the desert hunt, the island hunt, the cyberhunt—none will be successful without something more. And the deficit isn't the obvious falling behind in processing and making use of all the incoming information, though that problem haunts. When the Defense Science Board issued its report *Summer Study on the Transition to and from Hostilities* at the very time when wars in Afghanistan and Iraq were spawning more and more terrorism, it was mainly expressing a growing sense of a need to finish the two wars and just return to the hunt, the original mission. That in itself was the answer: extracting America from conventional war meant moving warfare even further into the shadows: close-access, terrestrial, as man-to-man as could be imagined to find and kill terrorists, manhunting perfected and, most of all, made invisible.

Somewhere along the way, the Data Machine and its growing capacity also facilitated (and maybe even demanded) the creation of two sets of rules—two sets that have profound consequences. One is open and the other is in the shadows, one subject to scrutiny by the news media and public opinion and even normal laws,

Gilgamesh taming a lion—on a relief taken from the palace of Sargon II in modern-day Khorsabad, Iraq. Pre-Judaism, the Sumerian king Gilgamesh became the subject of an epic poem, the first to struggle with questions of immortality and humanity. When the author discovered that Gilgamesh was also the name for a black box used on drones, the story—and the American military's ignorance of it—came to symbolize the continuing search, more than 5,000 years later, for security, a search undertaken in lands that the West fundamentally does not understand. (Photograph courtesy of Erich Lessing. "Statue of a hero taming a lion," Louvre, Département des Antiquités Orientales, Paris, France.)

Kandahar, early 2002: the author and his Afghan bodyguard at Objective Gecko, the bizarre compound of Mullah Omar, head of the Taliban, located in an off-limits and fortified notch outside the city. The compound was assaulted by special operations forces on October 19, 2001, and bombed and attacked by a Predator drone—the story of which grew into one of the first urban legends of this supposed new mode of perfect warfare. (William M. Arkin)

The star of every drone show, the now twenty-year-old Predator unmanned aerial vehicle (UAV), this one preparing for takeoff from Balad Air Base, northeast of Baghdad. In military jargon, Predator provides intelligence, surveillance, and reconnaissance, and in this MQ model, can strike with two laser-guided Hellfire missiles. Over the years, though, more and more black boxes have been attached to Predators (and other drones) to give them new ways of seeing and finding electronic signals. (USAF/Tech. Sgt. Sabrina Johnson)

The original Global Hawk drone, dwarfing two company employees from manufacturer Teledyne Ryan (later Northrop Grumman) in a hangar in San Diego before its rollout on February 20, 1997. Global Hawk flies at twice the altitude of Predator and Reaper and can loiter for more than twenty-four hours, imaging large geographic areas with a variety of black boxes. It can survey, in one day, an area equivalent to the state of Illinois (40,000 square nautical miles). A single Global Hawk—nicknamed Grumpy—was the unsung hero of the Iraq war, using its endurance and synthetic aperture radar to keep an eye on (and then target) Iraqi forces during the epic sandstorm of 2003. (David Gossett, courtesy of Teledyne Ryan Aeronautical)

All large drones are flown from remote ground control stations. Here is a training mock-up at Hancock Field Air National Guard Base in upstate New York, where air force, reserve, and National Guard men and women train as pilots and sensor operators of the Reaper drone. From New York, the 174th Fighter Wing also controls missions over the Middle East and Africa, a process called "reachback," where the majority of the activity supporting forward-deployed military forces takes place here in the United States. (USAF/Tech. Sgt. Ricky Best)

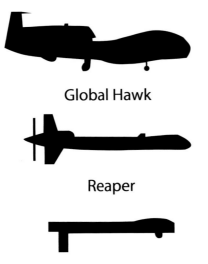

Global Hawk

Reaper

Predator

Raven

Silhouettes of the big three drones—the more than twenty-four-hour-flying Global Hawk, Reaper, and Predator—in comparison to the size of a human. Also shown is the most numerous drone, Raven, a handheld short-range "over the hill" spy plane assigned to army and marine corps troops. (William M. Arkin)

An army handheld Raven drone, here flown during a domestic exercise called Vigilant Guard in 2008. Thousands of Ravens have been issued to almost all service units down to the lowest echelon. The short-range systems are capable of looking over the next hill or scouting ahead on a highway, sending images back to a processing black box where they can be viewed by combat forces. (William M. Arkin)

The author's own version of Raven, an online-purchased Parrot drone. It has even shorter range, but has two cameras with higher definition. Here the author and his squadron pilot, Galen Richardson, prepare the first flight of their drone on Mount Desert Island in Maine. (William M. Arkin)

High-definition full-motion video imagery taken by a Special Operations Command Reaper drone. The sensor operator, or user on the ground, is able to zoom in to individual houses, automobiles, and even people; the cost being the amount of imagery collected and the pipelines of communications (called "bandwidth") needed to move and store all of that data. (Photograph obtained by the author from a confidential source.)

The bombed-out former home of Al Qaeda leader Mohammed Atef at Wazir Akbar Khan Street No. 13, as observed by the author in early 2002. Atef was killed in this strike, though it wasn't by a Predator drone — another urban legend of the early drone war. (William M. Arkin)

Part of the ubiquitous growth of the Data Machine is that every plat-form—not just dedicated drones and reconnaissance aircraft, but also nor-mal fighters and even transport planes—are equipped with pods and black boxes to collect ever more information. Here Major Olivia Elliott of the 40th Flight Test Squadron examines the Litening II advanced targeting pod mounted on her A-10 Thunderbolt II. (USAF/Samuel King Jr.)

The new (at the time) secretary of defense Robert M. Gates visits Creech Air Force Base in Nevada, on January 8, 2008, to see for himself whether the army's complaints of a lack of drone support are true. Here he is briefed by air force colonel Christopher Chambliss, commander of the 432nd Wing. Gates came away concluding that drone crew were second-class cit-izens and that the air force was not doing enough, ignoring the facts and missing the bigger problem of the gargantuan Data Machine. Five months later, Gates fired the air force chief of staff and civilian secretary, ostensi-bly over a nuclear scandal but really because someone had to be held accountable for losing in Afghanistan and Iraq. (USAF/Cherie A. Thurlby)

The lowest on the totem pole, the final warrior on the so-called edge of the network. Here a marine with Force Reconnaissance Platoon, 22nd Marine Expeditionary Unit (MEU), in Djibouti, East Africa, at the end of 2011. Using a ubiquitous black box called ROVER (and other black boxes), individuals at the edge of the network are able to simultaneously see what drones are seeing. (USMC/Cpl. Ricky J. Holt)

The killing machine got its start before 9/11 and before the Bush administration. A small group of Clinton counterterrorism hunters and bureaucrats began the long march to finding and killing Osama bin Laden and other terrorists threatening the United States. Here is annotated imagery from 2000 showing Tarnak Farms, east of Kandahar, where bin Laden was assumed to have a family home. It was the first target surveilled in the country in 2000. (Photograph obtained by the author from a confidential source.)

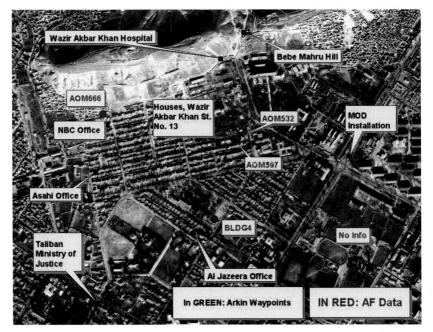

Data, as prepared by the author and the US Air Force lessons learned study team, on the night of November 13, 2001, when Al Qaeda leader Mohammed Atef was killed in a bombing attack and the Al Jazeera television office was also bombed. The killing of Atef was widely reported as having been carried out by a Predator drone but was clearly the result of bombing by a navy F/A-18 Hornet jet. (William M. Arkin)

More and more information and the increased computing capacities of the Data Machine led to the ability to create realistic simulations, allowing normal soldiers to then begin to master the capacities of the Data Machine. Here is a rendition of the Afghan village of Khairabad, as produced by the company MetaVR for the Pentagon—a meticulous simulation of a standard Muslim village that patrollers and targeters might face sometime in the future. (Image copyright © 2015 by MetaVR, Inc., Brookline, MA, USA. Used with permission.)

the other doing the dirty work that is often too difficult for humankind—the very articulation of what justifies unmanned systems in the first place—but also that which floats above written law. It isn't just bravado; there is literally a black-and-white special operations force, and there are even two sides of the CIA and the NSA and other institutions, one side that operates in accordance with laws and another that makes its own law in the name of security. And here is the ultimate irony: this other world of dead or alive, "bring me his head in a box," of waterboarding and secret prisons, of targeted killings, of indefinite detention, and even warrantless surveillance and bulk collection, tries to minimize harm in order to evade detection and intervention. It is not just political cynicism. Even the task of the x-men, or at least the driving factor in developing their black boxes and special reconnaissance capabilities—all of the enablers of fighting in the shadows—is articulated in official documents as having to be accomplished so that capabilities can be provided "without undue exposure of [friendly] personnel to risks."[27]

And manned versus unmanned? For all the talk of drones and black boxes, this hunt of the x-men is about as human as one could imagine. Yet when armed with so much information and so much power, it seems almost that remote and long-range begins to look pretty good in comparison. For to embody all of the attributes of military and civilian, soldier and policeman, surgeon and killer in one is essentially to create highly adaptive and essentially automated decision-making that leads to one answer, one continual answer. And it is hard not to condemn the enterprise as the toil of a rapacious Gilgamesh exercising the power of the gods.

Equipped with the greatest of real-world black boxes, sensors, communications, and weapons, with the Data Machine always at their beck and call, these x-men are the essence of imagined perfection — the x-men working at the edge also increase the level of confidence in the final decision. The willingness to make mortal sacrifices, the assumption of meticulous preparation, and the magic of the special ensure that commanders and decision-makers start from the assumption that the target is the most dangerous and deadly to friendly forces (and to the World), thereby justifying all of the effort, but also that once the penetration is made, they know enough detail to satisfy the unspoken color-of-the-socks test. As former air force chief scientist Dr. Mark Maybury says of the combination of persistence and closeness, they have "a very positive impact on increasing knowledge because you have a chance to loiter and see more things," bolstering with positive identification and reducing civilian casualties.[28]

That might just be the end of the story: assassins sent out, modern-day snipers creeping and hiding just a little bit closer to danger than less-skilled warriors, but even here, the Data Machine has changed everything and the warriors of special reconnaissance are valued more as collectors than killers, humans to be sure, but not valued for their cognitive abilities or language skills or even because they make a choice at the end whether to pull the trigger or not. No, here, "close" is the key word: the human operative is valued because getting close, putting an RFID device on a car, tagging an individual to follow him or her, slipping an intercept chip into a phone, fiddling with someone's computer or home router, picking up some cell phone call, or taking some picture; even just watching and listening to all of this activity peeping tom–style, is valued because it gains access and data that the central brain does not (yet) know. Yet the close-access operator is also merely a new platform and data processor for the unmanned.

The president and his advisors literally sit around the conference table at the White House Situation Room half a world away watching an operation unfold live because of these men. One might imagine that courageous political decisions are made in executing the mission that day, in taking whatever momentary risk there is in the willingness to take the heat for failure. But in approving the exccution — *We know the color of the socks! It's a go!* — the option of trial isn't even seriously considered; and in military terms, capture isn't even attempted. All these decisions are made a little easier because navy SEALs or other special operators are not quite soldiers. These are, after all, the elite of the elite, further obscuring all of the distinctions of military and civilian and just and unjust, a blurring that empowers other outlaw fighters to justify their own actions and their cause. From targeting Osama bin Laden down to designating the umpteenth al Qaeda number three to be killed, the machine facilitates a corrosive blight. The military mission from Desert Storm through this post-Iraq, post-Afghanistan period of no-name war is ever more obsessed with perfecting the process of finding and killing the target. Only the imprecision of using such a euphemism is left.

CHAPTER SEVENTEEN

Ring of Fiber

[...How can I keep silent?] How can I stay quiet?
[My friend, whom I loved, has turned] to clay,
my friend Enkidu, whom I loved, has [turned to clay,]
[Shall I not be like] him and also lie down,
[never] to rise again, through all eternity?
TABLET X, EPIC OF GILGAMESH

In early 2009, General David Petraeus signed Joint Urgent
Operational Need 336, a request to rapidly deploy the Battlefield Airborne Communications Node (BACN). BACN was a
system that filled an important gap in servicing soldiers operating
at the very edge.[1] It was a need specific to the mountains of
Afghanistan and Pakistan, where peaks and valleys inhibited normal communications and created a vaporous and unacceptable
nonnetworked space.[2] BACN would link to everyone who found
themselves out of range of the Data Machine. In addition, it
would be the military's own Internet to receive, bridge, and distribute data from satellite, radio, and data networks—a universal
relay and intelligence disseminator for standard and nonstandard
platforms alike.

To understand BACN, we have to take just a quick journey
back to the beginning, to the parts that make up the unmanned
machine. Every drone consists of four distinct elements: the plat-

form itself (whether aircraft, ground, or waterborne robot), the payload (what I call the black box—that is, the sensor or weapon), the control station (where the flight is directed from, whether it is on the ground or not), and the communications network that is required to control the platform and receive its product. External to the drone world are the processors (analysts or computers) who scrutinize the product and then the users (political decision-makers, commanders, special operatives, soldiers) who take action, the manned element of the unmanned system, who are hardly trivial.

If all of this were a tactical system—that is, simply serving one user—then the entire system could be relatively self-contained. But think of drones instead as a set of computing appliances (smartphones, tablets, laptops, desktops, etc.), all overlapping: some are indeed used offline and are personal, but the majority are connected to some network and then to the Data Machine, which demands constant data flowing through it like blood flowing through a living body. In the olden days, the military erected its own terrestrial and then space-based communications networks, and it still has many such networks today. But today, most military communications demand access to a network to operate. Where the networks are robust or can be supplemented by military-only systems, communicating is manageable. But where the network is lacking, or when the number of appliances connecting to it surpasses capacity, something different has to be created. And just as in the mid-2000s, when no operation would be undertaken without some drone flying overhead, now no one can be out of network range.

BACN, like other black box systems, really has no simple definition or description, no birth date, and no single identity. On October 24, 2003, its manufacturer, the defense giant Northrop Grumman, conducted a first set of communications between a

Global Hawk drone and a manned airborne command post in the skies above California.[3] Its system, called the Advanced Information Architecture, was a ROVER-like setup that allowed the drone to send imagery directly to the command aircraft but then also connected to everyone within range of the network to share what it was seeing. It facilitated not just faster and more personal provision of intelligence but also the automatic layering of different types of intelligence. By creating its own IP-based airborne network in the sky, BACN avoided the expensive and bandwidth-intensive transfer of imagery to processors far away. In short, BACN was a self-contained intelligence agency extending and speeding up the process, whatever it was.

Northrop got its first BACN contract in 2005, and it flew an experimental relay in February 2006. The black box was fitted onto a NASA-owned manned WB-57, the same plane used to map all of Afghanistan with hyperspectral precision. Flying over Southern California at 60,000 feet, BACN created a "forward-edge tactical server." Marines on the ground tapped into real-time imagery and intercepts from collectors near and far, pulling down common situational awareness displays and current intelligence, and gaining access to network-management services, including the ability to send e-mails and make cellular calls over a military-only network completely divorced from the commercial Internet.[4] In December 2008, a BACN-converted manned Bombardier business jet deployed to Afghanistan to serve as the quick-reaction capability to test the system operationally. Flying over a special operations or CIA mission otherwise taking place in a networked dead zone, the airplane could provide improvised connectivity for hours at a time. It could pull down what users at the edge needed directly from whatever was flying that possessed the right data. If a soldier queried the node and it did not have the requested data, its server would go out and poll other servers in the network to obtain it. BACN emerged not only to serve the soldiers at the edge and the new culture of constant contact but also because it was far cheaper and more flexible than leasing commercial communications. The Data Machine could now be extended anywhere, regardless of local capacity and without resort to commercial leases.

In June 2009, Northrop Grumman received a quarter of a billion dollars for three additional BACN Bombardiers, in addition to two unmanned Global Hawks, newly outfitted with BACN capabilities.[5] By November 2010, two Global Hawk BACNs, each with 300-mile-radius coverage when airborne, were providing about 50 percent of the requested 24/7 network support for the edge. The drones can stay up for days at a time. By the end of 2012, more than 3,000 missions had been flown.[6] In late 2011, a year after the last of 300,000-plus American soldiers and contractors left Iraq, the Pentagon formally christened the now multibillion-dollar converted Global Hawk the EQ-4.[7] No one noticed the party. In fact, in the eleven years of its existence from concept to deployment, from 2003 until this writing in late 2014, no mainstream media outlet has ever reported on the existence of this now-multibillion-dollar tool for waging war anywhere and anytime.

Perhaps one of the reasons for the media's silence is that this system—described by its manufacturer as platform agnostic, radio agnostic, and untethered—is virtually impossible to describe. Global Express is the closest one comes to a military nickname that sticks, but in a stroke of geographic indifference to mountainous Afghanistan, the overall system has been tagged Desert Express. So it is not a weapon, not a sensor, and though Global Hawk is host, it is not really a drone in the way most people think about drones. As simply as can be defined, it is an alternate and exclusive military Internet in the sky, essential to shore up a weak spot in the Data Machine but really a secret agent of the vision of precision without location, loitering transformed into perpetual war-making.

From the first night of Afghanistan bombing in October 2001, when everyone boggled over the all-seeing eye for the first time, decision-makers at the CIA, the Pentagon, the White House, and command centers near and far were glued to their own DNN, the drone news network, everyone fully in thrall. Video was of course the simplest explanation, spawning epithets of Predator porn and "CAOC crack,"[8] but what really appealed to a television-watching and image-obsessed generation was persistence. General Jumper called it the buzzword of the decade in 2003.[9] Arguably the most important strategy document that the Pentagon prepares, the *Quadrennial Defense Review*, in 2006 argued that future capabilities needed to favor "systems that have far greater range and persistence; larger and more flexible payloads for surveillance or strike; and the ability to penetrate and sustain operations in denied areas."[10] BACN is the facilitator of anywhere and always. Now all that was needed was all the time.

The concept of persistence requires yet another family of black box sensors. Predator is up there like no other, but it provided far less than the persistence that was envisioned, at least beyond extremely narrow individual targeting that came from looking through a soda straw. It's an "immediate-time kind of reporting," one air force officer said, "of viewing exactly what's going on with whatever your selected target is—whether that's a house, a building, a vehicle moving down the road, whatever that is—you are able to then sit there and watch that. It's very small. So I just see one vehicle or two or three vehicles at the most, but my field of view just isn't that big on the ground."[11] Not only did the Predator camera show a limited perspective, but the raw imagery from the moving platform proved not so easy to interpret, the thirty- to forty-five-degree angle constantly changing as the drone moved. Scientists went to work on better processing, developing software and hardware that would provide georeferences (what we today call metadata) and even a converted top-down perspective that matched a scene-based correlation, virtually all of the advances being borrowed from graphics processors used in gaming applications. The other two avenues of attack were increasing the breadth of the perspective (wide area) and providing higher resolution, thus allowing greater exploitation of each imaged scene by the naked eye.

Sonoma was the first experiment of widening the perspective, developed starting in 2003 by Lawrence Livermore National Laboratory in California. Using a novel mosaic-like sensor design that could view a wide area at high definition, the first prototype carried a 22-megapixel sensor (six times Predator's resolution), the second a 66-megapixel sensor, and the third a 176-megapixel sensor, each capable of imaging a larger and larger area in a single frame. Where that normal sensor on Predator can image the area of a city block, Sonoma 2 could cover an area the size of downtown Washington, DC, and Sonoma 3 could see the entire metropolitan area. Such wide-area high-definition imaging exposes every corner. In one of the initial Sonoma experiments, an IED scenario was created—Red Team Intent—that assumed that any car that slowed down to five miles per hour for more than 100 feet was suspicious. Software was written that highlighted the path of all vehicles matching this signature. Then, once the pattern was triggered, an analyst could rewind the video and discover where a suspicious vehicle came from. And Sonoma could track 8,000 simultaneous moving objects.

It was truly persistence, but in order for surveillance to be useful, an analyst must be able to see the data in real time. As the Livermore laboratory explained, "all data processing for one frame must be completed before the next frame is captured."

With data being collected at two frames per second, Sonoma's data exceeded the bandwidth of available communications by a factor of 100 to 10,000. So scientists applied various techniques, including data compression, to show only movement (or anomalies), while the georeferenced static background was only episodically transmitted to match what the sensor was seeing.[12]

Sonoma turned into the Mohawk Stare experiment for the army and then into Constant Hawk, and in 2006, a prototype Constant Hawk wide-area persistent surveillance (WAPS) system was quietly deployed in Iraq, owned and operated by contractors.[13] Constant Hawk could record and archive sensor data that allowed for playback of incidents, such as roadside IED bomb blasts, to be reviewed. Once an event occurred, the data was downloaded, and analysts attempted to backtrack from the incident, tracing bomb-makers and insurgents who might have deployed the IED and, if possible, following them backward even to their points of origin. They call this method of going backward to pick up clues forensic analysis. This was warfare completely turned on its head. Constant Hawk was an immediate hit. But the experimental black box was integrated on a manned airplane and not a drone, giving it limited time in the air. And it still produced enormous amounts of data, much more than could be moved very far, and in formats useful only for demonstration.[14]

Then, as these things go, the Los Alamos National Laboratory in New Mexico produced Angel Fire for the marines—smaller and more user friendly—and other wide-area and persistent programs came knocking.

More black boxes meant more data. And the introduction of wide-area surveillance, and particularly high definition,[15] exponentially increased the amount of information available. Collection outpaced the ability to move the information, store it, or process it.[16] As a result, the Pentagon admitted in 2009 that it was drowning in data. It was now looking at hundreds of terabytes of new data coming in every day. That's over 800 laptops with the typical 128-gigabyte solid state drive, and more than the total of all the terabytes collected by the Library of Congress Web teams.[17] "We're going to find ourselves in the not too distant future swimming in sensors and drowning in data," said Lieutenant General David Deptula, head of air force intelligence in January 2010. And within a couple of years, Reapers would be carrying their own wide-area black boxes that would be able to track up to twelve different targets simultaneously, delivering 84 million pixels twice a second. "The iteration after that will jump to 30 and there are plans to eventually reach 65. That's an increase from 39 possible video feeds [from Predators and Reapers] to more than 3,000 with a 50 cap force," Deptula said.[18] Data pipes were filled and storage was approaching saturation levels.[19]

The next month, BAE Systems announced successful flight tests of its ARGUS-IS, a 1.8-billion-pixel camera with a resolution of six inches that can see a minimum of sixty-five "Predator-like" video windows across more than 100 square kilometers.[20] And ARGUS would transmit at five times the frame rate of Constant Hawk, ten times a second.[21] One minute of high-definition video of a city block already demanded one gigabyte; an 800-megapixel image of a small city—that required to extract intelligence information at specific locations—demanded half of a terabyte per minute; ARGUS-IS, operating at 1,800 megapixels, could image a large city demanding half a petabyte per minute of bandwidth if all of the data was transmitted.[22]

BACN was pursued because everyone saw saturation coming, because there was a demand for far more bandwidth and data.

Part of the problem is the haystack itself. When 9/11 came, there were about 450 million Internet users and close to one billion mobile connections in use around the globe, sending about

10 billion electronic messages daily, 10 percent of them text messages. By 2014, the planet was closing in on two billion Internet users and the number of mobile connections was estimated at 7.5 trillion, with only about 5 percent of them in the United States. Internet use was no longer dominated by people sitting at computers; in most parts of the world, particularly in places like Afghanistan and Iraq, the vast majority of Internet access, including everything from communications to banking, was achieved using smartphones. By 2014, the number of electronic messages sent daily topped 500 billion. In the decade and a half after 9/11, the numbers multiplied many times over, with each development— digital DVDs replacing analog CDs, digital radio and television, high-definition, social media, and people living online—exerting greater and greater demands for bandwidth and presenting an infinite universe of data to be collected.

Everyone, including the custodians and residents of the Data Machine, is now drowning in information. The number of all kinds of manned and unmanned collection platforms tripled in the two years after 9/11 and continued to grow after the Iraq war started, increasing by over 200 percent from the end of the Bush administration until 2012.[23] Just in terms of combat flight hours, drones increased from a total of around 22,000 in 2001 to over 550,000 in 2011.[24] The demands for intelligence became so great, and the capacity to collect information proliferated so broadly, that by 2013, there were triple the number of platforms in Afghanistan than there had been at the height of operations in Iraq, despite the fact that the fighting force on the ground there was only one-fifth the number of troops that deployed to Iraq.[25]

Those in the know describe just the amount of visual data collected every day as five seasons' worth of every professional football game played—thousands upon thousands of hours. The data moves around the globe multiple times, first for "actionable" purposes, which means in support of an immediate high-value mission. The data then moves to be processed for second-phase and multi-INT exploitation. It then moves to contribute to geospatial products. It then moves to park itself somewhere on the network. And it then moves whenever someone pulses the system, secret Googles that go under names like Stone Ghost, Gemini, and Hercules. On a daily basis, the Data Machine produces hundreds of thousands of reports, many of which require no human intervention whatsoever.

All of this data is now constantly on and fully dynamic and moving from desktops to handheld ROVERs and ginormous video walls in fusion centers, occupying chat, e-mail, and Web services for processors and users all along the way. It is a wholesale change in culture that had quietly taken hold in the military and intelligence communities, one where information—data— came to dominate, where it was seen as key to soldier safety and discriminate warfare. Yet despite the coming end of the big wars in Iraq and Afghanistan, despite the directive to stop buying platforms, and despite the saturation that was affecting movement and storage, no one could seem to find a limit, a point when or where information ended. Years later, when Edward Snowden brought to light the NSA's infinite collection of signals, the broader impact (and appetite) of the Data Machine was lost in discussions of the legality and privacy of eavesdropping and cyberdata interception. The way the Data Machine itself works also wields enormous demands of its own, not just the post-9/11 cult of connect the dots and the kill chain perfected, but also the human factors—user friendliness and interactivity that make the machine workable for a generation of digital natives, seamless production values that now mask the drivel of most of the content.

CHAPTER EIGHTEEN

Command Post of the Future

For the king of Uruk-the-Town-Square,
the veil will be parted for the one who picks first;
for Gilgamesh, the king of Uruk-the-Town-Square,
the veil will be parted for the one who picks first.
TABLET II, *EPIC OF GILGAMESH*

Clustered along the Kabul-Gardez highway in the Char Asiab district and less than fifteen miles south of the city center of Kabul sits the hamlet of Khairabad, a dusty brown collection of wholly unexceptional houses and shops butting up against Afghan hills, the village itself at an altitude of 6,046 feet.

It was near Khairabad in 2005 that four Afghan policemen were killed just before nationwide elections were held. It wasn't the Taliban or al Qaeda; it was *Hizb-i-Islami*, literally meaning "Islamic Party," part political and part insurgent force, an organization that has opposed both the presence of American troops after 9/11 and the Karzai government. The organization is led by its founder, Gulbuddin Hekmatyar, a Sunni Pashtun and mujahideen whose résumé reads: Reagan-era freedom fighter, CIA proxy, prime minister, destroyer of Kabul, Taliban supporter, Taliban foe, al Qaeda affiliate, drug lord, officially designated terrorist, ally of everyone, ally of no one; the most-wanted everything, apparition who drifts across the border into Pakistan, even sometime resident of Iran. Since 9/11, Hekmatyar has added another honorific to his résumé—HVT, or high-value target—and he was the object of the third major CIA drone assassination attempt in May 2002.[1] *Hizb* insurgents were implicated in an attempt on the Afghan president's life in 2008. The group is also credited with one of the deadliest suicide bombings of 2013, one that killed fifteen, including two soldiers and four civilian contractors.[2] Long after US troops are gone, Hekmatyar (or one of his successors) will still be there.

Befitting its perch along the main transportation route to the Khyber Pass, Khairabad's status is also set in the giant brain of the Data Machine. It is enemy territory and an antigovernment stronghold, a place that the Afghan National Army might seek to pacify or just give up on, another pin on a global map. Home as it was to snipers and bomb-makers, for the United States, every transit through the village in the bad days represented the risk of an attack, if not by rifle or grenade launcher, then with a roadside IED. *Hizb* and other fighters would attack, blend into the homes and shops, alleyways and ditches, scurrying over rooftops and down tunnels, all with the exceptional guile of guerrillas defending their own turf.

To serve the Machine, Khairabad has also now been transformed into *Everybad*, a computer model created by a company that is itself virtual, its programmers working in a geographically distributed environment, with most civilian members of the team located in their home offices, modern-day Rosie the Riveters arming the men at the edge for duty in the war zone, here today and maybe gone from Afghanistan but somewhere else tomorrow.

With pinpoint accuracy, the United States has mapped every structure and compound in Khairabad, every mud hut, every wall, every path, and even every large rock. Like a set on a Hollywood studio lot (or yes, like a video game), Khairabad has been

rendered, actual mountains and complex terrain of varying eleva-
tions mixed in with everything man-made. MetaVR, Inc., the
company that built the Khairabad simulation for the US government, started with high-resolution commercial satellite imagery
and extensive ground photography, then supplemented those with
Internet research and actual intelligence from fights and incidents
to precisely model 520 structures that match the footprint of the
real village, its tree lines, its tunnel and cave entrances and networks, homes and courtyards, even furnished interiors. Even the
crops in the fields are simulated, plants digitally sculpted so that
their size and density change with the seasons. The effort is
meticulous, and the user experience behind the Khairabad simulation is meant to increase the odds for the United States and the
international side. But in the end, the geography is less important
than the operating skills. Mastering them is thought applicable to
any of thousands of Everybads in scores of places interchangeable
within dozens of training scenarios.

Simulators for high-speed pilot training have been around for
a long time, and flattened terrain is common in simulating urban
environments in both image generators and video games. Single-
player shooting games abound, and there are even sophisticated
immersion games used in large-scale simulations in controlled
environments. But it is only since the late 2000s that the density
and complexity of data needed to mimic a real world in 3-D have
been available for common use—no special computers and no
proprietary software are needed for a soldier to go to Khairabad.
The village and its surrounding mountainous terrain are optimized for conducting ground combat simulations: every potential
sniper nest, every observation point, every escape route, every
suspicious line of fire that can reach the road has been identified.
All of the wonders of a new generation of map products can be
developed for both operations and analysis. The randomness of

normal village life can be switched on, and entering the village, one can have an active roadside market, foot and vehicular traffic, villagers with pack animals, open doorways, translucent windows and blind stairways, character models and vehicles selected from Afghanistan-unique content libraries.

From another library, users can then select the insurgent stronghold scenario, the IED detection and defeat mission or the sniper attack, or they can practice in real time with air spotters and fighter aircraft flying overhead. Insurgents burying an explosive fitted with a cell phone detonator create simulated dust that is potentially visible from the air; patched roads are created to act as potential telltale signs; the buried demons are given distinct digital signatures to appear warmer to thermal sensors. They even are detectable on a molecular level through more sophisticated eyes in the sky. The simulation comes with the ability to visualize the same terrain in the form of magnified-view scopes and laser designators on board various aircraft; simulated data from simulated aircraft sensors speaking to simulated laptops through simulated networks. Drones are there, too, fully integrated into every scenario and yet also unexceptional in every way. As the second decade of US war in Afghanistan began, drones were hardly remarkable to the soldier in the field anymore. Small unmanned ground vehicles had also become ubiquitous, and MetaVR could boast of tunnels modeled with geometry and textures to allow simulated investigation by tiny robots, remotely controlled and monitored SUGVs, as the military calls them.[3]

Attack the network. Understand the enemy: with all of the superior technology and with all of the force of the Machine applied all the way to the edge, the upper hand doesn't go to the strong and good-looking—to some modern-day Gilgamesh and Enkidu armed to the teeth and itching to do battle. It goes to those who prepare. Preparation of the battlefield is the term du jour.

As is customary in the world of the military, preparation exists in accordance with new doctrine, and it is standardized and reduced to processes. Learn and follow the formal steps involved in Preparation of the Battlefield—Define the Battlespace Environment, Describe the Battlefield Effects, Evaluate the Threat, Determine Threat Courses of Action. It is a world of the same software, the same maps, the same symbology and terminology, the same in every unit, transposable anywhere, a training range that is not a shooting gallery yet is just as important, and even more so as troops and the real machines that we associate with war go home and the Data Machine remains behind. Preparation of the battlefield became so important that in 2004, the most elite special operations forces instituted rotations of the data as well as the soldiers. Units would collect onto portable hard drives the imagery and video and databases for their area of Iraq or Afghanistan, wiring a reachback loop so that the stateside unit could monitor, watch, study, and even sit in on video teleconferences of their replacements to keep up to date and focused.[4]

Absent a specific area of operations with real-world intelligence, PMESII is the universal base layer—political, military, economic, social information, infrastructure; data slotted into the proper fields of databases to deconstruct the operating environment into features, networks, and nodes turned ripe for further designation as "of interest" and finally as potential targets. On top of it all is layered the threat stream, the take from the satellites and aircraft and drones and aerostats and ground systems, from the human watchers and the remote collectors who reside in the digital domain. In a practical sense, this means reports and photographs and intercepts and alchemic discoveries all drifting through a stationary corner, a sort of pollen that adheres and a sediment that collects, ever so subtly revealing some Holmesian clue. Befitting an army that operates with the pretension that every soldier is a sensor and that throws around terms like "strategic corporal" to refer to the importance of interpersonal relations; and exemplifying an institution that can't help but systematize observation and relations into yet another acronym and process, the final layer is labeled the human terrain system.

When General Petraeus became Iraq commander, he pushed human terrain hard. Within weeks of the successful invasion of the country, the army admitted to itself that Iraq was an enigma to almost all American soldiers, and though there were a few Iraqi experts, they were almost exclusively assigned to the search for Saddam's WMDs.[5] With the preponderance of human activity in analysis and support of the Data Machine, just being in Iraq also didn't necessarily mean learning anything about the country. As one Predator pilot stationed at Balad Air Base wrote: "Miniature golf was about as close as a majority of the troops on base would ever get to the battlefield. Few would ever interact with the Iraqis; some would never even see an Iraqi." When Iraqi insurgents fired mortars onto the base, they nicknamed the base Mortaritaville. The odds against an individual getting hit by a mortar round were about the same as being struck by lightning somewhere inside the "Tornado Alley" of Oklahoma and Texas.[6] That also meant that those who did interact with the Iraqi population outside the fences were that much more likely to be injured or killed.

Hearts and minds, information operations, human factors, soft power, human terrain: it doesn't really matter what you call it. While the hunt was on and the insurgency was growing, and while counter-IED became the overwhelming mission, Petraeus's ivory tower goal to pacify the Iraqi population grew in competition with an overwhelming juggernaut. They tried: native speakers enlisted and contracted for their language skills were anointed cultural advisors. Anthropologists and social scientists were given jobs on the battlefield and sent out Margaret Mead–style to understand a people who had remained wholly foreign. Female engagement teams were formed to penetrate the fairer side; coalition and then even Afghan partners were brought into the secret spaces. The Pentagon created a cadre of AFPAK "hands," six-week wonders tutored in Dari and Pashto to man a burgeoning community of intelligence fusion centers. And back in Florida, CENTCOM activated an Afghanistan Pakistan Intelligence Center of Excellence. "Attack the network" also turned to human terrain. "Once coalition forces separate the enemy from the people, they bring in indigenous police forces to hold the security gains and then build trust and confidence as well as conduct reconstruction," wrote Brigadier General Anthony Tata, deputy director of the IED fight. "There is no greater ambassador for the American people than a war-fighter on the ground interfacing with the local population; and that works."[7]

It is such baseless pretension, this "working" at some village level because of a shared cup of tea, while at the same time the very power of the Machine and the attractiveness of the data are that the soldiers don't have to learn any actual human language. An extraordinary range of data appeared to turn the population into data: human terrain data and key leader engagements (KLEs) that collect data about tribes, family connections, language inflections. The connections and the sources of violence are all pooled into a single sociocultural knowledge base and then fed into the Combined Information Data Network Exchange (CIDNE, pronounced "Sidney"), a Middle East–wide events tracking system of the United States and NATO that seeks to record everything from commanders' local expenditures for school repairs to IED attacks. Thus, at every command brief, at every shift change, hourly, daily, weekly, and monthly, or on demand whenever, the significant activities (the SIGACTS) are gathered—the latest operational and enemy activity melded with human observations—

information that is constantly collected and entered into databases, where it is passed along to higher and subordinate headquarters.[8]

Everyday war is a challenge and "a roll of the dice," says one military intelligence officer of his typical experiences operating in Iraq. Getting from base to base and from camp to engagement areas, whether for resupply or combat, depended upon the arithmetic of the roll. In Iraq and Afghanistan, like a sophisticated game of Battleship or Minesweeper, intelligence at this level—at the village level—became almost exclusively focused on finding and neutralizing IEDs. "There are only so many avenues of approach into and out of the platoon and company patrol areas," says the officer. The trick was determining what routes and areas were dangerous; varying one's own routes so that patterns were less obvious, and then, most importantly, predicting which engagement area the enemy was going to use next so that forces could either attack it or avoid it.[9]

Though the systems available are an overwhelming word list of acronyms, there are basically two parts to the convention of getting through today and increasing the odds for tomorrow. In Everybad, wherever it is, pattern analysis has become the ubiquitous mission preparation: think all-news AM radio that provides traffic alerts "on the 8s" transformed into an automobile-mounted GPS that magically ingests slowdowns and accidents and then places it all in a life-and-death, no-mistakes instant navigator that not only provides warnings but also can assess the possibilities and dangers of alternate routes. Whether unit analysts input their SIGACTs into an older flattened Time/Event Plot Wheel or use the density plot software contained in the Distributed Common Ground System, the dual goal is not just to report bad traffic but to create a record of date, time, and location patterns to track enemy networks so as to know who is responsible for the jam and where they are at any given moment. And then the pseudoscience of this new type of warring is to predict where they will be next.

Any unit that ventures out into the unknown can create a mathematical grid: each kilometer of road is given a unique identifier within fixed named areas of interest, many of the latter as small as a two-block area; as many as 300 in a company area of operations may support about 180 infantrymen, masterminded by a handful of data gatherers. Every SIGACT is associated with a specific geographic point and instantly logged to show which grid is quiet, active, more active, and even more active; up to 10,000 SIGACTs at a time can be tracked at the unit level. With engagements plotted by location, and by hour and day of the week, and with percentages established by commanders for thresholds — say 15 percent to designate a high-risk area — windows of engagement with the highest probabilities of success are established: a location where indirect fire such as a mortar is known to have come from, a line of fire that snipers have consistently employed, IEDs that have been found and detonated. When it all comes together, when the data is collected and entered properly, when the servers serve and all the knowns are collected, the probability of success is increased: one NCO describes his experiences with convoy operations, remarking that the data in his area of operations showed that only about 5 percent of the roadside bombings occurred between the hours of 2400 and 0400, not only determining the optimum time to conduct movements but also providing immeasurable psychological reassurance to his soldiers.[10]

The SIGACTs system, which can precisely recount how many and precisely where suicide attacks or roadside bombings have occurred, is also overwhelmingly just a tactical reporting system. It is not intelligence per se, and though it is precise, it is little more than day-to-day reporting of data. Its corrosive influence at higher levels was seen in 2007 when Secretary Gates found "confusion over how the war was actually going," with wide divergences between Washington intelligence analysts and commanders on the scene, differences that some tried to repair by working together and sharpening the questions asked. By June 2008, Gates let loose in a videoconference: " 'I don't have a feel for how the fight is going!' he said. 'I don't think the president has a clear idea either....' "[11]

Contributing to the problem of assessment are the bifurcated objectives and missions. Military units on the ground only care about the SIGACTs, about force protection, about their immediate needs. Targeting and a bigger counterterrorism war, truly taken out of the hands of the conventional units, demand different data, and different decisions relating to Zarqawi-type high-value targets. Add to this that in intelligence terms, there has always been a tension between collection of information and the preservation of a capability to collect more. When something is found, when something is heard and geolocated, is it a clue to follow and understand, or is it a target to kill? In immediate self-defense, the answer is always "kill," but with so much data flowing, and the objective of the data itself not just to kill and not be killed but also to build, the pendulum seems to have swung almost completely over to the kill side.[12]

The initial battle against IEDs sought to reduce the number of soldier casualties and improve various direct methods of detecting the devices and jamming their detonation signals. And those efforts were largely successful, the math suggesting that the number of casualties declined even as the number of attacks escalated.[13] But the advantage still stayed with the stealthy attacker, and the area of interest wasn't limited to any set of finite Everybads. That is when going after the IED network itself—financiers, the makings of explosives, engineers, drivers—gained greater traction, even if in Iraq that meant Iran and in Afghanistan, that meant Pakistan. Then came Yemen, Saudi Arabia, Somalia, Syria,

Lebanon, Uganda, North Korea, China, Georgia, Uzbekistan, Turkmenistan, Russia, Everybad. It is no wonder that later on, every new country and every new insurgent or terrorist group present gigantic and constant political blind spots to the United States. Even in Iraq, knowledge would seemingly disappear in less than three years after the withdrawal of US forces, the activity given wholly over to a certain kind of intelligence that means data gatherers.

Wherever Everybad is, it is also about as far from the Pentagon as one can get, from the "analysis" done on high, from the intelligence centers and the war rooms with their eye-popping video walls, and from the conference rooms where decisions of life and death are so easily made (and not made). Here *the war* is wagered in the billions, the metrics of success as much a mix of data from the field, polling numbers, and atmospherics absorbed from the news media as they are based upon a captain's feel, or his commander's feel, or *his* commander's, and on and on. At the decision-making apogee, the words "national" and "strategic" aren't meant to be hierarchical or superior, but here, the pretensions hold, the big picture is located. Are we losing the war? That depends. Based upon the objectives laid down in the president's statement of *x-day*, based upon the political realities, based upon the resources applied, based upon comparison to yesterday or last year or ten years ago, based upon the absence of a 9/12, based upon consideration of all the limitations, the compromises, the fears?

Or based upon the reports from Everybads near and far, where all the high percentages can be made to appear so much bolder than all the lows. Stoplight charts—green, yellow, red—and other familiar templates turn complex data into an answer, an actual PowerPoint briefing that is meant to summarize all that is surveyed and the fortunes of battle at some moment in time. None of it is meant to deceive or mask when red is actually red, when things really are bad. But far away from Everybad, it is intrinsically a color-coded existence that analyzes and briefs never to get to red by combining all of the greens and the yellows with all of the other hues and their big-picture rationalizations to bring data and the politically desirable end color into alignment. Think a television commercial, necessary and instantly recognizable but also subliminal; sometimes just vacant space and the requisite stare, sometimes creative and heroic and noticed, sometimes an actual bathroom break. At the national level, there are simulations and there are choices made regarding which route to follow, but mostly the national SIGACTs are constructed to always be cautiously green or optimistically yellow, to always leave open the political options.

War has always had this divide, the view from the foxhole so different from that at the top. That is how even in the face of disastrous firefights and the perpetual Catch-22s of anytime and anywhere, a war can be going well to those higher up. And that is how, even when things are relatively quiet in the hooch, when thirty days without an accident tick by on the orderly room bulletin board and the PowerPoint briefing is solid green, things can also be for shit. When Afghanistan and Iraq descended into frontless battles, after the Taliban and Saddam were deposed, after al Qaeda was scattered, the battlefield literally became the domain of some infinite arithmetic. Terrorism remained the bigger threat, but the war became achingly local, and self-defense became seeking to get the enemy's unmanned robots *before* they maimed and killed.

An army marches on its stomach, and since the one thing that can't be stomached is too much hardship or friendly injury and death, protecting the force (known as force protection) became an industry in itself. Just as the IED and special operations worlds (and the CIA and the DEA) developed their own collection platforms, an entire other world of intelligence collectors emerged just to keep an eye on the bases and the soldiers—unmanned ground sensors, robots, closed-circuit television towers, tethered balloons. And all of this requires the unique parts and service personnel and engineers and the helium, another layer upon another layer, each with their own gizmos and hierarchies and economies behind them. More materiel to move from base to base, to network and serve, more unmanned helpers to relieve man of the risks, and yet to increase the risks intrinsically as Everybad feeds every new war. And all producing yet more data.

No matter how just the war, no matter the plan, no matter the weather, no matter how precise the weapons, even with all of the bandwidth and network pipelines open and all of the intelligence flowing all the way to the edge, the only things valued are the human qualities—eyes in the back of the head, sixth sense, intimacy, teamwork, leadership—and those are the very qualities that are also in smaller and smaller stock as these qualities shift to the technological realm. Short supply isn't affirmation of the constant political and Washington-based argument for more troops and more money, nor is it agreement with the poseurs who argue for a draft to make warfare more human, to spread around the costs and make it more painful for everyone with the hope that the cost of war-making will lessen its occurrence. More troops aren't "needed," particularly because technology extends the reach of everyone under arms, and computing replaces bodies, but more brains are needed, more brains to make sense of and use of everything that has now been accumulated but is so overlooked in a dialog that adheres to debates about troops and bodies and the multibillion-dollar industrial machines that are no longer at the center and yet take up so much space.

In creating the Khairabad simulation, no one means to dehumanize anyone. No one means to turn the Middle East or war merely into some video game. No one means to create some universal application that signals permanent war against the Muslim people. In fact, the desired outcome, more than anything else, is to minimize civilian exposure, whether friendly or enemy. If the hidden enemy can be more precisely identified and targeted, so the thinking goes, if the practices and protocols of superior identification can be imparted to the soldiers, then decision-making can be optimized and the dangers reduced.

Understand the village and its mood, find the anomalies, not just a hot spot or a patched roadway that wasn't there before, but also the qualities of people's stares, the level of nervousness of bystanders, the behavior of the young boys, the identities and presence and attitude of the key leaders. Learn the signs, smell the threats, pick up on the signals, know what to look for and what to see. Most important, do the right thing when you are the foreign organism introduced into this scenario: be smart, look smart, pass with honor, apply force as a last resort and only in proportion to the threat, be discriminating in whom you kill, leave in place the potential for a return to village life tomorrow. Protect yourself through training, prediction, and performance so that fewer civilians will die, so that fewer civilians will hate you, so that fewer civilians will side with the enemy, so that fewer will tolerate an insurgency or stateless violence in their midst, so that the pin on the map of this Everybad can change color and eventually be removed.

This is not just the laws of warfare or politics or the stuff of commendation medals; it is also intrinsic to orderly existence and self-preservation, a chain of understood behaviors — Gilgamesh the King is not just going to come in and take my bride on our wedding night — that goes back as far as there are stories of mankind and persists even in war, where even though the *enemy* does not honor any creed, the honorable fighters do. And they do so not just to live with themselves and maintain their humanity in the face of sanctioned killing, but also to forge a peace, to create the space for peace to return, for the sake of every good.

CHAPTER NINETEEN

Oh. Obama Was Elected.

[See] the tablet-box of cedar,
[release] its clasp of bronze!
[Lift] the lid of its secret,
[pick] up the tablet of lapis lazuli and read out
the travails of Gilgamesh, all that he went through.
TABLET I, *EPIC OF GILGAMESH*

On September 1, 2007, two IED bombers in northern Iraq were killed while lying in wait to detonate their roadside bomb the next time American soldiers passed by. The insurgents themselves were being watched by an army Hunter drone flying high overhead. Without any noise or warning, a weapon came out of the sky and killed the men. It was the first army weapon fired from one of its own drones in combat, organically able to spy and kill at the same time and all on its own.[1]

But the missile wasn't Hellfire, Predator's aptly named hunter-killer, nor was it one of the half dozen weapons configured for delivery by Reaper, just then newly flying over the skies of the Middle East.

It was Viper Strike. A glide weapon modified from a Cold War invention intended to attack massed armored formations with swarms of what were then called "brilliant" munitions, the recon-figured Viper Strike was reoriented as a single weapon for the

244

purpose of killing individuals. It weighs only a third of Predator's Hellfire, and has just 2.5 pounds of explosives, one-twentieth of even that small weapon's punch. Everything about Viper Strike is top-down. The weapon follows a trajectory that takes it directly over the target, setting itself up to make a steep dive nose-first, its warhead shaped and designed to explode with a focused downward-directed blast. With a laser seeker homing in on its quarry, it has a rated three-foot accuracy, meaning that friendly soldiers on the ground can be extremely close and still be safe in an attack.

Viper Strike was first tested in 2002 — another "quick reaction capability," of course — conceived for combat in places like Kabul or Baghdad where "urban canyons" exist. A small munition like Viper Strike reduces risk to nearby friendly soldiers, in addition to minimizing harm to civilian bystanders. Viper Strike is a kind of cop on the beat, turning loitering not just into observation of what goes on in the corners of Everybad but also into its own SWAT team, the full cycle completed in turning everyday soldiers into assassins for the Machine.[2]

GPS guidance and a data link were further added to Viper Strike's laser seeker in 2008, allowing the weapon to fly to the target vicinity, receive updates while in the air, and then use its laser seeker to home in on a designated spot.[3] Like a satellite-guided JDAM, the forty-pound missile could be launched indirectly and off-axis from as high as 31,000 feet, with operators and commanders on the ground and in helicopters watching its flight path through a constant video feed, another one of those truly brilliant inventions where the drone itself is the least important part. Unseen, unheard, and undetectable, Viper Strike offers a "covert capability." The weapon "does not have a plume; it is a stealthy glide weapon. You don't hear it coming," the program manager said.[4] As an army briefing expounds, Viper Strike is perfect for picking off one car in a motorcade or as a six-kilometer-range sniper for "Golden Shot" missions, which it describes as taking out a bad guy on a roof while leaving the roof intact or killing two guys hiding without any further skin off the hide.

When the 15th Military Intelligence Battalion fired Viper Strike from one of its twenty-year-old Hunters in September 2007, the earth moved for those once-lowly geeks, collectors, and analysts previously relegated to combat support.

As there is with all new weapons, there are shortcomings: Viper Strike has to be launched from a canister, and it doesn't operate in all weather conditions. And only about 1,200 Cold War BAT munitions could be converted into Viper Strikes, and even they have a limited shelf life. And, as with other spiral and ad hoc developments, the weapon, though approved by the army vice chief in 2002, came about without any validated military requirement. But with Secretary Gates on a tear criticizing the endless search for perfect weapons while soldiers were dying, the potential for Viper Strike to join the black box cavalcade unfolded. As early as 2004, the army was working on the Laser Homing Attack or Anti-Tank Missile (LAHAT), essentially an advanced follow-on to Hellfire at a third of the weight.[5] The air force followed the Viper Strike path and took another Cold War antitank weapon—called Skeet—and started a program of test-firing it from a drone.[6] The navy's weapons laboratory at China Lake developed Spike, the world's smallest guided missile. Weighing in at about 5.3 pounds and two feet in length, it could be fired from a small drone or from a shoulder launcher and travel two miles. And it could punch right through a window before exploding.[7] Another weapon under development was the Miniature Guided Bomb Unit (MGBU), weighing less than four pounds and designed for urban use from army Shadow and marine corps Blackjack/ Integrator drones.[8] Soon after, BAE Systems tested what it called the Advanced Precision Kill Weapon System (APKWS), doubling

Viper Strike accuracy to half a meter (or 1.5 feet) by adding a laser seeker to a 2.5-inch rocket.[9] The Lethal Miniature Aerial Munitions System (LMAMS) followed, a weapon that would fit on man-portable drones like Raven—"incapacitating effects using kinetic means," in other words, making it sound almost like no explosion was involved. Next came Griffin and then Pyros, both weapons with even more advanced targeting techniques that allowed for increased accuracy.

In early 2009, Spike was fired from a drone,[10] joining Viper Strike as another potential personal weapon and extending the possible number of armed drones into the hundreds. In March 2012, APKWS went to Afghanistan, initially qualified on marine corps helicopters, attack and utility, but slated for drones as well.[11] The air force acquired a LMAMS prototype that it called Anubis.[12] The army started shipping the tiny LMAMS, now called Switchblade, to Afghanistan in August 2012. It is described as the perfect hybrid of spying and killing—a "weapon designed for hand, tube, or aerial launch that could provide the warfighter with a rapid delivery to gather ISR information"—an expendable camera that goes beyond line of sight and gives the soldier the option to kill.[13] When LMAMS reaches the target, its camera allows an individual soldier to have not only "eyes on" the target but also the ability to wave the weapon off if the situation demands or if the soldier thinks the person being targeted is the wrong one. And then Switchblade can loiter for up to an hour in the air while the user searches for another person to kill.[14]

The marine corps also deployed Harvest Hawk in 2010, not a drone or a new weapon but another platform, this one a manned hybrid that could be called cousin to Global Hawk's BACN. Harvest Hawk is a black box that fits onto marine corps aerial refueling aircraft, giving them intelligence collection and weapons capabilities all in one. It is a black box of the future: one platform doing everything, as Harvest Hawk doesn't just collect—it also can carry Hellfire, Viper Strike, and Griffin.[15]

It would be stretching things beyond the innovation of each development to say that any of these weapons made much of a difference beyond the immediate ability to just kill the same target in a different way and with seemingly less immediate danger and harm to others. Given the efforts expended to reach this level of seeming perfection and equality, the numbers still don't support the image of a terrorist and insurgent class being eliminated.[16]

Granted, the war in Iraq had ended and the war in Afghanistan was winding down when Harvest Hawk first deployed, but the advances in spying and killing didn't and don't stand still. The production lines for drones stay open not because of the need to ship more to the fight but because they are becoming the standard equipment of every unit. If every army and marine corps division now needs its own complement of Predator-type drones, that is what determines the inventory. If every tactical unit is expected to go out with a Raven or a Puma, that is what establishes how many are required. If every base and every military police unit needs a certain number of drones or other unmanned surveillance gadgets in the form of balloons and towers and ground sensors for security and force protection, the number of bases in Afghanistan or Iraq or Djibouti or wherever determines how many. And none of this seemingly interferes with traditional missions or changes doctrine. Harvest Hawk is of value precisely because it is, as they say, "platform agnostic"—a black box and a weapon fitted to an airplane up there and flying anyhow. The plane is manned, but its unmanned spying and killing black box is more tied to the larger Machine than to the refuelers on board.

The military has been wholly transformed by these black boxes, and yet the army itself can't see what it has become. Any notion of centralized intelligence—of a temple of information leading a nation in an actual strategy—has disappeared. Information belongs to everyone, and the assassin's tool is increasingly at the beck and call of the decentralized god. The new aesthetic favored above all else is that no one puts their life at risk if a machine can do the job instead. And if soldiers have to work at the edge, they must be connected to the network and have personal ISR and weapons. Processing and bandwidth expand in service of the Data Machine, reachback continues because everyone serves the fighting man. No civilian leader or decision-maker—not Bush, Cheney, Rumsfeld, or Gates—seems to have the ability to see what has been created or question that the United States is stuck not just in this state of perpetual war but in a particular kind of war. No one has wrestled with the accumulated impact of the Data Machine and its erosion of distinction, nor the impact of its rampaging across cyberspace for five years or a decade and more. Unmanned, "attack the network," geolocation, reachback, a network for all, smaller and smaller weapons—each represents a huge but little-understood "advance" that stymies an understanding even of what is new and old, what is military and what is not. Harvest Hawk isn't married to just any airplane: it is married to a KC-130J tanker, a version of the venerable four-engine propeller C-130 transport, which is itself one of the oldest airplanes in the US inventory, surpassing fifty years of continuous production and upgrade, now souped up with black boxes to make it nothing like its ancestors. We can no longer measure combat capability merely in numbers of troops or platforms and ignore the black boxes and networks. But the arithmetic of the enemy also confounds, seemingly demanding hundreds of billions of dollars' worth of effort to merely keep a few thousand at bay.

Somewhere in the middle of all of this, a new president arrived in Washington. Everyone wants to believe that the Obama team decided to pursue some new tack against al Qaeda. [17] Critics from the left and right, even insiders, speak of "Obama's drone war" almost in an attempt to personalize this wholly automated and detached effort driven by the Data Machine.[18] Obama is labeled "assassin in chief," making personal life-and-death calls from the White House, micromanaging the military and intelligence community in a style reminiscent of Lyndon Baines Johnson. Dick Cheney can both express his affection for drones *and* criticize the Obama administration for being so weak that it has given up on trying to capture and interrogate the bad guys and instead just kills them.

It is true that drone activity over Pakistan accelerated in the year that overlapped the Bush-to-Obama transition, but in a historical sweep, it is the continuation of a policy predicated on a capability.[19] On January 30, 2009, the new administration asked the military's Joint Chiefs of Staff to cut the defense budget submission for Fiscal Year 2010 by more than 10 percent. Two months later, General Atomics delivered its 200th Predator to the air force.[20] Reaper, its eventual replacement, was moving steadily forward in production, deployed with Gilgamesh and Airhandler black boxes, and armed with its own wide-area sensor, called Gorgon Stare. Wide area widened even further with Constant Hawk, MAAS, Kestrel, and WAPS (the Wide Area Persistent Surveillance system), all coming off production lines in the new administration.

While Obama and his advisors debated Afghanistan surges and withdrawals, General Petraeus asked for more hyperspectral imagery, prompting Secretary Gates's ISR Task Force to search for an instrument "that was not a science project" and could be delivered quickly. The Advanced Responsive Tactically Effective Military Imaging Spectrometer (ARTEMIS) black box was launched into orbit barely four months after Obama was elected, collecting 480 different channels of data for each pixel in its view.[21] But the capability was so secret and so obscure that six months later, when ACES HY was approved, it was called the first.[22] Airborne Cueing and Exploitation System-Hyperspectral would fly on Predator in 2012, the thoroughbred successor to WARHORSE,[23] a 100-pound marvel that could be integrated and enable the drone to also carry its standard electrooptical/infrared ball.[24] Satellite-borne, unmanned, and even manned hyperspectral would join the Obama team: U-2s incorporated SPIRITT in 2010, the Spectral Infrared Remote Imaging Transition Testbed, optimized for its high-altitude mission.[25] Not one is an Obama initiative, not one is anything more than more.

Each ongoing emergency project, each quick-reaction capability, each experiment carried the most promising technology or black box forward. If there weren't enough drones and black boxes already in the fight, there was also each new discipline, like hyperspectral, that came on board. And then there were also "special communications" black boxes to support unmanned ground sensors and the x-men, some of the devices so secret-agent that they slip as much into the category of black bag as black box. In 2009, one company even touted an inflatable, airline-checkable, 2.4-meter satellite antenna system that would allow a secret agent to set up a remote high-bandwidth communications hub, perfect for infiltrating into a Pakistan or a Yemen or beyond.[26] As one set of top secret briefing slides says, the goal is "holistic integrated solutions," the ability to differentiate between terrorist and "indigenous activities" with the goal of "providing timely, actionable intelligence enabling disruption of terrorist kill chains."[27] The Data Machine drives an uninterrupted and never-ending search for novel techniques to detect and locate the signatures of terrorist activities, right down to their socks. Everybad is now reachable, and though we may debate "defense" as a set of choices of buying this or that industrial monster or pivoting to Asia, the reach to Everybad is political party and president agnostic.

In Obama's first year, Predator and Reaper inventories peaked at 228—174 Predators and 54 Reapers.[28] Two years later, at the height of all operations overseas, Predator-type drones had increased their daily schedules from three combat air patrols (orbits) to seventy-five-plus "caps" daily. And it wasn't just Predator and Reaper—there were Global Hawk and all the other drones and dozens of different types of manned aircraft. After 9/11, the United States accumulated hundreds of different types of wide-area and hyperspectral sensors on thousands of platforms capable of creating countless images daily. And try to fathom this: the next generation of wide-area motion imagery sensors will be capable of collecting 2.2 petabytes of data *per day*, bringing 450 percent more data into the network than all of Facebook adds on a typical day.[29] And the generation after that, "broad area" imaging, what is called persistent surveillance and is already happening, will demand twice that.[30]

In Pakistan, after the assassination of Benazir Bhutto, President Bush expanded the target list beyond al Qaeda to the Taliban and other "nexus" targets and increased the tempo of attacks; by the end of 2008 there had been forty-six drone strikes over the border.[31] Initially, Pakistani intelligence was consulted, but when US intelligence showed President Bush evidence that the targets might be receiving warnings, the United States started only to inform Pakistani officials concurrently. Bush also approved the employment of a more "attack the network" approach, bombing infrastructure and then tracking "squirters"—those who got away—to the next hideout.[32] X-men operating as part of Joint Expeditionary SIGINT Tactical Reconnaissance (JESTR) teams would infiltrate and get as close to potential targets with their

Swiss Army knife black box collection conducting "Charlie Ops" under the COHESIVE OVATION program. The operations were so successful that twenty additional ones were mounted between July and Obama's election. When Obama took over the program, drones were flying out of Pakistan and there were extensive plans to expand the area of permitted strikes and increase operations on the ground in Pakistan.[33] Deputy National Security Advisor Thomas Donilon told Bob Woodward that though Obama had campaigned against Bush's ideas and approaches, he underestimated the extent to which he had inherited George W. Bush's presidency—"the apparatus, personnel and mind-set of war making."[34]

In other words, Obama didn't accelerate anything. He just assumed "command" of greater capabilities to hit targets. That means also that the pretense of fewer troops can be sold as de-escalation of conflict or even success. The impression can be left behind that the American president himself sits at the joystick and the rest of the country has nothing to do with it. But that in itself is the triumph of the Machine. The unlaborers and the system are invisible, and so the Machine becomes platform agnostic—political platform agnostic as well.

When President Obama appeared before the cadets at West Point on graduation day 2014, his promise was a withdrawal from Afghanistan by a certain date, just as he had done in Iraq. The administration said that as the United States wound down its war in Afghanistan, it would keep a force of just 9,800 US service members in 2015. But "America's combat mission will be over," Obama said. And the United States would "have to develop a strategy that matches" the diffuse terrorism threat—"one that expands our reach without sending forces that stretch our military too thin, or stir up local resentments."[35]

Commentary on the president's speech dissected every nuance

about the American future, but black boxes are what makes that withdrawal possible, by allowing for a network that is less dependent on a human ground presence at the point of fighting. And because of the network, nearly ten thousand troops on the ground equals some hundreds of thousands of yesteryear. The nature of the Data Machine, moreover, including all of its mystifying classifications of military, civilian, and contractor; of overt, covert, clandestine, invisible, and just special, obscures what is the true commitment and activity on the ground and presents the illusion of demobilization and pulling back, when in fact that is not the reality. Find a president or a political decision in the continuity from Desert Storm to the mid-1990s to 9/11 and beyond: Clinton inherited Bush; Bush inherited Clinton; Obama, Bush. Our foreign policy itself is unmanned.

CHAPTER TWENTY

Pattern of Life

The axe at my side, in which my arm trusted,
the dirk at my belt, the shield at my face,
my festive garment, my girdle of delight...
TABLET VIII, *EPIC OF GILGAMESH*

I told my publisher that if I bought my own drone, I could tell the story, understand the allure, and perhaps even convey the complexity of the Machine.

My first stop was eBay, especially after I read that a Philippine man had pled guilty to trying to auction parts from a military reconnaissance drone on the website.[1] A search for "drone" yielded over 5,000 active listings as of mid-2013, including everything from women's clothing to action figures. The top listing, though, was a Parrot 2.0 App-Controlled Quadricopter, $293.95 or best offer—which I dismissed as a toy—followed by a $679 DJI Phantom. And then there was an Oktokopter DJI Wookong for $6,400. The cost was ten times as much as the Phantom but came with the caveat: "Please note that this equipment is not a toy."

Before your own eyes glaze over, let me say that I wasn't even sure if the Wookong had a camera, and I was hearing the voice of some fast-talking car salesman in my head: four on the floor, carburetor this, muffler that, souped up; the salesman in my head was lovingly stroking *this baby*. I've never really cared much about cars and don't have a pilot's license, and I'll admit that it was all pretty much Greek to me. So I plunked down my $300 and ordered the Parrot to start.

What a fabulous toy!

Without its Styrofoam bumpers—aka "the indoor hull"—protecting the four propellers, it looks like a big bug. Though it's not bigger than a laptop—a really small laptop—it has a forward-looking high-definition video camera *and* a non-high-definition video camera underneath. The attraction for a neophyte like me is that you can download the app and operate it with your iPhone or iPad. Charge the battery and it's ready to go.

In my living room, admiring my new Parrot, I joined the AR.Drone Academy online to track my flights and to find other Parrot users. I read the (surprisingly short) operator's manual (clearly, nobody reads anymore). I watched a variety of arty and instructional videos online that made it look really easy. And I decided on an inaugural indoor flight with the protective bumpers on. It looks pretty fragile, I thought. I'll just hover around the room, check out the controls, and see how the camera works.

My heart pumping, I hooked up the battery, tested the propellers as instructed, plugged in a USB thumb drive to store the recorded video, connected my iPhone via the drone's own wireless receiver, set the software for indoor flight, and put everything on the lowest possible speed and altitude settings. My Parrot took off and hovered; think tiny helicopter, the four propellers whirling in unison to provide lift and control direction. With thumbs on the two dots that simulate joysticks on the iPhone touch screen, I made the slightest movement and the Parrot darted away, almost twinkling at me like some Pixar character, animated and alive, as I later surmised, because it clearly had a mind of its own. Less than ten seconds into my first flight, I unceremoniously crashed into the window.

The second attempt was no better—I hit the chimney of the wood stove.

By now I was laughing and so was my wife, who was recording my endeavor. But it was very frustrating, and I told myself I'd get the feel for it.

The first flight outdoors didn't go much better. I was worried about the wind—*this baby* only weighs fourteen ounces, less than a small box of pasta. I set the maximum altitude at three meters just to be safe. The barn, two trees, the house, the driveway: before the battery ran down, I'd crashed into them all. I just couldn't get the hang of the controls and couldn't for the life of me figure out how to get the drone to come back once it darted away. Specks of dirt in the gears that turn the propellers were my first maintenance job, but other than that, my Parrot actually proved pretty hardy. And not only that, the video produced was beautiful and unintentionally hilarious.

The Parrot came to my brother-in-law's wedding in Maine the next week, where I hoped to find a big enough flat space far away from any water to practice. It's very pesky, I told my stepson, Galen, age eighteen, who badgered me to break it out so we could fly. I'm not going to let you fly it until you watch the instructional videos, I told him. Two minutes later, he was back and ready.

It wasn't like I was teaching him to shoot a gun, but as owner and commander of my own embryonic squadron, I became ridiculously officious, carefully showing him how to connect it to the phone, how to do the self-test, instructing him to land it on my command, fretting about the wind and using words like "aloft" like I knew what I was talking about. It was just breezy. Then I let him take the controls. The wind from the ocean definitely buffeted and pushed the Parrot around, but Galen almost effortlessly got the hang of it right away, flying it up to the top of the house we were staying in, crossing the road between two electrical wires — "Watch out!" I yelled — darting the Parrot back to the front lawn, flying it this way and that, and then landing it. He loved it, I loved it; I was humbled. When I debriefed Galen after this and other missions, he said the trick for him was calibrating himself to the rhythm of the drone, what actual pilots call "feeling" the plane, though unlike the pilot of a manned airplane, a drone pilot doesn't actually feel the inertia and acceleration caused by a gust of wind.[2]

They call Galen's generation "digital natives." His instinctive aptitude truly says something about our society, and about the expansive world of the Data Machine that drones represent. Whatever happens in the wiring of a brain that allows a young child to so easily pick up a second language, the digital natives have acquired a new way of absorbing and interacting with our wholly digital world.

Still, it drives me to distraction when I watch how Galen or any of his contemporaries operate; they have multiple things going on at once, on the laptop, on the iPod, on the phone, on the TV. They'll have several chat sessions open on a variety of appliances, texting on the phone as well; they'll be watching a show and watching a ball game; they'll have a YouTube video running; they're listening to music; and sometimes they'll have a couple of homework assignments going, sometimes involving real books but more often than not digital pablum and hands-on projects. The relentless demand to command all this data is only compounded by the speed at which music and videos are transmitted globally, not just to the home Wi-Fi network but also through the satellites and cables and fiberoptic networks needed to move it all. Galen and his generation didn't conform to the machinery of our day; the Machine conforms to their expectations.

And that wedding in Maine? It was truly beautiful. After a

week of dreary rain and fog, the sun shone brightly at the top of Cadillac Mountain at the moment of the ceremony, and everything went off without a hitch. Everyone, even my father-in-law, age eighty-four, had their own digital camera and was snapping away, the big old cameras with the bulging lenses dusted off, powered up, and brought out for the occasion as well, but more often than not it was just the ubiquitous smartphones, especially among the digital natives. There we were, recording everything, an NSA-like acquisition, each wedding participant—myself included—more comprehensive and efficient collectors than the old-fashioned single authoritarian wedding photographer of old, gigabytes upon gigabytes so easily collected, a massive and dispersed digital record. Those little LED screens also served, though, as a kind of obstacle, removing the participants by one step from the event. And then I saw our own family intelligence agency choking on data as everyone compiled their mass of photos and signals, the designated nerd spending hours on end putting them all on a DVD, the task of sorting through them all left to the bride and groom back at the family CIA.

As wedding turned to reception and after-party, the picture taking hardly slowed. This is my Parrot's way as well. In flight, one doesn't turn the video camera on and off—the data collection is automatic and constantly streaming like a data waterfall. Video continues, only constrained by onboard power, which constrains the flight. Movement of the video from camera to thumb drive to iPhone to computer (or the Web) is slow and intrusive to the operation of the drone itself. Storage being so cheap these days, I was able to use a 128-gigabyte USB thumb drive, its capacity exceeding the amount of video that could be shot by the drone in a single mission, given the thirty-minute life of the battery. And with my mighty thumb drive, I'd never run out of storage space. So my squadron's second requisition, after my ginormous data center, was going to have to be a second battery, and maybe a third, for sustained operations.

More drone flights followed; my friend Peter came to visit for the weekend, and to my surprise, he was fascinated with the drone. A decade older than me and a journalist and writer of the old school, which means two-finger typing and a deep love of musty archives—the real stuff—he'd never seemed to me to be much of a technology guy. So we went down to the school, where the size of the playing fields was sure to keep us out of trouble. I was getting better at flying, practice and help from Galen paying off. But on flight segment three, the Parrot sailed away and just kept going. It took us a good half hour to find it in the trees, ominously close to Barnard Brook.

My brother, an ultralight enthusiast who built and flies his own airplane in Virginia, asked if my new drone carried a weapon, certainly an apropos quip given how one type seems to rule over all others. I guess I could use it kamikaze style, I responded, but the weapon would have to be awfully light. He suggested attaching something called a servo and dropping a paintball, but I was thinking more of the aptly named and supersecret Pyros or some other variety of the forearm-sized weapons increasingly becoming the side arms of the uniformed digital natives.

Another training session with Galen, as he finally taught me how to just nudge the controls and get the Parrot to come back and we flew the drone higher and higher, over the roof of the house, peering now into all of South Pomfret village: the general store, the library, homes, and beyond. Winds at 120 feet required our smart little craft to constantly compensate to right itself, and the video, though beautiful at that altitude, was so jerky that watching it was enough to cause vertigo. But I was thinking that pretty soon I'd be able to bring the drone along to people's homes and parties, weather permitting, second battery now part of the unit supply, and do little surveys and demonstrations, and peer into neighbors' backyards, conduct some real espionage.

A short conversation with an attorney introduced me to tort law and the detail that Vermont might have some special rules. "If you look into a neighbor's yard it probably is not a violation of their privacy," he said, "but if you get on a ladder to do so…"

Now, in addition to needing an insufferable multitasking digital native assistant, and a budget, and someone to handle the accumulating mass of pictures and video, I also needed a squadron lawyer.

I'm afraid of my drone. There: I admit it. I still want to get that singular beautiful picture from a unique vantage point to serve as an illustration for this book, but I'm worried about trying to master something that isn't about anything except mastering something. And I'm worried about all that video: Why am I even keeping it all? It's a great illustration, my Parrot, of the fact that I don't want to spy on my neighbors, and though I own a new toy, I'm not really much of a hobbyist or a flier. I won't be getting my wings, but the drone has shown how the military and intelligence communities have impetuously moved forward with their drone acquisitions: You gotta fly it. You gotta communicate with it. You gotta keep it in good repair. You gotta have power and lots of it. You gotta point it at something and that's gotta have a reason. You gotta look at the video and you gotta store it and then be able to find it later. You can always use a better camera, which means more storage space and more issues with where and what you can record. And more range is useful, too, which means longer-range communications, which means a better controller, and maybe even a staff. Pretty soon, you've got a squadron; you've got dozens, hundreds, thousands.

Is that it? The acquisition of toys, toys turned into tools into weapons of war? Whatever you call it, we have created a killing Machine. We need to examine whether it is effective, to ask first of all two fundamental questions: whether it is even the right strategy to pursue to defend against terrorism, and whether it secures our future. And we also need to understand the Data Machine itself, whether it is spending our national treasure wisely or doing its given job well. But what if there are legality and economy and even oversight, no matter how effective or ineffective they might be? What if the making of the killing Machine in itself, the creation of this other black box–packed world of Gilgamesh's, changes the real world, changes us? That's my discovery with my own little Parrot and my deep descent into the world of the unmanned. We do have thousands of drones, and the Machine already rules. Somehow, though, it seems exactly what we want, what we crave in this life separated from the reality of war.

I went to look at the digital natives to seek an answer, and the sight was not pretty. One brainiac with a physics doctorate arrived in Kandahar in 2013 to serve as a kind of science officer with Combined Joint Task Force Paladin, the multinational counter-IED authority then still busily at work.

The Georgia Tech graduate's job title reads "operations research analyst": part staff officer, part intelligence analyst, part scientist, a new kind of government issue sent into combat, but a fighter who would be unrecognizable to an Eisenhower or even a Schwarzkopf. Put through his paces at basic in a coddled and lecture-filled predeployment training *building* in Maryland, the modern-day Poindexter is not an actual military officer or soldier or spy, nor is he one of those dreaded contractors; he's a bona fide army civilian employee, the kind that used to populate the arsenals in the rear areas doing the industrial weapons work but that now are essential unlaborers of the Data Machine. Like his volunteer brethren who serve in uniform, and yet totally different, he is there on the battlefield serving his own one-year combat tour because actual soldiers, no matter how good they are, need something beyond even the perfected Niagara of the user-friendly Machine to make sense of the big data of war.

Poindexter's focus is significant activities (SIGACTs) and statistical trends. He works alongside scores of others in the local intelligence fusion center. In each of the regions, there are counterpart centers and task forces with analysts and subject matter experts (SMEs) numbering in the hundreds who toil away, an activity duplicated endlessly in each of the districts and base hubs and units. They are backed up by thousands at higher headquarters, with more than half of the boots on the ground provided by men and women of statuses other than soldier. They are backed up by tens of thousands more working 24/7 shifts in the United States. More thousands populate similar fusion centers slightly different than counter-IED. There they wrestle with the reporting tools and databases of local and third-country national vetting and hiring, counterintelligence and insider threats ("green on blue"), counternarcotics, counter–threat finance, counter–human trafficking, countercorruption, warrant-based targeting, information security, physical security, and base and force protection. If a Poindexter supports the world of special operations, he does the same cubicle work that prepares and supports Village Stability Operations (VSO), Foreign Internal Defense (FID), Counterinsurgency (COIN), psychological operations, and irregular warfare. If he directly supports killers in the black world to find and fix the high-value targets and individuals, he resides in a similar world of the x-men. The higher any unlaborer goes, the more distinguished the arsenal of databases and networks—MagicDesk, Fire Truck, SKOPE, JIANT, SOIS, PDAS—the software and networks of the new gods.

Even as troops left Afghanistan, collection never faltered. Just in Kandahar, at just one enormous military and intelligence hub, more than a dozen different types of planes and drones flew at the end of 2013. Their black boxes are all the latest models. Hovering above all is the multi-INT Persistent Ground Surveillance Systems (PGSS), a combined balloon and unmanned ground sensor grid keeping watch on direct threats to every hub. Technicians fiddle with the latest black boxes in this world as well: the austere location force protection kits and the shooter detection systems. Also flowing in are the signals from fixed intercept sites and vehicle-mounted stations, even the take from the close-access technical reconnaissance of the x-men. Out on patrol, the actual warriors conduct sensitive site exploitations, collecting documents, hard drives and disks, cell phones and anything else that might provide a clue; they conduct meticulous forensics of what can only be called crime scenes; and they deal with the people, carrying out key leader engagements, interrogations, screenings, and background checks; and, most important these days to populate the databases for tomorrow, they collect biometric data.

This is a different kind of army: it doesn't advance per se, setting up camp and pitching pup tents as it halts for the night. The Poindexters and their subordinate plain old analysts are more like Dilbert technicians filling air-conditioned offices — planning, scheduling, monitoring, scanning, collating, translating, geolocating, data-pulling, processing, formatting, chatting, and briefing. Day in and day out, they prepare pattern of life studies, predictive analysis, historical threat analysis, District Narrative Assessments (DNA), intelligence preparation of the battlefield, Intelligence Summaries (INTSUMs) and graphic Intelligence Summaries (GRINTSUMs). They are literally the masters of software, valued for their digital acumen, almost all of them commercial products, technicians and unlaborers present and accounted for in attending to the Data Machine. There are dozens if not hundreds of additional black box software packages and databases of all of the three-letter agencies that connect the unlaborers. Their world is a self-contained and self-generating society within itself, not the real world.

In my experience of trying to tease out some intersect between the secret life of the information warriors and war, I discovered that video games and television series like *Game of Thrones* unite digital natives and their elder brethren-in-arms in some common and enduring language. And since I know nothing of the most current games or fads, I've tried to talk about *Star Trek* and have come up with an interesting conversation. Poindexter and his ilk can completely get into debating Spock versus Data, the next-generation science officer: who's smarter, who's a better character, who is more likable or who they would like to spend eternity with on a deserted planet. Amongst people of a certain generation — mine — Spock wins hands down, not just because he is a first love but also because he was an introduction to the future; charismatic and fearless, with that mystical otherworldly quality character-ized by all the Vulcan mumbo jumbo and the mind meld. To the digital natives of the Poindexter generation, Data is *the man*. He is not just Spock 2.0 but a walking thesaurus intrinsically more lov-able than the half-man with no emotions, a striver who wants external input and wants to collaborate, a techie who can learn at an astronomical rate, funny precisely because he is unfunny, an overtalking and eager *oid* that crosses the line from a that to a who.

There is no right answer in this debate, which is itself highly symbolic: an equal number of fanboy scholars seem annoyed that Data can babble on uncontrollably as are annoyed about Spock's monotone and the fact that his every line ends with the always anticlimactic "illogical." Data is endearing precisely because of his obvious almost-human flaws; it is in fact the nonmachine who seems more robotic.

The prime difference, of course, is that Data *is* a robot, an android with a positronic brain, a Hollywood tip of the hat to the great Isaac Asimov, who first conceived of such a brain in 1950s science fiction. Spock, on the other hand, is an alien from another galaxy, and though he has a human mother and a Vulcan father, in the end, he is not even on our historical horizon, while here is the truth: Data is completely logical.

Data the machine, on the other hand, can be more likened to the NSA or the Data Machine itself—he can literally listen to 100 separate songs at once and discern all of them. It is an incredible achievement and a necessary demonstration. Yet as a character, Data sought—with the processing of enough information—to be more like a human and even to tackle the human soul, a struggle not unlike the human struggle going back six thousand years to the time when the story of Gilgamesh was first conceived. Spock is in many ways another in a long line of Gilgameshes, that fantastic character that is only part human. In his detached way, he has to be likened to the modern-day national security wonk, the hyperexpert pursuing *über*-objectives with superhuman focus, the man or woman who will do almost anything to save lives, the unflappable officer you want on the bridge, unless it is a bridge to nowhere.

While science and society debate the potential of artificial intelligence and the limitations of actual software and models in becoming self-aware or producing humanlike reasoning, even the skeptics admit that a fusion agent like Data might be able to crunch the numbers with great accuracy to determine where a human target or an improvised explosive device might be hidden, even if, as one scientist friend says, it might also have nothing to say about what to do about it next. The popular nightmare and a staple of science fiction and movies going back to *2001: A Space Odyssey* is somehow that the machines go beyond their programming and threaten humans and humankind. Thus the egghead advisors in today's military formations don't even pretend to be working for the purpose of unlinking warfare from its human dimensions; it is merely that the Machine has already become too complex for ordinary humans to master.

Autonomy is coming precisely to solve this problem. The vigilant Data Machine already supports mission tasks that must be accomplished on a scale beyond human capability. Translation software, artificial intelligence, and electronic means of processing raw data—signals and imagery—are already managing the glut.[3] The military isn't shy about calling for "appropriate levels of autonomy"[4] in future development, with the increased use of autonomy and autonomous behaviors not just improving performance but also providing cost savings.[5] The increasing volume of data, combined with an ever-changing operational environment in the limitless number of possible Everybads, the air force says, demands innovative approaches in order to translate raw data into intelligence and deliver it rapidly.[6] It can all sound like another Gnat-750-to-Reaper continuum or a WARHORSE-to-ACES HY reduction in weight and improvement in performance, except that lurking in the dark corners are the mad scientists who do foresee "Complete Kill Chain Weapons," that is, machines that would make every decision from detection to the kill.

Though concerns about "killer robots" are valid, and there are already weapons that people should be concerned about that essentially kill automatically on the battlefield, the reality is that automated killing is inimical to military culture and the concepts of just warfare that most militaries rely on. Again, the military is quite aware of the shift and the danger, stressing the difference between performance and "execution," the military's actual word.

"Autonomous mission performance may demand the ability to integrate sensing, perceiving, analyzing, communicating, planning, decision-making, and executing to achieve mission goals versus system functions," the Pentagon says.[7] Systems, the military says, are "only as good as the software writer and developer because the control algorithms are created and tested by teams of humans." And that is where we will be as long as machines can't adapt to changes as well as predict what will happen next, as the human brain does. Killer robots are probably not the only place to look. Much more likely is human-robot teaming at the small-unit level: unmanned ground systems that guard bases or conduct logistics or even conduct missions such as remotely conducted, "nonlethal" crowd control; "dismounted offensive operations; and armed reconnaissance and assault operations,"[8] with everything under human control at some command post until that line is crossed or some undefined accretion of capability is achieved.[9]

Will the Machine someday decide who lives and dies? In some ways, the technologists can't contain themselves in seeing exponential growth and development in the future. Hence we hear not just of Complete Kill Chain Weapons but also of a future of "swarming" autonomous drones, actually operating "out of the loop," meaning without human intervention.[10] I simply wonder how different that really is from what we have today.

CHAPTER TWENTY-ONE

Warka

As for man, [his days] are numbered,
whatever he may do, it is but wind...
TABLET II, *EPIC OF GILGAMESH*

G ilgamesh's Uruk, Warka in modern-day Iraq, is about 185 miles south of Baghdad. It is mostly a wreck of a place, half buried and picked over by centuries of looters, largely unknown outside the world of archeology. Yet it has the distinction of being the first, largest, and longest-lived city from the most ancient period of Mesopotamia, perhaps even the oldest city in our entire world.[1]

Sometime during the first half of the third millennium BCE, in the early dynastic period of Sumerian civilization, a real Gilgamesh is said to have ruled there.[2] The city goes back even further, at least 2,000 years further. Within its 10-kilometer-long walls — claimed in the *Epic* to have been built by King Gilgamesh himself — were 500 acres where wheat was first successfully cultivated on a large scale, where the pottery wheel was developed, where time was first divided into units of sixty, where the first examples of writing were found, and where authorship was granted. This place *was* the ancient world until it disappeared — some say because of conquest, others because of the effects of overpopulation, others because of a change in the course of the great river and environmental challenges that followed.[3]

When Sumerian civilization disintegrated and Uruk perished, the *Epic of Gilgamesh* also disappeared. A lively oral history circulated throughout the Near East, and the story shaped countless others, but it wasn't until 1850 that the West discovered it. Tablets and fragments recording the *Epic* were found in the ruins of a royal Assyrian library at Nineveh, many hundreds of miles north of ancient Uruk, near today's Mosul.[4] Since then, almost 100 different caches of all or parts of the Gilgamesh story have been found from modern-day Iran to Turkey and into Palestine. And fragments are still being recovered.

Early translations, some hastily concluded and based on sparse understanding of the Akkadian language,[5] framed the story in the aesthetics and interests of the day. That mostly meant molding European Christian ideals and orthodoxy: the flood was a real event, and thus the Bible challenged the emerging theory of evolution.[6] Then, if you will, the intelligence improved. The "standard version" uncovered in Nineveh, missing some 575 of its total of 3,500 lines, was supplemented by parts of other tablets, some in other languages, some even from different epochs.[7] As one scholar points out, each subsequent translation and version that emerged was thus based on "steadily accumulated knowledge."[8]

Like a modern military PowerPoint briefing that is constantly fiddled with and always shifting, and now also like our entire world of interactive, ever-changing, and never static data, which masquerades as our "intelligence" explaining the world, each version of the *Epic* reflects the input, competence, interests, and biases of its author. That's why in academia there is a gay Gilgamesh and much dogma about everything from the origins of the gods to the rule of oppressive kings. Saddam Hussein even spoke of himself as a Gilgamesh in one of his last councils with his generals, the maniacal dictator born for and to a people who could rest assured that they had a unique history of giving birth to legends and heroes.[9] To me, Gilgamesh not only symbolizes our lack of understanding of the very lands in which we fight, but is also a seminal document that suggests the moral guidelines for making war, not just some heroic motif of comradeship in performing amazing feats and the brotherhood of Gilgamesh and Enkidu and their synergy in battle. Gilgamesh symbolizes the importance of thinking through *why* to undertake a fight, *how* to fight once we are in that battle, and then what the consequences of each conquest are, even in how we celebrate our victories.

When I discovered that there was a Gilgamesh black box, I tried to find out whether the person who named it had something in mind. Was it a wry acknowledgment of the futility of the modern endeavor? I didn't really expect to find the answer, but many of the military officers I asked, many of whom considered themselves historians and specialists on the Middle East, had never heard of the historic Gilgamesh or could only vaguely recount what the *Epic* was about. These *Iliad*-reading officers considered warfare's roots to lie in Greek heroes and battles that took place thousands of years after Sumeria. And though they were taught as young cadets that "the challenges and complexities associated with the moral and ethical dimensions of warfare can be traced back to ancient times," those times were never ancient enough to be associated with Uruk as an actual place.[10] Not only, then, do Western militaries fight in Gilgamesh's land largely oblivious to the stories of universal mankind, but the ways of the Data Machine ensure that as battles shift to any Everybad, the background becomes ever more irrelevant.

Intelligence collection and analysis, at least at the keyboard and monitor level, look awfully Googleized, an algorithm- and machine-determined imposition of what's important that seems to leave us as dumb as ever. I question how the practitioners of War 2.0 know the real world in all of its complexity or can possibly be learning anything. There is too-rapid turnover in assignments to any of a half dozen war zones for any geographic experience to develop among American military officers, and there is too much diversity of language and culture for any of them to truly emerge as an expert. Mastering the workings of the Data Machine and its never-ending shifts and changes is a full-time job.[11] An analyst or officer can shift from country to country, even from continent to continent, applying the same cultureless techniques. This is not even to mention that the job is targeting, not understanding. That is the essence of our unmanned world.

And as for that specific black box named Gilgamesh that sits on Predator and Reaper drones? The fact that this geolocating gizmo can reach right into cell phones and other communications devices to determine their precise location seems wholly unremarkable and transitory to the modern unlaborer. My friends in the military and intelligence worlds unanimously dismiss Gilgamesh and its ilk as the military equivalent of some digital crush and problem solver that is absolutely essential one day but accumulates in the back of the dresser drawer the next. These black boxes—so invisible—are not tangible fragments like ancient pieces of tablets and humanity, nor do they have any distinction in grasping why American war tends to unfold the way it does. Add to their unrewarded toil and mechanical dismissal the fact that technical proficiency doesn't have the same romance as any kind of human bravery, honor, or sacrifice. In other words, the unmanned are not worthy of an *Epic*.

When the US military found itself digging into these very lands in August 1990, confronting Iraq's invasion of Kuwait, it was probably the last place it ever expected to be. In describing the new battlefield, there were some news stories about the cradle of civilization and even mention of Iraq's Ur of the Chaldees as the birthplace of the biblical Abraham. The father of Judaism and the patriarch of Islam, if he existed at all, probably lived during the time of King Shulgi, maybe some 3,000 years after Gilgamesh. In modern-day southern Iraq there was still the millennia-old ziggurat of Ur, a wondrous archeological object that is unfortunately relegated to being little more than an entry in a database of objects that should be avoided; they are called no-strike targets.

Thirty-nine days of bombing in 1991 led to a complete rout of Saddam's army. Though most still can't believe it, modern airpower changed the human calculus: men and tanks clashing on the ground and mass slaughter were supplemented, some would even say replaced, by the technology of unstoppable remote attack. Organized war as it had been fought throughout history was finished. No one quite knew how to capture air war, it being so ahistoric and heroless. So the focus changed from battles to bombing, and the depiction became an endless stream of lifeless numbers of sorties and targets. Then the propagandists stepped in. Baghdad cried about hidden civilian casualties and collateral damage, actually scoring a hit when they unveiled an infant formula production plant that had been bombed, near a then little-known town called Abu Ghraib. Saddam Hussein even sat for his only wartime interview with Peter Arnett of CNN, and through a wordy and roundabout ninety-minute monologue, he promised "blood... lots of blood...let not fickle politicians deceive you once again by dividing the battle into air and land parts—war is war."[12]

American counterpropagandists retaliated. Imagery analysts spotted two Iraqi MiG-21 fighter jets parked next to the ruins of the ziggurat of Ur.[13] The archeological site was swallowed within the fence line of Tallil Air Base, one of Iraq's largest. Though the enemy planes had been towed more than a mile from the nearest runway and thus were a threat to no one, the picture illustrated Iraq's perfidy in trying to put the ziggurat within American cross hairs. Saddam was carrying out ploys to provoke civilian attacks, the United States bellowed. The White House even issued a terse statement: "This morning, we have documentation that two MiG-21s have been parked near the front door of a treasured archaeological site which dates back to the twenty-seventh century BC."[14] The White House was only off by twenty centuries.

And then, when American ground commanders concluded that those forces were defeated—Iraqi equipment was depleted by more than 50 percent—the glorious battle commenced. A still-industrial war machine advanced along a wide front, while the 24th Mechanized Infantry Division—a powerful force just being endowed with digital steroids—left-hooked right into ancient Akkad and even took Tallil Air Base, about the US Army's northernmost advance before swinging east toward Basra. In 100 hours, it was over, the *it* being the ground war, the only war that registered as real and legitimate, as honorable or historic.

By the time the second Iraq war came in 2003, the Data Machine had pumped up combat power enormously. Iraq's every electronic squawk and quiver was now exposed. Precision had started to transform the ground forces as well, as had computerization and miniaturization and digital everything. A force less than one-fifth the size of the force mobilized in 1990 gathered in Kuwait to get rid of Saddam. The little ground army jabbed, bobbed, weaved, and connected its way to Baghdad, a spry and lightning-fast welterweight David with superior vision rapidly overwhelming an archaic Goliath. Predator and Global Hawk were now fixtures of battle, and unrelenting 24/7 surveillance actually produced too much information, but again the narrative ignored drones and black boxes and all the instruments of the

Data Machine. Barely three US and British ground divisions, now half-digital and half-industrial, took down Saddam, shock and awe some faux crushing sideshow, victory secured by sweat and blood—absolute conventional victory. *The* history was the twenty-one-day dash of the ground forces—of men—to Baghdad. War was war and never changing, the generals and commentators agreed.

And they were oh so wrong.

In May 2003, President Bush declared "Mission accomplished," and though many would later guffaw over the error and the hubris, that was what it looked like to the *Iliad*-tutored officers. The 3rd Infantry Division to the west and the 2nd Marines to the east stood at the door of Akkad and then blasted through the land of Sumer, brushing aside Ur, driving through ancient Uruk on the way to Babylon and then on to Baghdad, a force armed with the greatest information and one that looked nothing like "divisions" of the past.

And yet every road and every landmark remained utterly foreign to the invaders. It wasn't just that the military didn't know the story of the *Epic* and the civilizations that lay beneath the actual places they'd been to, not once but twice. There were also true surprise and tragic unpreparedness in understanding the Iraqi people—Shia, Sunni, Kurd, tribal—just as there had been gross error in reading Afghanistan after Kabul and Kandahar fell. Then, the potential of the growing digital storm was shown in the rapid dislodgment of al Qaeda and the Taliban in barely a month of fighting. And the narrative then was just a few hundred American men with laptops on horseback vanquishing the enemy, despite the odds, despite the hand-wringing about those mountains being the graveyard of empires.

In both Afghanistan and Iraq, the Machine performed, suggesting and even portending what was to come: that no history or geography would get in its way. The drones emerged, as did GPS and the network, IR, SAR, MASINT, multispectral, ISR and nontraditional ISR, an acronymic multitude of INTs giving substance to a dream of an all-seeing and perfect execution. And then the crusaders stayed. They became occupiers and new subjugators, no matter how hard they actually strived to minimize civilian harm and fight a perfect war. When twenty-first-century assertions and chat sessions faded, the ways of the ancient times took over. In Afghanistan, the guerrillas regrouped, using all the advantages of geography and tribal relations. In Iraq, looting came and a locustlike swarm descended upon the tyrant's temples, even taking the artistic discoveries from Uruk: the massive Warka Vase, covered with relief carvings of a procession of offerings to the goddess Ishtar; and the life-sized limestone Face of a Woman, the oldest known sculptural depiction of the female face. Ignorance was simply framed as some Rumsfeldian or neoconservative failure, the civilized world tsk-tsking and finger-pointing as to too few troops or a diversion of attention, as if more men and more weight would have liberated, when in fact the peoples of these ancient lands were hardly yearning for the advances promised in the model of Western white and democratic civilization.

The public assumption remained that more troops were needed.[15] Yet boots on the ground and occupation no matter what the "strategy" also meant turning the nimble databird into a colossal dinosaur. The Machine initially stumbled on suicide bombers and the bloodlust of history and civil war and IEDs until it carved out enough of an information bubble for the ground army to actually withdraw. With Uruk and Iraq swept aside, expunging the world's evil became a matter of killing individuals. Slowly, the Machine armed itself with all of the black boxes to perfect its new appointed craft.

The terse recapping here isn't meant to impugn the US armed

forces and others who have sacrificed much and given life and limb in this awful fight. But no matter how many red lines the generals draw in the sand, no matter how many routes north and south are labeled with military precision to suggest battles of the past, no matter how many gaps in the defenses are studied for breaching, no matter how many counterinsurgency doctrines are written or how many cultural intelligence programs are created, the Data Machine has become the supreme authority and influential silent partner in all that has unfolded. After 9/11, the United States moved the Machine to Kuwait and the Gulf states, positioning it in obliging foreign lands to extend the unblinking eye and its accompanying broadband to dead spots on the globe, which then meant Afghanistan. It only made practical sense after the fall of Kabul not to close up the hot spot and send the network home.

That same Machine, growing in global capacity, then expanded into a targeted killing campaign in Pakistan and Yemen and Somalia and elsewhere, this time with no boots on the ground, at least not the boots of old. Drones were only a minor part of what emerged: the black boxes themselves accumulated and got better; then came every new platform from Constant Hawk to Harvest Hawk to space-based systems and even the cybervirtual that is body-worn. A permanent high-capacity global hot spot followed through the pumping up of satellite communications and the tetherless network, the be-anywhere air communications node. Combat troops left, but the Machine spiraled and perfected. And then, even as forces were withdrawn from Afghanistan, the pace of development didn't stop. Cemented into permanent and invisible space, the Machine could support global operations anywhere. But it was a particular kind of operation—targeting—and that in itself seemed to define both American involvement and its limits.

When the Syrian civil war came along in 2013, and when Iraq

War Number Three reared its head the next year, the Machine determined the response. Announcing American assistance as the Sunni group ISIS rampaged, the overall American task in Iraq, as laid out by President Obama, was some vague support to restore peace. It became clear that the actual activity acceded to the capacities of the Data Machine and the unmanned. American involvement would be given over completely to "intelligence, surveillance, and reconnaissance," specialized military jargon that even President Obama could throw about in prime time. Six times in a short press conference, Obama spoke of getting "a better picture" of what was going on in Iraq, wisdom pretended through the very suggestion of the word "intelligence." And then he spoke of his new Counterterrorism Partnerships Fund, which allocated $5 billion to work with Middle East governments to develop and improve their capacities to "fight the terrorists." That meant the professional protocols and capabilities of counter-this and counter-that, pure and simple, for there really wasn't anything that the American military and its intelligence cousins could teach or provide other than data and targeting. In short, the United States was assisting those governments, whether legitimate or not and regardless of the long-term outcome, in their capacity to improve their own targeting, with only a prayer and a hope that they would focus on the same targets.

More than anything else, though, Obama reassured the American people that American troops would not be "returning to combat," thus also evading the fact that indeed combat would be taking place and that the unmanned Machine would be doing the fighting previously done by men. "I have no greater priority than the safety of our men and women," Obama reassured in his Iraq speech.[16] The Data Machine would ensure the task in the immediate sense, with the safety of the men and women of the United States deferred.

Some might say that Obama's reluctance to send in troops is

political or even some expression of weakness or liberalism, when the reality is that it wholly matches American military style. This aesthetic has reigned throughout the precision age. "Yours is a society that cannot accept ten thousand casualties," Saddam said swaggeringly before the first Gulf war in 1990, baiting the United States to fight his version of some ancient grotesque bloody battle. Bush I did not. Through Bosnia and Kosovo, Clinton and company experimented with humanitarian intervention, some clamoring for boots on the ground and even arguing that the mere threat of a ground war achieved political outcomes (or even more bizarre, that ground forces were less destructive than precision airpower). Even before 9/11, terrorism became a national threat, and yet the response was almost completely given over to the hands-off technology, whether that meant Tomahawk sea-launched cruise missiles or the new Predators. When bombing began for the big public retribution campaign against al Qaeda and the Taliban after 9/11, Bush II never really loosened restrictions that were in place to safeguard American lives. In fact, Rumsfeld instituted policies that were as restrictive as those of his predecessors, the tandem goals being to take full advantage of technology while also not creating or provoking a hornets' nest of political controversy or backdraft. All through warring that would extend to Iraq and farther afield, the avoidance of risk to US forces (and the avoidance of the risk of civilian harm) was held up as a top priority. Critics might lament civilian casualties, but there is no denying that the numbers are historically low compared to wars of the past, that billions have been spent to develop intelligence and weapons capabilities specifically to minimize those casualties. Though again, the objective is tandem: fewer civilian casualties and fewer industrial accidents also mean that public interest wanes. The Data Machine counts and affirms constant progress, yet the numbers don't really matter in the same way.

Even at the height of frustration and American casualties in Iraq, even at the time of the hunting of Abu Musab al-Zarqawi and then later of Osama bin Laden, opportunities to kill even the worst terrorists were passed up because of the potential collateral harm to civilians — so deeply ingrained was a certain aesthetic promising perfection. When Zarqawi was killed in June 2006, the air force bragged that its pilots were assured "100 percent" that not only were all the socks in order, but no civilians were at risk in an attack.[17] When bin Laden was killed in May 2011, the mission was a careful balancing act that rejected manned bombing because of its potential for excessive damage. One might wonder how it is that such compromises can be made in the face of articulations of the extraordinary threats that these individuals pose. Even the most dovish commentaries about the laws of armed conflict accept that in cases of extreme military necessity, a balance can be struck between achieving a specific timely and important military objective and the potential civilian harm. And moreover, the most dovish commentaries accept that if the combatant hides amongst civilians, a certain immunity is lost *if* the target is deemed to be critical and timely.

The years-long hunt for Zarqawi and bin Laden was taken up with meticulous care in order to balance the amount of civil harm or collateral damage that was created in the interim. That is, if avoiding civilian deaths is an overriding objective, which I'm suggesting it can never be, then the far larger calculation has to be made as to the cost to society and humanity for even operating in this seemingly near-perfect way. Zero civilian casualties do not equal military necessity. Just war, which forms the basis of the law of armed conflict and US military doctrine, governs not only the justification to go to war but also the conduct of military operations during a war, all with the final conclusion — the only acceptable justification for using force — that not only is there no alternative, not only have all other options been exhausted, but the use of force will not create the conditions that would undermine the restoration of peaceful relations once war ends.

What Saddam Hussein said almost three decades ago is true: we *are* such a society that today cannot accept ten thousand deaths in battle (nor should we be). But if we are merely measuring progress and justness from each tiny Raven and Pyros that performs its magic task, then we might not be so brutal and bloodthirsty, but we are surely foolish and shortsighted. We have become a society that is largely divorced from our military, and that is partly due to its unmanning. And we have certainly, and even the political and military leadership has largely, divorced ourselves from the Data Machine. In other words, we have failed to keep up with its development and sway, and with the shift of warfare out of the millennia-long *Iliad* epoch.

Today, the Data Machine doesn't care where it is fighting. It doesn't matter whether targets are hiding in Hindu Kush caves or in villages of the Fertile Crescent. Nor does Predator care, or Reaper, or Global Hawk, or any other of our other aptly and awkwardly named all-seeing eyes. In fact, they don't care about anything: they are machines. But the men and women behind Gilgamesh the black box and behind the entire Machine also don't care, for every place is reduced to geographic coordinates that flash across a screen in seconds. Nations, armies, and even people are reduced to links and networks. Along the way, a popular and almost universally supported war against Osama bin Laden and al Qaeda diffused to one against high-value individuals, high-value targets, foreign regime elements, violent extremists, and anticoalition forces, names changed to match propaganda of the day but all atomized "targets" in the end. And this most modern technology and technique of digital war-making can be applied even in some of the most technologically backward places on earth—on the borderlands of Afghanistan and Pakistan, in Yemen and the "empty quarter" of the Arabian peninsula, in the Horn of Africa, in the stans, in the Sahel, in the Muslim archipelagoes, and even in the last pirate bastions.

Victory now means effective black boxes that work in whatever weather and whatever desert, mountain, or urban setting. Loitering drones and geolocating weapons just need the data. Everyone needs the global information grid and the Internet—or, more precisely, *an* internet. Actual battlefield geography and culture have become immaterial. The node and the network sentry become the determinant and the provocateur of action—all the way to the edge of the world, anywhere. Gilgamesh is sensing at the edge; the Epic temple of information at the core.

But here's where I don't fall: despite being of the generation of non-native-gamers, I also know something of the military—old and newfangled—and consequently, I don't yearn for the old days. I don't mean typewriters and carbon paper; I mean the industrial grind. When the Washington pundits and the New York movers and shakers and the Hollywood wannabes disparage the technology—video-game war, death TV, killer robots—I wonder what it is they *do* want. Eleven million men and women in uniform as in World War II? Thousands being killed at one time in battles and bombings? Some even suggest a draft—as if they are ready to serve themselves or serve their kids up for war—because equal risk might somehow tame some wild Enkidu out there, when the truth of the matter is that our own 2.0 way of war just doesn't demand that many bodies anymore, or at least not the traditional soldierly types. We are nowhere near being completely unmanned in our war-making, but a Data Machine doing the bulk of the work does and should change our picture of war and of shared sacrifice and risk. When all of the post-Afghanistan headlines announce that the US Army will be the smallest it's been since before World War II, the entire premise is cockeyed: we just don't need that many people anymore, particularly not in bringing lethal destruction to bear on some enemy. That's how good the technology of war is. But we do need armies of IT people and so-called analysts to conquer the increasingly infinite stockpiles of data, and that in itself makes the nature of the military, the nature of our economies, even the nature of our societies very different than they were in the past.

The semblance of Gilgamesh and Enkidu still tends to dominate how we see our world: the mighty bristling with muscles, and beautiful specimens to boot. It isn't that might makes right, as if it ever were. But it is the case that might is might. The 5,000-year-old story of Gilgamesh is still so powerful precisely because the heroic tale is so persistent and the universal lesson of the immortal quest so enduring. No matter how many conquests he accumulated, King Gilgamesh learned that he was going to die, that mortality and domination over the gods could never be achieved, and that the reality of mortal life demanded coexistence and wise leadership. Drones and their puppeteer, the Data Machine, may have developed from some sense of need and good, but no matter what, this Machine is going to kill, and it is going to make godlike decisions. In the end, having this Machine between us and the killing is making us less human. The illusion of perfect warfare is little more than a blaring video game endlessly played to higher and higher levels and higher scores, but one being played in a crumbling crack house.

The greatness of the Gilgamesh story, told and retold over millennia, is that it touches on the loss of human innocence, on the beauty of friendship, on the brevity of human life, on the rules for proper living while we are here on earth, and finally, on human striving, tragedy, and reconciliation. Focusing on any one of these narratives isn't wrong per se. The story's enduring power is that the tale is so grand and unifying that even as its interpretation has shifted over the years, the enduring core of the search that never ends is just that: it never ends. And not only that, but here is an ancient book that set down universal truths long before the Bible or the Qur'an, a tale from the very threshold between the days of legend and our era of historically grounded truth.

The *Epic of Gilgamesh* is about what it means to be human. In the original Sumerian version, laid down before Babylonian times, the king finds Utanapishti and receives not just the story of the flood but also long-lost information on practices and rituals that had fallen out of use after the deluge.[18] Gilgamesh returns to Uruk to restore the old ways and be more civilized, which means, amongst other things, ruling wisely and caring for a human community. A hero who at the beginning of the *Epic* is clearly closer to the gods than to ordinary mortals, a bumbling superpower labeled a "wild bull on the rampage," grows and learns that he is not all-powerful or all-knowing, that he will not live forever. He *is* a man, after all, even if he is divine. Beginning and ending with stanzas that emphasize the magnificence of the walls of Uruk, the whole narrative exudes the message that what man leaves behind is his only hope for immortality. And so there is also an epic scope in the Machine's striving—like its namesake's fruitless toils for immortality. The greatness of the *Epic of Gilgamesh*—the humanity of the endeavor—only comes in comprehending the arc from striving to failure to acceptance as that arc itself demonstrates our condition.

The Event

[For whom,] Ur-shanabi, toiled my arms so hard,
for whom ran dry the blood of my heart?
Not for myself did I find a bounty,
[for] the "Lion of the Earth" I have done a favor!
TABLET XI, *EPIC OF GILGAMESH*

On the day of the Event—that's all anyone ever called it—
the cloud started falling.

From New York to London to Berlin to Tokyo, signs of trouble appeared when the nanos and the micros went rogue. Thirty years earlier, scientists had perfected tiny machines that could emulate the biology and hive behavior of bees. The technobiological invention was combined with compact high-energy power sources and ultra-low-power computing and "smart" sensors, all tied together in a swarm algorithm to manage multiple, independent machines. They called them bats, butterflies, crickets, and hummingbirds—all manner of animation and affection had been endowed on them by their creators. Rejected and belittled at first as useless, they had become tolerated and accepted, almost invisible wireless helpers that had become a part of everyday life.

And yet on *that* day, almost simultaneously, as if the entire nanoworld had decided on a work stoppage, the swarms went their separate ways. In homes, at work, in stores, in hospitals, and in the streets, they were annoyingly swatted away. The worker bees began zipping through the air like a shower of juvenile rubber bands, people dodging and tripping over the clicking and skittering corpus as they began an en masse distress.

At first, at monitoring stations, technicians and security guards shook their vidocles and handheld controllers, and then even banged the sides of their monitors twentieth-century style to see what was wrong.

Most everyone at first thought there was some local connectivity break or a glitch in the wireless mesh. Nearly everyone trudged to reboot their systems or reached for the phone to call their service providers.

Authorities—at least those humans left to supervise the 911 call centers—took the first reports of a nationwide failure as mostly prank calls. But the reporting was steady and the Internet itself was poky, and then news reports started coming in: a massive satellite failure, a solar flare of epic proportions, a cyberattack, an enemy electromagnetic pulse, an IT blackout, no one knew for sure.

Then the service copters started dropping. From just beyond the rooftops and above the trees, they descended in a loud and jangling heap, all plastic and ceramic parts and wiring—quads, octorotors, hexocarts—smacking into whatever was in their way, hitting pedestrians and cars and structures, signaling a wide system failure. They were soon followed by the minis, most made of composites but some still fifty-pound chunks of metal, some idly parachuting down from even higher flight paths, the unguided ones like missiles, some wandering off into the trees, some with blades still whirring as they slashed their way to the ground. Like the litter at a stadium after a raucous match, sponsor names and company logos piled up, trashed and grounded.

Remote came home to roost, they'd later say. The nanos,

micros, copters, and minis were an immediate annoyance, but then they were followed by the mid-altitude workhorses, some the size of small cars, zigzagging lumps dropped dead on roofs, breaking windows, hitting power lines, littering highways, followed by flying glass and deadly debris. The mail carriers arrived on cockeyed schedules, their letters and packages landing wherever, scattering to the wind. Delivery craft let loose with groceries and store inventories at the most unpredetermined of points. Airvans and then the logistical megamovers sailed off their perfectly set and timed routes into missile trajectories, the formerly unseen moving parts of unmanned society becoming the new unannounced guests, some reverting to preprogrammed emergency flight paths that were built in when they went to "lost link" status, but others just speeding to earth without fail-safe systems or recovery pilots.[1]

For those who lived under the aerohighways, and for those in the major flight paths, the highfliers came down in abundance. Near the regional drone hubs, where the swarms went to refuel and line up for resupply and repair and modification, where the corporations had established the shipping centers run by the picker-packer robots and worker drones—*yep*, people would say in the latest affront of unmanned everything, *I've been replaced by a shelvie*—the scenes ended up close to the wreckage one might imagine from a tornado or a hurricane, the electronic carnage of hundreds of autocopters, superlights, hoverers, spanditos, and hypercarriers littering roads and fields and rooftops like some legendary bird kill.

The surveillance eyes and the police craft and the first responders and the preresponders arrived in a heap. At first, operations centers toggled off the net, activating their closed-loop disaster networks, but then the backup sky-borne communications nodes and airborne cell towers began to follow, booting up and meshing together for a moment to form their own government protocol networks, and then sputtering to silence as parts of the mesh tangled and floated to the ground. And then last came the photovoltaic-powered and solar and hydrogen sentinels, up there for weeks and months doing their work, lost and tetherless, gliding along like autumn leaves entangling in trees, on mountaintops, precariously settling on skyscrapers like splayed-out dormant moths.

Society's shrapnel storm continued for less than forty-five minutes, but even in the smallest towns, even in the most remote areas, there was wreckage. In the rural everywheres where people chose to live their lives intentionally to be as close to *manned* and away from the grid as possible in 2034, even with their seemingly uncluttered skies, the long arm of the network collapsed like a tottering colossus, the drones and robots more omnipresent and a hell of a lot closer than anyone had thought.

Not only was no one immune, but in the communities where people truly lived the 34.0 lifestyle, in the wireless burbs, the gated communities where unmanned meant complete 24/7 assistance and robotic security, blackout prisons were formed. Unmanned pets paralyzed and froze, the flying avatars literally dropping dead. In the gyms and on the tennis courts, the ball-playing roto-opponents took one last smack at the ball before collapsing.[2] Navigational signals on personal flypacks failed suddenly, schools of hovering strollers smacking into sidewalks and trees, babies and children upended, traumatized and injured. Sensors went blind, gates locked, spikes protruded; even the most granola of New Agers retreating into shutdown fortresses.

It was the same new, same new; except that those with the greatest levels of connectivity ended up being the most cut off. Landlines and wires were something grannies held on to, the once fortunate previously scoffed. Now the modern-day drone-nuts who'd gone over the digital edge discovered the menace of

X-Peller drones guarding golf courses and gated communities, normally chasing away birds and keeping the real mosquitos at bay from pools and yards.[3] They all mutinied as well, causing hundreds of injuries. Then the wireless set soon found that they didn't even have old-fashioned ambulances and rescuers to help anymore, none that weren't machines themselves.

Out in the middle of nowhere, where those who were prone to *I told you so* even before the Event, where "remote" merely meant a job that was too dull, dirty, or dangerous for real humans to do, there was no escape. Schools of electrical power and pipeline monitors and airborne wind turbines fell. The unmanned crop dusters exhausted themselves and puffed out their last toxic breaths. Aerotractors banged into the dirt. Picoherders ceased their buzzing, frightening and scattering cattle and sheep. The mighty X-loggers and the autominers crashed like giant trees in the woods and mountains, unseen and unheard.

The count wasn't a death count, though thousands of innocent bystanders were killed when the crash came. The conventional explanation—the predictable commentary that was as automatic as any mechanical recording—first screamed terror and cyberattack, except that word started coming in of the same thing happening in China and the Middle East. On-air analysts spoke of the flash crash of 2010, where still-inscrutable computer trading errors caused a 1,000-point drop in the Dow Jones; or the Yongbyon tragedy in the second Korean War, where a software miscalculation led a squadron of unmanned combat vehicles to attack the wrong targets, killing 4,000 civilians.

Predictable, said the experts: Moore's Law, the doubling of computer power every eighteen months—the theorem adopted in 1965—had been updated dozens of time through the 2020s, and now scientists spoke of a 32-million-times increase in performance,[4] a new opportunity to replace the mixed generations of unregulated machines, their only bond, their only government control the adherence to standard protocols. The technology is there, they said, almost licking their lips with a taste of investigation and repair. Public acceptance of an unmanned airline transport system just then hung in the balance—most commercial operators still employed pilots to monitor unmanned freight carriers to comply with civil aviation rules, completely autonomous and unmanned passenger travel being as much a political and cultural uncertainty as a systemic challenge.

As the numbers started coming in—over 22,000 medium- and high-altitude drones just in North America and Europe, as many as 70,000 worldwide, and that was the number that was just randomly up in the skies at 8:45 a.m. Greenwich Mean Time on a typical Tuesday—it was the realization of totality that signaled David's task against Goliath.[5]

There were just environmental and soil monitors, traffic eyes, news cameras, weather sniffers, data gatherers, refuelers, drone-haulers, energy aides, transponders, network bridges, drones on the way to and on the way back from work.

Rumors started flying, and so did the snapshots. In some places, it was like a scene out of *The Birds*, the litter of drones literally covering the streets. Everyone knew that the Skyguard network was up there, everyone had either hired or knew someone who had hired a private investigator to follow some cheating spouse or to spy on some neighbor, but again the wake-up was in the numbers. From police to homeland security, to NSA and NRO and even some foreign intelligence agencies, the pictures were astounding. Biomimicry had been enlisted by the intelligence community and law enforcement agencies to mask drones and emulate biological species, to aid low observability and deniability, but the pictures on the ground didn't lie.

The viral e-mails had photo attachments of the wreckage of

craft showing the logos of unknown government agencies and unheard-of corporations. There were fallen military and security and police spies, identified by international, national, and local logos of governments and corporations, strange cameras and sensors in unknown orbits. "Drones no more," someone wrote, a slogan that originated in what survivalists like to call the American redoubt, one that didn't need much translation, one that quickly took over personal walls and postings and the Web itself, a call to do *something*. It was the very opposite of the classic sci-fi cybernetic revolt of the robots. It wasn't machines taking over; it was mankind taking a stand.

Acknowledgments

Nothing about *Unmanned* really turned out as I expected. It is hardly a book about drones—that is, the drone "war" in Pakistan and the coming everything that saturates civilian society. And I didn't get the story I thought I would of how the military and intelligence worlds see drones, because, well, now that they've become controversial, there isn't a lot of enthusiasm for lifting the veil beyond the PR. Even more, as I discovered, it is the Machine that *is* the story, not the drones. Military and intelligence insiders seem oblivious to their captivity, or else they are so overwhelmed by the scourge of information overload that they can hardly see anything else.

Early on in my research I discovered Gilgamesh as the name of a black box and *that* gave the book and my own search some meaning. Tim Schultz and Watt Alexander were crucial stimulants who made me look deeper, but the *Epic* itself captivated me, particularly as I began to see parallels between the five-thousand-year-old story and our modern world. David Chappell engaged me in many challenging discussions. Tom Cochran and Regina Monaco helped with two vital scientific questions that were over my head. Jacques and Christine, Colleen and Clif, and Vicky Bippart also inspired and fed my spirit during the writing, as did Luciana. Thanks also to the unmentioned sources who guided me through the discoveries.

ACKNOWLEDGMENTS

Geoff Shandler, my former editor at Little, Brown, made the book possible. After he left, Ben George ably took over editing. Thanks also to the others I worked with at Little, Brown and Hachette, and to the production and editing team of Ben Allen and Barbara Perris, who I had the pleasure to work with on *American Coup* as well.

My whole world was turned upside down during the writing of this book, forcing me to go on my own search for the wind. Thanks to Kimberly, Chuck Gundersen, Nancy Spillane, Peter Pringle, David and Misa Chappell, Marianne Manilov, Daniel Stadler, and Sultana Khan for propping me up. And thanks as always to Kevin and Cory, Julia and Reed, Marianne Szegedy-Maszak, Stan Norris, Hans Kristensen, Bob Windrem, Steve Shallhorn, John Robinson, Chip Fleischer, and Tom Powers. Thanks also to my attorney and most trusted advisor, Jeffrey Smith.

During most of the time I worked on *Unmanned* I served as national security consultant to the *New York Times*. It was exhilarating and frustrating; none of it would have happened without the steady friendship of Eric Schmitt. To Leo, have fun with the Parrot. To Galen and Olivia, it's your future. To Rikki and Hannah, I love you.

Notes

INTRODUCTION

1. PowerPoint Briefing, General Atomics, Expanding the Capabilities of RPA, Presented to ISR Symposium, December 11, 2013; PowerPoint Briefing, General Atomics, Predator Aircraft Series Status Report: Military & Civilian Missions, Presented to RPAS 2012 June 2012.

2. I prefer to use the term "drone" throughout this book, even though in some ways it is both inflammatory and inaccurate. The standard dictionary defines a drone as "a pilotless airplane or ship controlled by radio signals." The term "drone" is said to have originated with a 1930s pilotless version of the British Fairey Queen fighter, the Queen Bee (see www .telegraph.co.uk/news/uknews/defence/9552547/The-air-force-men-who -fly-drones-in-Afghanistan-by-remote-control.html), and the term was in vogue through the 1950s. As drones shifted from aerial targeting and directed bombs to something resembling today's systems, the term "remotely piloted vehicle (RPV)" emerged. This distinguished new roles from those of merely taking out targets and remote-delivering bombs, and that term persisted through the Vietnam era into the 1980s. "Unmanned aerial vehicle (UAV)" then emerged, a break from the previous generation of technology and a shift back to a focus on conventional war. "Unmanned aerial systems (UAS)" became more popular after the computer network era to denote the entire system, including the flying element and its parts. Finally, in the middle of the 2000s, "remotely piloted aircraft (RPA)" emerged, a new designation favored by those wishing to stress the capabilities and complexities of third-generation systems and also to stress the involvement of people in their operation. "UAV/UAS" remains the most common term; "drone" is what is most commonly used in the mainstream press and in conversation.

3. US Congress, House Permanent Select Committee on Intelligence, Performance Audit of Department of Defense Intelligence, Surveillance, and Reconnaissance, April 2012.

The number grew from 167 UAVs in 2002 to 727 by 2004; to 2,962 by 2006; to 6,191 by 2008.

4. DOD, Unmanned Systems Integrated Roadmap 2013-2018, p. 20; DOD, Unmanned Systems Integrated Roadmap, FY 2011–2036, p. 23; "Putting the Army Together—Manned, Unmanned Aviation Teaming; Col. John D. Burke, Director, Unmanned Systems Integration (Deputy Director, Army Aviation), Army G-3/5/7; Presentation to AAAA Unmanned Aircraft Systems Symposium, 12 December 2006; Peter Finn, "Rise of the drone: From Calif. garage to multibillion-dollar defense industry," *Washington Post*, December 23, 2011; www.washingtonpost.com/national /national-security/rise-of-the-drone-from-calif-garage-to-multibillion -dollar-defense-industry/2011/12/22/gIQACG8UEP_story.html (accessed February 19, 2014).

5. CRS (Ronald O'Rourke), Unmanned Vehicles for U.S. Naval Forces: Background and Issues for Congress, Updated October 25, 2006.

6. DOD, Unmanned Systems Integrated Roadmap 2013-2018, p. 3; Power-Point Briefing, Future of Unmanned Aircraft Systems in a Fiscally Constrained Environment; Dyke Weatherington, OUSD(AT&L)/PSA; Deputy Director, Unmanned Warfare, n.d. (2011).

"The growing awareness and support in Congress and the Department of Defense for UAVs, investments in unmanned aerial vehicles, have been increasing every year. The Fiscal Year 2001 (FY01) investment in UAVs was approximately $667 million, while the FY03 funding totaled over $1.1 billion dollars. The Pentagon has asked for $1.39 billion in procurement and development funding for FY04, with much more planned for the out years"; CRS, "Unmanned Aerial Vehicles: Background and Issues for Congress," Report for Congress, April 25, 2003.

The Teal Group's "World Unmanned Aerial Vehicles Systems, Market Profile and Forecast 2008" research estimated that investment in unmanned aerial vehicles alone will reach $7.3 billion annually worldwide and total $55 billion between 2008 and 2018.

The U.S. International Trade Administration estimates that global unmanned aerial vehicle production will reach $8.8 billion annually by 2020. Some analysts predict that the civilian market will reach $400 billion in a few years.

7. The Joint Air Power Competence Centre (JAPCC) Flight Plan for Unmanned Aircraft Systems (UAS) in NATO, Version 5.4, March 15, 2007, p. 7.

NATO nations have approximately 51 HALE, 105 MALE aircraft, and over 3,300 tactical/mini aircraft that are developed and operated via national organizations.

8. Kari Hawkins, Assistant Editor, "People Profile; Unmanned aircraft systems deputy credits team effort," *Redstone Rocket* (Redstone Arsenal); Wednesday, June 4, 2014, 11:23 a.m.

9. Ian G. R. Shaw, Predator Empire: The Geopolitics of US Drone Warfare, Geopolitics, 2013 (DOI: 10.1080/14650045.2012).

10. www.cnn.com/2009/POLITICS/05/18/cia.pakistan.airstrikes/.

11. Dr. James Igoe Walsh, The Effectiveness of Drone Strikes in Counterinsurgency and Counterterrorism Campaigns, Army War College Strategic Studies Institute, September 2013, p. v.

12. On April 30, 2014, the State Department issued its latest Country Reports on Terrorism. Dealing with 2013, it states that the numbers of terrorists and acts of terrorism are increasing, including those associated with al Qaeda and its affiliates. In 2013, terrorist attacks worldwide rose 43 percent over 2012. Terrorists killed some 17,891 and wounded another 32,577. Nearly 3,000 people were kidnapped or taken hostage in 2013. In that year, the organization ISIS (the Islamic State of Iraq and Syria) doubled the number of people it had killed in 2012.

13. As of the end of 2013, General Atomics had delivered 575+ drones of the Predator, Reaper, Gray Eagle class; PowerPoint Briefing, General Atomics, Expanding the Capabilities of RPA, Presented to ISR Symposium, December 11, 2013.

14. Robert M. Gates, *Duty: Memoirs of a Secretary at War* (New York: Alfred A. Knopf, 2014), p. 133.

15. The Joint Air Power Competence Centre (JAPCC) Flight Plan for Unmanned Aircraft Systems (UAS) in NATO, Version 5.4, March 15, 2007, p. 7.
    Almost 80 percent of US flying drones weigh less than fifty pounds; 95 percent of NATO's drones are small unmanned aerial vehicles.

16. www.wilsoncenter.org/event/the-efficacy-and-ethics-us-counterterrorism -strategy.

17. I know this statistic invites incredulity, but the military is a pyramid, with tiny numbers of senior officers and enlisted leaders towering above the hundreds of thousands of soldiers (and unlaborers) at the bottom. The number of people in uniform who were in the military before 9/11 (fourteen years ago as of publication of this book) and are still in, is estimated to be less than 5 percent.

18. PowerPoint Briefing, Mike Kutch, SSC Atlantic Cyber Lead, Space and Naval Warfare Systems Center Atlantic, NDIA Fall Symposium, San Diego, October 6, 2010; PowerPoint Briefing, Mike Kutch, SSC Atlantic, Rethinking Cybersecurity Engineering and Innovation within the Fleet and Naval Enterprise, May 25, 2010.

19. "The recruiting pipeline is populated by digital natives, with an expectation of a multi-media rich training environment with evolving learning and communication technologies. This environment must be technologically intuitive, agile and globally accessible 24/7." DOD, Strategic Plan for the Next Generation of Training, September 23, 2010, p. 6.

20. Timothy J. Sundvall, Robocraft: Engineering National Security with Unmanned Aerial Vehicles, School of Advanced Air and Space Studies, Air University, Maxwell AFB, Alabama, 2006, p. v; Maj. Houston R. Cantwell, USAF, Beyond Butterflies: Predator and the Evolution of Unmanned Aerial Vehicle in Air Force Culture; School of Advanced Air and Space Studies, Air University, Maxwell AFB, Alabama, June 2007, p. 3.

21. DOD PowerPoint Briefing, Department of Defense Sustainability, n.d. (November 2009).

CHAPTER ONE Search of the Wind

1. The names used here, and the story line, derive from the dominant translations and adaptations, some of which are factual or accurate and some of which are fictional or take liberties or license. I researched the epic in the *Encyclopaedia Britannica* from the tenth edition (1902–1903) onward to the current *Encyclopedia Britannica* (online). The evolution of the understanding of the epic is well documented there.

    See David Damrosch, *The Buried Book: The Loss and Rediscovery of the Great Epic of Gilgamesh* (New York: Henry Holt and Company, 2007); Stephen Mitchell, *Gilgamesh: A New English Version* (New York: Free Press [paperback], 2004); Benjamin R. Foster, trans. and ed., *The Epic of Gilgamesh* (New York: Norton, 2001); *The Epic of Gilgamesh: A Prose Rendition Based Upon the Original Akkadian, Babylonian, Hittite and Sumerian Tablets*, Rendered and Annotated by John Harris (Writer's Club Press, 2001); Andrew George, *The Epic of Gilgamesh: A New Translation* (New York: Barnes and Noble Books, 1999); Andrew George, *The Epic of Gilgamesh: The Babylonian Epic Poem and Other Texts in Akkadian and Sumerian* (London: Allen Lane, 1999); Andrew George, trans., *The Epic of Gilgamesh* (Penguin Classics, 1999); N. K. Sanders, *The Epic of Gilgamesh,* an English translation with introduction (London: Penguin Books, 1964); Alexander Heidel, *The Gilgamesh Epic and Old Testament Parallels* (Chicago: University of Chicago Press, 1949); *The Epic of Gilgamesh*, translated by Maureen Gallery Kovacs and based on the standard Akkadian edition, but filled in with excerpts from the Old Babylonian where necessary; online at www.ancienttexts.org/library/mesopotamian/gilgamesh/. See also Theodore Ziolkowski, Gilgamesh: An Epic Obsession, November 1, 2011; www.berfrois.com/2011/11/theodore-ziolkowski-gilgamesh/.

2. *The Buried Book: The Loss and Rediscovery of the Great Epic of Gilgamesh*, p. 3.
3. In 1914 Edgar Rice Burroughs published *Tarzan of the Apes*, the story of a baby of English nobility who is raised by a band of African apes.
4. A number of reviewers have commented on my hyperbole here, but I stick by it.
5. See U.S. Cyber Command, PowerPoint Briefing, Cyberspace Operations, Prepared for the 18th International Command and Control Research and Technology Symposium, Major General Brett T. Williams, Director of Operations (J3), USCYBERCOM, June 6, 2013, UNCLASSIFIED//FOR OFFICIAL USE ONLY; obtained by the author.
6. Future Force: Joint Operations, Air Force Chief of Staff General John P. Jumper, Remarks to the Air Armaments Summit VI, Sandestin, Fla., March 17, 2004; obtained by the author.
7. "Interoperability challenges led to the advent of 'widgets' that can integrate ISR data from incompatible sensors. The Services and Combat Support Agencies have also started building software applications that translate the data from non-standard sensors to understandable formats"; US Congress, House Permanent Select Committee on Intelligence, Performance Audit of Department of Defense Intelligence, Surveillance, and Reconnaissance, April 2012, p. 20.
8. See, for instance, the description by Dana Priest, "Piercing the confusion around NSA's phone surveillance program," *Washington Post*, August 8, 2013; www.washingtonpost.com/world/national-security/piercing-the-confusion -around-nsas-phone-surveillance-program/2013/08/08/bdece566-fbc4-11e2 -9bde-7ddaa186b751_story.html (accessed August 9, 2013).
9. Department of Defense Directive (DODD) 5250.01, "Management of Intelligence Mission Data in DOD Acquisitions," defines Intelligence Mission Data (IMD) as: "the DOD intelligence used for programming platform mission systems in development, testing, operations, and sustainment including, but not limited to, the functional areas of:
   - Signatures
   - Electronic Warfare Integrated Reprogramming (EWIR)
   - Order of Battle (OOB)
   - Characteristics and Performance (C&P)
   - Geospatial Intelligence (GEOINT)."
10. DOD, IMD Cost Methodology Guidebook, February 2013, p. 3.
11. DOD, IMD Cost Methodology Guidebook, February 2013, p. 12.
12. "Part of my goal in these conversations has been to bring back to reality many of the inflated expectations of what can be done with predictive analytics: predictive analytics is a powerful approach to finding patterns in data, but it isn't magic, nor is it fool-proof." Dean Abbott, "The NSA, Link Analysis and Fraud Detection," Smart Data Collective (Blog), July 25,

2013; http://smartdatacollective.com/deanabbott/136376/nsa-link-analysis
-and-fraud-detection (accessed August 1, 2013).

13. The official was Harold Hongju Koh, former dean of the Yale Law School
and State Department legal advisor and one of the key Obama administration participants in decisions relating to targeted killings; quoted in *Kill or
Capture*, p. 201.

14. Even for someone like Robert Gates, who describes his visit to the drone
main operating base Creech Air Force Base in Nevada early in 2008, saying, "The whole enterprise resembled a very sophisticated video arcade—
except these men and women were playing for keeps." See *Duty*, p. 131.

CHAPTER TWO   Dead Reckoning

1. Mark Anthony Phelps, "Roads and bridges in ancient Mesopotamia," in
Encyclopedia of Society and Culture in the Ancient World (New York: Facts On
File, Inc., 2008); *Ancient and Medieval History Online*, Facts On File, Inc.;
www.fofweb.com/activelink2.asp?ItemID=WE49&iPin=ESCAW572&
SingleRecord=True (accessed October 8, 2013).

2. The story of Iraq's use of its Scud-type missile in the 1991 war is complex
and little understood. Most of the attention (and much of the postwar narrative) is focused on western Iraq and the missiles that were in striking
range of Israel.

Less than twenty-four hours after Desert Storm bombing commenced, Iraq launched a missile at Israel in the early-morning hours of
January 18, 1991. The Scud didn't come from one of twenty-eight launch
sites in western Iraq, fixed installations that US intelligence had carefully
mapped and bombers had rushed to destroy, but from a mobile launcher, a
huge multi-ton vehicle that trundled through the vast western desert,
scooting to firing sites at night and then hiding during the day.

But Scud missiles had also been fired south from the Amarah area of
eastern Iraq, aimed at US and coalition forces in Saudi Arabia and the gulf
states.

3. Barry Watts writes "in Desert Storm U.S. forces had virtually no success
killing mobile launchers for Iraq's modified 'Scuds,' even after they had
revealed themselves to nearby aircrews by firing a missile"; Barry D.
Watts, The Evolution of Precision Strike, CSBA, 2013, p. 12.

An interesting updated assessment of the 1991 campaign as compared
to 2003, though it focuses exclusively on western Iraq (Amarah is in southeastern Iraq) is Major Brook J. Leonard, USAF, "How the West Was
Won: The Essence of Network-Centric Operations (NCO)," School of
Advanced Air and Space Studies, Air University, Maxwell AFB, Al; June
2006, pp. 32ff. "Because of the poor resolution of the LANTIRN targeting pod and a lack of training among aircrew in how to identify SCUDs,

they could not identify and employ ordnance against a target more than 80 percent of the time. Based on postwar assessment, the other 20 percent of the time, when the aircrews did employ ordnance, they hit either decoys or support vehicles;" ibid, p. 34.

4. "During Operation Desert Storm, China Lake increased Gator weapon delivery by a factor of four. Gator performed so well that United States forces employed more than 1,000 Gators to limit the mobility of the Iraqi Army and hamper Iraqi movement in areas known to hide Scud missile launchers." Naval Air Warfare Center Weapons Division, China Lake and Point Mugu, California, *Arming the Fleet*, third edition, p. 42.

5. Aircraft patrolling from medium and high altitudes randomly delivered cluster bombs on roads and highways, and around culverts and bridges suspected of being missile traveling routes or hide-sites. F-16 aircraft primarily delivered CBU-87 CEMs in eastern Iraq as part of these operations, and the F-111F aircraft delivered CBU-89 Gator antitank and antipersonnel mines in western Iraq; Department of the Air Force, Gulf War Airpower Survey (GWAPS), Volume IV, Part I, pp. 43, 48.

From February 19 onward, in addition, B-52 heavy bombers flying at extremely high altitudes dropped cluster bombs in potential Scud launch areas, traveling down roads and releasing bombs at timed intervals. See GWAPS, Volume IV, Part I, p. 290.

Toward the end of the war, B-52 bombers, together with many types of tactical fighter aircraft, also delivered cluster bombs on tank and vehicle columns retreating from Kuwait, including at the so-called "highway of death" north of Kuwait City, but also at the main highway due north out of Basra, which crossed the Euphrates River at al Qurnah and continued through Amarah on the way to Baghdad. See GWAPS, Volume IV, Part I, p. 231.

6. Department of the Air Force, *Reaching Globally, Reaching Powerfully: The United States Air Force in the Gulf War: A Report*, September 1991, p. 36.

7. See, e.g., R. Jeffrey Smith, "Numerous US Bombs Probably Missed Targets," *Washington Post*, February 22, 1991, p. A1.

8. W. Andrew Terrill, Nationalism, Sectarianism, and the Future of the U.S. Presence in Post-Saddam Iraq, Army Strategic Studies Institute, July 2003.

9. "Further on Saddam Interview with Turkish Paper, Third Installment," FBIS-NES-92-030, February 13, 1992, p. 22.

10. "Because of the enemy air defense systems, allied manned aircraft were forced to fly too high, well above their useful sensor ranges for viewing targets of this size. Other data show that humans are not good at search in high stress, multi-tasking scenarios, even with good sensor inputs. Thus, it can be argued that Allied aircraft would not have found their targets any better even if they had been able to fly lower." See The Development and Deployment of Precision Guided Munitions (PGMS) for Standoff Attack, Richard H. Van Atta and Ivars Gutmanis; in IDA, Transformation and

Transition: DARPA's Role in Fostering an Emerging Revolution in Military Affairs, Volume 2—Detailed Assessments, p. V-24.

11. Major Brook J. Leonard, USAF; "How the West Was Won: The Essence of Network-Centric Operations (NCO)," School of Advanced Air and Space Studies, Air University, Maxwell AFB, Alabama; June 2006, p. 33.

12. The "kill chain" was later defined as "find, fix, track, target, engage, assess." See Air Force Doctrine Document 2-1.9, Targeting, June 8, 2006.

CHAPTER THREE   Fire and Forget

1. "On February 27, 1991, when a Pioneer detected two Iraqi patrol boats off Faylaka [sic] Island, naval aircraft were called in to destroy the craft. Seeing the drone and thinking they were about to be attacked, Iraqi soldiers on the island surrendered to the Pioneer! It was the first recorded surrender of enemy troops to an unmanned vehicle." See Norman Polmar and Thomas B. Allen, *Spy Book—The Encyclopedia of Espionage* (New York: Random House, 1998), p. 466.

   "When the battleships sent their Pioneers on a low-level surveillance of Faylaka [sic] Island after pummeling its defenders with 16-inch gunfire, the surviving Iraqis were observed waving bed sheets in an effort to 'surrender' to the UAVs!" See John Barry and Evan Thomas, "Up in the Sky, an Unblinking Eye: The hundreds of drones cruising over Iraq and Afghanistan have changed war forever," *Newsweek*, June 9, 2008.

   "Noisy as a lawn mower, the Pioneer was scarily effective in the 1991 gulf war, when Iraqi soldiers learned to fear the barrage of missiles that would quickly follow its buzz. One Pioneer shot footage of a squadron of Iraqi soldiers waving their shirts in the air, likely the first unit ever to surrender to a drone"; Bill Yenne, *Attack of the Drones: A History of Unmanned Aerial Combat* (St. Paul: Zenith Press, 2004), p. 53.

2. Coskun Kurkcu and Kaan Oveyik, U.S. Unmanned, Aerial Vehicles (UAVs) and Network- Centric Warfare (NCW): Impacts on Combat Aviation Tactics from Gulf War I through 2007 Iraq, Naval Postgraduate School, March 2008, p. 24.

3. Bill Yenne, *Attack of the Drones: A History of Unmanned Aerial Combat*, p. 54.

4. "At the outset of the air campaign, the USAF and USN employed target drones to confuse and disrupt Iraqi air defenses. Following the initial F-117 and cruise missile strikes, Navy A-6s launched 25 Tactical Air Launched Decoys and USAF ground crews launched 44 BQM-34C target drones. Thinking the decoys and drones were incoming strike packages, Iraqi air defenses turned on their radars and engaged them, only to be attacked by radiation homing missiles"; Christopher J. Bowie, Robert P. Haffa, Jr., and Robert E. Mullins; Future War: What Trends in America's

Post-Cold War Military Conflicts Tell Us About Early 21st Century Warfare, Northrop Grumman Analysis Center, 2003, p. 55.

5. Major Christopher A. Jones, USAF; Unmanned Aerial Vehicles (UAVS): An Assessment of Historical Operations and Future Possibilities; A Research Paper Presented to the Research Department, Air Command and Staff College, AU/ACSC/0230D/97-03, March 1997, p. 19; IDA, Transformation and Transition: DARPA's Role in Fostering an Emerging Revolution in Military Affairs, Volume 1: Overall Assessment, p. S-8.

6. On one mission, a low-altitude Pioneer melded its close-in observations with the wide-area radar contact data generated by the brand-new Joint Surveillance and Target Attack Radar System (JSTARS), a lumbering airplane flying far overhead and hundreds of miles away in Saudi Arabia. At the end of the battle, a Pioneer flying under the obscuration of the smoke from oil fires set by Iraqi forces also spotted a tank unit poised to ambush at the northern edge of the international airport, a tip-off that led to merciless bombing and naval gunfire. One account described how "UAVs were used to map Iraqi minefields and bunkers, thus allowing the Marines to slip through and around these defenses in darkness, capture key command sites without warning, and speed the advance into Kuwait City by as much as two days." The attack on the Iraqi-held Kuwaiti Airport provides another illustration of the utility of UAVs. During that encounter, "a live Pioneer UAV picture showed a battalion of Iraqi tanks poised on the north end of the airfield for a counterattack. The armored force was broken up by naval gunfire and air attacks before it could strike the advancing Marines"; David A. Fulghum, "UAVs Pressed into Action to Fill Void," *Aviation Week & Space Technology*, August 19, 1991, p. 59.

    See also Defense Airborne Reconnaissance Office (DARO), Unmanned Aerial Vehicles (UAV) Program Plan, April 1994, For Official Use Only markings removed, pp. 2-2, 2-3.

7. Quoted in Defense Airborne Reconnaissance Office (DARO), Unmanned Aerial Vehicles (UAV) Program Plan, April 1994, For Official Use Only markings removed, p. 3-1.

8. DOD, UAV 1994 Master Plan, n.d. (1993), p. 3-9.

9. Cesar E. Nader, An Analysis of Manpower Requirements for the United States Marine Corps Tiers II & III Unmanned Aerial Systems Family of Systems Program, Naval Postgraduate School, June 2007, pp. 8–9.

10. Coskun Kurkcu and Kaan Oveyik, U.S. Unmanned, Aerial Vehicles (UAVs) and Network-Centric Warfare (NCW): Impacts on Combat Aviation Tactics from Gulf War I through 2007 Iraq, Naval Postgraduate School, March 2008, p. 24.

11. CNA, Desert Storm Reconstruction Report, Volume XIV, pp. v, 8–10; partially declassified and released under the FOIA to the author; David S.

Steigman, "Big guns' last hurrah aids allied triumph," *Navy Times*, March 11, 1991, p. 12.

12. DOD, Final Report to Congress: Conduct of the Persian Gulf War, Pursuant to Title V of the Persian Gulf Conflict Supplemental Authorization and Personnel Benefits Act of 1991 (Public Law 102-25), April 1992, pp. 341, 722–725, 796–797.

    During Desert Storm, Navy Pioneer UAVs flew 64 sorties for 213 hours while providing naval gunfire support (NGFS) for 83 missions.

    A total of 1,102 sixteen-inch rounds were expended on an average of nineteen projectiles per mission, more than half estimated against targets on Faylakah Island. The first firing took place on February 3, the first battleship sixteen-inch gun firing since the Korean War.

13. RAF, Air Power UAVs: The Wider Context, p. 31.

14. RAF, Air Power UAVs: The Wider Context, p. 30.

15. Defense Airborne Reconnaissance Office (DARO), Unmanned Aerial Vehicles (UAV) Program Plan, April 1994, For Official Use Only markings removed, pp. 2-2, 2-3.

16. Introduction to Unmanned Aircraft Systems, p. 14.

17. Defense Airborne Reconnaissance Office (DARO), Unmanned Aerial Vehicles (UAV) Program Plan, April 1994, For Official Use Only markings removed, pp. 2-2, 2-3; DOD, OSD UAV Reliability Study—Section 2, UAV Reliability Data, February 2003, pp. 12–13; Introduction to Unmanned Aircraft Systems, pp. 14–15.

18. Dr. Daniel L. Haulman, Air Force History Research Agency, U.S. Unmanned Aerial Vehicles in Combat, 1991–2003, June 9, 2003.

19. PH3 Todd Frantom, "Eyes in the Sky," *All Hands* (US Navy magazine), March 2005, p. 16.

20. "PAVEWAY III (GBU-24) Low Level Laser Guided Bomb (LLLGB) consists of either a 2,000-pound MK-84 general purpose or a BLU-109 penetrator bomb modified with a PAVEWAY III low-level laser-guided bomb kit. The LLLGB was developed in response to improved enemy air defenses, poor visibility, and low ceilings. The weapon is designed for low altitude delivery with an improved standoff capability of more than 10 nautical miles. The PAVEWAY III also has increased seeker sensitivity and a larger field of regard. Another guided bomb development was the GBU-27, a 2,200-pound laser-guided bomb designed specifically for use by the F-117 Stealth Fighter. It is a highly accurate, hard-structure munition compatible with the F-117's advanced target acquisition/designator system. The GBU-27 uses a BLU-109 improved performance 2,000-pound bomb developed in 1985 under the project name HAVE VOID, designed for use against hardened structures. The GBU-27 was used extensively during Desert Storm with a claimed hit probability of over

70 percent." See The Development and Deployment of Precision Guided Munitions (PGMS) for Standoff Attack, Richard H. Van Atta and Ivars Gutmanis; in IDA, Transformation and Transition: DARPA's Role in Fostering an Emerging Revolution in Military Affairs, Volume 2 — Detailed Assessments, p. III-14.

21. The army also employed the Pointer micro-UAV in Desert Storm, but poor weather and high winds made it even less effective than the Pioneer; McDaid and Oliver, p. 60.

22. Barry D. Watts, The Evolution of Precision Strike, CSBA, 2013, p. 8.

23. See The Development and Deployment of Precision Guided Munitions (PGMS) for Standoff Attack, Richard H. Van Atta and Ivars Gutmanis; in IDA, Transformation and Transition: DARPA's Role in Fostering an Emerging Revolution in Military Affairs, Volume 2 — Detailed Assessments, p. III-19.

24. Operational Requirements Document (ORD), Joint Direct Attack Munitions (JDAM), CAF 401-91-II-A (ORD324), 1991.

The kit includes a Global Positioning System (GPS)–aided Inertial Navigation System (INS), consisting of a power supply, an Inertial Measurement Unit (IMU), a GPS receiver, and an autopilot. The Guidance Control Unit (GCU) provides guidance commands to the tail actuator system of the bomb, which steers the weapon to the target. It communicates with the aircraft through the MIL-STD-1760 interface to receive initialization data and mission-specific guidance information. It also sends GCU and fuse status information back to the aircraft. See USAF Weapons School, Nellis AFB, Nevada; Student Paper: Joint Direct Attack Munition and the F-15E, for F-15E Class 96 AIM, by Captain Daniel F. Holmes, 4 FW, Seymour Johnson AFB, North Carolina, May 1996.

The initial accuracy goal for JDAM was 13m CEP. Even during testing, that goal was surpassed.

25. USAF Weapons School, Nellis AFB, NV; Student Paper: All Weather PGMS for the F-16 for F-16 Class 98-AIF, by Captain Matthew R. Dana; 51 FW, Osan AB, ROK, 13 June 1998.

"The second part of the alignment process is the initialization of the GPS...the JDAM gets GPS almanac data from the DTC. If the host aircraft has no GPS or the GPS is not functioning, the JDAM needs to be provided date and time data to know where to look for the satellites. This is done by entering the time (in GMT) and date on the Up Front Control (UFC) time page. Once the bomb is released, it uses the almanac data and the time/date data to begin its search for the satellites. If the host aircraft is GPS equipped and tracking satellites when the weapon is released, the position of the satellites being tracked by the aircraft and time/date information is passed to bomb. This greatly decreases the time required for the weapon to acquire satellites after release. The free flight state of the JDAM involves separation from the aircraft, fuse arming, GPS satellite acquisition, guidance optimization, trajectory adjustment, and impact. When the weapon is released, the fins are locked in position for one second to allow for safe separation. Once the fins unlock, bomb orientation rotates to place the stationary fin down. Guidance commands are phased in during the first 250 msec after the fins are unlocked. The weapon then attempts to achieve Optimal Guidance. The Optimal Guidance law computes the minimal control effort to go from the present position and velocity state to impacting the target at the desired flight path and approach angle. If all the planned impact conditions cannot be achieved, the guidance law trades off impact velocity first, then angle/azimuth, and finally impact point. The JDAM does not begin self-tracking satellites until after it is released. The acquisition process starts three seconds after release. This is to prevent the aircraft from 'shadowing' the satellites from the weapon. The weapon uses five channels for satellite acquisition. Channels one through four are used to track four satellites. The fifth channel is used to obtain correction computations. The fifth channel is also used to search for and receive data on reserve satellites. The maximum amount of time needed before the weapon will start guidance from the GPS is 27 seconds."

26. "The 422 TS is 89% confident that the true CEP based on the F-16 employment is nine meters (+/- 20%). Twenty-nine live drops, 90% of which were between 20,000 and 25,000 feet MSL, confirmed this. This CEP is based on a 7.2meter TLE. JDAM's accuracy rivals that of the GBU-10/12." See USAF Weapons School, Nellis AFB, NV; Student Paper: F-16 JDAM Accuracy vs. Terminal Threats for F-16 Class 99 AIF, by Captain Todd A. Murphey, 27 FW, Cannon AFB, New Mexico, 6 June 1999.

USAF Intelligence Targeting Guide, Air Force Pamphlet 14-210, 1 February 1998, p. 74.

27. Even in the face of jamming and other countermeasures, 100-foot accuracy would still be produced through the inertial measurement unit in each JDAM.

"JDAM accuracy is dependent upon the accuracy of target coordinates and the acquisition of GPS satellites. The design tolerances against horizontal targets call for a 13meter CEP for GPS guidance and a 30meter CEP for INS guidance...(T.O. 1-1M-34, 1-72.25). When using INS guidance, INS drift can effect bomb accuracy depending on the length of time-of-fall. The error assumed to achieve the 13meter or 30meter CEP is based on a target location error (TLE) of 7.2meters.

"If JDAM never acquires GPS, it guides to the target using its INS with degraded accuracy. In these cases, JDAM will still hit at the programmed impact angle and heading. Potential causes for not acquiring

GPS can vary from a short time of fall to no acquisition due to GPS jamming. It should be noted that JDAM does not have wings and cannot glide to the target. Instead, it falls similar to a GP bomb where some lift is provided by the strakes and its flight path is adjusted with the tail assembly. Therefore, the more JDAM must maneuver to hit the target, the closer the aircraft must be for the release. USAF employs from 20,000–25,000 feet MSL due to targeting pod limitations and GPS accuracy. However, this is no longer a factor with JDAM. Climbing higher and flying faster, pilots can drop JDAM from much farther away while still maintaining high accuracy"; see USAF Weapons School, Nellis AFB, NV; Student Paper: F-16 JDAM Accuracy vs. Terminal Threats for F-16 Class 99 AIF, by Captain Todd A. Murphey, 27 FW, Cannon AFB, New Mexico, 6 June 1999.

28. Air Land Sea Application Center, Targeting: The Joint Targeting Process and Procedures for Targeting Time-Critical Targets, FM 90-36, MCRP 3-16.1F, NWP 2-01.11, AFJPAM 10-225, July 1997, p. II-1.

29. PowerPoint Briefing, B-1B Team, MPE-960221-1480, 22 July 1996.

30. Lieutenant General Buster C. Glosson, USAF; Impact of Precision Weapons on Air Combat Operations, presentation made at the 1992 Armament Symposium at Eglin AFB, Florida, 23 September 1992.

31. U.S. Congress, House Armed Services Committee, Subcommittee on Military Procurement, Hearing on the Performance of the B-2 Bomber in Kosovo, 30 June 1999. At the time of the Kosovo war, no fighter was able to drop JDAMs because they had not yet received the proper interface; PowerPoint Briefing, Kosovo Lessons Learned, General John P. Jumper, n.d. (1999).

32. USAF Weapons School, Nellis AFB, NV; Student Paper: F-16 JDAM Accuracy vs. Terminal Threats for F-16 Class 99 AIF, by Captain Todd A. Murphey, 27 FW, Cannon AFB, New Mexico, 6 June 1999.

33. USAF Weapons School, Nellis AFB, NV; Student Paper: Future Developments in Conventional Weapons for F-16 Class 95 BIF, by Captain Stephen A. Langford, 522 FS, Cannon AFB, New Mexico, November 1995.

34. William M. Arkin, Special to *Defense Daily*, 9 February 2000.

35. USAF Intelligence Targeting Guide, Air Force Pamphlet 14-210, 1 February 1998, p. 74.

"JDAM is only as accurate as the target coordinates given to it. Getting coordinates accurate within 7.2 meters during mission planning will require sensitive sources, which in past conflicts have not always been accessible to fighter aircrew due to security issues. Anyone who has ever fought with Intel to get target area imagery knows this is a problem."

"...To achieve its advertised 13 meter accuracy, JDAM requires 3 dimensional target coordinates in the WGS-84 Datum. These coordinates must have a Target Location Error (TLE) of 7.2 meters or less.... The primary source of coordinates this accurate will be the Defense Mapping Agency's Database, although other sources, such as reconnaissance aircraft, do exist. These coordinates could be given to aircrew via the Air Tasking Order or through Intel's mission planning computer system, the Combat Intelligence System (CIS). Aircrew planning with the air force Mission Support System (AFMSS) will expedite getting these coordinates as the CIS can be linked to AFMSS and targets selected from imagery can be converted to accurate coordinates quickly. If the coordinates you receive have no TLE associated with them, weapon accuracy becomes questionable. A good rule of thumb to use for coordinates with no associated TLE is if they have three or more numbers after the decimal point, they have the required TLE for JDAM." See USAF Weapons School, Nellis AFB, Nevada; Student Paper: Joint Direct Attack Munition and the F-15E, for F-15E Class 96 AIM, by Captain Daniel F. Holmes, 4 FW, Seymour Johnson AFB, North Carolina, May 1996.

CHAPTER FOUR   Trojan Spirit

1. The most detailed story of Predator's origin is contained in Whittle, *Predator: The Secret Origins of the Drone Revolution* (New York: Henry Holt and Company, 2014).

   See also Frank Strickland, "The Early Evolution of the Predator Drone," *Studies in Intelligence*, Vol. 57, No. 1 (Extracts, March 2013); Houston R. Cantwell, Major, USAF, RADM Thomas J. Cassidy's MQ-1 Predator: The USAF's First UAV Success Story, Air Command and Staff College, Maxwell AFB, Alabama, April 2006; Major Houston R. Cantwell, USAF; Beyond Butterflies: Predator and the Evolution of Unmanned Aerial Vehicle in Air Force Culture; School of Advanced Air and Space Studies, Air University, Maxwell AFB, Alabama, June 2007, p. 19; Walter J. Boyne, How the Predator Grew Teeth, *Air Force Magazine*, July 2009 (Vol. 92, No. 7); Richard Whittle, Predator's Big Safari, Mitchell Papers 7, August 2011.

   As Deputy Secretary of Defense, William Perry championed the establishment of the Defense Airborne Reconnaissance Office (DARO), which was also commanded by Congress to bring some advocacy and organization to a floundering program. "The DARO will be responsible for the development and acquisition of manned and unmanned platforms, their sensors, data links, data relays, and ground stations," Perry directed in the establishing memo; Deputy Secretary of Defense Memorandum, "Establishment of the Defense Airborne Reconnaissance Office (DARO)," November 6, 1993.

2. See, e.g., Ashley Collman, "Marilyn the Riveter: New photos show Norma Jean working at a military factory during the height of World War II," *Daily Mail Online* (UK), July 27, 2013; www.dailymail.co.uk/news/article

-2380152/Marilyn-Monroe-photos-young-Norma-Jean-working-WWII
-factory.html (accessed July 27, 2013).

"First delivered to the US Army Air Corps in November 1939, the Radioplane Model RP-4 was designated as OQ-1. It would be the first of a family of drones for which Radioplane would earn fleeting fame. Until the interest in UAVs later in the twentieth century sparked a resurgence of interest, Radioplane drones were merely a forgotten footnote to World War II"; Bill Yenne, *Attack of the Drones: A History of Unmanned Aerial Combat*, p. 16.

3. See, e.g., John Barry and Evan Thomas, Up in the Sky, an Unblinking Eye: The hundreds of drones cruising over Iraq and Afghanistan have changed war forever, *Newsweek*, June 9, 2008.

4. Whittle, *Predator: The Secret Origins of the Drone Revolution* (2014), pp. 85–86; Rand, The Predator ACTD: A Case Study for Transition Planning to the Formal Acquisition Process, 1997, p. 22.

5. For references to June 1994, see, e.g., Bill Yenne, *Attack of the Drones: A History of Unmanned Aerial Combat*, p. 60.

6. Under the code name Red Wagon, the unmanned program began in 1959. In Vietnam, from August 1964 until their last combat flight on 30 April 1975, the air force's 100th Strategic Reconnaissance Wing launched 3,435 Ryan reconnaissance drones over North Vietnam and its surrounding areas, at a cost of about 554 UAVs lost to all causes during the war. See RAF, Air Power UAVs: The Wider Context, p. 30.

In comparison with manned aircraft, during the Vietnam War, unmanned reconnaissance drones produced about a 40 percent mission effectiveness rate, meaning that for every 100 targets to be photographed, they would come back with about 40 (after film canisters were successfully recovered and the film was developed). Manned platforms performed at about 70 percent. The cost of mounting an unmanned mission, including operating the launching and recovery aircraft and a higher rate of attrition, was about $40,000 per sortie, compared to about $6,500 for a manned mission. See Major Houston R. Cantwell, USAF; Beyond Butterflies: Predator and the Evolution of Unmanned Aerial Vehicle in Air Force Culture; School of Advanced Air and Space Studies, Air University, Maxwell AFB, Alabama, June 2007, pp. 11–12.

7. This included the application of "stealth," when engineers figured that by putting screen mesh over engine inlets and using special blankets and radar-absorbing paints they could make the drones more difficult for radar to detect. Major Christopher A. Jones, USAF; Unmanned Aerial Vehicles (UAVS): An Assessment of Historical Operations and Future Possibilities; a Research Paper Presented to the Research Department, Air Command and Staff College, AU/ACSC/0230D/97-03, March 1997, p. 12.

8. Unmanned Aerial Vehicles, Richard H. Van Atta, Jack Nunn, Alethia Cook, and Ivars Gutmanis; in IDA, Transformation and Transition: DARPA's Role in Fostering an Emerging Revolution in Military Affairs, Volume 2—Detailed Assessments, pp. VI-18 to VI-28; Thomas P. Ehrhard, Air Force UAVs: The Secret History, p. 20; Bill Yenne, *Attack of the Drones: A History of Unmanned Aerial Combat*, p. 67.

9. "Flown in 1973, the Developmental Sciences R4 SkyEye was a remarkably advanced UAV for its day. During the 1980s, the army flew them operationally in covert missions in Central America and possibly elsewhere"; Bill Yenne, *Attack of the Drones: A History of Unmanned Aerial Combat*, pp. 36, 39.

10. Major Houston R. Cantwell, USAF; Beyond Butterflies: Predator and the Evolution of Unmanned Aerial Vehicle in Air Force Culture; School of Advanced Air and Space Studies, Air University, Maxwell AFB, Alabama, June 2007, pp. 5, 18.

11. Thomas P. Ehrhard, Air Force UAVs: The Secret History, pp. 5–6. Ehrhard writes that the US intelligence community was the single greatest contributor to US operational UAV development. From the period 1960 through 2000, roughly forty years, "the intelligence community budget funded more than 40 percent of the total US UAV investment, double that of the next greatest contributor."

   See also comments by Robert Gates, who as CIA director in 1992 tried to get the air force to participate in development of advanced drones; *Duty*, p. 128.

   "To say that the Predator program lacked any coherent development plan would be an understatement. From its roots a consistent theme emerges. Predator's success did not result from any strategic long-term plan, but instead, occurred from cumulative short-term decisions made 'on the fly.' Even the air force's initial interest in Predator came rather abruptly. During the early stages of the ACTD process, the air force demonstrated little interest in participation. This lack of interest left the army largely responsible for operating the Predator during the 1995 Roving Sands exercise and the Nomad Vigil deployment to Europe later in 1995"; Major Houston R. Cantwell, USAF; Beyond Butterflies: Predator and the Evolution of Unmanned Aerial Vehicle in Air Force Culture; School of Advanced Air and Space Studies, Air University, Maxwell AFB, Alabama, June 2007, p. 21.

12. Thomas P. Ehrhard, Air Force UAVs: The Secret History, p. 49. Whittle, in *Predator: The Secret Origins of the Drone Revolution* (2014), p. 71, says that President Clinton himself was frustrated with the quality of the intelligence available.

   In Bosnia specifically, manned reconnaissance was also shown to have significant limitations, "mainly due to bad weather, roughness of the Bosnian terrain, camouflage skill of the Serbs, and limited availability and flexibility." See Lieutenant Colonel Richard L. Sargent, Chapter 8: Aircraft Used in Deliberate Force, p. 226; in Department of the Air Force, *Deliberate Force: A Case Study in Effective Air Campaigning.*

13. Unmanned Aerial Vehicles, Richard H. Van Atta, Jack Nunn, Alethia Cook, and Ivars Gutmanis; in IDA, Transformation and Transition: DARPA's Role in Fostering an Emerging Revolution in Military Affairs, Volume 2 — Detailed Assessments, p. VI-24; Major Houston R. Cantwell, USAF; Beyond Butterflies: Predator and the Evolution of Unmanned Aerial Vehicle in Air Force Culture; School of Advanced Air and Space Studies, Air University, Maxwell AFB, Alabama, June 2007, p. 17.

14. "The dronefather; Abe Karem created the robotic plane that transformed the way modern warfare is waged — and continues to pioneer other airborne innovations," *The Economist*, December 1, 2012; www.economist .com/news/technology-quarterly/21567205-abe-karem-created-robotic -plane-transformed-way-modern-warfare (accessed October 2, 2013).

15. Frank Strickland, "The Early Evolution of the Predator Drone," *Studies in Intelligence*, Vol. 57, No. 1 (Extracts, March 2013). See also the detailed history in Whittle, *Predator: The Secret Origins of the Drone Revolution* (2014), pp. 68ff.

16. Richard M. Clark, Uninhabited Combat Aerial Vehicles: Airpower by the People, for the People, but Not with the People; A Thesis Presented to the Faculty of the School of Advanced Airpower Studies, for Completion of Graduation Requirements, School of Advanced Airpower Studies, Air University, Maxwell AFB, Alabama, June 1999, p. 53.

17. Richard M. Clark, Uninhabited Combat Aerial Vehicles: Airpower by the People, for the People, but Not with the People; A Thesis Presented to the Faculty of the School of Advanced Airpower Studies, for Completion of Graduation Requirements, School of Advanced Airpower Studies, Air University, Maxwell AFB, Alabama, June 1999, p. 53; Unmanned Aerial Vehicles, Richard H. Van Atta, Jack Nunn, Alethia Cook, and Ivars Gutmanis; in IDA, Transformation and Transition: DARPA's Role in Fostering an Emerging Revolution in Military Affairs, Volume 2 — Detailed Assessments, p. VI-23.

18. Congressional Research Service (Richard A. Best), "Intelligence Technology in the Post-Cold War Era: The Role of Unmanned Aerial Vehicles (UAVs)," July 26, 1993, p. 10.

19. Peter W. Merlin, Ikhana: Unmanned Aircraft System Western States Fire Missions, NASA History Office, 2009, p. 1; John David Blom, Unmanned Aerial Systems: A Historical Perspective, Occasional Paper 37, Combat Studies Institute Press, September 2010, p. 94.

Prior to Deliberate Force, the Gnat had seen service during Deny Flight operations, unlike Predator. During Deliberate Force, the Gnat launched and recovered from Dezney, Turkey, and inside Croatia. In all, the Gnat-750 attempted twelve launches and flew seven successful flights.

During Deliberate Force, Lofty View and Condor aircraft based at Dezney, Turkey, flew nine sorties, logging more than fifty-two hours of recce and surveillance time; Lieutenant Colonel Richard L. Sargent, Chapter 8: Aircraft Used in Deliberate Force, p. 227; in *Deliberate Force: A Case Study in Effective Air Campaigning.*

One source says that Gnats followed UN convoys and took pictures of artillery and surface-to-air missile sites. See John David Blom, Unmanned Aerial Systems: A Historical Perspective, Occasional Paper 37, Combat Studies Institute Press, September 2010, pp. 93–94.

20. Rand, The Predator ACTD: A Case Study for Transition Planning to the Formal Acquisition Process, 1997, p. 20.

21. With a wingspan of 48.7 feet and a weight of approximately 2,250 pounds, the Predator A had an operational altitude of 7,000 to 22,000 feet, a loitering airspeed of 85 knots cruising and 120 knots maximum, and endurance of 16 to 22 hours (out to 500 nautical miles. It can carry approximately 450 pounds internally and 200 pounds externally).

See Frank Strickland, "The Early Evolution of the Predator Drone," *Studies in Intelligence*, Vol. 57, No. 1 (Extracts, March 2013). Predator can carry a larger payload than the Gnat-750's (450 pounds versus 140 pounds) and is a heavier vehicle (1,873 pounds versus 1,140 pounds); see Rand, The Predator ACTD: A Case Study for Transition Planning to the Formal Acquisition Process, 1997, p. 9.

22. Matt J. Martin with Charles W. Sasser, *Predator: The Remote-Control Air War over Iraq and Afghanistan: A Pilot's Story* (Minneapolis: Zenith Press, 2010), p. 20.

23. As Whittle, in *Predator: The Secret Origins of the Drone Revolution* (2014), p. 95, points out, though: "The first dish installed was merely a placeholder, a UHF (ultra-high-frequency) antenna with too little bandwidth to handle the amount of data required both to control the aircraft and stream video."

See also Glenn Goodman, Evolving the Predator; Interview: Thomas J. Cassidy Jr, President and CEO General Atomics Aeronautical Systems, Inc., *Intelligence, Surveillance & Reconnaissance Journal*, July 2004, p. 26.

24. Rand, The Predator ACTD: A Case Study for Transition Planning to the Formal Acquisition Process, 1997, pp. 21–22.

25. In August 1995, engineers retrofitted the initial three Predators with Ku-band capability (which they did not initially have). "After the retrofitting, the UAV could provide real-time motion video to ground sources"; Rand, The Predator ACTD: A Case Study for Transition Planning to the Formal Acquisition Process, 1997, p. 25; see also Thomas P. Ehrhard, Air Force UAVs: The Secret History, p. 49.

26. CBO, Options for Enhancing DOD's UAV Programs, September 1998, p. 13; Linda Shiner, "Predator: First Watch: Lesson learned: never send

a man to do a machine's job," *Air & Space* magazine (Smithsonian), May 2001.

27. The payload on Predator, the black box, was the MX-14 Wescam, a stabilized gimbal (or sensor ball) turret slung underneath the chin and containing a visible color and infrared video camera. Predator delivered daylight and nighttime full-motion video (FMV). Additionally, Predator squeezed a form of compressed FMV into existing bandwidth—akin to the same signal going through a dial-up pipeline, as opposed to broadband. Before Predator, at least in the military, the norm for manned reconnaissance was 8-by-10-inch glossy images that took an hour or so to process and much longer to distribute. See Glenn Goodman, Evolving the Predator; Interview: Thomas J. Cassidy Jr, President and CEO General Atomics Aeronautical Systems, Inc., *Intelligence, Surveillance & Reconnaissance Journal*, July 2004, p. 26.

Motion imagery is defined as an imaging system that collects at a rate of one frame per second (1 Hz) or faster; DOD/IC//National System for Geospatial Intelligence, Motion Imagery Standards Board, Motion Imagery Standards Profile, Version 5.4, December 3, 2009.

Full-motion imagery (FMV) refers to motion imagery at twenty-four frames per second or higher. This is generally considered the minimum frame rate required to appear fluid to the human eye. The Motion Imagery Standards Board notes that "Historically... FMV has been that subset of motion imagery at television-like frame rates (24–60 Hz)"; See Rand Corporation (Lance Menthe, Amado Cordova, Carl Rhodes, Rachel Costello, Jeffrey Sullivan), The Future of Air Force Motion Imagery Exploitation: Lessons from the Commercial World, 2012, p. 3, fn. 14. For background on FMV, see also the excellent paper by Lieutenant Colonel Mark A. Cooter, USAF, Airborne Armed Full Motion Video: The Nexus of Ops/Intel Integration in the Joint/Coalition Environment, Joint Forces Staff College, Joint Advanced Warfighting School, 25 May 2007.

28. Glenn Goodman, Evolving the Predator; Interview: Thomas J. Cassidy Jr, President and CEO General Atomics Aeronautical Systems, Inc., *Intelligence, Surveillance & Reconnaissance Journal*, July 2004, p. 26.

29. Frank Strickland, "The Early Evolution of the Predator Drone," *Studies in Intelligence*, Vol. 57, No. 1 (Extracts, March 2013).

30. Peter Finn, "Rise of the drone: From Calif. garage to multibillion-dollar defense industry," *Washington Post*, December 23, 2011; www.washingtonpost.com/national/national-security/rise-of-the-drone-from-calif-garage-to-multibillion-dollar-defense-industry/2011/12/22/gIQACG8UEP_story.html (accessed February 19, 2014); Quoted in Ian Shaw, History of U.S. Drones: The Rise of the Predator Empire: Tracing the History of U.S. Drones, Understanding Empire (Blog), 2013; http://understandingempire

.wordpress.com/2-0-a-brief-history-of-u-s-drones/ (accessed March 27, 2013).

31. Lieutenant Colonel Richard L. Sargent, Chapter 8: Aircraft Used in Deliberate Force, p. 226; in *Deliberate Force: A Case Study in Effective Air Campaigning.*

    Major Mark Biwer, The Joint Broadcast Service Supporting Bosnia: Value to the Warrior and Lessons Learned, A Research Paper Presented to the Research Department, Air Command and Staff College, March 1997, gives specific examples of Predator's use in Bosnia, see pp. 27–28.

32. American Forces Press Service, Linda D. Kozaryn, Predators Bound for Bosnia, February 8, 1996.

33. On August 11, 1995, Bosnian Serbs shot down one Predator. "The unlucky aircraft had descended to 4,000 feet to get beneath a cloud layer and had lingered in a valley for about an hour at the behest of commanders in Naples, Italy. Its loss was virtually inevitable. Another Predator crashed a few days later because its engine quit." Rumor has it that the Bosnian Serb military was able to shoot down the Predator by firing a machine gun out the open side door of a helicopter.

    On August 14, 1995, technicians destroyed a second Predator when it developed engine problems and lost power over Bosnia.

    See Linda Shiner, "Predator: First Watch: Lesson learned: never send a man to do a machine's job," *Air & Space* magazine (Smithsonian), May 2001; James Risen and Ralph Vartabadian, "Spy plane woes create Bosnia intelligence gap," *Los Angeles Times*, December 2, 1995; Larry Ernst, "Predator: our experience in Bosnia using UAVs in combat," Proc. SPIE 2829 Airborne reconnaissance XX (131) (1996).

34. Matt J. Martin with Charles W. Sasser, *Predator*, p. 24.

35. "The RQ-1 is a remotely operated single engine propeller driven aircraft capable of speeds to 120 knots, altitudes to 25,000 feet, and airframe endurance in excess of 24 hours (clean). Takeoffs and landings utilize a forward mounted nose camera. The RQ-1 is the legacy airframe from which the MQ-1 was developed, and it lacks weaponized capability. All future procurements will be of the MQ-1 variant, and the RQ-1 will be phased out through attrition. The RQ-1 employs the Wescam 14 payload sensor and internal SAR with 0.3 meter resolution. The Wescam 14 employs EO and Medium Wave IR (MWIR) sensors. The RQ-1 is capable of performing limited Killer Scout and FAC(A) without laser designation capability. The RQ-1 employs a military standard (Mil Std) 1553 avionics bus"; ACC, Concept of Employment for the MQ-1 and MQ-9 Multi-role Endurance Remotely Operated Aircraft, 2 May 2002, FOUO (obtained by the author), p. 4.

    See also Major Christopher A. Jones, USAF; Unmanned Aerial Vehicles (UAVS): An Assessment of Historical Operations and Future Possibilities; A

Research Paper Presented to the Research Department, Air Command and Staff College, AU/ACSC/0230D/97-03, March 1997, pp. 32–33.

36. See the criticisms leveled in Bosnia, in Whittle, in *Predator: The Secret Origins of the Drone Revolution* (2014), pp. 113ff.

37. See Rand, The Predator ACTD: A Case Study for Transition Planning to the Formal Acquisition Process, 1997, pp. 21–22.

38. George Galdorisi, Robin Laird, and Rachel Volner, Taking the Next Step: From "Unmanned" to True Autonomy, Abstract for 17th ICCRTS, "Operationalizing C2 Agility," US Navy, Space and Naval Warfare Systems Center (SPAWAR) Pacific, p. 3.

39. "The only cost figure the JPO [Joint Program Office] considered during the ACTD was associated with the aerial vehicle. The JPO estimated the flyaway target cost for the Predator in the $3–$3.5-million range. However, in April 1996, the Predator TIPT reported that the cost of a Predator system, including four aerial vehicles, a ground control station, one Trojan Spirit II system, operator training, and logistics support, was around $30 million. Prior to the release of this information, the air force...did not realize that significant life-cycle costs would be associated with the entire system." See Rand, The Predator ACTD: A Case Study for Transition Planning to the Formal Acquisition Process, 1997, pp. 43–44.

40. See Richard M. Clark, Uninhabited Combat Aerial Vehicles: Airpower by the People, for the People, but Not with the People; A Thesis Presented to the Faculty of the School of Advanced Airpower Studies, for Completion of Graduation Requirements, School of Advanced Airpower Studies, Air University, Maxwell AFB, Alabama, June 1999, p. 53.

"Three Predators equipped with a color video camera and an electro-optical/infrared camera, conducted 128 missions each totaling 850 hours (and with 6.6 hours average endurance—more than double what the Pioneers averaged in *Desert Storm*)....In November 1995, the Predators, still in limited supply, were fitted with synthetic aperture radars and redeployed to Bosnia to provide detailed radar images in adverse weather. By May 1998, Predators had logged more than 600 sorties and 3800 flying hours over Bosnia"; Christopher J. Bowie, Robert P. Haffa, Jr., and Robert E. Mullins; Future War: What Trends in America's Post-Cold War Military Conflicts Tell Us About Early 21st Century Warfare, Northrop Grumman Analysis Center, 2003, pp. 55–56.

41. Lieutenant Colonel Richard L. Sargent, Chapter 8: Aircraft Used in Deliberate Force, p. 228; in Deliberate Force: A Case Study in Effective Air Campaigning.

42. DOD, UAV Annual Report FY 1996, 6 November 1996, p. 9.

43. Bill Yenne, *Attack of the Drones: A History of Unmanned Aerial Combat*, p. 63.

44. Major Christopher A. Jones, USAF; Unmanned Aerial Vehicles (UAVS): An Assessment of Historical Operations and Future Possibilities; A

Research Paper Presented to the Research Department, Air Command and Staff College, AU/ACSC/0230D/97-03, March 1997, pp. 32–33.

45. Whittle, *Predator: The Secret Origins of the Drone Revolution* (2014), pp. 104, 114–115.

46. Unmanned Aerial Vehicles, Richard H. Van Atta, Jack Nunn, Alethia Cook, and Ivars Gutmanis; in IDA, Transformation and Transition: DARPA's Role in Fostering an Emerging Revolution in Military Affairs, Volume 2 — Detailed Assessments, pp VI-21 to VI-22.

47. Rand, The Predator ACTD: A Case Study for Transition Planning to the Formal Acquisition Process, 1997, p. 33.

48. Houston R. Cantwell, Major, USAF, RADM Thomas J. Cassidy's MQ-1 Predator: The USAF's First UAV Success Story, Air Command and Staff College, Maxwell AFB, Alabama April 2006, p. 14.

49. The impact of PowerPoint is still an issue today, at least with the wise guys of Washington. Robert Gates writes that PowerPoint briefings became "the bane of my existence in Pentagon meetings"; *Duty*, p. 82.

CHAPTER FIVE   Dialogue of the Deaf

1. Quoted in JCS, Joint Publication 2-01, Doctrine for Joint and National Intelligence Support to Military Operations, October 7, 2004, p. III-27.

2. In 1975 the idea of arming RPVs for strike operations was discussed in the final report of the Long Range Research and Development Planning Program. The LRRDPP's employment concept was that armed RPVs would employ standoff precision munitions to penetrate enemy air defenses and, then, in the case of a major target such as an oil refinery, make a kamikaze strike against the facility; Barry D. Watts, The Evolution of Precision Strike, CSBA, 2013, pp. 17–18.

3. Thomas P. Ehrhard, Air Force UAVs: The Secret History, p. 21.

4. General Ronald Fogleman, who became chief of staff of the air force in 1994 — mid-development of the Predator — made an argument that the UAV was all about the mission, neither technological determinism nor bureaucratic triumph. Even though the air force hadn't looked at Predator in much detail, with the retirement of dedicated reconnaissance jets and a questionable future for the manned SR-71, and with oversubscribed national satellites capable of only episodic coverage of the battlefield, he personally pushed for the new loitering drones to fill the gap; Richard Whittle, Predator's Big Safari, Mitchell Papers 7, August 2011, p. 9; Whittle, *Predator: The Secret Origins of the Drone Revolution* (2014).

Thomas P. Ehrhard, Air Force UAVs: The Secret History, pp. 50–51, makes a much more convincing institutional and opportunistic argument about the air force's newfound enthusiasm after Bosnia.

5. Quoted in Major Christopher A. Jones, USAF; Unmanned Aerial Vehicles (UAVs): An Assessment of Historical Operations and Future Possibilities, Air Command and Staff College Research Paper, March 1997, p. 23.

It is important to note that Predator can fly at 25,000 feet but actually flies most of its missions at 10,000 to 15,000 feet.

6. In April 1996, Secretary of Defense William Perry stated, "The Predator has proved its ability to provide a significant and urgently needed reconnaissance capability in many mission areas and the continued participation of each Service must be maintained." Quoted in Houston R. Cantwell, Major, USAF, RADM Thomas J. Cassidy's MQ-1 Predator: The USAF's First UAV Success Story, Air Command and Staff College, Maxwell AFB, Alabama, April 2006, p. 14.

7. Chris Bowie estimates that the United States had spent about $21 billion between 1950 and 1998 on unmanned aerial vehicles; Chris Bowie (then Northrop Grumman Analysis Center), PowerPoint Briefing, UAV Lessons Learned, 1950–2001, n.d. (Version 5, 2001).

8. SAR sensors are different than passive electrooptical sensors that do not provide their own illumination.

9. Kazuo Ouchi, "Review: Recent Trend and Advance of Synthetic Aperture Radar with Selected Topics," Remote Sens. 2013, 5, pp. 716–807; ACC, Concept of Employment for the MQ-1 and MQ-9 Multi-role Endurance Remotely Operated Aircraft, 2 May 2002, FOUO (obtained by the author), p. 4; Robert Hendrix, "Aerospace System Improvements Enabled by Modern Phased Array Radar," Northrop Grumman Electronic Systems, Baltimore, Maryland, October 2002; "Northrop Grumman Delivers First TUAVR Radars and Spares to the Army," July 17, 2001; American Forces Press Service, Linda D. Kozaryn, Predators Bound for Bosnia, February 8, 1996.

The AN/ZPQ-1 TESAR used a radar signal in the 10-20 GHz J-band. Strip map imaging observes terrain parallel to the flight path or along a specified ground path. Resolution depends on range and swath width. At ground speeds from 25 to 35 m/sec, the swath width is 800 meters. Spot map mode observes 800 x 800 meter and 2400 x 2400 meter tiles. In MTI mode, moving targets are overlaid on a digital map.

"The TESAR [Tactical Endurance Synthetic Aperture Radar (SAR)] system uses four algorithms in its three-stage algorithmic approach to the detection and identification of targets in continuous real-time, 1-ft-resolution, strip SAR image data. The first stage employs a multitarget detector with a built-in natural/cultural false-alarm mitigator. The second stage provides target hypotheses for the candidate targets and refines their angular pose. The third stage, consisting of two template-based algorithms, produces final target-identification decisions"; Dalton S. Rosario, "End-to end performance of the TESAR ATR system," Proc. SPIE

4053, Algorithms for Synthetic Aperture Radar Imagery VII, 677 (August 24, 2000).

10. David A. Fulghum, Washington; Global Hawk Crashes in UAE After Afghanistan Mission, *Aviation Week & Space Technology*, January 7, 2002.

There was a major perception that the sensors were not operating as anticipated, due to lack of pilot experience, to poor visibility, and "to a misunderstanding of how imagery is collected and analyzed." See Rand, The Predator ACTD: A Case Study for Transition Planning to the Formal Acquisition Process, 1997, pp. 24–25.

11. Four NATO allies (France, Germany, Italy, and the UK) also flew their own new unmanned drones: Mirach, CL-289, Phoenix, and Crecerelle. See Air Force PowerPoint Briefing, U.S. Air Force Unmanned Aerial Vehicles, Capt. Dan Callahan, Chief, UAV Operations, HQ AF/XOIRC, n.d. (2000); DOD/JCS, Joint Statement on the Kosovo After Action Review, 14 October 1999; Tony Capaccio, "JSTARS Led Most Lethal Attacks on Serbs," *Defense Week*, July 6, 1999, p. 13.

12. Hunter did as well. Pioneer and Crecerelle sent motion imagery back to a ground control station for processing and further distribution; the CL-289 and Phoenix transmitted infrared imagery to line of sight users.

13. Whittle, *Predator: The Secret Origins of the Drone Revolution* (2014), p. 131.

14. Quoted in Christopher J. Bowie, Robert P. Haffa, Jr., and Robert E. Mullins; Future War: What Trends in America's Post-Cold War Military Conflicts Tell Us About Early 21st Century Warfare, Northrop Grumman Analysis Center, 2003, pp. 55–56.

15. Linda Shiner, "Predator: First Watch: Lesson learned: never send a man to do a machine's job," *Air & Space* magazine (Smithsonian), May 2001.

16. As told in Major Houston R. Cantwell, USAF; Beyond Butterflies: Predator and the Evolution of Unmanned Aerial Vehicle in Air Force Culture; School of Advanced Air and Space Studies, Air University, Maxwell AFB, Alabama, June 2007, p. 25. See also RAF, Air Power UAVs: The Wider Context, pp. 37–38; Richard Whittle, Predator's Big Safari, Mitchell Papers 7, August 2011, p. 12.

Many others would tell anecdotes reflecting the same or similar problems, perhaps also adding even a little antiunmanned bias: Lieutenant Colonel David Nichols, commander of the 510th Fighter Squadron at Aviano Air Base, Italy, during Allied Force, provided the following vignette on the use of the Predator UAV: "The Predator would give us an 8 by 10 picture of a tank. We would ask 'Where is it?' And they would say 'Well, it's in Serbia!'.... pilots and command staffs had to improvise during the conflict to find ways of making Predator's capabilities beneficial to the squadrons flying the missions." See Major Kathy B. Davis, USAF; Operation Allied Force: Reachback and Information Processes; AU/

ACSC/031/2002-04; Air Command and Staff College; Maxwell AFB, Alabama, March 2002, pp. 9–10.

17. The story as it gets told is that Lieutenant General Michael Short, Jumper's subordinate and the direct commander of the air campaign in Italy, had a son who was an A-10 pilot flying over Kosovo. He told Dad of the problems of talking the pilots onto the target, and Short then talked to Jumper, who called General Ryan in Washington, who called in Snake and the other subject matter experts to solve the problem. But Richard Whittle pretty much determines that this was urban legend. See telling in Richard Whittle, Predator's Big Safari, Mitchell Papers 7, August 2011, p. 13; and Whittle, in *Predator: The Secret Origins of the Drone Revolution* (2014), p. 132.

18. Richard Whittle, Predator's Big Safari, Mitchell Papers 7, August 2011, pp. 13–14.

19. Walter J. Boyne, How the Predator Grew Teeth, *Air Force Magazine*, July 2009 (Vol. 92, No. 7).

20. Houston R. Cantwell, Major, USAF, RADM Thomas J. Cassidy's MQ-1 Predator: The USAF's First UAV Success Story, Air Command and Staff College, Maxwell AFB, Alabama, April 2006, pp. 24–25; Richard Whittle, Predator's Big Safari, Mitchell Papers 7, August 2011, p. 14.

21. Using its infrared camera, a Predator tracked a Serb military vehicle driving into a shed, shooting its laser at the spot, the A-10 then hitting the building with a 500-pound laser-guided bomb. Whittle, *Predator: The Secret Origins of the Drone Revolution* (2014), p. 141. See also Richard Whittle, Predator's Big Safari, Mitchell Papers 7, August 2011, p. 15.

22. USAF, RQ-1A Predator Unmanned Aerial Vehicle (UAV) System, 1999 DOTE report, p. v-153; Richard Whittle, Predator's Big Safari, Mitchell Papers 7, August 2011, p. 15.

23. Bill Yenne, *Attack of the Drones*, p. 86.

24. Richard Whittle, Predator's Big Safari, Mitchell Papers 7, August 2011, p. 17.

25. RAF, Air Power UAVs: The Wider Context, pp. 37–38; Walter J. Boyne, How the Predator Grew Teeth, *Air Force Magazine*, July 2009 (Vol. 92, No. 7).

26. USAF, RQ-1A Predator Unmanned Aerial Vehicle (UAV) System, 1999 DOTE report, p. v-153.

CHAPTER SIX   Another Plane

1. Michael Scheur, *Through Our Enemies' Eyes: Osama bin Laden, Radical Islam and the Future of America* (Dulles, Virginia: Potomac Books, 2006, revised edition), pp. 124–125; Lawrence Wright, *The Looming Tower* (New York: Knopf, 2006), pp. 158, 195, 210, 247; CNN broadcast, interview of Bin Ladin [sic] by Peter Arnett on March 20, 1997.

2. *Looming Tower*, p. 188.

3. On August 23, 1996, bin Laden issued an 11,500-word "fatwa" authorizing attacks against Western military targets in the Arabian Peninsula. See Usama Bin Ladin [sic], "Declaration of War Against the Americans Occupying the Land of the Two Holy Places," August 23, 1996; *Looming Tower*, pp. 232ff. According to *Through Our Enemies' Eyes*, p. xvi, the declaration of war on the United States is actually published on September 2, 1996, in the Movement for Islamic Reform in Arabia's *al-Islah* newsletter.

4. An al Qaeda videotape appeared on Al Jazeera on June 21, 2011, presenting recorded statements of Osama bin Laden. "With small capabilities, and with our faith, we can defeat the greatest military power of modern times. America is much weaker than it appears," bin Laden says. He reassures potential martyrs: "You will not die needlessly. Your lives are in the hands of God," and encourages the killing of Israelis and Americans: "We will see again Saladin carrying his sword, with the blood of unbelievers dripping from it."

5. CIA director George Tenet, in a top secret memo after the embassy bombings, even declared "war" against al Qaeda. DCI memo to deputies at the CIA, December 4, 1998: "We are at war...I want no resources or people spared in this effort, either inside CIA or the Community...We must now enter a new phase in our effort against Bin Ladin [sic]...we all acknowledge that retaliation is inevitable and that its scope may be far larger than we have previously experienced...."

Tenet additionally writes: "I want Charlie Allen [Deputy Director] to immediately chair a meeting with NSA, NIMA [now NGA], CITO [our clandestine information technology organization] and others to ensure we are doing everything we can to meet CTC's [counterterrorist center] requirements." See George Tenet with Bill Harlow, *At the Center of the Storm* (New York: HarperCollins, 2007), p. 119.

6. 9/11 Commission Report, p. 203.

7. *Looming Tower*, pp. 265–266.

8. John Rizzo, *Company Man: Thirty Years of Controversy and Crisis in the CIA* (New York: Scribner, 2014), p. 165.

9. 9/11 Commission Report, Chapter 6, Footnote 112, p. 506.

10. *At the Center of the Storm*, p. 112; 9/11 Commission Report, p. 112.

11. Written Statement for the Record of the Director of Central Intelligence, Before the National Commission on Terrorist Attacks Upon the United States, March 24, 2004.

12. 9/11 Commission Report, pp. 131–132. The four were Secretary of State Albright, Secretary of Defense Cohen, Attorney General Reno, and chairman of the Joint Chiefs General Shelton.

13. 9/11 Commission Report, p. 189.

14. Daniel Benjamin and Steven Simon, *The Age of Sacred Terror* (New York: Random House, 2002), p. 344.

15. Mark Mazzetti, *The Way of the Knife* (New York: Penguin Press, 2013), p. 92.
16. *Age of Sacred Terror*, p. 321; Richard Whittle, Predator's Big Safari, Mitchell Papers 7, August 2011, p. 19.
17. Whittle, *Predator: The Secret Origins of the Drone Revolution* (2014), p. 154.
18. Saudi Arabia is merely the author's best guess as to the location of the second base. In Richard Whittle, Predator's Big Safari, Mitchell Papers 7, August 2011, p. 21, he says "another country that was located within the beam footprint of a [communications] satellite in orbit over Southwest Asia." George Tenet later testified before the 9/11 Commission that: "indications were that the host country would be unlikely to tolerate extensive operations, especially after the Taliban became aware, as it surely would, of that country's assistance to the United States." See Written Statement for the Record of the Director of Central Intelligence, Before the National Commission on Terrorist Attacks Upon the United States, March 24, 2004.
19. 9/11 Commission Report, p. 189.
20. 9/11 Commission Report, p. 189.
21. Whittle, *Predator: The Secret Origins of the Drone Revolution* (2014), p. 157.
22. 9/11 Commission Report, p. 190; *At the Center of the Storm*, p. 127; Richard A. Clarke, *Against All Enemies* (New York: Free Press, 2004), p. 220; *The Way of the Knife*, p. 93.
23. Written Statement for the Record of the Director of Central Intelligence, Before the National Commission on Terrorist Attacks Upon the United States, March 24, 2004.

    After a second sighting of the "man in white" at the compound on September 28, intelligence community analysts determined that he was probably Bin Laden; 9/11 Commission Report, p. 190. The footnote reads: "The CIA's Ben Bonk told us he could not guarantee from analysis of the video feed that the man in the white robe was in fact Bin Ladin, but he thinks Bin Ladin is the 'highest probability person.' (Bin Ladin is unusually tall.)" Ben Bonk briefing (March 11, 2004). Intelligence analysts seem to have determined that this might have been Bin Ladin very soon after the September 28 sighting; two days later, Clarke wrote to Berger that there was a "very high probability" Bin Ladin had been located. NSC note, Clarke to Berger, "Procedures for Protecting Predator," September 30, 2000.

    Tenet later testified: "During two missions the Predator may have observed Usama bin Ladin. In one case this was an after-the-fact judgment. In the other, sources indicated that Bin Ladin would likely be at his Tarnak Farms facility, and, so cued, the Predator flew over the facility the next day. It imaged a tall man dressed in white robes with a physical and operational signature fitting Bin Ladin. A group of 10 people gathered around him were apparently paying their respects for a minute or two." Written Statement for the Record of the Director of Central Intelligence,

Before the National Commission on Terrorist Attacks Upon the United States, March 24, 2004.

24. 9/11 Commission Report, Chapter 6, Footnote 120, p. 507.

25. *Age of Sacred Terror*, p. 322.

26. On May 1, 2000, General Jumper, then commander of Air Combat Command (ACC), sent a message to Headquarters Air Force, the office of Air Force Secretary F. Whitten Peters, AFMC, and other relevant commands. "Chief, ACC has internalized the Predator lessons learned from Operation Allied Force and is changing the direction for the Predator program," the May 1 message began. "The original construct of the Predator as just a reconnaissance surveillance target acquisition asset no longer applies. ACC will employ Predator as a FAC-like resource, with look-out, target identification, and target acquisition roles using the inherent and proposed EO/IR/laser targeting/designation capabilities and upgrades. Also, ACC, AFMC, and the Air Armament Center (Eglin) are moving out on the next logical step for USAF UAVs using Predator—weaponizing UAVs." See Richard Whittle, Predator's Big Safari, Mitchell Papers 7, August 2011, pp. 17–18.

In the spring of 2000, a weaponization working group was formed including air force and army representatives. Big Safari assumed stewardship of the weaponization effort in late summer and a CONOPS for the multirole Predator was drafted, finalized in August 2001. See Briefing, Colonel Larry L. Felder, Commander, UAVB; Unmanned Aerial Vehicle Battlelab, 5 January 2005 (FOUO); obtained by the author.

27. Richard Whittle, Predator's Big Safari, Mitchell Papers 7, August 2011, p. 19; 9/11 Commission Report, p. 189.

28. Richard Whittle, Predator's Big Safari, Mitchell Papers 7, August 2011, pp. 21–22. On December 21, 2000, the Office of the Secretary of Defense signed the armed Predator's "Compliance Certification," resolving the treaty issues.

29. See, e.g., *Against all Enemies*, p. 220; Written Statement for the Record of the Director of Central Intelligence, Before the National Commission on Terrorist Attacks Upon the United States, March 24, 2004.

30. See Whittle, *Predator: The Secret Origins of the Drone Revolution* (2014), p. 157, for the story of the sighting on the seventh and not the first flight. Then see also 9/11 Commission Report, p. 190; *At the Center of the Storm*, p. 127; *Against all Enemies*, p. 220; and *The Way of the Knife*, p. 93.

"In the Predator's very first trial run…we observed a tall man in flowing white robes walking around surrounded by a security detail"; *At the Center of the Storm*, p. 127.

Even Whittle in his initial Predator study accepted the first flight/fight sighting tale: "Big Safari began flying Afghan Eyes missions over

Afghanistan on Sept. 7, 2000. On its first flight over Bin Laden's Tarnak Farms compound outside Kandahar, the Predator's camera spotted a man intelligence analysts believed to be the Al Qaeda leader himself." See Richard Whittle, Predator's Big Safari, Mitchell Papers 7, August 2011, p. 21.

Later CIA analysts concluded that the camera had captured bin Laden in the second mission flown but only after analysis later; Whittle, *Predator: The Secret Origins of the Drone Revolution* (2014), p. 160.

31. *Company Man*, p. 178.

32. By September 2001, nineteen of the sixty-eight Predators that had been delivered had been lost in operations, as many because of operator error as due to weather; the Pentagon operational evaluation office criticized the drone for its vulnerability to "visible moisture such as rain, snow, ice, frost or fog." Bill Yenne, *Attack of the Drones: A History of Unmanned Aerial Combat*, pp. 64–65.

33. Major Christopher A. Jones, USAF; Unmanned Aerial Vehicles (UAVS): An Assessment of Historical Operations and Future Possibilities; A Research Paper Presented to the Research Department, Air Command and Staff College, AU/ACSC/0230D/97-03, March 1997, p. 33.

34. Major Houston R. Cantwell, USAF; Beyond Butterflies: Predator and the Evolution of Unmanned Aerial Vehicle in Air Force Culture; School of Advanced Air and Space Studies, Air University, Maxwell AFB, Alabama, June 2007, p. 24.

From March 1996 through April 1997, out of the 315 Predator missions tasked, weather and system cancellations kept nearly two-thirds (60 percent) on the ground. Of the remaining missions that were launched, slightly under one-half were subsequently aborted. These aborts were due to system (29 percent), weather (65 percent), and operational issues (6 percent) that included airspace conflicts, operator errors, and crew duty limitations.

Data indicates that 38 missions (12 percent) were scrubbed due to system failures, and that there were an additional 18 system aborts (6 percent) that did not result in mission cancellation (due to launch of another aircraft or weather hold), as well as other issues that kept the Predator on the ground 6 times (2 percent). See DOD, UAS Roadmap 2005, Appendix H—Reliability, pp. H-5 and H-6.

Of 128 Predator sorties scheduled during Operation Allied Force over Kosovo in 1999, 84 were launched, 30 had to return to base (20 due to weather, 4 for maintenance problems, 6 for communications). And of the remaining 54, a total of 41 missions were shortened or canceled due to weather, 4 for maintenance. See Air Force PowerPoint Briefing, Weaponized UAV Demonstration, Brigadier General Kevin Sullivan, AAC Vice Commander, 16 March 2000; obtained by the author.

35. The DOD Director of Operational Test & Evaluation went further in his 2001 annual report, declaring, "The Predator UAV system is not operationally effective or suitable as tested during IOT&E." DOT&E Annual Report FY2001, February 2002, p. V-100 and V-101; www.dote.osd.mil /pub/reports/FY2001/.

36. Written Statement for the Record of the Director of Central Intelligence, Before the National Commission on Terrorist Attacks Upon the United States, March 24, 2004.

   On September 30, 2000, "the Taliban issued press statement on unknown aircraft seen over Kandahar allegedly looking for UBL. NSC note, Clarke to Berger, "Procedures for Protecting Predator," September 30, 2000. Clarke pointed to a silver lining: "The fact that its existence has become at least partially known, may for a while change the al Qida movement patterns," he wrote, but "it may also serve as a healthy reminder to al Qida and the Taliban that they are not out of our thoughts or sight." See 9/11 Commission Report, Chapter 6, Footnote 119, p. 507.

37. The 9/11 Commission report later said that after the October attack on the USS *Cole* in Yemen, just weeks later: "Bin Laden anticipated U.S. military retaliation. He ordered the evacuation of al Qaeda's Kandahar airport compound and fled—first to the desert area near Kabul, then to Khowst and Jalalabad, and eventually back to Kandahar. In Kandahar, he rotated between five to six residences, spending one night at each residence. In addition, he sent his senior advisor, Mohammed Atef, to a different part of Kandahar and his deputy, Ayman al Zawahiri, to Kabul so that all three could not be killed in one attack." 9/11 Commission Report, p. 191.

38. Stealth Combat Aircraft—Michael J. Lippitz and Richard H. Van Atta; in IDA, Transformation and Transition: DARPA's Role in Fostering an Emerging Revolution in Military Affairs, Volume 2—Detailed Assessments, p. I-7.

39. George Tenet writes: "neither our intelligence nor the FBI's criminal investigation could conclusively prove that Usama bin Ladin and his leadership had had authority, direction, and control over the attack. This is a high threshold to cross.... What's important from our perspective at CIA is that the FBI investigation had taken primacy in getting to the bottom of the matter." *At the Center of the Storm*, p. 128.

40. *Against all Enemies*, p. 223.

41. *Age of Sacred Terror*, pp. 323–324.

42. *Against all Enemies*, p. 224.

43. John Miller and Michael Stone with Chris Mitchell, *The Cell* (New York: Hyperion, 2002), p. 225; Bill Gertz, *Breakdown* (Washington, DC: Regnery Publishing, 2002), p. 51.

44. *Looming Tower*, p. 331.

CHAPTER SEVEN Inherit the Wind

1. *At the Center of the Storm*, p. 143.
2. 9/11 Commission Report, Chapter Six, Footnote 190, p. 511.
3. Written Statement for the Record of the Director of Central Intelligence, Before the National Commission on Terrorist Attacks Upon the United States, March 24, 2004.
4. Air Force PowerPoint Briefing, Requirements Pull: Predator-Hellfire, n.d. (2001); obtained by the author; Richard Whittle, Predator's Big Safari, Mitchell Papers 7, August 2011, p. 23. See also Sue Baker, Aeronautical Systems Center Public Affairs, "Predator Hellfire Missile tests 'totally successful,'" March 1, 2001; Whittle, *Predator: The Secret Origins of the Drone Revolution* (2014), p. 191.
5. Randy Roughton, "Rise of the Drones—UAVs After 9/11: 9/11 and war on terror sparked an explosion in unmanned aerial vehicle technology," *Airman* magazine, September 2011.
6. Richard Whittle, Predator's Big Safari, Mitchell Papers 7, August 2011, p. 18.
7. Jumper issued that order on June 21, 2000; Richard Whittle, Predator's Big Safari, Mitchell Papers 7, August 2011, p. 7. See also Houston R. Cantwell, Major, USAF, RADM Thomas J. Cassidy's MQ-1 Predator: The USAF's First UAV Success Story, Air Command and Staff College, Maxwell AFB, Alabama, April 2006, p. 23.

   At an Air and Space Conference in 2002, Jumper talked about the problems he had in getting service officials to agree to a proposal for arming Predator with Hellfire. "People blanked out and fainted" about the proposal, Jumper said, noting that opponents said that it would cost "tens of millions of dollars." Instead, it cost $3 million, he said. Those attached to the intelligence field in the service thought a Hellfire capability would make Predator unflyable, but Jumper said that putting air force technicians familiar with close air support on the problem solved such issues quickly. See Marc Strass, "Air Force Stands Up First Armed Predator UAV Squadron," *Defense Daily*, March 11, 2002.
8. Mark Mazetti says that with this test, "The age of armed, remote-controlled conflict had begun," but this is an exaggeration; *The Way of the Knife*, p. 97.
9. Richard M. Clark, Uninhabited Combat Aerial Vehicles: Airpower by the People, for the People, but Not with the People; A Thesis Presented to the Faculty of the School of Advanced Airpower Studies, for Completion of Graduation Requirements, School of Advanced Airpower Studies, Air University, Maxwell AFB, Alabama, June 1999, p. 2; Richard Whittle, Predator's Big Safari, Mitchell Papers 7, August 2011, p. 18.
10. Richard Whittle, Predator's Big Safari, Mitchell Papers 7, August 2011, p. 23; Walter J. Boyne, How the Predator Grew Teeth, *Air Force Magazine*, July 2009 (Vol. 92, No. 7).

11. Written Statement for the Record of the Director of Central Intelligence, Before the National Commission on Terrorist Attacks Upon the United States, March 24, 2004. See also 9/11 Commission, p. 211; referring to NSC memo, Hadley to McLaughlin, Wolfowitz, and Myers, "Re: Predator," July 11, 2001; *At the Center of the Storm*, p. 158.

12. Whittle, *Predator: The Secret Origins of the Drone Revolution* (2014), p. 202.

13. Whittle, *Predator: The Secret Origins of the Drone Revolution* (2014), p. 199; Richard Whittle, Predator's Big Safari, Mitchell Papers 7, August 2011, pp. 22–23.

14. Richard Whittle, Predator's Big Safari, Mitchell Papers 7, August 2011, pp. 23–24.

15. The CIA was also flying its Gnat-750 drones, which it had operated from fourteen sites worldwide, but clearly it was on a path to adopting the Predator as its standard as well.

16. After OAF, the 11th Reconnaissance Squadron remained at Tuzla for several months, and they returned for periodic deployments in 2000 and early 2001. See Bill Yenne, *Attack of the Drones: A History of Unmanned Aerial Combat*, p. 64.

17. Thomas P. Ehrhard, Air Force UAVs: The Secret History, p. 52.

18. Global Hawk stems from the Long-Endurance Reconnaissance, Surveillance, and Target Acquisition (RSTA) Capability mission need statement (MNS) endorsed by the Joint Requirements Oversight Council (JROC) in January 1990; Rand, Global Hawk and DarkStar in the HAE UAV ACTD, p. 7.

19. The ACC CONOPS states: "The Global Hawk system's long dwell capabilities increases the likelihood of detecting, identifying, and locating with precision (less than 20 meters CEP), high value ground targets of a time-critical nature. Typical targets in this class are tactical missile launchers, mobile air defense elements, supply convoys, and mobile command and control centers. It is critical that such time-critical targets be targeted before they move again. The combination of SAR/EO/IR with GMTI carried by Global Hawk provides the tools to facilitate immediate attack by air or ground elements, provided the target data (not necessarily an image) can be delivered immediately to the appropriate tactical forces." Air Combat Command (ACC) Concept of Operations for Global Hawk Unmanned Aerial Vehicle (UAV), August 2000, Version 2.0, p. ix; DOD, UAS ROADMAP 2005, p. 3-10.

20. The DarkStar program was canceled in January 1999, before it had completed its full demonstration.

21. Basic background on Global Hawk comes from Air Combat Command (ACC) Concept of Operations for Global Hawk Unmanned Aerial Vehicle (UAV), August 2000, Version 2.0.

22. Air Combat Command (ACC) Concept of Operations for Global Hawk Unmanned Aerial Vehicle (UAV), August 2000, Version 2.0, p. ix; DOD, UAS ROADMAP 2005, p. 6.

23. Global Hawk's airborne systems are designed to identify, isolate, and compensate for a wide range of possible system failures and also autonomously take actions.

24. The initial order called for the air force to acquire fifty-one, with the first six to be delivered through the end of 2002.

25. Rand, Innovative Management in the DARPA HAE UAV Program, p. 56.

26. Rand, Global Hawk and DarkStar in the HAE UAV ACTD, p. 27.

27. GAO-06-447 Unmanned Aircraft Systems, p. 12; Bill Yenne, *Attack of the Drones*, p. 76.

28. Rand, Global Hawk and DarkStar in the HAE UAV ACTD, pp. 38–39.

29. On August 27, Baghdad claimed that it shot down a Predator over southern Iraq; another was reported downed in Afghanistan before the shooting started; http://news.bbc.co.uk/1/hi/world/middle_east/1511540.stm.

30. Written Statement for the Record of the Director of Central Intelligence, Before the National Commission on Terrorist Attacks Upon the United States, March 24, 2004.

31. 9/11 Commission Report, p. 211.

32. *At the Center of the Storm*, p. 158; Written Statement for the Record of the Director of Central Intelligence, Before the National Commission on Terrorist Attacks Upon the United States, March 24, 2004.
   "Following the attacks on 11 September 2001, the United States rapidly fielded the armed Predator into an environment that not only lacked a clear delineation of the command and control framework, but one where there existed no direct policy on who, when, where, and how to use this new asset. Military commanders can and do fill in the blanks in a situation like this, however, with the current trend of rapid technology development, a more forward looking approach in which policy makers address the questions faster than technological achievements occur will minimize the holes needing to be filled in." See Major Matthew C. Crowell, "Unmanned Warfare: Second and Third Order Effects Stemming from the Afghan Operational Environment between 2001 and 2010," Master's Thesis, US Army Command and General Staff College, 6 October 2011, pp. 39–40.

33. *American Soldier*, p. 258.

34. *Inside Centcom*, p. 23.

35. Richard Myers and Malcolm McConnell, *Eyes on the Horizon* (New York: Pocket Books, 2009), p. 164.

36. www.washingtonpost.com/ac2/wp-dyn?pagename=article&node=&contentId=A64802-2002Jan30&notFound=true; According to Bradley Graham: "The contrast between the extent of Pentagon and CIA readiness

became clear at...Camp David...A Defense Department paper prepared for the Camp David briefing book had again raised the prospect of hitting Iraq....It would afford the Pentagon a chance to spearhead a complementary effort to what was shaping up as an unconventional war in Afghanistan led by the CIA." See Bradley Graham, *By His Own Rules: The Ambitions, Successes, and Ultimate Failures of Donald Rumsfeld* (New York: PublicAffairs, 2009), p. 290.

37. Woodward, p. 101; 9/11 Commission Report, pp. 333, 335.

38. Peter L. Bergen, *Manhunt: The Ten-Year Search for Bin Laden from 9/11 to Abbottabad* (New York: Crown, 2012), p. 25.

39. Whittle, *Predator: The Secret Origins of the Drone Revolution* (2014), pp. 240–245.

40. 9/11 Commission Report, p. 331.

41. *Air Power Against Terror: America's Conduct of Operation Enduring Freedom*, p. 67.

42. *Eyes on the Horizon*, p. 169.

43. www.airpower.maxwell.af.mil/airchronicles/cc/marion.html

44. General Tommy Franks with Malcolm McConnell, *American Soldier* (New York: Regan Books/HarperCollins, 2004), p. 273.

45. Gary Schroen, *First In: An Insider's Account of How the CIA Spearheaded the War on Terror in Afghanistan* (New York: Presidio Press, 2005), pp. 113, 136.

46. The ministry wasn't actually an invention of the Taliban, which is to say that the capital crime committed by Mullah Mohammed Omar, the first high-value target ever to be attacked by the United States of America, was hosting al Qaeda; violating human rights and preventing vice Taliban-style were certainly repugnant but not worth a war before 9/11. In the five years after the commander of the faithful consolidated his rule and gained some degree of international recognition as head of a failed state, his day-to-day existence took on that furtive and protective reclusion we associate with despots.

47. The story is told from the vantage point of the operators in Whittle, *Predator: The Secret Origins of the Drone Revolution* (2014), pp. 280ff. See also Richard Whittle, Predator's Big Safari, Mitchell Papers 7, August 2011, p. 8; Lieutenant Colonel Mark A. Cooter, USAF, Airborne Armed Full Motion Video: The Nexus of Ops/Intel Integration in the Joint/Coalition Environment, Joint Forces Staff College, Joint Advanced Warfighting School, May 25, 2007, p. 1; Christopher J. Bowie, Robert P. Haffa, Jr., and Robert E. Mullins; Future War: What Trends in America's Post-Cold War Military Conflicts Tell Us About Early 21st Century Warfare, Northrop Grumman Analysis Center, 2003, p. 58.

48. The first combat shot is confirmed in Air Force PowerPoint Briefing, ISR Innovations and UAV Task Force Directorate, NDIA Conference, November 4, 2008.

49. Seymour M. Hersh, "King's Ransom," *The New Yorker*, October 22, 2001, p. 38.

   According to General Delong, Franks's deputy commander, in his autobiography *Inside Centcom* (Washington, DC: Regnery Publishing, 2004), pp. 37–38, CIA director Tenet and Franks discuss the attack:

   "'I'm not convinced that's him,' Franks said, 'and the collateral damage issues are significant.'

   "'We think it is him,' Tenet said.

   "CENTCOM's Rules of Engagement were strict: You had to be sure. Franks wasn't sure, and neither were the CENTCOM staff or the CENTCOM lawyers. Omar was a big fish, but we did not want to kill innocent civilians.

   "Franks answered, 'We're going to wait.'"

   General Franks gives a different version of events. He says the convoy included three vehicles and a motorcycle, and was detected at around 4:30 a.m. local time. Brigadier General Jeff Kimmons, the CENTCOM J-2, says "the convoy profile fits Taliban leadership." The CIA also states that the target had "all of the characteristics of a leadership convoy." The CENTCOM JAG navy captain Shelly Young pronounces the convoy a "valid target." Given the probability of kill with a moving convoy of only 30 percent, Franks requests that the CAOC check to see whether aircraft are in the area and available. The convoy enters Kandahar and the passengers enter a compound, removing large cases of what General Franks believes are shoulder-fired SAMs. Before the Predator shot can be lined up, the convoy leaves, drives some forty minutes, and stops "in a courtyard of a mosque, a large, domed building surrounded by mud huts and several two- and three-story structures, upscale homes by Afghan standards." Franks orders the Predator to attack a car, perhaps to persuade the people to leave the mosque "and give us a shot at the principals." Cars and trucks speed away to the northeast, stopping about half a mile away at a multistory house. General Franks decides to call Secretary Rumsfeld to get clearance to hit "a high collateral damage target." Rumsfeld gets permission from the president within five minutes. But the CIA says it thinks the building is a mosque, and some of the people have left the building. Franks orders F/A-18 Hornets, which have arrived on station, to attack the building, which is destroyed. See *American Soldier*, pp. 288–295.

   General Charles ("Chuck") Horner, the air war chief in Desert Storm, provides yet another version of events, cockeyed factually, but nevertheless revealing about the underlying issues:

   "In Afghanistan we saw examples of both schools: the 'centralizers,' who seek to accumulate data at the senior level in order to guide the actions of those operating in battle, and the 'decentralizers,' who push data down or at least make it readily available to those locked in battle.

An example is vivid pictures of General Franks operating in Tampa, Florida. He is viewing the movement of individuals at night walking in a compound in Afghanistan attempting to identify Mullah Omar and next determine if he should be shot by a missile from a Predator aircraft operating immediately overhead. Alternatively, the video/audio tape of an AC-130 demonstrates the capacity of a virtual network that provides those with their hands on the trigger almost unimaginable support. In this case an intelligence officer in California is pointing out which of the structures in the AC-130 thermal sensor's field of view is a Mosque and which houses al-Qaida gunmen. At the same time linguists in Georgia provide commentary about the identity of the individuals walking from the Mosque and their intentions. In theater support for both General Franks and the AC-130 aircrew includes an array of overhead assets: EC-130, EC-135, E-3, EP-3, and E-8 manned aircraft and Global Hawk and Predator unmanned aircraft. All are tied together by a vast array of communications links providing all the capability to reach forward or reach back"; General (retired) Charles A. Horner, Men and Machines in Modern Warfare, n.d. (2002), provided to the author.

50. *Eyes on the Horizon*, p. 192.
51. *American Soldier*, p. 303.
52. According to General Franks, "by the 20th of October, virtually all of the air defenses and early warning systems in Afghanistan had been destroyed by airpower. And so, perhaps at that point, conditions were set for us to move in to conduct some special operations work that was done on the ground—the introduction of our Special Forces. I think it was about the 20th of October [actually the 19th] that we put the first high-end direct action raid into the very home of Mullah Omar in downtown Khandahar [sic]. What a remarkable feat!" See General Tommy R. Franks, Commander in Chief, U.S. Central Command, AFA National Symposium—Orlando, February 14, 2002.
53. Major Joseph Campo, USAF; Information Dominance or Information Overload?, Naval War College, 3 May 2010, p. 8.
54. Franks says Jumper, the air force chief of staff, had been watching the Predator video feed from the Pentagon. Franks says he then requests that the Predator feed be removed from the Pentagon; see *American Soldier*, pp. 288–295.

CHAPTER EIGHT   My Back Is Killing Me

1. Atef played some role in training or equipping anti-American fighters in Somalia in 1992–1993, was the military commander of the Embassy bombings in 1998, and was the primary operational head above Khalid Sheikh Mohammed for the planning of 9/11. He was a member of the *maj-*

lis al shura (or consultation council) of al Qaeda and became head of its military committee in 1996. He was responsible for supervising the terrorist training of al Qaeda members and identifying targets for terrorist attacks that would be carried out.

2. The best description of this important event is given by Richard Whittle in *Predator: The Secret Origins of the Drone Revolution*, pp. 276–290. The account is written mostly from the recollections of air force participants stationed at the CIA.

See also Chris Cole, "The Drone Wars Briefing," Drone Wars UK, January 2012, p. 2; quoting Mary Ellen O'Connell, Seductive Drones: Learning from a Decade of Lethal Operations, *Journal of Law, Information & Science*, Notre Dame Law School, August 2011, pp. 4–5; MedAct (UK), which states: "a CIA-operated Predator drone was used in combat for the first time to assassinate Mohammed Atef, an alleged al-Qaeda leader in Afghanistan," *Drones: the physical and psychological implications of a global theatre of war*, MedAct (UK), 2012, p. 2.

"A drone was used in November 2001, to launch a missile to kill al-Qaida's Mohammed Atef in the eastern Afghan city of Jalalabad"; Mary Ellen O'Connell, Robert and Marion Short Professor of Law, Research Professor of International Dispute Resolution—Kroc Institute, Notre Dame Law School, "Unlawful Killing with Combat Drones; A Case Study of Pakistan, 2004–2009," Legal Studies Research Paper No. 09-43, Final Draft: July 2010.

"The targeted killing operations have successfully killed a number of senior Al-Qaeda members, including its chief of military operations, Mohammad Atef"; Gabriella Blum and Philip Heymann, "Law and Policy of Targeted Killing," *Harvard National Security Journal*, Vol. 1, June 27, 2010, p. 151.

"However, on November 3, 2001, a missile-carrying Predator drone killed Mohammed Atef, al Qa`ida's chief of military operations, in a raid near Kabul"; Testimony of William C. Banks before the Subcommittee on National Security and Foreign Affairs, Committee on Oversight and Government Reform, United States House of Representatives, April 28, 2010; quoting James Risen, "A Nation Challenged: The Terror Network," *New York Times*, December 13, 2001, p. A1.

See also Christopher Bolkcom and Kenneth Katzman, "Military Aviation: Issues and Options for Combating Terrorism and Counter-insurgency," CRS Report for Congress, 2005, p. 14; Dennis Larm, "The Unmanned Aerial Vehicle's Identity Crisis," Army War College, May 3, 2004, p. 3.

Kenneth Chang, "A Crafty, Deadly Predator," *New York Times*, November 23, 2001, p. B3; Judith Miller and Eric Schmitt, "Ugly duckling turns out to be formidable in the air," *New York Times*, November 23, 2001,

p. B1; "Sources Report Death of Mohammed Atef," CNN.com, transcript of interview by CNN anchor Bill Hemmer with CNN national correspondent Mike Boettcher, November 16, 2001.

"During the November 2001 invasion of Afghanistan, CIA predator drones attacked a high-level al Qaeda meeting in Kabul, missing Osama bin Laden but killing his military chief, Mohammed Atef"; John Yoo, *War by Other Means* (New York: Atlantic Monthly Press, 2006), p. 49. Note: This is no evidence whatsoever that Osama bin Laden was anywhere near Atef on November 12–13.

See also Bill Yenne, *Attack of the Drones: A History of Unmanned Aerial Combat*, p. 9; Dennis M. Gormley, "New Developments in Unmanned Air Vehicles and Land-Attack Cruise Missiles," in *SIPRI Yearbook 2003 — Armaments, Disarmament and International Security* (Oxford: Oxford University Press, 2003), p. 417.

3. *The Secret History of al Qaeda*, p. 24.

Atef is an alias for Tayseer Abu Sitah, AKA Abu Hafs al-Masri ("The Egyptian") and Subhi Abu Sitah. He was born in 1944 in Egypt; he was a police officer by training and one of the original members of Egyptian Islamic jihad before becoming an al Qaeda man.

4. Associated Press (Kabul), Kathy Gannon, "Arab satellite channel Al-Jazeera's office in Afghan capital destroyed by missile," 12 November 2001.

5. Rear Admiral Quigley, Deputy Spokesman, Department of Defense, Briefing at the Foreign Press Center, Tuesday, Nov. 13, 2001 — 3:16 p.m. EST, www.defenselink.mil/transcripts/2001/t11142001_t1113fpc.html.

6. Vernon Loeb, "U.S. Bombs Hit Kabul TV Station," *Washington Post*, November 14, 2001, p. A13.

7. AP (Kathy Gannon), "Arab satellite channel Al-Jazeera's office in Afghan capital destroyed by missile." November 13, 2001; Vernon Loeb, "U.S. Bombs Hit Kabul TV Station," *Washington Post*, November 14, 2001, p. A13. Hoey said that the bombing of Serb television in Belgrade during the Kosovo conflict was a different issue; there, he said, the targets in question "appeared to have government facilities associated with them."

Another Pentagon spokesman, Marine Corps Lieutenant Colonel Dave Lapan, said: "We hit an al-Qaeda facility...we don't know what al-Jazeera was doing there." See Julia Scheeres, "Trolling the Web for Afghan Dead," *Wired*, January 4, 2002; www.wired.com/news/conflict /0,2100,49475,00.html.

It was a "command and control facility," another Pentagon spokesman said. Matt Wells in Barcelona, "Al-Jazeera accuses US of bombing its Kabul office," *The Guardian* (UK), November 17, 2001.

8. Letter, General Tommy R. Franks, to Ann Cooper, Committee to Protect Journalists, n.d. (21 June 2002).

9. Committee to Protect Journalists, "United States: CPJ asks Pentagon to explain Al-Jazeera bombing," New York, January 31, 2002.

10. The attack is reported variously to have occurred between 1:30 and 3:00 a.m. local time on November 13, 2001. The Committee to Protect Journalists says that the incident occurred at 1:30 a.m. Kabul time; Committee to Protect Journalists news alert, "Afghanistan: U.S. Airstrike Destroys al-Jazeera Office in Kabul," November 13, 2001. The managing director of Al-Jazeera, Mohammed Jassim al-Ali, has been quoted as saying that the strike occurred around 3 a.m. Kabul time; AP (Kathy Gannon), "Missile destroys al-Jazeera office," November 13, 2001. CENTCOM says the attack occurred at 3:40 p.m. EST Monday.

11. See, in particular, the account in *Predator: The Secret Origins of the Drone Revolution*, pp. 276–290.

12. Nik Gowing, "Full text of Nik Gowing's al-Jazeera feature," *The Guardian* (UK), April 8, 2002.

13. Nik Gowing, "Full text of Nik Gowing's al-Jazeera feature," *The Guardian* (UK), April 8, 2002.

14. *The Secret History of al Qaeda*, p. 25.

15. Department of the Air Force, Operation Anaconda: An Airpower Perspective, 2005, p. 15.

16. Ali H. Soufan, *The Black Banners: The Inside Story of 9/11 and the War Against al-Qaeda* (New York: W. W. Norton, 2011), p. 345. Soufan says Atef was killed with seven other al-Qaeda members.

17. Bergen, *Manhunt*, p. 37.

18. 9/11 Commission Report, Notes to Chapter 7, p. 527.

19. See Charles N. Cardinal, Timber P. Pagona, and Edward Marks, The Global War on Terrorism, A Regional Approach to Coordination, *Joint Force Quarterly* (*JFQ*), Autumn 2002, p. 49: "Perhaps the earliest successes in the regional campaign were arrests in Singapore and Malaysia of *Jemaah Islamiya* cells that were well rehearsed in the press. The arrests occurred in December 2001 after evidence of operational planning against U.S. and allied targets in Singapore was found in the residence of Mohamed Atef in Afghanistan."

20. Ben Lambeth, certainly one of the premier contemporary air historians today, wrote a very official and sanctioned history of the Afghanistan air war under air force sponsorship. Conducting what he called the longest fighter combat mission in history—15.8 hours—an air force F-15E Strike Eagle (not a navy F-18 Hornet) killed Mohammed Atef, he says, hitting the targeted house in Kabul with a laser-guided bomb. A hero, finally, were it only so. See Ben Lambeth, *Air Power Against Terror: America's Conduct of Operation Enduring Freedom* (Rand Corporation, 2005), p. 137.

21. *Predator: The Secret Origins of the Drone Revolution*, pp. 276–290.

22. *Eyes on the Horizon*, p. 199.

23. Bergen, *Manhunt*, pp. 38, 287.

24. When in the 2003 Iraq war the United States unambiguously bombed Al Jazeera in Baghdad, again on the justification of it being a command and control target, the story of November 13 grew ever more complex than just a bomb directed at a single al Qaeda digit.

25. See *Air Power Against Terror: America's Conduct of Operation Enduring Freedom*, p. 137.

CHAPTER NINE   The Machine Builds

1. DOD Transcript, Press Briefing, Statement of Secretary Rumsfeld on Anti-Terrorism Strike; Rumsfeld and Myers Briefing on Enduring Freedom, October 7, 2001.

2. DOD Transcript, Secretary Rumsfeld Interview with *CBS Evening News*, October 9, 2001.

3. US Air Forces in Europe (USAFE) PowerPoint Briefing, USAFE and Strategy, Lieutenant Colonel Marc "Homer" Jamison, Chief, Strategy Division, n.d. (2004) (obtained by the author); Lieutenant Colonel Mark A. Cooter, USAF, Airborne Armed Full Motion Video: The Nexus of Ops/Intel Integration in the Joint/Coalition Environment, Joint Forces Staff College, Joint Advanced Warfighting School, 25 May 2007, p. 15.

4. Richard Whittle, Predator's Big Safari, Mitchell Papers 7, August 2011, p. 25; Randy Roughton, Rise of the Drones—UAVs After 9/11: 9/11 and war on terror sparked an explosion in unmanned aerial vehicle technology, *Airman* Magazine, 3 October 2011; http://science.dodlive.mil/2011/10/03/rise-of-the-drones-uavs-after-911/ (accessed May 2, 2013).

5. Robert Wall, "Space Reformers Juggle War, Acquisition Demands," *Aviation Week & Space Technology*, April 8, 2002, p. 80.

6. USMC, Task Force 58 Operations in Afghanistan [lessons learned narrative], n.d. (2005); obtained by the author.

7. *Air Power Against Terror: America's Conduct of Operation Enduring Freedom*, pp. 253–254.

8. *Air Power Against Terror: America's Conduct of Operation Enduring Freedom*, pp. 253–254.

9. *First In*, p. 155.

10. *First In*, pp. 161–162.

11. "During our many discussions, the President, the senior military officers, and the civilian officials involved determined that the first wave of attacks should avoid all urban areas to minimize collateral damage." See *Eyes on the Horizon*, p. 180.

12. *American Soldier*, p. 301.
13. *By His Own Rules*, p. 302; *Manhunt*, p. 151.
14. Central Command, Operation Enduring Freedom Update, 16 October 2001.
15. Richard Whittle, Predator's Big Safari, Mitchell Papers 7, August 2011, pp. 25–26.
16. Rebecca Grant, "The Rover," *Air Force Magazine*, August 2013.
17. *First In*, p. 169; *By His Own Rules*, p. 302.
18. U.S. Special Operations Command, History: 1987–2007, p. 90; U.S. Special Operations Command, History 6th Edition, p. 93; A Different Kind of War: The United States Army in Operation ENDURING FREEDOM (OEF), October 2001–September 2005, pp. 95–96; Dr. Rebecca Grant, The Afghan Air War, September 2002, pp. 17–18; DOD, Two Soldiers Killed; Special Forces Assault Taliban Sites; www.defenselink.mil/news/Oct2001/n10202001_200110201.html; DOD, DOD Officials Won't Confirm U.S. Ground Troops in Afghanistan; www.defenselink.mil/news/Oct2001/n10192001_200110193.html; Rebecca Grant, "The War Nobody Expected," *Air Force Magazine*, April 2002; www.afa.org/magazine/April 2002/0402airwar.asp.
19. Lieutenant Colonel Eric E. Theisen, Ground-Aided Precision Strike Heavy Bomber Activity in Operation Enduring Freedom, Maxwell Paper No. 31, July 2003, p. 1.
20. Despite their value, not all of the special operations teams had JTACs. "While some SOF teams had a JTAC from the beginning others did not bring a JTAC with them until the military recognized that results were not meeting expectations and ordered their integration. Operationally, the joint special operations task force (JSOTF) headquarters did not have a mechanism for integrating joint fires with all of the different SOF teams and the various task force headquarters spread throughout Afghanistan"; Major Brook J. Leonard, USAF; "How the West Was Won: The Essence of Network-Centric Operations (NCO)," School of Advanced Air and Space Studies, Air University, Maxwell AFB, Alabama; June 2006, p. 32.
21. The United States Army in Afghanistan: Operation Enduring Freedom, pp. 11–12.
22. *By His Own Rules*, p. 305.
23. On October 30, Bill Kristol wrote an op-ed in the *Washington Post* in which he said that too many self-imposed constraints in Afghanistan had produced "a flawed plan." On October 31, R. W. Apple wrote a front-page article in the *New York Times* asking whether Afghanistan would become another "military quagmire" like Vietnam.
24. *Air Power Against Terror: America's Conduct of Operation Enduring Freedom*, p. 125.

25. *First In*, pp. 311–312, 325.
26. Department of the Air Force, Operation Enduring Look, Chapter 16, Implications for Transformation (U), UNCLASSIFIED WORKING PAPER, FINAL COORD 22 January 2003.
27. Bill Yenne, *Attack of the Drones*, p. 88.
28. Dr. Daniel L. Haulman, Air Force History Research Agency, U.S. Unmanned Aerial Vehicles in Combat, 1991–2003, June 9, 2003.
29. Rebecca Grant, "Eyes Wide Open: The lone Global Hawk flying above Iraq was one busy, busy bird," *Air Force Magazine*, November 2003.
30. Matt J. Martin with Charles W. Sasser, *Predator*, p. 21. See also *The Way of the Knife*, pp. 100–101.
31. Kevin Peraino, "Low-Key Leader: Lt. Gen. David McKiernan is the soft-spoken soldier with the hard job of commanding U.S. ground forces in Iraq," *Newsweek* (Web exclusive), March 19, 2003.
32. Megabits per second (Mbps) refers to the transfer speed and is commonly used in networking technologies to represent the speed at which a transfer takes place. Everything—satellite communications, phone-line networks, wireless communications, and data networks like the Internet—transfers information based upon the number of bits per second the data travels. An old 56k modem transferred data at 56 kilobits per second (Kbps). A typical home Ethernet network supports data rates up to 10 Mbps, while Fast Ethernet provides 100 Mbps. To get a sense of the military differences, for those who can't remember the old days when the last of the manned, triple-tailed, bug-eyed OV-1 Mohawk spy planes ceased monitoring the Korean DMZ in the early 1990s, sending one picture back to the United States via satellite communications took about 30 seconds.

    Ron Graham and Alexander Koh, *Digital Aerial Survey: Theory and Practice* (Whittles Publishing, 1st edition, 2002), p. 184; John Sotham, "The Last of the Mohawks: Grumman's triple-tail, bug-eyed, heat-seeking camera platform," *Air & Space* magazine (Smithsonian), March 1997.

    Kodak created the first digital camera prototype in 1975 and was the first to introduce a commercial professional-level digital SLR camera, the DCS 100, in 1992.

    See Operation Enduring Look, QUICK LOOK REPORT, Air Force Space Command, Satellite Communications Support, January 2003; Defense Science Board Study on Unmanned Aerial Vehicles and Uninhabited Combat Aerial Vehicles, February 2004, p. 24.

    In Desert Storm, coalition military forces numbered 542,000, and they had 99 megabits per second of bandwidth available.
33. Operation Enduring Look, QUICK LOOK REPORT, Air Force Space Command, Satellite Communications Support, January 2003.

34. In addition to Predator, two army Hunter drones flew from Macedonia, and each one required an additional 6 Mbps of bandwidth.

35. Lieutenant Colonel Kurt A. Klausner, USAF; Command and Control of Air and Space Forces Requires Significant Attention to Bandwidth, *Air & Space Power Journal*, Winter 2002.

36. Major Kathy B. Davis, USAF; Operation Allied Force: Reachback and Information Processes; Air Command and Staff College; AU/ACSC /031/2002-04; Maxwell AFB, Alabama, March 2002, p. 5.

37. Patrick Rayermann, "Exploiting Commercial SATCOM: A Better Way," *Parameters* (Army War College), Winter 2003–2004, pp. 54–66.

38. Of the 700 Mbps in bandwidth capacity provided to the initial Afghanistan operations, almost 400 Mbps came from commercial satellites; Operation Enduring Look, QUICK LOOK REPORT, Air Force Space Command, Satellite Communications Support, January 2003.

39. Operation Enduring Look, QUICK LOOK REPORT, Air Force Space Command, Satellite Communications Support, January 2003.

40. Operation Enduring Look, Chapter 16, Implications for Transformation (U), UNCLASSIFIED WORKING PAPER, FINAL COORD 22 January 2003, p. 16-3.

41. *Eyes on the Horizon*, pp. 214–215.

42. Larry J. Dodgen, Space: Inextricably Linked to Warfighting, Military Review, January/February 2006; Defense Science Board Study on Unmanned Aerial Vehicles and Uninhabited Combat Aerial Vehicles, February 2004, p. 24.

43. Quoted in Lieutenant Colonel Kurt A. Klausner, USAF; Command and Control of Air and Space Forces Requires Significant Attention to Bandwidth, *Air & Space Power Journal*, Winter 2002.

44. When Predator itself switched to remote split operations in 2002, moving the mission control element back to the United States, the global communications network demanded even more. See Major Houston R. Cantwell, USAF; Beyond Butterflies: Predator and the Evolution of Unmanned Aerial Vehicle in Air Force Culture; School of Advanced Air and Space Studies, Air University, Maxwell AFB, Alabama, June 2007, pp. 27–28.

45. Defense Science Board Study on Unmanned Aerial Vehicles and Uninhabited Combat Aerial Vehicles, February 2004, p. 23.

46. Operation Enduring Look, QUICK LOOK REPORT, Air Force Space Command, Satellite Communications Support, January 2003; John M. Donnelly, "Panel Probes Military's Fight for Radio Waves," *Defense Week*, no. 17 (22 April 2002), p. 3.

CHAPTER TEN The Split

1. The system was called Special Operations Tactical Video System (SOTVS).
2. Richard Whittle, Predator's Big Safari, Mitchell Papers 7, August 2011, pp. 27–28; Evaluation of U.S. Air Force Preacquisition Technology Development, National Academies Press, 2011, p. 67; Rebecca Grant, "The Rover," *Air Force Magazine*, August 2013; USAF PowerPoint briefing, Remotely Operated Video Enhanced Receiver Capabilities Brief, A2Q ISR Innovations, Lieutenant Colonel Chuck Menza, n.d. (2012); Air Force PowerPoint Briefing, ISR Innovations and UAV Task Force Directorate, NDIA Conference, November 4, 2008.
3. Air Force F-111F aircraft carried and used the Pave Tack (AN/AVQ-26) to deliver LGBs. Pave Tack included a laser and FLIR, plus a videotape recorder for poststrike BDA. The Navy A-6E had the Target Recognition and Attack Multisensor (TRAM) (AN/AAS-33) system built in under the nose, providing a FLIR, laser, and video recorder. RAF Buccaneers carried the Pave Spike (AN/AVQ-23E), which allowed the aircraft to "buddy lase" for other aircraft firing LGBs.
4. Air Force Fact Sheet, August 2007; www.af.mil/factsheets/factsheet.asp ?id=111.
5. LANTIRN also includes a missile boresight correlator for automatic lock-on of imaging infrared Maverick missiles (AGM-65D).

   Single-role Navy F-14 Tomcats were also modified to carry LANTIRN, and a software update enabled the aircraft to acquire mensurated target coordinates accurate enough for delivery of GPS-guided JDAMs.

   The initial LANTIRN targeting version pod has a unit cost of $3.2 million; the air force inventory eventually built up to some 300 pods. The navy procured about 75. Though a significant amount of money has been spent on LANTIRN and other pods, including constant upgrades, the cost per platform, and the increasing elimination of a second weapon systems officer, afforded additional savings and marshaling of resources.
6. Jake Melampy, *The Modern Hog Guide: The A-10 Warthog Exposed* (Trenton, Ohio: Reid Air Publications, 2007), p. 110.
7. NITE stands for Navigation IR Targeting Equipment. The Nite Hawk (AAS-38) is being phased out and replaced with new ATFLR (ASQ-228) pods.
8. F-16 Fighting Falcon Units of Operation Iraqi Freedom, p. 13; F-15C/E Eagle Units of Operation Iraqi Freedom, pp. 21, 26–27; F-15E Strike Eagle Units in Combat: 1990–2005, pp. 38–39; U.S. Navy Hornet Units of Operation Iraqi Freedom: Part One, pp. 12–13.

9. Dedicated reconnaissance pods introduced during this period included:
   - The Tactical Airborne Reconnaissance Pod System (TARPS) pod, which was successfully utilized by the navy in Desert Storm. Digital TARPS capability was first used in 1996. The initial TARPS and interim capabilities were replaced by the TARPS CD in 2000, adding a digital imagery capability with higher resolution and full datalinks, allowing digital imagery able to be transmitted in real time to the Battle Group Commander.
   - The F/A-18D also introduced the Advanced Tactical Airborne Reconnaissance System (ATARS), which provides multiple sensor capabilities, including electrooptical, infrared, and synthetic aperture radar, selectable by the aircrew in flight.

   Air National Guard F-16s initially flew with the MMSA (Multi-Mission Sensor & Avionics) pod, another dedicated reconnaissance system, introduced in April 1995; this was replaced by the more capable Theater Airborne Reconnaissance System (TARS) (AN/ASD-11).

10. "To ask someone to do something outside of what they have planned to do requires a different mind-set. For a Block 52 [F-16] guy to be told, 'I want you to fly to this destination and "take a picture" of this…' would seem to most fighter pilots a total waste of time. They didn't think it was an effective use of their capabilities, and at that point in time the value of this mission was misunderstood." See F-16 Fighting Falcon Units of Operation Iraqi Freedom, p. 13.

11. American Forces Press Service, "Nontraditional Fighter Missions Provide Eyes in the Sky," 24 March 2006; www.defenselink.mil/news/news article.aspx?id=15070.

12. Michael W. Isherwood, Roadmap for Robotics, *Air Force Magazine*, December 2009.

13. The first AF DGS weapon system node (DGS-1) was activated in July 1994; DGS-2 at Beale AFB, California, was activated in July 1995; DGS-3 in South Korea was activated in November 1996; DGS-NV in October 2001; DGS-4 in Ramstein, Germany, was activated in February 2003; DGS-5 in October 2004; DGS-KS in July 2006; and DGS-AL and DGS-AR in November 2006.

14. In 1995, DGS-2 forward deployed from California in support of Balkan operations, this time, though, with a line of sight ground relay station called MOBSTR, for MOBile STRetch. With the relay station, the DGS site could establish communications with a data-linked drone or airplane hundreds of miles away. Delivery of a second MOBSTR package meant that the preponderance of the workers could leave Saudi Arabia. See Adam J. Hebert, "Operation Reachback," *Air Force Magazine*, April 2004;

www.airforcemag.com/MagazineArchive/Pages/2004/April%202004
/0404reach.aspx (accessed October 14, 2013).

15. In October 2002, DGS network expansion continued with Site 8, DGS-3 at Osan AB, Korea. The Warrior Alpha site was added in January 2003.

16. In November 2002, the MASINT Initial Operating Capability (IOC) was achieved in AF DCGS. IOC criteria was the demonstrated capability within AF DCGS to exploit tactical imagery generated by the U-2 Advanced Synthetic Aperture Radar System (ASARS) and produce MASINT products.

17. A sense of the ad hoc nature is seen in Evaluation of U.S. Air Force Preacquisition Technology Development, National Academies Press, 2011, p. 67: "Big Safari program director was briefed on a concept that would provide ground troops the capability to receive video feeds from Predator unmanned aircraft in flight. By October, the Remotely Operated Video Enhanced Receiver (ROVER) working group was formed, including members of the U.S. Special Operations Command, the army's Special Forces Command, and other government agencies. In order to meet full system specifications, Special Operations Tactical Video System (SOTVS) transmitters and receivers would have had to be installed on the Predator aircraft. Instead, the Big Safari team traded the fully integrated solution for an 80 percent capability. The team decided that decoupling a receiver from an aircraft would be the quickest way to deploy the system. The modified system with proven Technology Readiness Level (TRL) 7 maturity quickly established a one-way link from Predator aircraft to ground units. In fact, this decision enabled Big Safari to deliver a successful prototype of the ROVER system to the C Company, 3rd Special Forces Group (Airborne) within just 2 weeks."

18. See Major Royce Frengle, USAF; "Beyond Afghanistan: Effective Combined Intelligence, Surveillance and Reconnaissance Operations," A Research Report Submitted to the Faculty in Partial Fulfillment of the Graduation Requirements, Maxwell Air Force Base, Alabama, April 2010, pp. 11–13; USAF PowerPoint briefing, Remotely Operated Video Enhanced Receiver Capabilities Brief, A2Q ISR Innovations, Lieutenant Colonel Chuck Menza, n.d. (2012).

19. These included the United Kingdom, France, Australia, Germany, Norway, New Zealand, Canada, Portugal, Italy, Spain, Sweden, Belgium, and the Netherlands.

20. Marine Corps PowerPoint Briefing, VMU Overview, Gunnery Sergeant Charles "Cookie" Cook, n.d. (August 2011).

21. "VORTEX is a multiband capable radio and supports AES/NSA Type 1 encryption. VORTEX Phase I is a USSOCOM PoR managed by Aero-

nautical Systems Center (ASC), Medium-Altitude Unmanned Aircraft Systems (ASC/WII) and includes encrypted C and S Band (AES/NSA Type 1), is multiwaveform (e.g., CDL, ROVER 466ER, VORTEX Native Waveform), dual channel, 5-band (C, L, S, Ku, and UHF), and transmit only. The first retrofits for MQ-1 started in the third quarter of FY12 with additional retrofits for MQ-9 occurring in the third quarter of FY13. VORTEX Phase II is an ASC/WII PoR and includes an integrated software solution for the MQ-1 that will enable frequency and crypto control from the GCS.

"The VORTEX program is a spiral development effort that integrates hardware to support duplex LOS operations and tactical IP communications using the NET-T firmware upgrade as a primary means of FMV LOS dissemination. Future upgrades include software that enables in-flight configuration changes and improved encryption technologies." *U.S. Air Force (USAF) Remotely Piloted Aircraft (RPA) Vector—Vision and Enabling Concepts: 2013–2038*, February 2014, p. 71.

22. Broadly speaking, "processing" refers to the conversion of collected information into forms suitable for the production of intelligence; "exploitation" to the analysis of this information and the production of intelligence; and "dissemination" to the delivery of this intelligence to the end users. See JCS, Joint and National Intelligence Support to Military Operations, Joint Publication 2-01, Appendix II, October 7, 2004.

23. *Air Power Against Terror: America's Conduct of Operation Enduring Freedom*, p. xxix.

24. Adam Hebert, "Army Change, Air Force Change," *Air Force Magazine*, March 2006.

25. Richard J. Newman, "The Little Predator That Could," *Air Force Magazine*, March 2002.

26. See, e.g., William M. Arkin, *American Coup: How a Terrified Government Is Destroying the Constitution* (2013).

27. Hugh Lessig, "At Langley, a classified unit quietly marks the end of Iraq war," *Daily Press*, December 19, 2011; http://articles.dailypress.com/2011 -12-19/news/dp-nws-langley-iraq-drones-20111219_1_iraq-war-war-zone -msr-tampa (accessed October 15, 2013).

CHAPTER ELEVEN   The Explosion

1. Dr. Daniel L. Haulman, Air Force History Research Agency, U.S. Unmanned Aerial Vehicles In Combat, 1991–2003, June 9, 2003; Defense Science Board Study on Unmanned Aerial Vehicles and Uninhabited Combat Aerial Vehicles, February 2004, p. 4; Rebecca Grant, "Iraqi Freedom and the air force," *Air Force Magazine*, March 2013.

In February 2003, the worldwide DOD inventory of UAVs was 163 airframes.

2. Rebecca Grant, "Eyes Wide Open: The lone Global Hawk flying above Iraq was one busy, busy bird," *Air Force Magazine*, November 2003.

3. Charles E. Kirkpatrick, Joint Fires as They Were Meant to Be: V Corps and the 4th Air Support Operations Group During Operation Iraqi Freedom, Association of the US Army, Land Warfare Papers No. 48, October 2004.

4. Rand Corporation, Counterinsurgency in Iraq (2003–2006), p. 7. The analysts explained: "Saddam regarded Kurds and Shi'ites backed by Iran as more immediate threats than an unlikely U.S. invasion. Therefore, he kept most of his forces opposite Kurds and Iranians, leaving the invasion corridor through Kuwait to the vicinity of Baghdad largely unprotected. Baghdad was defended by Republican Guard divisions deployed around the city, but even they offered only sporadic resistance. Saddam and his two sons issued amateurish and confusing orders to their military commanders, who were not allowed to exercise any initiative. The Iraqi Army was neglected, demoralized, and poorly trained even by regional standards. Moreover, the Iraqi soldiers knew from experience that U.S. forces were overwhelmingly superior, and therefore most of them deserted before making contact."

See also Joint Center for Operational Analysis and Lessons Learned, Joint Forces Command, Iraqi Perspectives Project: A View of Iraqi Freedom from Saddam's Senior Leadership, 2006.

5. Lieutenant General Walter E. Buchanan III, the air component commander, told the House Armed Services Committee in 2004 that "prior to launching the first weapons to rid Iraq of Saddam Hussein, Predators flew above Baghdad gathering data, monitoring HVTs and providing us real-time intelligence information." See Walter E. Buchannan III, "Intelligence, Surveillance, and Reconnaissance," Statement Before the House Armed Services Committee, Subcommittee on Tactical and Land Forces regarding unmanned combat air vehicles (UCAV) and unmanned aerial vehicles (UAV), March 17, 2004.

6. Charles E. Kirkpatrick, Joint Fires as They Were Meant to Be: V Corps and the 4th Air Support Operations Group During Operation Iraqi Freedom, Association of the US Army, Land Warfare Papers No. 48, October 2004.

7. "Even when the advance into Iraq was held up by fierce sandstorms, use of Global Hawks flying well above or offset from the storms enabled a constant stream of intelligence to be provided, ensuring that coalition commanders were not left making educated guesses based upon a mixture of partial information, experience and instinct"; RAF, Air Power UAVs: The Wider Context, p. 41.

8. Charles E. Kirkpatrick, Joint Fires as They Were Meant to Be: V Corps and the 4th Air Support Operations Group During Operation Iraqi Freedom, Association of the US Army, Land Warfare Papers No. 48, October 2004.

9. Future Force: Joint Operations, Air Force Chief of Staff General John P. Jumper, Remarks to the Air Armaments Summit VI, Sandestin, Florida, March 17, 2004; obtained by the author.

10. PowerPoint Briefing, Colonel Mace Carpenter, Fast and Final: Operation Iraqi Freedom, March 22, 2004; obtained by the author.

11. Charles E. Kirkpatrick, Joint Fires as They Were Meant to Be: V Corps and the 4th Air Support Operations Group During Operation Iraqi Freedom, Association of the US Army, Land Warfare Papers No. 48, October 2004.

12. PowerPoint Briefing, Major General Dave Deptula, HQ ACC/XP, Airpower Lessons from Operation Iraqi Freedom, October 2003; obtained by the author.

13. Rebecca Grant, "Eyes Wide Open: The lone Global Hawk flying above Iraq was one busy, busy bird," *Air Force Magazine*, November 2003.

14. John A. Tirpak, "The Blended Wing Goes to War," *Air Force Magazine*, October 2003.

15. Rebecca Grant, "Iraqi Freedom and the air force," *Air Force Magazine*, March 2013.

16. Michael Isherwood, Global Hawk and Persistent Awareness: Sizing the Global Hawk Fleet, Northrop Grumman Assessment Center, August 2008, p. 28.

The Defense Science Board later wrote that "one Global Hawk in the Iraqi theater from 8 March 03 to 23 April 03 accounted for 55% of the Time Sensitive Targets generated to kill air defense equipment. In missions, Global Hawk located 13 Surface-to-Air Missiles (SAM), 16 batteries, 50 SAM launchers, over 70 SAM transport vehicles and over 300 tanks." Defense Science Board Study on Unmanned Aerial Vehicles and Uninhabited Combat Aerial Vehicles, February 2004, pp. iii–iv.

Predator also scored a couple of notable hits, one an urban attack in Baghdad that its proponents crowed could only be done by the sharpshooter with its Hellfire missile, given the strict constraints imposed on avoiding collateral damage.

According to a UK RAF study: "While the destruction of an Iraqi ZSU-23-4 self-propelled anti-aircraft gun near al-Amarah by a Hellfire launched by a Predator attracted press attention, the work of ISTAR [ISR] UAVs tended to go unnoticed. Yet again, however, the scale of information that could be obtained from the unmanned platforms provided commanders with the ability to make informed decisions based upon near-real time or real time reconnaissance product." See RAF, Air Power UAVs: The Wider Context, p. 40.

17. Charles E. Kirkpatrick, Joint Fires as They Were Meant to Be: V Corps and the 4th Air Support Operations Group During Operation Iraqi Freedom, Association of the US Army, Land Warfare Papers No. 48, October 2004; Defense Science Board Study on Unmanned Aerial Vehicles and Uninhabited Combat Aerial Vehicles, February 2004, p. 4; Defense Science Board Study on Unmanned Aerial Vehicles and Uninhabited Combat Aerial Vehicles, February 2004, p. 28.

18. Defense Science Board Study on Unmanned Aerial Vehicles and Uninhabited Combat Aerial Vehicles, February 2004, pp. 9–10.

19. Defense Science Board Study on Unmanned Aerial Vehicles and Uninhabited Combat Aerial Vehicles, February 2004, p. 4.

20. The U.S. Unmanned Aerospace Vehicle Industry: Transformational Capabilities in the Making; Presentation by the Deputy Under Secretary of Defense (Industrial Policy), 1st AIAA Unmanned Aerospace Vehicles, Systems, Technologies, and Operations Conference, Portsmouth, Virginia, Tuesday, May 21, 2002.

21. Defense Science Board Study on Unmanned Aerial Vehicles and Uninhabited Combat Aerial Vehicles, February 2004, p. 18.

22. Defense Science Board Study on Unmanned Aerial Vehicles and Uninhabited Combat Aerial Vehicles, February 2004, p. 24.

The air force made similar recommendations: "The roles of UAVs are continuing to dynamically change, but their integration ability with other CAF assets is falling behind. UAVs need better integration into the Link 16 network to improve their role in SCAR and other missions." See USAF, 2004 CAF Tactics Review Board/Weapons and Tactics Conference Final Report, UAV MDS Working Group, UAV Chair: Capt. Nick Devereaux, Det 4, 53 TEG/DO, n.d. (2004).

23. One of the board's recommendations was: "Build on the Defense Advanced Research Projects Agency (DARPA) program base (AJCN and others).... Airborne relays will be needed to link mobile forces in the field and other UAVs." It went on to say "This need was recognized in the ASD (C3I), (ASD (NII)), study on Unmanned Aerial Vehicles as Communications Platforms, dated 4 November 1997. Major conclusions were:
   • Tactical communications needs: can be met much more responsively and effectively with Airborne Communications Nodes (ACNs) than with satellite;
   • ACNs can effectively augment theater satellite capabilities by addressing deficiencies in capacity and connectivity."

See Defense Science Board Study on Unmanned Aerial Vehicles and Uninhabited Combat Aerial Vehicles, February 2004, p. 24.

24. Defense Science Board Study on Unmanned Aerial Vehicles and Uninhabited Combat Aerial Vehicles, February 2004.

25. Defense Science Board Study on Unmanned Aerial Vehicles and Uninhabited Combat Aerial Vehicles, February 2004, p. 8.

26. Defense Science Board Study on Unmanned Aerial Vehicles and Uninhabited Combat Aerial Vehicles, February 2004, pp. ix, x.

27. Mr. Dyke Weatherington's Testimony to HASC Subcommittee on Tactical Air and Land Forces, March 3, 2006; www.dod.mil/dodgc/olc/docs/test03-03-26Weatherington.doc.

28. Rand Corporation, Counterinsurgency in Iraq (2003–2006), p. xiv.

29. Rand Corporation, Counterinsurgency in Iraq (2003–2006), pp. xviii, 9, 33.

30. Soon after Operation Iraqi Freedom (OIF), it was recognized that "mission need to rapidly produce a high volume of precise and accurate mensurated geolocation coordinates to support the employment of precision-guided munitions." See Air Force, Common Geopositioning Services (CGS) Technical Requirements Document, July 16, 2004.

CHAPTER TWELVE   Flock of Birds

1. Pioneer was son of Scout, an Israeli-designed unmanned aerial vehicle (UAV) born of the 1982 invasion of Lebanon. For the army, Pioneer became successor to Aquila, a princely billion-dollar propeller-driven aircraft that died in 1987 at the age of eight. Hundreds of the $850,000 Pioneers ended up being acquired by the services; the last retired from Iraq duty as they became increasing unsupportable in 2007.

    See the excellent summary of the history and characteristics of Pioneer at the Smithsonian National Air and Space Museum website, Pioneer RQ-2A UAV; http://airandspace.si.edu/collections/artifact.cfm?object=nasm_A20000794000 (accessed April 27, 2014). The Smithsonian, unfortunately, repeats the story of Iraqi soldiers surrendering to a Pioneer in 1991, not quite an accurate story (see Chapter 4).

2. Pioneer didn't directly give birth to Shadow. On the way were Heron 26, which Pioneer beat in a flying competition, and Hellfox and Outrider, both of which died in development. And there were Prowler II and Sentry, both of which lost out to Shadow in competitive fly-offs to determine which drone would become the new standard. Bill Yenne, *Attack of the Drones: A History of Unmanned Aerial Combat*, p. 71.

3. The exact range difference was 67 nm (125 km) for Shadow (RQ-7B) and 100 nm (185 km) for Pioneer (RQ-2B).

4. "Small UAS support broader multi-sensor ISR missions than Micro UAS. They are less sensitive to meteorological conditions than Micros as well as have greater range, endurance and payload capabilities. These vehicles also possess the ability to carry stores for delivery, including target marking and ordnance delivery. In terms of the DOD this can be a Tier I or Tier II System for the army and Marines and does fulfill the role of a Class I and Class II System in the Future Combat System parlance for small military tactical units." See UAS Service Demand 2015-2035, August 2013, pp. 101–102.

5. Army PowerPoint Briefing; David Milburn, Sigmatech Contractor, Spectrum Manager, Unmanned Aircraft Systems Project Office, PACOM 2012, July 2012.

6. DOD, UAS Roadmap 2005, p. 27; AFSOC PowerPoint Briefing, AF Flight Plan for Small UAVs, June 21, 2004.

7. The army bought four AeroVironment FQM-151 Pointer UAVs in 1999, for military operations in urban terrain (MOUT), then the rage, and as part of the Pathfinder ACTD (advanced concept technology demonstration) program. In November 2003, Congress approved an additional $9.3 million to purchase a mix of Pointer and next-generation Raven UAVs, also from AeroVironment (58 systems: 16 Pointer, 42 Raven). The Pointer served the marine corps from 1990 until it was replaced by the Group 1-equivalent RQ-14 Dragon Eye in 2003, which was replaced by Raven.

Pointer was used by Navy SEALs in the 2003 invasion of Iraq, but it was already well on the way to being retired.

See also Peter Finn, "Rise of the drone: From Calif. garage to multibillion-dollar defense industry," *Washington Post*, December 23, 2011; www.washingtonpost.com/national/national-security/rise-of-the-drone-from-calif-garage-to-multibillion-dollar-defense-industry/2011/12/22/gIQACG8UEP_story.html (accessed February 19, 2014).

8. The Flashlight small UAV (SUAV) flew for the first time in October 2001. After successive feedback and development, Flashlight yielded the initial variant of the RQ-11 Pathfinder Raven UAV, which then became Raven.

9. "Weighing in at approximately five pounds, the Dragon Eye carries two color cameras and can be outfitted with chemical and biological sensors in the nose cone. The UAV also offers night-vision capabilities that are especially valuable for force protection and SOF operations. USS Albany had complete control of the UAV, utilizing systems within the Type 18 periscope. The UAV has a payload capacity of 12 ounces and researchers are developing lightweight zoom lenses to further improve the vehicle's value and utility. The aircraft can fly at altitudes up to 10,000 feet, over a range of 40 kilometers, for approximately one hour—all on a single battery charge. The Albany launch followed a successful demonstration in Febru-

ary of the UAV's capabilities at Naval Submarine Base Kings Bay. A prototype UAV was launched and controlled by force protection personnel
ashore to search out the waters ahead of a submarine as it entered port.
Although the modular UAV is designed to be a "throw-away" item, some
have been flown and recovered successfully more than 30 times. The new
UAV design is ideal for stealth, due to its ultra-quiet electric motor and
small size." www.navy.mil/navydata/cno/n87/usw/issue_28/albany.html.

10. Air Force Fact Sheet, Wasp III, published November 1, 2007; www.af.mil
/AboutUs/FactSheets/Display/tabid/224/Article/104480/wasp-iii.aspx
(accessed April 29, 2014); John D. Gresham, "SOF Persistent ISR: The
SOCOM UAS Roadmap," Special Operations—2008 Edition; www.blue
toad.com/display_article.php?id=32988 (accessed April 27, 2014).

11. In winter 2008, Raven B was introduced to marine corps operating forces
as a replacement for the Dragon Eye UAS, which was first fielded in 2004.

12. The mission operator (MO) uses the laptop for map-based control of the
vehicle, limited to setting parameters of the various waypoints (the waypoints are labeled A, B, C, D, E, L O1, O2, O3, and H). The vehicle operator (VO) has no map display (video only) but has full control of the vehicle.
The MO can display the live video but cannot control the vehicle in any
mode other than NAV mode, which is used for waypoint control. See
Nicholas Stroumtsos, Gary Gilbreath, and Scott Przybylski, "An intuitive
graphical user interface for small UAS," Space and Naval Warfare Systems Center Pacific, SPIE Proc. 8741: Unmanned Systems Technology
XV, Baltimore, MD, May 1–3, 2013.

13. Marine Corps PowerPoint Briefing, VMU Overview, Gunnery Sergeant
Charles "Cookie" Cook, n.d. (August 2011).

14. Marine Corps PowerPoint Briefing, VMU Overview, Gunnery Sergeant
Charles "Cookie" Cook, n.d. (August 2011).

15. Air Force PowerPoint Briefing, UAV Battlelab Overview to Weapons and
Tactics Conference, January 15, 2002.

16. Marine Corps Center for Lessons Learned, (U) Unmanned Aircraft System: RQ-11B Raven Group I Employment in OIF (U//FOUO) Lessons
and Observations from 1st Battalion, 4th Marines and 2d Battalion, 23d
Marines, December 2009; released under the Freedom of Information Act.

17. Raven B was equipped with a protected GPS signal, improved optics, and
an infrared illuminator (to mark targets on the ground). Raven B begat
Raven B eight channel, which begat Raven B DDL—for digital data
link—in 2009, which begat Raven B Gimbal the next year, replacing the
fixed cameras with electronic stabilized pan-tilt-zoom functionality, the
ball "ruggedized for nose impact," that is, crash landing. Digital data link
(DDL) replaced Raven's analog command link and video, replacing the
original four-channel (or later eight-channel) analog setup, increasing

channels by a factor of four (or eight). DDL thus supports sixteen Ravens operating simultaneously in the same area. Additional upgrades include digital/encrypted Full-Motion Video (FMV) and aircraft control, and future interoperability with Unmanned Ground Vehicles (UGV) and Unattended Ground Sensors (UGS); see USAACE Info Paper, TCM-UAS RQ-11B Raven UAS, March 22, 2010.

See also Army PowerPoint Briefing; David Milburn, Sigmatech Contractor, Spectrum Manager, Unmanned Aircraft Systems Project Office, PACOM 2012, July 2012.

18. The gimbaled payload has a price range of $30,000 to $48,000 (depending on the quantity purchased); see Digital Raven Enhanced with New Gimbaled Payload, Image Processing, *Defense Update*, April 2, 2012; http://defense-update.com/20120402_raven_gimballed_eo_payload.html (accessed April 28, 2014).

19. Puma AE (All Environment) begat Puma AECV (All Environment Capable Variant) for Special Operations Command, which also begat Aqua Puma, a perfect companion for Navy SEALs, as it was waterproof. In 2012, the 1,000th Puma came off the production lines, and Sweden ordered some of its own Pumas and WASPs.

20. After Iraq duty, Hunter begat no one. A prospective Hunter II was canceled in favor of Warrior (later Gray Eagle). See Army PowerPoint Briefing; David Milburn, Sigmatech Contractor, Spectrum Manager, Unmanned Aircraft Systems Project Office, PACOM 2012, July 2012.

21. 2nd Lieutenant Matthew Polek, "Supplementing Shadow's ISR Capabilities with an Expeditionary TUAS," *Military Intelligence Professional Bulletin*, April–June 2013, p. 15.

22. ScanEagle exceeded 4,000 combat hours in Iraq by July 2005 and 1,000 flight hours rented by the Australian Army in Iraq in 2007. Overall, in February 2006, ScanEagle surpassed 10,000 combat flight hours in less than two years.

23. Richard Whittle, DoD Tries Buying Pixels, not Planes, for Flexible ISR; "It Ain't Leasing," *AOL Defense*, 7 May 2012.

24. Lieutenant Colonel Mark A. Cooter, USAF, Airborne Armed Full Motion Video: The Nexus of Ops/Intel Integration in the Joint/Coalition Environment, Joint Forces Staff College, Joint Advanced Warfighting School, 25 May 2007, p. 7.

25. Robert A. Masaitis, Jr., Advancing Under Fire: Wartime Change and the U.S. Military, Naval Postgraduate School, December 2008, pp. 92–93; John Barry, Michael Hastings and Evan Thomas, "Iraq's Real WMD," *Newsweek*, March 27, 2006.

Abizaid wasn't the only military official to use such hyperbole. Lieutenant General James N. Mattis, Marine Corps Combat Development Command commander and later Abizaid's replacement, "lamented the failure of American science to vanquish the roadside bomb. "If we could prematurely detonate IEDs, we will change the whole face of the war," he said. For "a country that can put a man on the moon in ten years, or build a nuke in two and a half years of wartime effort, I don't think we're getting what we need from technology on that point"; quoted in Rick Atkinson, "Left of Boom; 'You Can't Armor Your Way out of This Problem,'" *Washington Post*, October 2, 2007, p. A1 (Part 3 in a series).

26. On Point II: Transition to the New Campaign: The United States Army in Operation Iraqi Freedom, May 2003–January 2005, pp. 100–102, 110–112.

27. On Point II: Transition to the New Campaign: The United States Army in Operation Iraqi Freedom, May 2003–January 2005, p. 113.

28. Cristina Cameron Fekkes, "Defining Conditions for the Use of Persistent Surveillance," Naval Postgraduate School, December 2009, p. 54.

29. Bill Yenne, *Attack of the Drones*, p. 83.

30. The Joint Air Power Competence Centre (JAPCC) Flight Plan for Unmanned Aircraft Systems (UAS) in NATO, Version 5.4, March 15, 2007, p. 5.

31. "OEF Route Clearance Teams to Receive Puma-AE," *Eyes Beyond the Horizon (EBTH)* (magazine of the JUAV Program Office), August 2010, pp. 30–31; Adam Baddeley, "With unblinking eyes," *CBRNE World*, Spring 2008, p. 40.

32. Rand Corporation, Counterinsurgency in Iraq (2003–2006), pp. 45–46.

33. Lieutenant Colonel Mark A. Cooter, USAF, Airborne Armed Full Motion Video: The Nexus of Ops/Intel Integration in the Joint/Coalition Environment, Joint Forces Staff College, Joint Advanced Warfighting School, 25 May 2007, p. 11.

34. Lieutenant Colonel Mark A. Cooter, USAF, Airborne Armed Full Motion Video: The Nexus of Ops/Intel Integration in the Joint/Coalition Environment, Joint Forces Staff College, Joint Advanced Warfighting School, 25 May 2007, p. 19.

35. Lieutenant Colonel Mark A. Cooter, USAF, Airborne Armed Full Motion Video: The Nexus of Ops/Intel Integration in the Joint/Coalition Environment, Joint Forces Staff College, Joint Advanced Warfighting School, 25 May 2007, p. 36.

36. Rick Atkinson, "Left of Boom; 'You Can't Armor Your Way out of This Problem,'" *Washington Post*, October 2, 2007, p. A1 (Part 3 in a series).

37. Rand Corporation, Counterinsurgency in Iraq (2003–2006), pp. 45–46.

38. *Duty*, p. 119.

39. William H. McMichael, "Head of Anti-IED Agency Says It's Been Effective: Now takes more bombs to get same level of casualties, *Army Times*, May 21, 2007, p. 24. See also comments by General McChrystal about promiscuous buying; in General Stanley McChrystal, *My Share of the Task* (New York: Portfolio/Penguin, 2013), p. 155.

CHAPTER THIRTEEN   Mind-Set over Mind

1. *Duty*, p. 129.
2. *Duty*, p. 128; Remarks to Air War College (Montgomery, AL), as Delivered by Secretary of Defense Robert M. Gates, Maxwell-Gunter Air Force Base, Montgomery, Alabama, Monday, April 21, 2008.
3. *Duty*, pp. 115, 126, 129–130.
4. On Point II: Transition to the New Campaign: The United States Army in Operation Iraqi Freedom, May 2003–January 2005, p. 160.
5. On Point II: Transition to the New Campaign: The United States Army in Operation Iraqi Freedom, May 2003–January 2005, p. 191.
6. On Point II: Transition to the New Campaign: The United States Army in Operation Iraqi Freedom, May 2003–January 2005, pp. 196–201.
7. Major General James O. Barclay III, commanding general of the United States Army Aviation Center of Excellence and the commanding general of Fort Rucker, Alabama; in Emerson Pittman/OCPA Plans, "Unmanned aircraft systems leading fight," Army News Service, October 7, 2009.
8. *Duty*, p. 128.
9. Quoted in Defense Science Board, Report of the Defense Science Board Task Force on Fulfillment of Urgent Operational Needs, July 2009.
10. That history is wonderfully told in Whittle, *Predator: The Secret Origins of the Drone Revolution*, pp. 90–108, 118.
11. *Duty*, p. 130.
12. *Duty*, p. 105.
13. One fascinating aside is the decision of the Joint Requirements Oversight Council (JROCM 283-05: MQ1 Orbit Demand Study) that tasked the joint arena and the air force to examine Predator supply to the combatant commander in the 2010–2011 time frame, a study that just predated Gates. The purpose was to set spending for the Fiscal Year 08 Program Objective Memorandum (POM), which determines how the air force can spend money. In other words, the air force was fulfilling the tasking it had been given when Gates came into office.
14. Christopher B. Carlile and William S. Larese, "Manned-Unmanned Aircraft Teaming Making the Quantum Leap," *Army Aviation*, October 31, 2009.
15. Army Vice Chief of Staff General Richard A. Cody established Task Force Observe, Detect, Identify, and Neutralize (TF ODIN) in June 2006. See David Pugliese, "Task Force ODIN: In the Valleys of the Blind," *Defense Industry Daily*, January 15, 2009; Jon W. Glass, "Taking Aim in Afghanistan," *CISR Journal*, February 5, 2009.
16. Cristina Cameron Fekkes, "Defining Conditions for the Use of Persistent Surveillance," Naval Postgraduate School, December 2009, p. 41.
17. Matt J. Martin with Charles W. Sasser, *Predator*, p. 147.

18. In his first briefing from the ISR Task Force in April 2008, Gates says he learned that of over nearly 4,500 drones worldwide, only a little more than half were in Iraq and Afghanistan; he completely missed the reality that almost all of the drones not forward were small drones assigned to army and marine corps units who also weren't there. See *Duty*, pp. 132–133.

19. General Atomics News Release, "The Army IGnat UAV Operationally Available 24/7 in Iraq," September 24, 2004. In February 2005, a contract for two more IGnat-ER systems was placed. By then, the original three systems had completed over 850 combat missions in Iraq.

20. According to the GAO, "both the air force and the Joint Staff responsible for reviewing Sky Warrior's [later the program's name] requirements and acquisition documentation raised concerns about duplicating existing capability—specifically, capability provided by Predator. Nevertheless, the program received approval to forgo an analysis of alternatives that could have determined if existing capabilities would meet its requirements. The Army noted that such an analysis was not needed and not worth the cost and effort. Instead, it conducted a source selection competition and began the Sky Warrior development program, citing battlefield commanders' urgent need for this capability." GAO, Opportunities Exist to Achieve Greater Commonality and Efficiencies among Unmanned Aircraft Systems, July 2009, GAO-09-520, p. 16.

21. Del C. Kostka, "Moving Toward a Joint Acquisition Process to Support ISR," *Joint Forces Quarterly* (*JFQ*), issue 55, 4th quarter 2009.

22. General T. Michael Moseley, CSAF's *Scope* on Unmanned Aerial Vehicles (UAVs), May 21, 2007; www.af.mil/specials/scope/archive/uav.html; see also *Birds of Prey: Predators and America's Newest UAVs in Combat*, p. 84.

    Lieutenant General Raymond Odierno, commander of Multinational Forces—Iraq and Petraeus's replacement after he was promoted, took a further shot at this in 2008: drones and other ISR assets should be consolidated under the army corps commander. The conventional army could be more unconventional—like special operations—the future army chief of staff argued, by using the ODIN model across the theater. "ISR is working in Iraq because tactical leaders are maximizing the effectiveness of a limited resource," Odierno wrote, arguing for decentralized control and the greatest flexibility at the lowest level. The army corps, he said, was "really the highest level at which this can be done with a true feel for what is going on at all levels," not some distant command center. See Raymond T. Odierno, Nichoel E. Brooks, and Francesco P. Mastracchio, "ISR Evolution in the Iraqi Theater," *Joint Forces Quarterly* (*JFQ*), issue 50, 3rd quarter 2008, p. 52.

23. *Duty*, p. 127.

24. *Duty*, p. 129.

25. *Duty*, p. 130.
26. *Duty*, p. 130.
27. Major Scott R. Cerone, USAF; "How Should the Joint Force Handle the Command and Control of Unmanned Aircraft Systems? A Monograph," School of Advanced Military Studies, United States Army Command and General Staff College, Fort Leavenworth, Kansas, 2008.
28. *Birds of Prey: Predators and America's Newest UAVs in Combat*, p. 85.
29. Admiral Edmund Giambastiani (Vice Chairman of the Joint Chiefs of Staff), "Memorandum for the Deputy Secretary of Defense regarding Executive Agency for Medium and High Altitude Unmanned Aircraft Systems," July 16, 2007.
30. DOD, USD (ATL), Department of Defense Report to Congress on Addressing Challenges for Unmanned Aircraft Systems, September 2010; *Birds of Prey: Predators and America's Newest UAVs in Combat*, p. 86.
31. *Duty*, p. 127.
32. *Duty*, p. 127.
33. Statement by Brigadier General Stephen Mundt; Director, Army Aviation Directorate, Deputy Chief of Staff, Army G-3/5/7, before the House Armed Services Committee, Tactical Air and Land Forces Subcommittee, United States House of Representatives on US Army Unmanned Aerial Vehicle Programs, June 4, 2006.
34. Remarks to Air War College (Montgomery, Alabama), as Delivered by Secretary of Defense Robert M. Gates, Maxwell-Gunter Air Force Base, Montgomery, Monday, April 21, 2008.

    On April 4, Gates sent a memo to Mullen asking for an update on increasing ISR support and for proposals on how to increase more over the ensuing thirty to ninety days. Mullen said that a more comprehensive approach was needed, and Gates decides to establish the ISR task force. See discussion in *Duty*, pp. 131–132.
35. Air Force News Service, "Predator Combat Air Patrols Double in 1 Year," May 6, 2008; Associated Press (AP), "Defense Secretary Gates Says Air Force must step up efforts in Iraq, Afghanistan," April 21, 2008; General T. Michael Moseley, Memorandum for the Deputy Secretary of Defense regarding Executive Agency for Medium- and High-Altitude Unmanned Aerial Vehicles (UAVs), March 5, 2007.
36. DOD, USD (ATL), Department of Defense Report to Congress on Addressing Challenges for Unmanned Aircraft Systems, September 2010.
37. *Duty*, pp. 132–133. Another example of Gates's disregard for his own supposed standards comes in the MRAP decisions he also made. In 2004, Rumsfeld established the Joint Rapid Acquisition Cell (JRAC), an office that was supposed to have already ensured that any wartime requests be expedited. The process began with a joint urgent operational need (JUON). Once approved at the JRAC, any parochial service objections

were overridden by top-level reprogramming. As one observer notes, Gates's MRAP accomplishments began with JUONs submitted to the JRAC, "a process wholly enabled by Rumsfeld's policies, which prevented the service black holes lamented by Gates. Curiously, Gates belittles the JUON and ignores the JRAC." See www.defensenews.com/article/2014 0217/DEFREG02/302170032/Commentary-Faulty-MRAP-Recollections ?odyssey=mod/newswell/text/FRONTPAGE/p.

38. See US Congress, House Permanent Select Committee on Intelligence, Performance Audit of Department of Defense Intelligence, Surveillance, and Reconnaissance, April 2012, p. 6; ISR Leader Q&A: Ensuring War-fighters Have the Intelligence Support They Require, Lieutenant General John C. Koziol, Deputy Under Secretary of Defense, Joint and Coalition Warfighter Support; Director, DOD ISR Task Force, Geospatial Intelligence Forum (GIF 8.6), September 2010, p. 21; *Duty*, pp. 132–133.

39. In June 2007, General Atomics flew for the first time a company-owned Block 0 Predator derivative, which would join army combat operations in early 2008. Erik Schechter, "Rush to the sky; U.S. Army quickens the pace of its new UAV program," *Defense News*, June 1, 2008; General Atomics Press Release, "First Pre-Production Sky Warrior Aircraft Takes Flight; Maiden Flight Marks Important Milestone in Execution of U.S. Army ER/MP Contract," June 14, 2007.

40. In response to April 2008 "SECDEF" direction, the program split into two Quick Reaction Capability sets (QRC 1 and QRC 2), each consisting of four aircraft. DOD, Selected Acquisition Report (SAR), MQ-1C UAS GRAY EAGLE as of December 31, 2010.

41. "Quick Reaction Capability-1; Fielding UAS Assets to Ground Commanders Faster," *Eyes Beyond the Horizon* (Army UAS PO), January 2010.

42. Timothy M. McGrew, Army Aviation Addressing Battlefield Anomalies in Real Time with the Teaming and Collaboration of Manned and Unmanned Aircraft, Naval Postgraduate School, December 2009, pp. 17–22.

43. Air Force PowerPoint Briefing, Lieutenant General Dave Deptula, Deputy Chief of Staff, Intelligence, Surveillance and Reconnaissance; Air Force Unmanned Aerial System (UAS) Flight Plan, 2009-2047, n.d. (2009).

44. *Duty*, p. 133.

45. PowerPoint Briefing, UAS Operations and Comparison, Lieutenant Colonel Bruce "Shadow" Black, USAF UAS Task Force, as of March 17, 2010 (ver13).

And of course, following the spiral habit, the air force actually sent two YMQ-9 experimental Reapers to Afghanistan in 2005. See Colonel (USAF) Chris R. Chambliss, "MQ-1 Predator and MQ-9 Reaper Unmanned Aircraft Systems: At a Crossroads," *Air & Space Power Journal*—Español Cuarto Trimestre 2008,1 January 2009.

46. PowerPoint Briefing, UAS Task Force, HQ AF/A2, "Air Force and Army UAS," March 9, 2009; Paul Fiddian, "U.S. Military's UAV Mission Increasing," *Armed Forces Journal*, February 2008.
47. Captain Jessica Martin, 926th Group Public Affairs, "Reservist member of Predator's 500,000-hour milestone crew," Air Force News Service, February 25, 2009.
48. PowerPoint Briefing, HQ AF RPA/UAS Airspace Integration, Steven Pennington, AF/A3O-B, April 15, 2010.
49. Jeffrey Kappenman, "Army Unmanned Aircraft Systems: Decisive in Battle," *Joint Force Quarterly* (*JFQ*), Issue 49, 2d Quarter 2008; "Army Weapons," *Army*, October 2010, p. 322.
50. *Duty*, p. 243.
51. *Duty*, p. 243.

CHAPTER FOURTEEN   Gilgamesh Calling

1. Jack Anderson and Dale Van Atta, "The Soul of Gen. Schwarzkopf," *Washington Post*, February 24, 1991, p. C27.
2. The air force part of the story is taken from "Talking Points on Air Force's Efforts in the Bombing and Death of Al Zarqawi, Based on the transcript of Lt Gen [Gary] North," June 8, 2006, obtained by the author; PowerPoint Briefing, "Warfighting Integration, ITAA Defense Committee Meet," David Tillotson III, SES, Deputy Chief of Warfighting Integration and Deputy Chief Information Officer, n.d. (March 2009); obtained by the author. See also Michael W. Isherwood, "Airpower for Hybrid War," *Air Force Magazine*, October 2009; F-16 Fighting Falcon Units of Operation Iraqi Freedom, p. 14.
3. Much has been written about Zarqawi and his background. See, in particular, Ely Karmon, "Al-Qa'ida and the War on Terror After the War in Iraq," *Middle East Review of International Affairs*, Vol. 10, No. 1 (March 2006).

   Zarqawi's status as a *national* target elevated because US and foreign intelligence agencies had concluded that he was behind biological and chemical weapons plots. In June 2002, the Jordanian intelligence service notified Baghdad that al-Zarqawi (aka Ahmad Fadeel al-Nazal al-Khalayleh) was in Baghdad under an assumed identity after he and his commanders had conducted crude chemical and biological training experiments at the remote Khurmal camp in northeastern Iraq, in the Kurdish zone and near the Iranian border. Iraqi intelligence told the Jordanian government it could not find Zarqawi. Independent of al Qaeda, he had operated in Herat Camp in Afghanistan under Taliban rule, and had been convicted in absentia for planning the assassination of US diplomat Laurence Foley in Amman, Jordan.

On January 5, 2003, after an arrest in London, the Zarqawi "network" was implicated in a plot to use ricin poison on the Underground. Further arrests in Europe confirm evidence of crude poisons and toxins.

In his February 5, 2003, presentation at the United Nations, Secretary of State Colin Powell named Zarqawi and others as part of poison cells in the United Kingdom, Spain, France, and possibly Italy.

4. Elsa Walsh, "Learning to Spy: Can Maureen Baginski save the FBI?," *The New Yorker*, November 8, 2004.

5. General Michael Hayden, Air Warfare Symposium Speech, February 2, 2006; www.afa.org/media/scripts/AWS06_Hayden.html (accessed November 11, 2006).

6. James Bamford, *Body of Secrets: Anatomy of the Ultra-Secret National Security Agency* (New York: Anchor Books , 2002), p. 329.

7. When a signal arrives at two moving, spatially separated receivers, the receivers measure a difference in phase and frequency. The time when a signal arrives at two spatially separate receivers also yields helpful information. These characteristics are the basis for four methods of geolocation: (1) the angle of arrival (AOA) method, which locates a position using the directional angle of a signal, (2) the frequency difference of arrival (FDOA), which determines the position of the emitter from the difference in frequency of the signal measured between two receivers, (3) the time of arrival (TOA) technique, which calculates the position of the emitter using the precise time the signal arrives at multiple receivers, and (4) time difference of arrival (TDOA), which uses the difference in time when a signal is received at two or more receivers to determine the location of an emitter.

8. Volkan Tas, Optimal Use of TDOA Geo-Location Techniques Within the Mountainous Terrain of Turkey, Naval Postgraduate School, September 2012; Myrna B. Montminy, Captain, USAF; "Passive Geolocation of Low-Power Emitters in Urban Environments Using TDOA," Air Force Institute of Technology, AFIT/GE/ENG/07-16, March 2007.

9. *My Share of the Task*, pp. 144–145.

10. Though most sources, including McChrystal in *My Share of the Task*, refer to TF 714, there is a mind-boggling list of other secret organizations that were involved: Task Force 145 North, Task Force 170, the SOCOM J-239 Information Operation (OI) shop, and Project Sovereign Challenge.

11. *Top Secret America*, pp. 221–255.

12. PowerPoint Briefing, "Operational ISR in the CENTCOM AOR," Colonel Terri Meyer, USCENTAF/A2, Shaw AFB, South Carolina, Al Udeid AB, n.d. (December 2004); obtained by the author.

13. *My Share of the Task*, p. 155.

14. PowerPoint Briefing, "Operational ISR in the CENTCOM AOR," Colonel Terri Meyer, USCENTAF/A2, Shaw AFB, South Carolina, Al Udeid AB, n.d. (December 2004); obtained by the author.
15. *My Share of the Task*, p. 154.
16. *My Share of the Task*, p. 157.
17. *My Share of the Task*, p. 149.
18. *My Share of the Task*, p. 156.
19. Jeremy Scahill and Glenn Greenwald, "The NSA's Secret Role in the U.S. Assassination Program," The Intercept (website), February 10, 2014, 12:03 AM EDT; https://firstlook.org/theintercept/article/2014/02/10/the-nsas -secret-role/ (accessed July 9, 2014).
20. *Top Secret America*, p. 242.
21. Jeremy Scahill and Glenn Greenwald, "The NSA's Secret Role in the U.S. Assassination Program," The Intercept (website), February 10, 2014, 12:03 AM EDT; https://firstlook.org/theintercept/article/2014/02/10/the-nsas -secret-role/ (accessed July 9, 2014).
22. PowerPoint Briefing, USAF FMV Needs, Initiatives, & Requirements, Robert T. "Bo" Marlin, DISL; Deputy Director, ISR Capabilities (AF/ A2C), May 22, 2013; obtained by the author.
23. Rick Atkinson, "Left of Boom; 'If You Don't Go After the Network, You're Never Going to Stop These Guys. Never.'" *Washington Post*, October 3, 2007, p. A1 (Part 4 in a series).
24. See On Point II: Transition to the New Campaign: The United States Army in Operation Iraqi Freedom, May 2003–January 2005, p. 191; Michael T. Flynn, Rich Juergens, and Thomas L. Cantrell, "Employing ISR; SOF Best Practices," *Joint Forces Quarterly* (*JFQ*), issue 50, 3rd quarter 2008.
25. *My Share of the Task*, p. 156.
26. Michael T. Flynn, Rich Juergens, and Thomas L. Cantrell, "Employing ISR; SOF Best Practices," *Joint Forces Quarterly* (*JFQ*), issue 50, 3rd quarter 2008.
27. Rebecca Grant, "Iraqi Freedom and the air force," *Air Force Magazine*, March 2013.
28. Stew Magnuson, Military 'Swimming in Sensors and Drowning in Data,' *National Defense*, January 2010.
29. Michael W. Isherwood, "Roadmap for Robotics; USAF expects unmanned aircraft to play a huge role in future warfare," *Air Force Magazine*, December 2009; Sean D. Naylor, "Inside the Zarqawi Takedown; Persistent Surveillance Helps End 3-Year Manhunt," *Defense News*, June 12, 2006, p. 1.
30. DOD PowerPoint Briefing, Department of Defense Sustainability, n.d. (November 2009).

31. PowerPoint Briefing, "Persistent and Evolving Threats," Deputy Chief of Staff, G-2 LTG John F. Kimmons, MICA Luncheon, Fort Huachuca, Arizona, October 31, 2005; obtained by the author.
32. *My Share of the Task*, p. 165.
33. *My Share of the Task*, p. 153.

CHAPTER FIFTEEN   Beyond the Speed of War

1. The Signatures Support Program (SSP), under the purview of the Defense Intelligence Agency, was previously called the National Signatures Program (NSP). See Chadwick T. Hawley, "Signatures Support Program," in Atmospheric Propagation VI, edited by Linda M. Wasiczko Thomas and G. Charmaine Gilbreath, Proc. of SPIE (2009), Vol. 7324-17.
2. Chadwick T. Hawley, "Signatures Support Program," in Atmospheric Propagation VI, edited by Linda M. Wasiczko Thomas and G. Charmaine Gilbreath, Proc. of SPIE (2009), Vol. 7324-17.

   "The Signatures Support Program (SSP) leverages the full spectrum of signature-related activities (collections, processing, development, storage, maintenance, and dissemination) within the Department of Defense (DOD), the intelligence community (IC), other Federal agencies, and civil institutions. The enterprise encompasses acoustic, seismic, radio frequency, infrared, radar, nuclear radiation, and electro-optical signatures. The SSP serves the war fighter, the IC, and civil institutions by supporting military operations, intelligence operations, homeland defense, disaster relief, acquisitions, and research and development. Data centers host and maintain signature holdings, collectively forming the national signatures pool. The geographically distributed organizations are the authoritative sources and repositories for signature data; the centers are responsible for data content and quality. The SSP proactively engages DOD, IC, other Federal entities, academia, and industry to locate signatures for inclusion in the distributed national signatures pool and provides world-wide 24/7 access via the SSP application."
3. Matthew Edward Fay, Major, United States Marine Corps; An Analysis of Hyperspectral Imagery Data Collected During Operation Desert Radiance, Naval Postgraduate School, June 1995, p. 5.
4. MASINT is defined as "Intelligence obtained by quantitative and qualitative analysis of data (metric, angle, spatial, wavelength, time dependence, modulation, plasma, and hydromagnetic) derived from specific technical sensors for the purpose of identifying any distinctive features associated with the emitter or sender, and to facilitate subsequent identification and/ or measurement of the same. The detected feature may be either reflected or emitted."

MASINT is information derived from measurements of physical phenomena intrinsic to an object or event. Measurements/signatures resulting from the shift, change, vibration, fluctuation, existence of, or the lack of any of these states for a given phenomenon:

- Electro-Optical: examples infrared, laser, spectral,
- Radar,
- Polarimetric,
- High-Power or Unintentional Radio Frequency Emanations,
- Geo-Physical: examples seismic, acoustic, magnetic, gravimetric, infrasonic;
- Chemical,
- Biological,
- Nuclear, and
- Biometrics: relies on unique signatures of human beings.

See PowerPoint Briefing, National MASINT Management Office (NMMO), MASINT/Common Sensor COI, April 2009; obtained by the author.

5. "Non-literal exploitation is the analysis of measurable, quantifiable, repeatable data collected by remotely-located sensors to produce information of intelligence value that cannot be interpreted by the human eye and cognitive system." See NGA.IP.0006_1.0 2011-07-27 Implementation Profile for Tactical Hyperspectral Imagery (HSI) Systems, 2011, pp. 16–17.

"A hybrid definition of nonliteral imagery exploitation can be found in Joint Pub 1-02 [the official military dictionary]....The process of extracting non-spatial information from image data, automatically or semi-automatically, using non-traditional, advanced processing techniques, employing models, measurements, signatures (spectral, textual, temporal, polarization), or other features to detect, locate, classify, discriminate, characterize, identify (material, unit, function), quantify (material, time, physical), track, predict, target, or assess objects, emissions, activities, of events represented in the imagery." See Matthew Edward Fay, Major, United States Marine Corps; An Analysis of Hyperspectral Imagery Data Collected During Operation Desert Radiance, Naval Postgraduate School, June 1995, p. 2.

6. Spatial resolution is the smallest distance between two ground points such that both points can be resolved by the sensor. Spectral resolution is the number and dimension (size) of specific wavelength intervals in the electromagnetic spectrum to which a remote sensing instrument is sensitive. See Christopher Burt, Detection of Spatially Unresolved (Nominally Sub-Pixel) Submerged and Surface Targets Using Hyperspectral Data, Naval Postgraduate School, September 2012, p. 15.

7. A pixel is defined as: "The atomic element of an image having a discrete value. Although a pixel value represents a minute area of an image, the generic use of the term does not specify the exact shape or symmetry of the area (circle, oval, square, rectangle, other) represented by the value." Information received from NGA, 2014.

   Pixel size is a direct indicator of the spatial resolution of the sensor because pixels are the smallest elements that can be detected by the sensor. Spatial resolution is a measure of the smallest angular or linear separation between two objects that can be resolved by the sensor. More simply put, it is the smallest separation between two objects on the ground that can be detected as a separate object.

8. The electromagnetic spectrum extends from the short-wave cosmic ray region to the long-wave TV and radio-wave region and includes, among others: gamma rays, X-rays, ultraviolet, visible, near infrared, thermal infrared, microwave, and radio waves (TV and radio bands). The wavelengths of visible light range from 400 to 700 nanometers (nm), near-infrared wavelengths range from 700 to 1100 nm, and short-wave infrared wavelengths range from 1400 to about 3500 nm.

9. Henry Canaday, "Seeing More with Hyperspectral Imaging," *Geospatial Intelligence Forum* (GIF) 11.2, p. 21.

10. Paul J. Pabich, Lieutenant Colonel, USAF; Hyperspectral Imagery: Warfighting Through a Different Set of Eyes, Occasional Paper No. 31, Center for Strategy and Technology, Air War College, October 2002, p. 4.

11. A number of multispectral sensors were developed, particularly by NASA, but it was not until the Airborne Visible/Infrared Imaging Spectrometer (AVIRIS) was flown aboard a specially configured U-2 in 1989 that hyperspectral information extraction was achieved, with AVIRIS imaging 224 contiguous spectral bands at a resolution of 10 nanometers. See Matthew Edward Fay, Major, United States Marine Corps; An Analysis of Hyperspectral Imagery Data Collected During Operation Desert Radiance, Naval Postgraduate School, June 1995, pp. 9–10.

12. Spectral imaging as opposed to the more familiar visible-light imagery, that is, photography, can distinguish many objects from their surroundings by strong reflection, or lack thereof, in parts of the electromagnetic spectrum but are washed out in a photographic view. The distinguishing reflectance (or emittance) in a small portion of the spectrum may be undetectable when an entire portion of the spectrum, such as the visible-light portion, is observed as a whole.

13. Paul J. Pabich, Lieutenant Colonel, USAF; Hyperspectral Imagery: Warfighting Through a Different Set of Eyes, Occasional Paper No. 31, Center for Strategy and Technology, Air War College, October 2002, pp. 1–2.

14. Christopher Burt, Detection of Spatially Unresolved (Nominally Sub-Pixel) Submerged and Surface Targets Using Hyperspectral Data, Naval Postgraduate School, September 2012, pp. 9–10.

15. See discussion in Andrew C. Rice, Context-Aided Tracking with Adaptive Hyperspectral Imagery, Air Force Institute of Technology, AFIT/GE/ENG/11-43, June 2011, pp. 1–9.

16. Paul J. Pabich, Lieutenant Colonel, USAF; Hyperspectral Imagery: Warfighting Through a Different Set of Eyes, Occasional Paper No. 31, Center for Strategy and Technology, Air War College, October 2002, p. 13.

17. Jeffrey H. Bowles, John A. Antoniades, Mark M. Baumback, John M. Grossmann, Daniel Haas, et al., "Real-time analysis of hyperspectral data sets using NRL's ORASIS algorithm," Proc. SPIE 3118, Imaging Spectrometry III, 38 (October 31, 1997); Matthew Edward Fay, Major, United States Marine Corps; An Analysis of Hyperspectral Imagery Data Collected During Operation Desert Radiance, Naval Postgraduate School, June 1995.

18. Deploying a hyperspectral sensor in space was not a seamless task. The Lewis spacecraft was launched in August 1997 with a 384-channel sensor but did not succeed in demonstrating hyperspectral technology. Soon after launch, the spacecraft developed a slow spin, rendering the solar array unusable. The spacecraft could not be recovered, and it reentered Earth's atmosphere in September 1997.

   Ten days after 9/11, the air force's satellite-borne Warfighter 1 hyperspectral package on board a civilian satellite was destroyed when its launch vehicle failed.

19. In cases where targets were located in environments that masked or distorted the signature spectra of the target, even when objects were overtly exposed, some sensors were not able to discriminate the target. See Jeffrey D. Sanders, Target Detection and Classification at Kernel Blitz 1997 Using Spectral Imagery, Naval Postgraduate School, December 1998.

20. Naval Research Laboratory, "NRL Demonstrates First Autonomous Real-Time Hyperspectral Target Detection System Flown Aboard a Predator UAV," October 31, 2000; www.nrl.navy.mil/media/news-releases /2000/nrl-demonstrates-first-autonomous-realtime-hyperspectral-target -detection-system-flown-aboard-a-predator-uav#sthash.UuOUzpv4.dpuf (accessed April 30, 2014).

21. Data from a nadir-looking visible hyperspectral sensor were analyzed by an onboard real-time processor. A three-band false-color waterfall display of the hyperspectral data with overlaid target cues, along with the corresponding high-resolution image chips, was transmitted to a ground station in real time.

   The push-broom sensor consisted of a grating spectrometer and a 1024x1024 custom charge-coupled device (CCD) camera. The sensor operated at a frame rate of 40 Hz and provided 1,024 cross-track spatial pixels and 64 wavelength bands (450 to 900 nm). The panchromatic imaging sensor operated in the visible-wavelength region and consisted of a CCD line scanner and a large-format lens (300 mm). This sensor operated at a frame rate of 240 Hz and provided high-resolution imagery via 6,000 cross-track spatial pixels. A high-frame-rate video frame grabber and custom demodulation software decoded the transmitted data, which consisted of a false-color waterfall display, target cue information, and corresponding high-resolution image chips.

See Naval Research Laboratory, "NRL Demonstrates First Autonomous Real-Time Hyperspectral Target Detection System Flown Aboard a Predator UAV," October 31, 2000; www.nrl.navy.mil/media/news-releases /2000/nrl-demonstrates-first-autonomous-realtime-hyperspectral-target -detection-system-flown-aboard-a-predator-uav#sthash.UuOUzpv4.dpuf (accessed April 30, 2014).

22. Paul J. Pabich, Lieutenant Colonel, USAF; Hyperspectral Imagery: Warfighting Through a Different Set of Eyes, Occasional Paper No. 31, Center for Strategy and Technology, Air War College, October 2002, p. 16.

23. Chadwick T. Hawley, "Signatures Support Program," in Atmospheric Propagation VI, edited by Linda M. Wasiczko Thomas and G. Charmaine Gilbreath, Proc. of SPIE (2009), Vol. 7324-17.

24. Matthew Edward Fay, Major, United States Marine Corps; An Analysis of Hyperspectral Imagery Data Collected During Operation Desert Radiance, Naval Postgraduate School, June 1995, pp. 1–2.

25. Over Afghanistan, Hyperion was used to give researchers "a unique opportunity to compare hyperspectral images of targets before and after they were bombed, adding to the store of signature data that can be used in applying the technology to targeting and post-attack damage assessment"; Paul J. Pabich, Lieutenant Colonel, USAF; Hyperspectral Imagery: Warfighting Through a Different Set of Eyes, Occasional Paper No. 31, Center for Strategy and Technology, Air War College, October 2002, p. 17.

26. Paul J. Pabich, Lieutenant Colonel, USAF; Hyperspectral Imagery: Warfighting Through a Different Set of Eyes, Occasional Paper No. 31, Center for Strategy and Technology, Air War College, October 2002, p. 7.

27. Amy Butler, "USAF Turns to Hyperspectral Sensors in Afghanistan: New sensors provide new edge in finding explosives in Afghanistan," *Aviation Week & Space Technology*, September 19, 2011; Paul J. Pabich, Lieutenant Colonel, USAF; Hyperspectral Imagery: Warfighting Through a Different Set of Eyes, Occasional Paper No. 31, Center for Strategy and Technology, Air War College, October 2002, p. 7.

28. USAF, HyCAS ACTD Management Plan, January 7, 2003.

29. "Using a National Aeronautics and Space Administration (NASA) WB-57 aircraft flown at an altitude of approximately 15,240 meters (roughly

50,000 feet), 218 flight lines of hyperspectral data were collected over Afghanistan between August 22 and October 2, 2007. These HyMap data were processed, empirically adjusted using ground-based reflectance measurements, and georeferenced to Landsat base imagery. Each pixel of processed HyMap data was compared to reference spectrum entries in a spectral library of minerals, vegetation, water, ice, and snow in order to characterize surface materials across the Afghan landscape." See USGS Projects in Afghanistan, Hyperspectral Surface Materials Maps; http://afghanistan.cr.usgs.gov/hyperspectral-maps (accessed May 12, 2014).

30. Shannon O'Harren, Trude V. V. King, Tushar Suthar, and Kenneth D. Cockrell, "Information-driven Interagency Operations in Afghanistan," *Joint Forces Quarterly* (*JFQ*), Issue 51, 4th quarter 2008.

31. Chadwick T. Hawley, "Signatures Support Program," in Atmospheric Propagation VI, edited by Linda M. Wasiczko Thomas and G. Charmaine Gilbreath, Proc. of SPIE (2009), Vol. 7324-17.

32. Henry Canaday, "Seeing More with Hyperspectral Imaging," *Geospatial Intelligence Forum* (GIF) 11.2, p. 22. See also National Air Intelligence Center PowerPoint Briefing, Hyperspectral Collection and Analysis System (HyCAS) ACTD, n.d. (June 2003).

33. SpecTIR Government Solutions (SGS), GEOINT | MASINT | IMINT; *SpecTIR Spectator*, Quarterly Newsletter, Vol. 1, 2012.

The SpecTIR Hyperspectral Automated Processing and Exploitation System (SHAPES) is described by its manufacturer as a highly rugged ground-based hyperspectral remote-sensing capability in a trailer. SHAPES's sensor can complete a scan in thirty seconds, and then SHAPES takes twenty to forty seconds to process, exploit, and generate a report from scanned data. Processing includes radiometric calibration, atmospheric compensation, and target detection. See Henry Canaday, "Seeing More with Hyperspectral Imaging," *Geospatial Intelligence Forum* (GIF) 11.2, p. 22.

34. Henry Canaday, "Seeing More with Hyperspectral Imaging," *Geospatial Intelligence Forum* (GIF) 11.2, p. 21.

35. National Air Intelligence Center PowerPoint Briefing, Hyperspectral Collection and Analysis System (HyCAS) ACTD, n.d. (June 2003); DOD, Exhibit R-2, RDT&E Budget Item Justification: PB 2012 Office of Secretary of Defense, PE 0604648D8Z: Joint Capability Technology Demonstration Transition (JCTD), February 2011, p. 4.

36. USAF, HyCAS ACTD Management Plan, January 7, 2003.

37. "Combat Identification is the process of attaining an accurate characterization of detected objects in the battle space to the extent that a high confidence, timely application of tactical options, and weapons resources can occur. Depending on the situation and the tactical decisions that must be made, this characterization will be at least, but may not be limited to, 'friend,' 'enemy,' or 'neutral.' Combat identification functions encompass

cooperative and non-cooperative identification capabilities"; see JCS, Joint Pub 3-01, February 5, 2007.

38. Department of the Army, Military Intelligence Reference Guide, MI Publication 2-0.1, June 2010, p. B-1.

39. PowerPoint Briefing, Tom Dee, Director, Defense Biometrics, OSD AT&L, DDR&E; DOD Biometrics; Information Technology Association of America (ITAA), April 22, 2008.

40. "The committee understands that there are also additional 'soft' biometrics, such as gait, keystroke, or analysis of body markings, which could also be useful in identifying specific individuals, and could be done from greater stand-off distances. The committee notes that some research has been conducted by the air force Research Laboratory, as well as other civilian research agencies to better characterize the utility and operational challenges of such modalities, but that the current biometrics architecture does not yet integrate any of these capabilities. The committee encourages the Department to examine all biometric modalities as it develops its future biometrics architecture." See U.S. Congress, House of Representatives, National Defense Authorization Act for Fiscal Year 2014, Report of the Committee on Armed Services, June 7, 2013, p. 129.

41. SOCOM PowerPoint Briefing, Bonny Heet, SBIR Program Manager, Overview of the USSOCOM Program Executive Offices, USSOCOM/ SORDAC-ST, March 20, 2013; PowerPoint Briefing, Dr. Thomas Killion, Director, BIMA; Biometrics: Impact, Opportunities & Challenges, 2012 EUCOM 3rd Annual Information, Innovation, Integration, and Technology (i3T) Conference, February 16, 2012; PowerPoint Briefing, Tom Dee, Director, Defense Biometrics, OSD AT&L, DDR&E; DOD Biometrics; NDIA Disruptive Technologies, September 5, 2007.

42. PowerPoint Briefing, Tom Dee, Director, Defense Biometrics, OSD AT&L, DDR&E; DOD Biometrics; NDIA Disruptive Technologies, September 5, 2007.

43. "Technical, geospatial, and intelligence information derived through interpretation or analysis using advanced processing of all data collected by imagery or imagery-related collection systems. Amplification: This definition of AGI, also known as Imagery-Derived MASINT, includes all types of information technically derived from the processing, exploitation, and non-literal analysis (to include integration or fusion) of spectral, spatial, temporal, radiometric, phase history, and polarimetric data. These types of data can be collected on stationary and moving targets by electro-optical, infrared, radar, and related sensor programs (both active and passive). AGI also includes both ancillary data needed for data processing/exploitation and signature information (to include development, validation, simulation, data archival, and dissemination). (Joint Pub 2-03 Draft Feb 2006)." See NGA, National System for Geospatial Intelligence,

Geospatial Intelligence (GEOINT) Basic Doctrine, Publication 1-0, September 2006, p. 45.

44. Keith J. Masback, USGIF from the Desk of the President, *Geospatial Intelligence Forum* (GIF) 8.6, p. 5.

CHAPTER SIXTEEN   X-Men

1. Paula Pomianowski, Richard Delanoy, Jonathan Kurz, and Gary Condon, "Silent Hammer," *Lincoln Laboratory Journal*, Volume 16, Number 2, 2007; Marianna J. Verett, Performance and Usage of Biometrics in a Testbed Environment for Tactical Purposes, Naval Postgraduate School, December 2006, p. 11.

2. See *Age of Sacred Terror*, p. 319. Shelton later expressed respect for Richard Clarke, the main memo-writer of the Clinton administration, but does say "he would come in from watching a Rambo movie or something and present some wild-haired idea that would brief well—but when you looked at the reality of it, of what it would really take to pull it off, it was far better suited for an episode of *NCIS* than a real-life situation in which lives were on the line"; Hugh Shelton with Ronald Levinson and Malcolm McConnell, *Without Hesitation* (New York: St. Martin's Press, 2010), p. 353.

3. Mazzetti in *The Way of the Knife*, p. 89, tells the tale repeated in the 9/11 Commission report, and I'll repeat it here, though other sources have also told me that it wasn't Clinton who expressed such sentiment but one of his subordinates.

4. "Madeleine's War," *Time* magazine, May 17, 1999.

5. The year is 1995 or 1996: "The CSG [the White House Counterterrorism Security Group] also considered direct action, examining options for attacks on bin Laden's and/or Turabi's facilities in and around Khartoum [in Sudan]. The White House requested the Pentagon to develop plans for a U.S. Special Forces operation against al Qaeda-related facilities in Sudan. Weeks later a Pentagon team briefed National Security Advisor Tony Lake and other Principals in Lake's West Wing office....While the Joint Staff dutifully briefed the plan, they recommended against it.... [Lake responds that the plan is nothing short of war. "The military briefing leader nodded: That's what we do, sir. If you want covert, there's the CIA."]; Richard Clarke, *Against all Enemies*, p. 141.

6. See Michael A. Sheehan, *Crush the Cell* (New York: Crown, 2008), p. 120; *Age of Sacred Terror*, p. 319.

7. The Special Reconnaissance Capability (SRC) Program "exploits, leverages, and integrates DOD's service and agency efforts to improve surveillance and reconnaissance tools (unattended sensors, tagging devices, data infiltration/exfiltration, remote delivery, and mobility/delivery of sensors), while providing risk reduction for DOD and other agency technol-

ogy and development programs. The SRC Program identifies, integrates, and operationalizes the technical tools for the collection of actionable information against a variety of targets and mission requirements, including Global War on Terrorism (GWOT), and maintains DOD's on-line catalog of tools in order to minimize crisis response time for special reconnaissance and surveillance." DOD, FY 2007 Exhibit R-2, RDT&E Budget Item Justification, SOLIC Advanced Development—PE 0603 12 1 D8Z, February 2006.

Within the budgetary and procurement world of U.S. Special Operations Command, SRC is also referred to as Special Reconnaissance, Surveillance, & Exploitation (SRSE).

8. Department of the Army, Intelligence, FM 2-0, May 2004, pp. 4–9; Terms & Definitions of Interest for Counterintelligence Professionals, October 2013, p. GL-284, quoting JP 3-05, Special Operations, April 18, 2011.

9. William Murray, "Tagging, Tracking & Locating: TTL Systems Empower SOF to Spot and Eliminate Dangers," Special Operations Technology (SOTECH 11-1), February 2013.

10. Defense Science Board 2004 Summer Study on Transition to and from Hostilities, December 2004, pp. 158–160.

11. "Argos Doppler tags (known as platform transmitter terminals, or PTTs) are electronic tags that send periodic signals to Argos transmitters on polar-orbiting satellites. Receiving stations located around the globe collect the data from the satellites and send it to a processing center, where location estimates are made by measuring the Doppler shift on the signals sent by the tag. The location estimates are typically much less accurate than those made with a GPS, but the tags can be much lighter than GPS units and can also be used to transmit GPS locations if the tag is properly equipped. Compared to the types of tags described below, these tags are relatively expensive and heavier, but allow for location measurements from anywhere on the globe." Information from Movebank, "a free, online database of animal tracking data hosted by the Max Planck Institute for Ornithology"; www.movebank.org/ (accessed May 19, 2014).

12. "AIT is a collection of enabling technologies including linear and two-dimensional bar codes, radio frequency identification (RFID), smart cards, memory cards, laser cards, touch memory, voice and biometrics identification. These technologies provide timely and accurate automatic capture, aggregation and transfer of data to management information systems with minimal human involvement." See DOD FY 2000 Budget Request, OPAF/ Other Base Maintenance & Support Equipment, February 1999.

13. "This system was capable of delivering GPS position reports every five minutes and sends messages both among users and to various higher headquarters. It utilizes a software program called TracerLink mapping software and MTS Messenger simultaneously so that users can send messages

and view their position (and the position of others in their group) at the same time. These software programs are viewed as pop-up windows through the use of the Windows based operating systems. This first rendition of MTS used an external Precision Lightweight GPS Receiver (PLGR) for GPS locations, a COMTECH Mobile Transceiver model MT2010/MT2011 transceiver, and a Paravan computer." See Department of the Army, Capability Production Document for Movement Tracking System (MTS), Increment: 1, Draft Version 1.0, March 13, 2009.

14. PowerPoint Briefing, Product Manager Joint-Automatic Identification Technology, Lieutenant Colonel P. Burden, November 29, 2007.

15. DARPA ITO Sponsored Research, 2001 Project Summary, Operational CONOPS development and experimentation in support of HUMAN ID at a Distance in Reconnaissance and Surveillance applications, Chenega Technology Services Corp., n.d. (January 2002).

16. MITRE Corporation, Technology Assessment for the State of the Art Biometrics Excellence Roadmap; Volume 2 (of 3) Face, Iris, Ear, Voice, and Handwriter Recognition; v1.3, March 2009, p. 2-34.

ENCORE TASK ORDER (TO) STATEMENT OF WORK (SOW) as of 18 November 2003, Contract Number: DCA200-02-D-5014, Human Interface Security (HIS) Biometrics Solutions Integration Research Support.

The goal of this task is to develop a prototype of a CMSS that will be integrated with the Acsys Biometrics Corporation's facial recognition system (FRS) framework to support the following capabilities:

- Support one-to-many facial identification scenarios, such as identifying people in a crowd
- Support real-time operation in identification mode for a minimum of 50,000 enrolled subjects
- Enrollment in the field (FRS client) and biometric template generation at the FRS central server
- Support for LAN, WAN, cellular wireless and web-based communication between the FRS central server and the FRS client modules to support operation in the field
- Highly portable and provides covert deployment

The proposed system will be comprised of a wearable computer module (WCM) receiving and processing video stream input from a covert camera. The user interfaces during normal field operation will be provided through microphone/earphone and a head-mounted display (HMD). A wireless PDA and/or speech recognition module will serve as the control input interface to the wearable computer. The WCM will provide wireless communications to both the FRS central server and mobile or stationary alarm annunciation/monitoring stations. The capability to import and store up to 50,000 biometric templates at the FRS client will also be provided. The user of the system will be able to acquire facial targets, identify the target subject if they exist within the local client database, and store acquired images for subsequent post analysis. The WCM and batteries will be worn on the waist and the camera components will be blended into standard sunglasses or other concealed locations on the user.

17. 2013 Program Management Updates, Special Operations Technology (SOTECH 11.4), p. 33.

18. DOD, Fiscal Year (FY) 2005 Budget Estimates, SO/LIC Advanced Development, PE 0603121D8Z, DOD, R-1 Shopping List Item No. 26, February 2004, p. 1 of 9.

19. Defense Science Board 2004 Summer Study on Transition to and from Hostilities, December 2004, pp. xvi, xvii.

20. After the 2005 Quadrennial Defense Review confirmed a commitment to increase the number of special operators by a third; and the study called for even more investment in tagging, tracking, and locating (TTL); the top-level affirmation for a Manhattan-like project geared toward micro-miniaturization was given. See Michael Vickers, Implementing GWOT Strategy: Overcoming Interagency Problems, 15 March 2006, p. 4. SOCOM conducted a Capability Gap Analysis to determine specific hardware needs and on February 28, 2006, its commander, General Bruce Brown, approved the TTL program as the highest-ranked capability to be developed. A 2006 USSOCOM/DDR&E TTL Roadmap attempted to lay out a strategic plan and portfolio of capabilities then existing and under development.

21. 2011 SOCOM Program Management Updates, Special Operations Technology (SOTECH) 9.4, p. 28.

22. One example is the Ground SIGINT Kit, or GSK, 150 hand-built systems optimizing power, heat, and weight issued to the most expert and covert of the black collectors, each item of software-definable receivers (Nanoceptor and Picoceptor) Digital Receiver Technology (DRT) being manufactured or calibrated exactly for the signals being sought and tailored to fit.

23. William Murray, "Tagging, Tracking & Locating: TTL Systems Empower SOF to Spot and Eliminate Dangers," Special Operations Technology (SOTECH 11-1), February 2013.

24. USSOCOM Posture Statement 2007, n.d. (February 2007), p. 21.

25. Statement Testimony of Honorable John J. Young, Jr., Director of Defense Research and Engineering, Before the United States House of Representatives, Committee on Armed Services, Subcommittee on Terrorism, Unconventional Threats and Capabilities; March 21, 2007.

26. SOCOM PowerPoint Briefing, Bonny Heet, SBIR Program Manager, Overview of the USSOCOM Program Executive Offices, USSOCOM/SORDAC-ST, March 20, 2013.

27. SOCOM PowerPoint Briefing; Doug Richardson, SOAL-T WSO, Continuous Clandestine Tagging, Tracking, and Locating (CTTL), September 5, 2007; obtained by the author.
28. Randy Roughton, Rise of the Drones—UAVs After 9/11: 9/11 and war on terror sparked an explosion in unmanned aerial vehicle technology, *Airman* magazine, October 3, 2011; http://science.dodlive.mil/2011/10/03/rise-of-the-drones-uavs-after-911/ (accessed May 2, 2013).

CHAPTER SEVENTEEN Ring of Fiber

1. On May 28, 2009, the deputy secretary of defense directed the acceleration of two BACN payloads onto RQ-4A/B UAS Global Hawk Block 20 aircraft to support Joint Urgent Operational Need 336.
2. The JUON actually began as an Advanced Concept Technology Demonstration (ACTD) in 2006 to meet the challenges associated with operating in mountainous terrain, such as limited line of sight, and was melded into the already existing BACN.
3. In November 2003, the ScanEagle drone also demonstrated communications relay with Enhanced Position Locating and Reporting System (EPLRS).
4. Maryann Lawlor, "Technology Takes Flight," *Signal Magazine* (AFCEA), June 2006. See also Northrop Grumman, BACN CDMA Subsystem Test Results, June 2, 2006.
5. On June 24, 2009, the USAF awarded Northrop Grumman Defense Mission Systems Inc., of San Diego a $276.3-million cost-plus-fixed-fee urgent requirement contract for its Battlefield Airborne Communications Node (BACN) System. The contract funded fielding in three long-range Bombardier BD-700 Global Express jets and two Global Hawk RQ-4B Block 20 UAVs. It will also fund the company's support for continuing operations of the existing BACN-equipped BD-700, which the air force deployed to the front lines in December 2008.
6. Through additional experimentation and natural gold plating, BACN was "enhanced"—a SIGINT black box and a secure data link that would allow F-22 Raptors to communicate with other platforms without compromising its stealth were added.

   Air Force, Air Force Programs, Global Hawk High-Altitude Long-Endurance Unmanned Aerial System (RQ-4), January 2012, pp. 221–224; Air Force Materiel Command, Patty Welsh, "Contract award helps keep BACN airborne," November 21, 2012. See also Idaho National Laboratory, Analyzing Options for Airborne Emergency Wireless Communications, March 2008.
7. On November 3, 2011, the Battlefield Airborne Communications Node (BACN) platforms were officially designated. The manned Bombardier

BD-700 aircraft were designated E-11As, and the modified Global Hawk Block 20 platforms were designated EQ-4Bs.

8. CAOC crack refers to the Coalition (or Combined) Air Operations Center (the CAOC, pronounced "kay-ock"), the operational command center where air warfare is overseen.

9. General John P. Jumper, Air Force chief of staff; Space Architecture and Integration—Challenges for the Future; Speech to the 19th National Space Symposium, Colorado Springs, Colorado, April 10, 2003.

10. DOD, *Quadrennial Defense Review Report*, 2006, p. 45.

11. Maggie Ybarra, "USAF Unmanned Aircraft Could Benefit from Army Surveillance Capability," Insidedefense.com, April 2, 2013.

12. "Surveillance on the Fly," *Science and Technology Review* (*S&TR*, Livermore National Laboratory), October 2006, pp. 4–5.

13. "Wide area persistent surveillance is defined as the ability to provide surveillance over as much of the region known to be associated with a specific activity in order to increase the chance of detecting and observing the activity, identify the entity, track the entity forward in real time or backwards forensically. In most cases, the activity of interest can be identified as a transaction between locations"; PowerPoint Briefing, RRTO sponsored BAA on Persistent Surveillance Exploitation Technologies, Seeking new strategies and methodologies to leverage wide area EO and GMTI data, n.d. (2008).

14. Jack E. Huntley, "Advancing GEOINT Standards Across the NSG," *Pathfinder*, January/February 2009;Tom Vanden Brook, "Spy technology caught in military turf battle," *USA TODAY*, October 2, 2007; www.usatoday.com /news/military/2007-10-02-angel-fire_N.htm (accessed October 15, 2009).

15. "AFSOC modified four [Reaper] aircraft and three GCSs to perform HD operations in December 2011 per JROCM 066-10. In April 2012, AFSOC modified three additional aircraft and one GCS to support HD operations. The first phase implements target location accuracy (TLA), which will support enhanced data exploitation tools, including real-time display of target coordinates, digital data archiving, digital video recorder playback capability, and image mosaicking. The first phase also integrates the Raytheon Community Sensor Model (CSM), which separates 'key length value' metadata for LOS/BLOS links, integrates CSM in the GCS, and provides 'near-frame synchronous' metadata. The final fielded TLA (-3) MTS-B turret will enable 'frame synchronous' metadata and 720p HD IR." *U.S. Air Force (USAF) Remotely Piloted Aircraft (RPA) Vector—Vision and Enabling Concepts: 2013–2038*, February 2014, pp. 83–84.

16. PowerPoint Briefing, "Disruptive Technologies; Innovation or Disruption? The Impact of Changing Technology upon ISR Capabilities"; Jim Martin, Director ISR Programs, Under Secretary of Defense for Intelligence, October 11, 2010.

17. PowerPoint Briefing, RRTO sponsored BAA on Persistent Surveillance Exploitation Technologies, Seeking new strategies and methodologies to leverage wide area EO and GMTI data, n.d. (2008).

18. Stew Magnuson, "Military 'Swimming in Sensors and Drowning in Data,'" *National Defense,* January 2010.

19. PowerPoint Briefing, "Disruptive Technologies; Innovation or Disruption? The Impact of Changing Technology upon ISR Capabilities"; Jim Martin, Director ISR Programs, Under Secretary of Defense for Intelligence, October 11, 2010.

20. This contract was competitively procured via a broad agency announcement by the Naval Air Warfare Center Aircraft Division in Lakehurst, New Jersey (N68335-10-C-0064).

21. Rand Corporation (Lance Menthe, Amado Cordova, Carl Rhodes, Rachel Costello, Jeffrey Sullivan), The Future of Air Force Motion Imagery Exploitation: Lessons from the Commercial World, 2012, p. 3.

    The pod design employs 368 visible band CCD imaging sensors, each with 5 megapixel resolution, grouped into four camera systems, to provide an aggregate ability to simultaneously image up to 1.8 Gigapixels. The CCD imaging chips are of a type used in mobile phone cameras, with a frame update rate of 12–15 frames per second, about half the frame rate required at broadcast quality. The ARGUS-IS internal data processing system with 28 parallel processors is claimed to be able to handle 400 Gigabits/sec of data. The prototype pod was carried on a YEH-60B Blackhawk helicopter, but is intended for drone employment. The demonstrator employs a 274 mbps downlink to transmit imagery to a ground station, a compressed and fractured data rate well below that of the sensor package.

22. PowerPoint Briefing, "Disruptive Technologies; Innovation or Disruption? The Impact of Changing Technology upon ISR Capabilities"; Jim Martin, Director ISR Programs, Under Secretary of Defense for Intelligence, October 11, 2010.

23. From 2001 to 2003, U.S. manned and unmanned intelligence, surveillance, and reconnaissance flight hours of all kinds (not including satellites) increased more than 5,000 percent. But even that number is misleading, for small drones of Raven size and below are not even being counted; intelligence sources say that at any one moment worldwide, it is estimated that close to 1,000 drones are in the air. And even this number is misleading, for every day, the drones and manned aircraft join with satellites and ground systems and computer-network-based systems, all collecting massive volumes of raw information, from voice transmissions to e-mails and texts to data movements to electrooptical, infrared, synthetic aperture radar, full-motion video, and spectral information.

24. US Congress, House Permanent Select Committee on Intelligence, Performance Audit of Department of Defense Intelligence, Surveillance, and Reconnaissance, April 2012, p. 27.

   About 90 percent of the total number of hours was flown in direct support of combat operations. Less than 10 percent was flown inside the United States.

25. www.theskywardblog.com/2012/08/auvsi-blog/.

CHAPTER EIGHTEEN   Command Post of the Future

1. Thom Shanker and Carlotta Gall, "U.S. Attack on Warlord Aims to Help Interim Leader," *New York Times*, May 9, 2002; BBC, CIA "tried to kill Afghan warlord," Friday, 10 May 2002, 03:26 GMT 04:26 UK; http://news.bbc.co.uk/2/hi/south_asia/1978619.stm; Airpower Against Terror, p. 202; John Yoo, *War by Other Means*, p. 49.

2. Matthew Rosenberg, "Memo from Afghanistan: A Group Taking Politics and Military Strategy to the Same Extremes," *New York Times*, May 21, 2013; www.nytimes.com/2013/05/22/world/asia/in-afghanistan-hezb-i -islami-takes-its-extremism-into-politics.html?pagewanted=all&_r=0 (accessed August 15, 2013); Lisa Lundquist, "Hizb-i-Islami Gulbuddin suicide bomber in Kabul kills 6 Americans, 9 Afghans," *Long War Journal*, May 16, 2013; www.longwarjournal.org/archives/2013/05/this_morning _in_kabu.php#ixzz2c2qQInsM (accessed August 15, 2013); Scott Baldauf, "In crucial step toward democracy, Afghans vote for lawmakers: Violence before Sunday's election left seven candidates and six poll workers dead," *Christian Science Monitor*, September 19, 2005.

3. MetaVR News, "26.A, MetaVR's New 3D Afghanistan Terrain," Volume XIII, Issue 1, April 29, 2009; "Virtual Afghanistan Village; www.metavr .com/technology/afghan_village.html (accessed August 15, 2013).

   The overall imagery resolution of the virtual terrain of the whole country is 2.5 meters. The terrain, built with MetaVR's Terrain Tools for ESRI ArcGIS, includes an area of 1,120 sq km of 60 cm Digital Globe commercial satellite source imagery and 90 meter elevation posts. Within this area is the highly detailed 2 sq km terrain of the 3D "geospecific Afghan village," Khairabad. All 3-D content was created in Autodesk 3ds Max, and is referenced by the terrain's cultural feature file at run time; the content is rendered by VRSG at run time as part of the terrain.

4. *My Share of the Task*, p. 144.

5. On Point II: Transition to the New Campaign: The United States Army in Operation Iraqi Freedom, May 2003–January 2005, pp. 114, 193, 195.

6. Matt J. Martin with Charles W. Sasser, *Predator*, p. 188.

7. Anthony Tata, "IEDs: Combating Roadside Bombs," *Washington Post*, October 2, 2007.

8. The SIGACT report is the cornerstone of event reporting in CIDNE. This report is the method by which event information is transmitted through the chain of command and eventually made visible to all users. The SIGACT report can be completed at any echelon and submitted through a user-defined validation chain for publication. The SIGACT report contains the information regarding any event that happens to a unit. Only six fields are required to be entered before submitting a SIGACT report; however, the report can collect well over 100 data points on any given event. Completing as many fields as possible provides a clearer picture of the event to the data consumer.

9. Andrew G. Schlessinger, Advanced analysis techniques: the key to focused ISR, Military Intelligence Professional Bulletin (US Army), July 2010.

10. Long Hard Road: NCO Experiences in Afghanistan and Iraq, US Army Sergeants Major Academy, October 2007, p. 161.

11. *Duty*, pp. 199, 205–209.

12. Network-centric warfare and the concept of everything being a network originated in electronic warfare and nodal targeting at the start of the computer age, when the exponential impact of network-level modes of attack over physical attack was first recognized. Attacking the network became the priority. And that meant targeting, spying, and killing. See Colonel Joseph Yavorsky and Mike Hamilton, "Unit of action NET-WORK MAPEX: Testing the network in a virtual warfight," *Army Communicator* (US Army), Summer 2003.

13. William H. McMichael, "Head of Anti-IED Agency Says It's Been Effective: Now takes more bombs to get same level of casualties," *Army Times*, May 21, 2007, p. 24; "U.S. Forces Clearing Half of All Combat Area IEDs Before Detonation," *Inside the Pentagon*, March 22, 2007, p. 5.

CHAPTER NINETEEN   Oh. Obama Was Elected.

1. Timothy M. McGrew, Army Aviation Addressing Battlefield Anomalies in Real Time with the Teaming and Collaboration of Manned and Unmanned Aircraft, Naval Postgraduate School, December 2009, p. 16.

2. Information on Viper Strike is taken from PowerPoint Briefing, Northrop Grumman, Rick Schultz, Aircraft w/Viper Strike—Transformational Weapon System for Today's Operational Environment, October 13, 2004; PowerPoint Briefing, Small Guided Munitions Program Office, Small Guided Munitions Path Ahead, March 11, 2009; Army PowerPoint Briefing, Steve Borden, DPM [Deputy Program Manager] Submunitions, Viper Strike, April 2006; Shelby G. Spires, *Huntsville* [Alabama] *Times*, "Cold War-Era Weapon Is Hot Again; Viper Strike concept uses BAT on an unmanned aerial vehicle," June 23, 2004.

A test Hunter dropped four Brilliant Anti-Tank (BAT) submunitions at WSMR, New Mexico, in October 2002 and achieved four hits in four attempts. It then dropped laser-guided Viper Strike munitions in March/July 2003, the Hunter drone self-lazing the target. On March 8, 2004, the army G3 (Operations Deputy) signed an Operational Needs Statement (ONS) for weaponized Hunter to be used in Iraq.

The Congressional Research Service wrote in 2005: "It was widely reported in 2002 and 2003 that the army had already deployed two weaponized Hunter UAVs, but recent press reports quote Army spokesmen denying this, and saying that classification issues prohibited any further elaboration." CRS, Report for Congress, Military Aviation: Issues and Options for Combating Terrorism and Counterinsurgency, January 24, 2005.

3. Fiscal Year (FY) 2013 President's Budget Submission, Navy, Justification Book Volume 1, Weapons Procurement, Navy, January 24, 2012.

4. Dan O'Boyle, "Stealthy glide weapon strikes like viper: Viper Strike submunition augments Army's arsenal," *Redstone Rocket* (Redstone Arsenal, Alabama), April 9, 2008.

5. DOD, Unmanned Systems Integrated Roadmap 2013–2018, p. 73.

6. Briefing, Colonel Larry L. Felder, Commander, UAVB; Unmanned Aerial Vehicle Battlelab, January 5, 2005 (FOUO); obtained by the author.

7. *Arming the Fleet*, p. 98; DOD, Unmanned Systems Integrated Roadmap 2013–2018, pp. 73–74.

8. *Arming the Fleet*, p. 98.

9. DOD, Unmanned Systems Integrated Roadmap 2013–2018, p. 74.

10. *Arming the Fleet*, p. 67.

11. APKWS Is a Hit, *Precision Strike Digest*, 1st Quarter, 2013.

12. *U.S. Air Force (USAF) Remotely Piloted Aircraft (RPA) Vector—Vision and Enabling Concepts: 2013–2038.*

13. DOD, Unmanned Systems Integrated Roadmap 2013–2018, pp. 74–75.

14. Army Acquisition Support Center, "Direct fire munition increases lethality, reduces collateral damage," January 2, 2013; http://asc.army.mil/web/access-st-direct-fire-munition-increases-lethality-reduces-collateral-damage/ (accessed July 13, 2014); Paul McLeary, "U.S. Army Wants More Switchblades: Remote-Control Munitions Are Small, Lethal," *Defense News*, February 12, 2013.

15. Staff Sergeant Christopher Flurry, "KC-130J Harvest Hawk: Marine Corps teaches old plane new tricks in Afghanistan," Marine Corps News, April 1, 2011; www.cherrypoint.marines.mil/News/NewsArticleDisplay/tabid/4890/Article/66147/kc-130j-harvest-hawk-marine-corps-teaches-old-plane-new-tricks-in-afghanistan.aspx (accessed July 13, 2014).

The Harvest Hawk system, fitted on existing KC-130J aircraft, includes a version of the target sight sensor used on the AH-1Z Cobra attack helicopter (the AN/AIQ-30 Targeting Sight System), as well as a complement of four AGM-114 Hellfire, 10 Griffin, or Viper Strike munitions. The "mission kit"—the black box—reconfigures any KC-130J aircraft rapidly into a platform capable of performing persistent targeting ISR. See USMC, Deputy Commandant for Aviation, FY2011 Marine Aviation Plan, p. 3-3; Fiscal Year (FY) 2013 President's Budget Submission, Navy, Justification Book Volume 1, Weapons Procurement, Navy, January 24, 2012.

16. Since 9/11, only about 1,700 Hellfire missiles had been expended and only two dozen Viper Strikes were fired in combat.

   "More than 100 of the APKWS rockets have been fired in action in Afghanistan since the Marines first deployed the weapon in March 2012. None of the APKWS rockets fired has missed its target due to failure after launch"; APKWS Is a Hit, *Precision Strike Digest*, 1st Quarter, 2013.

17. *Company Man*, p. 280.

18. "Obama's advisers were fascinated by the CIA's targeted killing program and the ruthlessly effective use of drones. At a second meeting…they peppered these hosts with questions: How Many al Qaeda leaders have been neutralized? What was the civilian death toll? They were awed by the precision and lethality of the strikes.…John Rizzo, a longtime CIA lawyer known for his bespoke tailoring and sardonic wit, came away from the meeting thinking Obama would keep the program, and might even step it up. 'I guess they're not a bunch of left-wing pussies after all,' he thought to himself." See *Kill or Capture*, p. 32.

19. Under President Bush, the CIA carried out two targeted killing drone strikes in Pakistan in 2006 and three in 2007. In July 2008, Bush increased the number of drone strikes, totaling thirty-four attacks by the end of the year.

20. General Atomics, Air Force MQ-1 Predators Achieve 500,000 Flight Hours; GA-ASI Predator A Deliveries to USAF Nears 200, 3 March 2009.

21. The Raytheon-built ARTEMIS—the Advanced Responsive Tactically Effective Military Imaging Spectrometer—was launched by the air force in May 2009 aboard the TacSat-3 satellite built by ATK. ARTEMIS performed well enough that in June 2010, STRATCOM declared the sensor operational, clearing the way for analysts to feed processed intelligence products to forces in Afghanistan. Ben Iannotta, "Afghan war brings call for new Predator sensor," *Defense News*, July 1, 2011; Amy Butler, "USAF Turns to Hyperspectral Sensors in Afghanistan: New sensors provide new edge in finding explosives in Afghanistan," *Aviation Week & Space Technology*, September 19, 2011.

22. Ben Iannotta, "Afghan war brings call for new Predator sensor," *Defense News*, July 1, 2011; Henry Canaday, "Seeing More with Hyperspectral Imaging," *Geospatial Intelligence Forum* (GIF) 11.2, p. 21.

23. Air Force PowerPoint Briefing, USAF FMV Needs, Initiatives, & Requirements; Robert T. "Bo" Marlin, DISL Deputy Director, ISR Capabilities (AF/A2C), May 22, 2013, U/FOUO; obtained by the author.

   In September 2010, the air force and Raytheon completed flight testing of ACES HY on a manned Twin Otter aircraft used as a surrogate for Predator. Raytheon received its initial production contract for ACES HY in 2011.

24. Amy Butler, "USAF Turns to Hyperspectral Sensors in Afghanistan: New sensors provide new edge in finding explosives in Afghanistan," *Aviation Week & Space Technology*, September 19, 2011.

25. Amy Butler, "USAF Turns to Hyperspectral Sensors in Afghanistan: New sensors provide new edge in finding explosives in Afghanistan," *Aviation Week & Space Technology*, September 19, 2011.

26. GATR Demonstrates world's only inflatable, 2.4m satellite solution at Trident Spectre, Norfolk, Virginia, May 11, 2009.

27. Office of Secretary of Defense, Exhibit R-2, RDT&E Budget Item Justification: PB 2013 Office of Secretary of Defense, PE 0603618D8Z: Joint Electronic Advanced Technology, February 2012. See also Department of Defense Fiscal Year (FY) 2014 President's Budget Submission, Office of Secretary of Defense, Justification Book Volume 3 of 3, Research, Development, Test & Evaluation, Defense-Wide, PE 0603618D8Z: Joint Electronic Advanced Technology, April 2013.

28. Rebecca Grant, "Iraqi Freedom and the air force," *Air Force Magazine*, March 2013.

29. Air Force PowerPoint Briefing, Air Force ISR Reach Back: Distributed Common Ground Systems; Colonel Mike Shortsleeve, Commander, 497th Intelligence, Surveillance and Reconnaissance Group (DGS-1), n.d. (2013); obtained by the author.

30. Air Force PowerPoint Briefing, Air Force Acquisition Issues, Challenges, and Opportunities, AFCEA Luncheon, February 12, 2012; obtained by the author.

31. Mazzetti, *The Way of the Knife*, pp. 103–109. "The first strike in the FATA took place in South Waziristan on 18 June 2004, with the full support of President Musharaff's government, when Nek Muhammad, a Taliban commander knowingly misrepresented by the US as an 'al Qaeda facilitator' was killed along with four of his companions. He was marked by Pakistan and its Inter-Services Intelligence Agency as an enemy of the state, and his death was the price the CIA agreed to pay Islamabad for its tacit consent to 'covert' drone strikes in the FATA."

32. Bob Woodward, *Obama's Wars* (New York: Simon & Schuster, 2011), pp. 4–5.

33. Woodward, *Obama's Wars*, pp. 208–209.

34. Woodward, *Obama's Wars*, p. 281.

35. Remarks by the president at the United States Military Academy Commencement Ceremony, US Military Academy-West Point; West Point, New York; May 28, 2014.

CHAPTER TWENTY   Pattern of Life

1. Raven Parts Seller on eBay Pleads Guilty, UAV Vision (Blog), posted on July 29, 2011, by The Editor; www.uasvision.com/2011/07/29/raven-parts -seller-on-ebay-pleads-guilty/#more-5836; Spencer Ackerman, What Not to Sell on eBay: Drones, Wired, 03.29.11 [March 29, 2011]; www.wired .com/dangerroom/2011/03/what-not-to-sell-on-ebay-drones/; eBay Raven Seller Faces 20 Years Jail, UAV Vision (Blog), posted on April 4, 2011, by The Editor; www.uasvision.com/2011/04/04/ebay-raven-seller-faces-20 -years-jail/#more-2400.
2. See, e.g., Matt J. Martin with Charles W. Sasser, *Predator*, pp. 22ff.
3. *U.S. Air Force (USAF) Remotely Piloted Aircraft (RPA) Vector—Vision and Enabling Concepts: 2013–2038*, p. 39.
4. *U.S. Air Force (USAF) Remotely Piloted Aircraft (RPA) Vector—Vision and Enabling Concepts: 2013–2038*, pp. iii–iv.
5. *U.S. Air Force (USAF) Remotely Piloted Aircraft (RPA) Vector—Vision and Enabling Concepts: 2013–2038*, p. 13.
6. ISR Leader Q&A: Ensuring Warfighters Have the Intelligence Support They Require, Lieutenant General John C. Koziol, Deputy Under Secretary of Defense, Joint and Coalition Warfighter Support; Director, DoD ISR Task Force, Geospatial Intelligence Forum (GIF 8.6), September 2010, p. 21.
7. DOD, Unmanned Systems Integrated Roadmap 2013–2018, pp. 66–68.
8. DOD, Unmanned Systems Integrated Roadmap 2013–2018, p. 24.
9. DOD, Unmanned Systems Integrated Roadmap 2013–2018, p. 29.
10. PowerPoint Briefing, UAS Operations and Comparison, Lieutenant Colonel Bruce "Shadow" Black, USAF UAS Task Force, as of March 17, 2010 (ver13).

CHAPTER TWENTY-ONE   Warka

1. It should be noted that some scholars suggest that Karal in Peru might be as old as Uruk, and there are other sites in northern Mesopotamia and Syria that vie for the honor of being first city; others argue in favor of Çatalhüyük in Turkey.
2. "Attempts to identify Gilgamesh in art are fraught with difficulty. Cylinder seals from the Old Akkadian period (ca. 2334–2154 B.C.) onward showing nude heroes with beards and curls grappling with lions and bovines cannot be identified with Gilgamesh. They are more likely to be associated with the god Lahmu ('The Hairy One'). A terracotta plaque in

the Vorderasiatisches Museum, Berlin, depicts a bearded hero grasping an ogre's wrist while raising his right hand to attack him with a club. To his left, a beardless figure pins down the monster's arm, pulls his hair, and is about to pierce his neck with a knife. This scene is often associated with the death of Humbaba. The Babylonian Gilgamesh epic clearly describes Enkidu as being almost identical to Gilgamesh, but no mention is made of the monster's long hair, and although Gilgamesh is said to strike the monster with a dagger, he holds an axe rather than a club in his hand. The scene on the Berlin plaque may reflect the older Sumerian story wherein Enkidu is described as a companion rather than a double of the hero. In this older tale, Enkidu is the one who 'severed [Huwawa's] head at the neck.' Similar images appear on cylinder seals of the second and first millennium B.C." See Gilgamesh, Heilbrunn Timeline of Art History, Metropolitan Museum of Art; www.metmuseum.org/toah/hd/gilg/hd_gilg .htm (accessed August 1, 2013).

3. According to the British Museum, "The earliest evidence for writing in Mesopotamia was discovered in Eanna, though it is difficult to date precisely: the writing is on clay tablets that had been used as packing for foundations of later buildings. The city was surrounded by a wall that, according to later accounts, was built by Gilgamesh, a legendary king of the city. After the third millennium BC Uruk declined politically but it remained an important religious centre and its shrines were embellished by many of the later rulers of Mesopotamia. From 1912 onwards, major excavations have been undertaken by the Deutsche Orient-Gesellschaft" (see The British Museum, Uruk; www.britishmuseum.org/explore/high lights/articles/u/uruk_iraq.aspx; accessed March 31, 2014).

"After the end of Ur III [the third Mesopotamian dynasty], the city declined only to revive in the 1st millennium when its temples controlled vast agricultural estates, and flourished well into the Seleucid and Parthian periods, being finally abandoned before the Arab conquest in 634 AD." See Central Command/Center for Environmental Management of Military Lands (CEMML) at Colorado State University, Cultural Property Training Resources, Site 115. Warka (ancient: Uruk); www .cemml.colostate.edu/cultural/09476/iraq05-115.html, accessed March 31, 2014). See also BBC News, "Gilgamesh tomb believed found," April 29, 2003; http://news.bbc.co.uk/2/hi/science/nature/2982891.stm.

4. The story of the tablet's discovery and unveiling is a thrilling and sometimes sordid tale of perseverance, treacheries, racism, professional and institutional ambitions, and finally of religious supremacy and empire, the hubris of Western custody of a backward people, "the very proprietorship of the past." See, especially, *The Buried Book: The Loss and Rediscovery of the Great Epic of Gilgamesh*, pp. 35ff, 86, 149.

5. None are in the original language, Sumerian, which linguists call a "language isolate" because it belongs to no known family and died with that ancient civilization. The Nineveh tablets were written in Akkadian, a Semitic language in a family connecting ancient Babylonian and Assyrian and modern Arabic and Hebrew. Mesopotamian-era writing of this family became not just the means to administer the first organized empire but also a way of preserving a human narrative. Thousands upon thousands of clay tablets and fragments have been recovered, recording everything: "receipts for oxen, slaves, and casks of wine, petitions to the Assyrian kings, contracts, treaties, prayers, and reports of omens the gods had planted in sheep's livers." *The Buried Book: The Loss and Rediscovery of the Great Epic of Gilgamesh*, p. 10.

6. *The Buried Book: The Loss and Rediscovery of the Great Epic of Gilgamesh*, pp. 60–61.

7. See *The Epic of Gilgamesh: A New Translation*, pp. xxvii–xxxviii.

8. *Gilgamesh: A Verse Narrative by Herbert Mason with an Afterword by John H. Marks*, p. 98.

    For an interesting tale of how our understanding of Mesopotamia continues to evolve through science, specifically declassified satellite imagery from the 1960s and 1970s, see Eric Rupley, "Science in a Complex World: Declassification of data important to future science," *The New Mexican* (Santa Fe), Sunday, February 2, 2014; www.santafenewmexican .com/news/local_news/science-in-a-complex-world-declassification-of -data-important-to/article_1687dbb5-71d0-5537-88b5-0fb860044bb0 .html (accessed February 2, 2014).

9. *The Buried Book: The Loss and Rediscovery of the Great Epic of Gilgamesh*, p. 254.

10. Army Infantry Center, Maneuver Self Study Program; Moral, Ethical, and Psychological Dimensions of War; www.benning.army.mil/mssp /MEPDOW/ (accessed October 9, 2013).

    See also J. E. Lendon, *Soldiers and Ghosts: A History of Battle in Classical Antiquity* (New Haven: Yale University Press, 2005).

11. Robert Gates makes the observation about the rapid turnover in *Duty*, p. 37.

12. When Arnett asked Hussein what he hoped for with the interview, he thanked "those people who are coming out onto the streets, demonstrating against this war." Iraqi propagandists had filled the prewar airwaves with endless programs about antiwar protests in the United States and around the world as a means to mobilize public opinion to see Bush as the culprit in the face of popular opposition. Saddam was evidently a victim of his own propaganda; Peter Arnett, *Live from the Battlefield: From Vietnam to Baghdad—35 Years in the World's War Zones* (New York: Simon & Schuster, 1994), pp. 401–402.

13. CENTCOM SITREP for 122115Z February 1991 (February 12, 1991), referred to in An Air Staff Chronology of Desert Shield-Desert Storm, p. 323; Gulf War Air Power Survey (GWAPS), Volume V, Part II, p. 211.

14. See "White House Statement on the Bombing," *Washington Post*, February 14, 1991; UPI (Washington), "Cheney Says Saddam Using Holy Site to Protect Arsenal," February 14, 1991; UPI (Northern Saudi Arabia), "Schwarzkopf Defends US Bombings," February 14, 1991; Warren Strobel, "US scrutinized after bombing Iraqi civilians," *Washington Times*, February 14, 1991.

    See also DOD News Briefing, Mr. Pete Williams, Lieutenant General Thomas Kelly, USA, Rear Admiral Mike McConnell, USN, Saturday, February 16, 1991, 3:30 PM EST; DOD News Briefing, Mr. Pete Williams, Lieutenant General Thomas Kelly, USA, Rear Admiral Mike McConnell, USN, Tuesday, February 19, 1991, 3:30 PM EST.

15. See, in particular, Fred Kaplan, *The Insurgents: David Petraeus and the Plot to Change the American Way of War* (New York: Simon & Schuster, 2013), a lively and incisive though completely myopic narrative.

16. The White House, Office of the Press Secretary, Remarks by the President on the Situation in Iraq, James S. Brady Press Briefing Room, June 19, 2014, 1:32 p.m. EDT.

17. Talking Points on Air Force's Efforts in the Bombing and Death of Al Zarqawi, Based on the transcript of Lieutenant General [Gary] North," June 8, 2006, obtained by the author.

18. *The Buried Book: The Loss and Rediscovery of the Great Epic of Gilgamesh*, pp. 222–226.

EPILOGUE   The Event

1. "As a safety feature of most UAS autopilots, the system can perform a 'lost-link' procedure if communication becomes severed between the ground control station and the air vehicle. There are many different ways that these systems execute this procedure. Most of these procedures involve creating a lost-link profile where the mission flight profiles (altitudes, flight path, and speeds) are loaded into the memory of the system prior to aircraft launch. Once the aircraft is launched, the autopilot will fly the mission profile as long as it remains in radio contact with the ground control station. The mission or lost-link profile can be modified when necessary if connectivity remains during flight. If contact with the ground station is lost in flight, the autopilot will execute its preprogrammed lost-link profile." See Introduction to Unmanned Aircraft Systems, p. 20.

2. Inside the Quadrotor Thunderdome, UAV Vision (Blog), www.uasvision .com/2011/04/04/inside-the-quadrotor-thunderdome/ (posted on April 4, 2011).

3. BirdXPeller Predator Drone Scares Off Real Birds; UAV Vision (Blog), www.uasvision.com/2011/03/24/birdxpeller-predator-drone-scares-off -real-birds/ (posted on March 24, 2011).

4. RAF, Air Power UAVs: The Wider Context, p. 50.

5. "The DoD expects its inventory of aircraft, both conventionally manned as well as unmanned, to grow to 27,000 vehicles by 2035, including 8,000 traditional aircraft, 14,000 UAS of all sizes and types, and 5,000 new air-craft with UAS technologies for pilot augmentation or optional pilot replacement." UAS Service Demand 2015–2035, August 2013, p. 3.

   "Between 2015 and 2035, it is expected that federal agency UAS fleets will grow from a few hundred to approximately 10,000, with over 90 per-cent of these vehicles categorized as Nano, Micro, or Small UAS." UAS Service Demand 2015–2035, August 2013, p. 5.

   "From the modest acquisition of a few hundred UAS in 2015, state UAS inventories are expected to grow to 10,000 vehicles by 2035. These estimates include modest UAS inventories at colleges and universities.

   "All told, the federal and state sectors are forecast to be collectively operating some 36,000 UAS vehicles by 2035. This number is comparable to the Nano, Micro, and Small UAS forecasts for local governments; espe-cially including some 18,000 metropolitan police departments and other first responders. The number of UAS vehicles forecast for first respond-ers jumps from a few hundred in 2015 to a number almost equal to all others except the commercial sector—some 34,000 UAS vehicles by 2035. This means an expected population of 70,000 state and local public UAS by 2035." UAS Service Demand 2015–2035, August 2013, p. 6.

   "As markets are defined and refined, it is expected that beginning in the 2022 to 2023 period commercial sales of UAS vehicles, including products and services, will experience accelerated growth with total UAS vehicles approaching 250,000 by 2035, of which 175,000 will be in the commercial marketplace." UAS Service Demand 2015–2035, August 2013, p. 7.

Index

About the Author

WILLIAM M. ARKIN is one of America's premier military experts, having started his forty-year career in national security serving in army intelligence in West Berlin during the Cold War. He has written more than a dozen books and been instrumental in countless exposés. At the *Washington Post* he conceived and coauthored the landmark "Top Secret America" investigation, and cowrote the national bestseller of the same name. He has been a columnist for the *Los Angeles Times* and national security consultant to the *New York Times* and NBC News. He is also the author, most recently, of *American Coup*. He lives in Vermont.